LANGUAGE, CULTURE, AND SOCIETY

Language, our primary tool of thought and perception, is at the heart of who we are as individuals. Languages are constantly changing, sometimes into entirely new varieties of speech, leading to subtle differences in how we present ourselves to others. This revealing account brings together twelve leading specialists from the fields of linguistics, anthropology, philosophy, and psychology, to explore the fascinating relationship between language, culture, and social interaction. A range of major questions are discussed: How does language influence our perception of the world? How do new languages emerge? How do children learn to use language appropriately? What factors determine language choice in bi- and multilingual communities? How far does language contribute to the formation of our personalities? And finally, in what ways does language make us human? *Language, Culture, and Society* will be essential reading for all those interested in language and its crucial role in our social lives.

CHRISTINE JOURDAN is Professor of Anthropology in the Department of Sociology and Anthropology at Concordia University in Montreal. Trained in linguistics and anthropology, her work focuses on theories of culture and social change, on pidgins and creoles, and on linguistic representation of cultural knowledge. She has published books and articles on Solomon Islands Pijin, urbanization in the Pacific, and socio-cultural creolization.

KEVIN TUITE is *Professeur titulaire* (full Professor) of Anthropology at the Université de Montréal. He specializes in the languages and cultures of the Caucasus, especially those of the Republic of Georgia, where he has conducted fieldwork since 1985. He has published a number of books and journal articles on language and culture, in journals such as *Anthropological Linguistics*, *Anthropos*, and *Lingua*.

STUDIES IN THE SOCIAL AND CULTURAL FOUNDATIONS OF LANGUAGE

The aim of this series is to develop theoretical perspectives on the essential social and cultural character of language by methodological and empirical emphasis on the occurrence of language in its communicative and interactional settings, on the socioculturally grounded "meanings" and "functions" of linguistic forms, and on the social scientific study of language use across cultures. It will thus explicate the essentially ethnographic nature of linguistic data, whether spontaneously occurring or experimentally induced, whether normative or variational, whether synchronic or diachronic. Works appearing in the series will make substantive and theoretical contributions to the debate over the sociocultural-function and structural-formal nature of language, and will represent the concerns of scholars in the sociology and anthropology of language, anthropological linguistics, sociolinguistics, and socioculturally informed psycholinguistics.

Editors	*Editorial Advisers*
Judith T. Irvine	Marjorie Goodwin
Bambi Schieffelin	Joel Kuipers
	Don Kulick
	John Lucy
	Elinor Ochs
	Michael Silverstein

A list of books in the series can be found after the index.

LANGUAGE, CULTURE, AND SOCIETY

KEY TOPICS IN LINGUISTIC ANTHROPOLOGY

CHRISTINE JOURDAN
Concordia University

KEVIN TUITE
Université de Montréal

CAMBRIDGE
UNIVERSITY PRESS

CAMBRIDGE UNIVERSITY PRESS
Cambridge, New York, Melbourne, Madrid, Cape Town, Singapore, São Paulo

Cambridge University Press
The Edinburgh Building, Cambridge CB2 8RU, UK

Published in the United States of America by Cambridge University Press, New York

www.cambridge.org
Information on this title: www.cambridge.org/9780521849418

© Cambridge University Press 2006

First published 2006

A catalogue record for this publication is available from the British Library

ISBN 978-0-521-84941-8 hardback
ISBN 978-0-521-61474-0 paperback

Transferred to digital printing 2008

In memory of Roger M. Keesing, a *passe-muraille* of the best kind.

CONTENTS

vii

TABLES

CONTRIBUTORS

CHARLES TAYLOR, Department of Philosophy, McGill University

JOHN LEAVITT, Department of Anthropology, Université de Montréal

REGNA DARNELL, Department of Anthropology, University of Western-Ontario

PENELOPE BROWN, Max Planck Institute for Psycholinguistics, Netherlands

PAUL KAY, Department of Linguistics, University of California, Berkeley

MONICA HELLER, CREFO, OISE, Université de Toronto

ELINOR OCHS, Department of Applied Linguistics, University of California, Los Angeles

BAMBI SCHIEFFELIN, Department of Anthropology, New York University

ELIZABETH POVINELLI, Department of Anthropology and the Institute for Research on Women and Gender, Columbia University

PAUL FRIEDRICH, Committee on Social Thought, University of Chicago

ACKNOWLEDGMENTS

We would like to thank the authors of this collection for their collaboration on this project, and Andrew Winnard, from Cambridge University Press, for his support. Thanks also to the Department of Sociology and Anthropology at Concordia University in Montreal for a small grant used for the preparation of the manuscript. Finally we owe special thanks to Alexandrine Boudreault-Fournier and Catherine Bélair, two graduate students in the department of Sociology and Anthropology at Concordia University, for their creativity, enthusiasm, flexibility, and professionalism in the preparation of the manuscript.

INTRODUCTION:
WALKING THROUGH WALLS

CHRISTINE JOURDAN AND KEVIN TUITE

In an interview recorded in 1994, André-Georges Haudricourt described himself as a "passe-muraille," a person capable of walking through walls (Bertrand 2002: 251). The *passe-muraille*, best known to French readers from the short story of that name by Marcel Aymé, is both marvelous and disquieting, a transgressive being – in both senses of the word – who refuses to acknowledge the barriers that contain and channel the movements of others. Haudricourt clearly had this complex of senses in mind when he chose the word to characterize his atypical career in French academia: an agronomy graduate who subsequently studied under Marcel Mauss, Haudricourt went on to conduct important research in such diverse fields as ethnoscience, phonological theory and the history of agriculture, often to the discomfiture of his more sessile colleagues.

For much of the past century, to say nothing of the present one, there has been a great deal of talk about the desirability of interdisciplinarity, and of breaking down the walls that impede communication between adjoining academic fields. The discipline of anthropology, as conceived (and exemplified) by Franz Boas, was to be just such a wall-less meeting place, where ethnologists, archaeologists, linguists, and physical anthropologists would collaboratively grapple with the complexities of human diversity (see, e.g. Boas 1899). Boas's vision took institutional form as the "four-field" or "Boasian" anthropology departments of many North American universities, where course offerings, faculty recruitment, and even the composition of internal committees conform to the principle of an asymmetrical confederation of canton-like subdisciplines, with social-cultural anthropology as the *primus inter pares*. Admirable as this Boasian plan might have been at the time of its conception, it has been increasingly subject to criticism and attempts at reconfiguration. Johannes Fabian (1993: 53) – himself a notorious *passe-muraille* – questioned the continued relevance of "that decisively modernist conception of a 'four-fields approach'" in the contemporary intellectual landscape of reflexive anthropology, cultural studies, postprocessual archaeology, the various recent developments in human genetics, creole studies and sociolinguistics. To this list one might add the troublesome fault line running between "scientific" and "critical" stances within the discipline. It is a telling sign of the times that when the anthropologists at Stanford University split into separate "Anthropological Sciences" and "Cultural and

1

Social Anthropology" departments, the new wall cut across three of the four Boasian fields.

Where something akin to the Boasian configuration is maintained, one detects evidence of "the contemporary marginalization of linguistic anthropology" in North American academia (Darnell, this volume). Many leading anthropology departments now recognize only three subdisciplines, with linguistic anthropology either blended into a combined "socio-cultural and linguistic" section (e.g. NYU), or relegated to institutional invisibility (e.g. Columbia, Harvard).

Depending on the venue and the time, linguistic anthropologists have a room of their own, bunk with the ethnologists, are split apart by new departmental configurations, or fade into the background of institutionally unrecognized specializations like kinship or political economy. Nonetheless, the history of anthropology, and especially of North American anthropology, is to a significant degree marked by its relations with linguistics. As Keesing (1992) noted, the relationship has not always been a tranquil one. It has been a *pas-de-deux* where the partners approach, then separate, then approach again as the internal dynamics of each discipline shift, and as research focus oscillates between particularism and universalism, culturalism and mentalism. The relationship has at times fostered the sharing of models and exchanging of paradigms, the rejecting or borrowing of concepts, all of which has been beneficial to both disciplines: consider such offspring of crossbreeding as ethnoscience and ethnosemantics, structuralism, and more recently, cognitive anthropology, the dialogic principle and cultural creolization. Even if some of these approaches have not been as productive as had been hoped, and even if some have been the targets of intense criticism (ethnoscience and structuralism, for example), they have informed the anthropological practice of generations of researchers, and therefore, have become part of the history of the field.

This book has its roots in a special issue of the Québec journal *Anthropologie et sociétés*, published in 1999. The two editors, Christine Jourdan and Claire Lefebvre, were commissioned to assemble an "état des lieux" of ethnolinguistics, a term – more common in French usage than in English – for the study of the embeddedness of language in social and cultural life, in "ways of being." "État des lieux" is routinely translated "state of the art," but in fact the French and English phrases have very different connotational fields. "State of the art," especially when used as an adjective, brings up images of cutting-edge, top-end technology (audio equipment, for example), with all of the attendant bells and whistles. "État des lieux," which has a second sense referring to the inventory of rented property done at the beginning and end of a lease, evokes the far humbler scene of a landlord inspecting chipped paint and carpet stains. These contrasting perspectives are in fact well represented in the current discourses of linguistic anthropology – the high-theoretical, terminologically daunting writings of the semiotic functionalists, on the one hand, the repeated handwringing over the peripheral status of the field, on the other – but in the end, we decided to go with neither orientation for the expanded English-language version of the *Anthropologie et sociétés* collection. The width of focus varies considerably from one chapter to the next, as do the historical depth, manner of presentation (or argumentation), and comprehensiveness of coverage. Summaries of past accomplishments and present debates are juxtaposed to forward-looking proposals, and even the surveying of new terrain to explore.

Like the self-described "vagabond" Haudricourt, many of the authors contributing to our collection followed atypical pathways across academic fields or indeed outside of them. The two senior authors in this volume are particularly dramatic exemplars of the *passe-muraille* profile. Alongside their multidisciplinary careers within the university, Paul Friedrich has published volumes of poetry, and Charles Taylor has been an active participant in Canadian politics. (In 1965 he ran – unsuccessfully – for a parliament seat against Pierre Trudeau.) It may be difficult – and is almost certainly beside the point – to specify in what manner Friedrich's activity as a poet has been reflected in his varied work as an anthropologist and linguist, or to what degree Taylor's hands-on involvement in debates over multiculturalism or the future of Québec has colored his sensitivity to the interdependance of language and ways of being. The same could be said, *mutatis mutandis*, of each of the *passe-muraille* represented in this book. It is not the point of this collection either to explain each contributor's research in terms of his or her education, career trajectory or interests, nor to carve the field of linguistic anthropology, or ethnolinguistics, into the set of subjects treated in the collection.

The ethnolinguistic perspective

Europe, 1937. Nazi Germany rearms, "enemies of the people" die before Soviet firing squads, the Luftwaffe tests its weapons on the Basque city of Guernica. Aldous Huxley watches two cats preparing to fight:

> balefully the eyes glare; from far down in the throat of each come bursts of a strange, strangled noise of defiance . . . Another moment and surely there must be an explosion. But no; all of a sudden one of the two creatures turns away, hoists a hind leg in a more than fascist salute and, with the same fixed and focused attention as it had given a moment before to its enemy, begins to make a lingual toilet . . . Such as it is, the consistency of human characters is due to the words upon which all human experiences are strung. We are purposeful because we can describe our feelings in rememberable words, can justify and rationalize our desires in terms of some kind of argument. Faced by an enemy, we do not allow an itch to distract us from our emotions: the mere word "enemy" is enough to keep us reminded of our hatred, to convince us that we do well to be angry.
>
> (Huxley 1937: 84)

Erudite as he was, Huxley may well have had Herder in mind when he penned this passage, although he did not refer to him, or any other eighteenth-century thinker for that matter, in his essay. What was clear to him is the fundamental difference between the wordless, reactive living-in-the-present of animals, and the thought world of language-using humanity. As Charles Taylor shows in his revisiting of Herder's critique of Condillac, the former's "constitutive" (or constitutive-expressive) theory of language is a necessary preliminary to an appreciation of how "language transforms our world," endowing all that surrounds us with meaning, enabling us – through expressive language, and also the nonverbal codes of gesture, stance and dress – to create new "ways of being" in the world, with their associated sets of values.

Although this insight into the intimate relation between language and what we understand as the essence of humanness goes back two centuries, there have been repeated moves in the subsequent history of linguistics to represent language as an object of study in isolation from its users and situations of use. Advances in historical-comparative linguistics, especially with regard to phonetics, contributed to mid nineteenth-century Neo-grammarian models of mechanical, "exceptionless" sound laws "decontextualized from their circumstances of use and any link to their users" (Tuite, this volume). To this narrow-scope, natural-scientific approach to the reconstruction and explanation of language change, Hugo Schuchardt opposed a wider-scope historical method which drew upon ethnographic and sociological data, information on naming practices and the expressive use of language, as well as the findings of historical phonetics and semantics. In the early years of the twentieth century, Ferdinand de Saussure, a historical linguist who studied under the leading Neo-grammarians at Leipzig, proposed his celebrated contrast between *parole* and *langue*, "a rigorous methodological distinction between language seen as the constantly changing speech habits of a community and language as a *system*, a virtual structure extracted from time and from the minds of its speakers" (Tuite, this volume). The Saussurean project of studying the virtual structures underlying linguistic competence has been carried forth most notably by the various schools of formalist grammar, whose models of language are characteristically situated in what two linguists recently dubbed "Chomskiania, the land of idealized speaker-hearers," these being a "uniform population modelled by a single solipsist speaking to himself" (Pierrehumbert and Gross 2003).

In view of the dominance of what are often – and perhaps inaccurately – called Saussurean models in the field of linguistics, the ethnolinguistic perspective could be characterized as the refusal to decontextualize language. Such a description, however, gives the false impression that linguistic anthropology is a reactionary movement, with goals defined in opposition to the methodology of whatever happens to be the leading paradigm in formalist linguistics. Some of the authors represented here do, it is true, contrast purely language-centered explanations to those which make reference to speakers as social agents, the internal dynamics of speech communities, and the situated use of language (Heller on bilingualism and codeswitching, Jourdan on creolization, Ochs and

Schieffelin on the acquisition of grammatical competence). Nevertheless, we wish to point out to any linguists who might be reading this that the ethnolinguistic perspective is not to be equated with what is commonly called "functionalism," that is, attempts to supplant all or part of formalist theories of innate, specialized linguistic competence with explanations that invoke more generalized cognitive capacities, or design exigencies related to the various uses to which language is put. Much work by linguistic anthropologists is compatible with – or, in any case, does not contradict – the putative existence of an innate language organ and dedicated mental modules (Chomsky 1980; Fodor 1983). Like ethnology, linguistic anthropology is a hermeneutical enterprise; in William Foley's words, "it is an interpretive discipline peeling away at language to find cultural understandings" (1997: 3). Ethnolinguistic inquiries tend to cluster around two grand approaches to the relation between culture and language, which had long been regarded as mutually exclusive: language depends on culture; language organizes culture. Although contemporary researchers no longer attach the same significance to this formal distinction, it is nonetheless at the basis of the division between the research methods of linguistic anthropology and sociolinguistics, narrowly defined: cultural interpretation on the one hand, linguistic markers and social correlates, on the other. If linguistic anthropologists observe language with a wide-angle lens, they do not always focus on the same field of view, nor from the same standpoint. In this collection, the following themes – and probably others as well – can be adduced as points of convergence, drawing the attention of more than one author, and sometimes being subjected to quite different treatment by each: linguistic relativity, expressivity and verbal art, language socialization, translation and hermeneutics, language contact, and variation and change.

Linguistic relativity

On hearing the term "linguistic anthropology," the first thing that comes to many readers' minds is the Sapir–Whorf hypothesis, generally understood as the principle that language conditions habits of speech which in turn organize and generate particular patterns of thought. But linguistic anthropology has likewise a contribution to make to the debate between particularism and universalism, which is once again a subject of interest in many sectors of American anthropology. One sign of this renewal of attention is the return to the classic works of authors linked to particularism, notably Edward Sapir (for example, Darnell 1990 and Sapir 1994; also Lucy's [1992a] important re-reading of the foundational texts on linguistic relativity). It is true that the linguistic relativity hypothesis has played a central role in the history of North American linguistic anthropology, in that the deep, organic relation that it postulates between language and culture is of central relevance to debates on the nature of the mutual determination of language, mental representations, and social action.

John Leavitt situates the linguistic relativity concept in an intellectual history going back to Herder and Humboldt, and forward to our own times. He delineates two grand perspectives on human nature, the one universalist, seeking natural-scientific laws to account for the important features of cognition; the other pluralistic and essentialist, inspired by Romanticism and the human sciences, according to which each language (and culture) has its own essence and "indwelling principle that cannot be classified into any general category, any more than a human being or a human face" (W. v. Humboldt "Von dem grammatischen Baue der Sprachen", translated by Leavitt). Within linguistics, the natural-scientific stream came to the foreground in the Neo-grammarian doctrine of sound laws, and continued on to Chomsky and generative grammar. The other, Humboldtian, stream is less well known to anglophone readers, but, as Leavitt demonstrates, it represents a highly significant component of the intellectual backgrounds of Franz Boas and Edward Sapir.

Boas received his early training in physics, then moved into the fields of psychophysics and geography. According to Leavitt, he began his intellectual activity "right on the cusp of th[e] antinomy" between the natural and human sciences. Unlike most of his predecessors on both sides of the divide, however, Boas "rejected the evolutionist package on every level," as well as "any ranking of languages and cultures according to a fixed standard." This led to accusations, from neo-evolutionists in particular, that Boas's "radical empiricism" and emphasis on individual difference made him irreconcilably hostile to sociological and anthropological theorizing (Wax 1956). Leavitt draws an original and useful parallel between Boas's ethnology and Marx's critique of political economy; with regard to the rejection of evolutionism, one might also juxtapose Boas and the German linguist A. F. Pott, the founder of modern etymological practice. The etymological study of word histories can be conceived as being, in microcosm, an enterprise comparable to the investigation of culture, insofar as etymologists operate at the interface of the law-like regularities of historical phonetics and analogical change, on the one hand, and the messiness of history, social networks and human creativity, on the other. Sitting, like Boas, astride the divide between the *Natur-* and *Geisteswissenschaften*, Pott likewise inveighed against those who applied natural-scientific models in a heavy-handed and simplistic way, especially when such theories were informed by unexamined Eurocentrism (Pott 1856).

Despite the difficulties of operating "within a pre-existing discursive field massively oriented either to universalism or to essentialism," Boas, Sapir, and Whorf developed a means of conceptualizing the relation between language and (habitual) thought that was "pluralist but not essentialist," in that linguistic relativity – like Einstein's celebrated theory in physics – does not privilege any single point of view, nor any fixed standard (such as Indo-European had been taken to be) for assessing the adequacy of human languages.

In her contribution to the present volume, Regna Darnell presents the career of Benjamin Lee Whorf, and the role he played in pre-war American linguistic anthropology. An atypical and original character in an academic landscape succumbing to the economic downturn of the Great Depression, Whorf drew the remarkable observations that guided his thinking about the relation between language structure and habitual thought as much from his professional experience as a fire-insurance investigator as from the study of "exotic" societies. Darnell offers the intriguing hypothesis that Whorf's celebrated formulation of linguistic relativity may have not been so much "a new theory or methodology but a pedagogical effort to translate the linguistic work of Sapir and his students so that it would be comprehensible to non-linguists." Whorf died young, before he could give his intuitions the extended treatment that they required. Nonetheless, his work has drawn enormous attention, and criticism, since his death. It is clear that many interpretations and utilizations of the "Whorfian hypothesis" go well beyond anything Whorf himself appeared to have intended. Darnell warns her readers against simplistic readings of Whorf, which present his hypothesis as holding that linguistic categories mechanistically constrain thought. She limpidly delineates the differences between the approach of Boas and that of Sapir. This section of her chapter is important for what it reveals of the foundations of the Americanist tradition of linguistic anthropology, which will eventually steer it in the direction of culturalist and cognitivist frameworks: phonemic models, theories of mind, the ontological relation between language and culture.

Cognitive anthropology, earlier known under the labels "new ethnography," "semantic ethnography" or "ethnoscience," coalesced toward the end of the 1950s in the context of a movement in linguistic anthropology seeking to revise the notion of culture then favored by ethnographers. The new movement insisted on methodological rigor and the necessity of identifying fundamental cultural categories. As explained by Penelope Brown in her contribution to this volume, the notion of culture, until then primarily derived from the study of "behavior or artifacts," should be replaced by one which foregrounds the role of systems of knowledge and mental dispositions. Brown summarizes the forty-year history of cognitive anthropology's examination of the relation between language (and other semiotic systems) and thought, the role of language in organizing knowledge, etc. These questions have been at the center of vigorous debates between "(i) those who emphasize universals of human cognition vs. those who stress the importance of cultural differences, and (ii) those who treat cognition as 'in the head' vs. others who insist on its embodied, interactional, and contextually dependent nature." The first part of the chapter presents an overview of the initial approaches and goals of cognitive anthropology through the 1970s. The second part is concerned with the North American tradition of research on cultural models. The third section presents some new approaches to the issue of linguistic relativity, especially those which focus on spatial language and cognition. The author concludes by looking toward the future of the program of cognitive anthropology, suggesting some areas where fruitful research might be undertaken.

The article contributed by Paul Kay is in response to the debates provoked by the hypotheses presented in Berlin and Kay (1969) on the typology of the basic color terms of the world's languages. Their conclusions appeared to contradict standard interpretations of the Whorfian hypothesis. They imply, first of all, that a set of no more than eleven perceptual categories can account for the referential range of the basic color terms of any human language. Secondly, more elaborate color term systems evolve from less elaborate ones in a partially fixed order. In his chapter in the present volume, Kay responds to three objections raised by John Lucy, Anna Wierzbicka and others: (1) In many (perhaps all) languages, lexemes used to denote chromatic features also denote non-color properties, such as ripeness or succulence; (2) The basic color lexemes of many languages do not constitute a distinct formal class, in terms of morphology or syntactic properties; (3) The findings reported by Berlin and Kay (1969), and similar investigations in the "Universals and Evolution" tradition of research, are an artifact of the methodology used by these approaches. Kay presents a vigorous and detailed rebuttal to these criticisms in his paper, drawing upon his more than three decades of research on color terms, as well as the contributions of numerous other scholars who have looked at this lexical subsystem in various languages.

While much of the research on linguistic relativity has focused on readily delimitable semantic domains such as color, number, and space, the average learner of a foreign language is struck by differences less amenable to psycholinguistic testing: the expressive potential of the new language, the tropes and metaphors preferred by its speakers, the distinctive forms of verbal art and conversational genres. Edward Sapir – a "minor poet and a major phonologist," in Paul Friedrich's characterization – once wrote that "the understanding of a simple poem . . . involves not merely an understanding of the single words . . . but a full comprehension of the whole life of the community as it is mirrored in the words, or as it is suggested by their overtones" (Sapir 1929a [1949]: 162). Language is, by its very nature, a competence shared by a community; a phonology, grammar and lexicon structured in ways that are comparable to, but different from, those of other languages; an expressive and constitutive medium through which "we present, enact, and thus make possible our way of being in the world and to others" (Taylor, this volume). According to Jakobson's (1960) communication-theoretic model, the poetic function of speech is oriented toward the message itself, the linguistic form *as* form. Dry and technical it may be, but Jakobson's definition can be extraordinarily fruitful if one uses it, as Friedrich does, as a standpoint for viewing the multiple interactions and relations among language, the social group, and the individual. The ethnopoetic project has as its goal, one might say, the working out of the manifold implications of "form about form" for both individual creativity, and what Friedrich calls "linguaculture," a neologism intended to capture the fundamental fact that "culture is a part of language just as language is a part of culture" (Friedrich: 219). Among the facets of ethnopoetics explored in this chapter are: (1) the aesthetic and expressive potential of language structure (phonetics, morphology, etc.); (2) the dilemma of universalism and linguacultural situatedness; (3) the inevitability, yet impossibility, of translation; (4) the poetics of "nonpoetic" texts. In his concluding sections, Friedrich reflects on the possibility of reconciling philosophical and poetic conceptions of truthfulness, and the political nature of poetic texts.

Language contact

The phenomena that are described by the term *contact* in anthropology and in linguistic anthropology have challenged conceptions of culture and language as whole, bounded and organic entities. At the core of that challenge lie two issues: first, how to understand the processes of contact itself with regard to such a reified understanding of culture; and second, how to analyze the effects of contact-induced change. These two questions have forced anthropologists to engage with the issue of change as an inherent part of culture and language, and thus to apprehend social and linguistic realities in terms of processes and not simply in terms of traits and features. Central to this discourse on change are "otherness" and an understanding of the effects that alterity has on the conception of self, on group identity, and on cultural positioning. Interpretation of the other is the key feature of the contact situation. Permanent exposure to "otherness" through contact with neighboring groups may lead to various linguistic practices that have been described in the literature in terms of interference, interlanguage, bilingualism, multilingualism, language shift, language crossing, obsolescence, pidginization, and creolization. In some cases, sustained contact has led to an exacerbated sense of group identity that may be symbolized through the enhancement of linguistic differences (as in the Amazon basin or Melanesia). Anthropologists interested in contact-induced cultural change have focused on cultural borrowing, diffusion, reinterpretation, syncretism, translation, and acculturation; but also on biculturalism and multiculturalism and, more recently, on cultural creolization and on the effect of globalization on local cultures. Some forms of contact, such as colonization and forced displacements of population, are extreme types that, through imposition of new ideologies and modes of life, have severely altered, and often destroyed, the pre-existing balance of power among neighboring groups. They have often brought about the birth of new languages (such as pidgins and creoles), but also the death or attrition of others. Under colonization, or any other form of hegemonic conditions, the cultural anchoring of languages is challenged and often shattered, compelling individuals and groups to adopt the language spoken by the dominant power, or whatever language that will allow them to survive socially. In most cases, the question of choice is irrelevant.

In this volume, two chapters address some of the linguistic effects of cultural contact: Jourdan presents an analysis of the genesis of pidgin and creole (PC) languages, while Heller discusses bilingualism with regard to linguistic and cultural theory.

Jourdan tackles the question of PC genesis from the angle of culture, power and meaning. Convinced as she is that the birth of new languages cannot be dissociated from the social condition of their genesis, and that the impetus for PC genesis is found in the lived experience of their makers, she seeks to identify the cultural components of this experience that have led to, and shaped, the development of these new languages. Considering primarily those pidgins that have evolved in plantation societies of the Atlantic and Pacific, and starting with the concept of culture, Jourdan revisits the conditions prevalent in these social worlds. A discussion of the social organization of the plantations and of the work practice on plantations, as well as of practices of cultural retention on the part of the workers, leads her to propose that *work*, and work-related activities, have been among the main loci of pidgin genesis. Special consideration of the power relationships that were characteristic of plantation societies allows her to shed light on the conflictual and consensual relationships that have made pidgins possible. She further suggests that in situations of liminality or cultural alienation, the birth of a new language may be constitutive of a form of resistance against hegemony. She concludes that, given human agency and the social conditions that served as their matrix, the birth of pidgins and creoles was inevitable.

One outcome of sustained contact between ethnocultural groups has been bilingualism or multilingualism, a phenomenon that has been often portrayed as a pragmatic response to local sociolinguistic realities. In her chapter, Monica Heller moves away from such a functionalist approach to bilingualism, and instead examines it from the points of view of linguistic theory, the demands of the nation-state and the political economy of culture. Her own research on codeswitching demonstrates the challenges it poses to core tenets of linguistic theory. Whether it is considered from the perspective of universal grammar, or from an interactionist theory of language, codeswitching challenges the conception of language as an autonomous system. She asks: "What if grammar were the order speakers impose, more or less successfully, on their linguistic resources?" But bilingualism also challenges directly the organicity of the nation-state conceived as the bounded collective space where the unity of language and ethnicity takes place, a representation which has driven many a language-policy reform. More interestingly, bilingualism is seen as a resource deployed by speakers in making meaning, and on this basis Heller calls for a reassessment of traditional tenets in linguistic anthropology concerning language, identity and culture. In her view, language is best seen as a complex and fuzzy social construct, that is not evenly distributed socially, and which is associated by speakers with disparate goals, values and intentions, in the course of social practice. Bilingualism can be conceptualized as a set of ideologically loaded resources through which speakers, as social actors, not only replicate existing conventions and relations, but also create new ones.

Language socialization

Sentences such as "I declare the meeting adjourned," or "I bet you $50 the Cubs will win the World Series before the end of the century" are known to philosophers as performatives, in that the speaker performs the act of adjourning a meeting or making a bet by the very fact of having uttered these words. As analyzed by Austin (1975), performatives conventionally presuppose the conditions for their successful performance, and have conventional entailments, i.e. their successful performance brings about a specific state of affairs. Anyone can *say* "I declare the meeting adjourned," but the utterance will only be efficacious if there is in fact a meeting going on, the speaker has the floor, he or she has been invested with the authority of chairperson, and so forth. The importance of Austin's analysis for anthropologists is that it can in principle be extended to *any* utterance. Silverstein (1976) has combined the notion of performativity with Peircian semiotics (the concept of indexicality, in particular), to create a powerful tool for investigating the context-dependence of speech. Even a blandly routine "Nice day, isn't it?", said to a neighbor one passes on the sidewalk, is laden with indices pertaining to the social identity of the speaker (variables of pronunciation or form correlated with sex, age, social class, ethnicity, etc.), that of the interlocutor (casual or formal style, mode of address), and the nature of the interaction (phatic communion, rather than an earnest request for meteorological data). Each element of the phrase presupposes an appropriate context, if only on the grammatical level, and entails certain consequences for subsequent talk. On-going speech can be imagined as a point of intersubjective focus moving forward in time, surrounded by more or less shadowy concentric circles of presupposable knowledge, from the most immediate, local and ephemeral, to the most general, durable and "cultural."

Best known to anthropologists for their research on language socialization, Elinor Ochs and Bambi Schieffelin have also made important contributions to linguistics and to the study of child language acquisition. Psycholinguists have long known that children achieve grammatical mastery of their native languages at about the same age, regardless of the structure of the language, the degree of explicit training they receive from their care-givers, or the use of simplified registers such as mainstream North American "motherese." But children are not just maturing language organs acquiring the principles and parameters of the target language. They are also becoming competent social actors and interactants, learning not only what to say, but when and to whom to say it. In other words, children are picking up the indexical associations, the presuppositions and entailments of language forms – their performative component – along with their grammatical structure. In this paper, an updated version of one written a decade ago for the *Handbook of child language* (Ochs and Schieffelin 1995), Ochs and Schieffelin, drawing on their long-term ethnographic studies of language acquisition in Samoa and highland New Guinea, demonstrate the degree to which "children's use and understanding of grammatical forms is culturally reflexive – tied in manifold ways to local views of how to think, feel, know, (inter)act, or otherwise project a social persona or construct a relationship." Based on their fieldwork, they show that children readily acquire age-, status- and gender-appropriate forms that are rarely used by the adults around them, while not employing more frequently heard grammatical constructions that are not deemed appropriate for children. "Even very young children," they conclude, "appear to be sensitive to the ways in which grammatical constructions within a code index social identity," as demonstrated by their selection of linguistic forms that, in accordance with communal norms that often operate below the level of conscious awareness, signal – and construct – their identity as children, as members of a kingroup, as male or female.

Elizabeth Povinelli's contribution builds upon Ochs and Schieffelin's work on language socialization, despite the impression the reader might get from the opening scene, set in the Australian outback over a century ago. Two European men and a group of Arrente speakers are portrayed engaging in a cross-language encounter reminiscent of the late W. V. Quine's well-known parable on the inscrutability of reference (Quine 1969). The two parties attempt to bridge the radically different conceptual and cultural arrays that have been brought into momentary contact by the European's finger pointing to "that" field-of-action, which he understands as "sex," explained as necessary to keep the head decorations from coming loose during a corroboree. The anthropologist who points to a passing rabbit, and the native who says "gavagai" are presented by Quine as engaged in a simple act of reference and predication.

The scene reconstructed by Povinelli is far less innocent. The Arrentes, forced from their land and hunted like animals, offer ethnographic data in exchange for food and protection. In this highly asymmetric context of communication, the bridge opened by Spencer and Gillen's extended fingers and sketches in the sand is not destined for an equitable two-way flow of information. The utterances and performances of the Arrentes supply the ethnographers with comparative data, and perhaps a few titillating or exotic excerpts to be reframed for mass consumption. As for the Aborigines, the English term "sex," accompanied by its Victorian-era ideological baggage, "slowly rearticulated the total order of indigenous semantic and pragmatic meaning, entextualizing new value-laden references and predications." This story of the impression of meanings and norms onto minds (and bodies) under asymmetric power relations is a jumping-off point for Povinelli's thought-provoking and original exploration of the emergence of the pre-linguistic subject into the symbolic order. It is at this stage that the child's "intimate grammar" begins to form, as "traumas and corporeal sensations" are laminated onto language along with socially approved (or, in any case, care-giver-approved) norms of speech, behavior and the presentation of self. Some readers may still grit their teeth whenever the name of Lacan is invoked within earshot, but there is no doubt that Povinelli's ambitious attempt to wed key notions from Lacanian psychology to the analytical tools of contemporary anthropology, sociolinguistics, and pragmatics will draw new attention to the crucial, but understudied, developmental phase in early childhood where language, gender identity, and desire emerge.

Translation and hermeneutics

Leaving aside what the Arrentes might have thought about their encounter, the ethnographers Spencer and Gillen probably considered themselves to have been engaged in the work of translation, or rather hermeneutics, the interpretation of difficult, chronologically or culturally distant texts. Habermas (1983: 258) distinguished three major stances among social scientists with regard to the project of interpretation. The first, "hermeneutic objectivism," continues to pin its hopes on what Dilthey called "empathy" (Einfühlung), the sympathetic reading of distant texts undistorted by the reader's own cultural, linguistic and historical situation. In reaction, some philosophers (Richard Rorty, for example) opposed a relativist "radical hermeneuticism" to the naïve, and potentially ethnocentric, traditional approach, accompanied by the renouncing of claims to objectivity and explanatory power. Habermas himself staked out the middle ground, favoring a "hermeneutic reconstructionism" which does not claim absolute neutrality, yet seeks, through a dialogic back-and-forth between the reader's horizon and the distant one of the text, to arrive at "some sort of objective and theoretical knowledge."

The question of the grounding of interpretation across distinct linguacultural horizons, or of its very possibility, lies at the heart of the ethnolinguistic enterprise, indeed, that of anthropology as a whole. The contributors to this volume touch on this matter from their particular standpoints, and the lack of consensus within the confines of these pages is representative of the field at large. Some cognitive scientists and psycholinguists anchor their understanding of hermeneutics in intensional universals: patterns, concepts and categories of thought common to all humanity, presumably as infrastructural features of the mind determined by our common genetic heritage. The very different semantic universalisms of Jerry Fodor and Anna Wierzbicka are extreme cases in point, but it is safe to say that few people nowadays still take radical-empiricist, *tabula rasa* models of mind seriously. Most scholars also assume some measure of extensional universals, these being features not just of the world "out there," but also the much closer-to-home commonalities of the human body, human life cycles, the expression of emotional states (for example, Paul Ekman's work on facial expressions), etc.

In what was to be his last conference paper, Roger Keesing (1993) accused anthropologists of exaggerating "the gulfs between culturally constructed worlds of thought and experience" in the face of mounting evidence from cognitive science and linguistics, and indeed from the daily experiences of the Kwaios with whom he had lived in the Solomon Islands, as they shuttle back and forth between the mountain shrines of their ancestors, and the shops, schools, and video parlors of the capital, and between their indigenous Austronesian language and Solomons Pidgin and/or English. (A less dramatic, almost reflex-like, shuttling between languages is a daily occurrence here in Montréal, and doubtless many other bilingual or polyglot societies the world over. We have noted from our own experience – and numerous acquaintances have related similar stories – that it is quite possible to recall, in great detail, the content of a conversation one had at lunch, or of a program seen on television, without remembering what language(s) it was in.) Yet however rich, specific and hard-wired the pan-human common ground might be, the differences are there, they are evident to everyone, and they serve as expressive resources, and occasions of adventure and aesthetic appreciation, not just obstacles to perfect understanding. Friedrich asserts that "translation is linguistically and mathematically impossible," yet it has been attempted since the dawn of civilization, and doubtless long before then. Taylor points out the inevitability of "Sapir–Whorf incommensurabilities" across languages and cultures, in social institutions, values, practices and virtues, yet in the same sentence, he avers that they are "the very stuff of life in multicultural, 'globalizing' societies." If Povinelli's hypothesis about intimate grammars is on the mark, minor (and perhaps not-so-minor) incommensurabilities may lurk beneath the surface of face-to-face encounters between two people who, by all appearances, speak the same language and participate in the same culture. Being a *passe-muraille* is a conscious stance for some, a necessity for others, and – to a greater or less degree – part and parcel of everyone's social life, whether or not one realizes it.

Variation and change

Hermeneutics originated as the methodology for interpreting ancient texts, such as the Bible and the Homeric epics. Although many philosophers interested in hermeneutic theory have turned their attention toward the difficulties of interpreting across contemporary social and linguistic divides, new advances in this area can be brought to bear once again on the study of the past. In his chapter, Kevin Tuite considers the consequences of treating historical linguistics – and in particular, its somewhat rarefied subfield of etymology – as a member in full standing of the historical social sciences. Linguists hypothesizing sound changes in the distant past, and etymologists studying word origins, are practitioners of historical reconstruction and historiography. This being the case, what can historical linguists learn from recent debates on narrativity, the poetics of historical writing or archaeological methodology? In his paper, Tuite looks at recent work on variation and change in language, specifically, that done within the framework of variationist sociolinguistics. It is an inherent characteristic of language, as a shared competence that continually emerges and renews itself through communicative interaction, that it is constantly changing, and that no speech community, nor even the speech repertoire of a single individual, is completely uniform. As Labov and his colleagues have documented, the ubiquity of variation entails a constant source of distinguishing variables which can take on indexical loadings of all sorts. Ethnographic work by sociolinguists has begun to reveal the networks through which new pronunciations spread, and the identity-marking (and identity-making) strategies underlying the deployment of speech variables. Much work remains to be done, and the circumstances surrounding linguistic innovation remain obscure. Can Ochs and Schieffelin's research on language socialization, Friedrich's ethnopoetic inquiry into the creative potential of all speakers (not just poets), or Povinelli's work on the uneasy interface between intimate and social grammars, help us further explore the murky and porous boundary between the communal and the individual? One thing, at least, is certain: it will take a *passe-muraille* . . .

I

AN ISSUE ABOUT LANGUAGE

CHARLES TAYLOR

How to understand language? This is a pre-occupation going back to the very beginning of our intellectual tradition. What is the relation of language to other signs? to signs in general? Are linguistic signs arbitrary or motivated? What is it that signs and words have when they have meaning? These are very old questions. Language is an old topic in Western philosophy, but its importance has grown. It is not a major issue among the ancients. It begins to take on greater importance in the seventeenth century, with Hobbes and Locke. And then in the twentieth century it has become close to obsessional. All major philosophers have their theories of language: Heidegger, Wittgenstein, Davidson, and all manner of "deconstructionists" have made language central to their philosophical reflection.

In what we can call the modern period, from the seventeenth century, there has been a continual debate, with philosophers reacting to and feeding off each other, about the nature of language. I think we can cast light on this debate if we identify two grand types of theory. I will call the first an "enframing" theory. By this I mean that the attempt is made to understand language within the framework of a picture of human life, behaviour, purposes, or mental functioning, which is itself described and defined without reference to language. Language is seen as arising in this framework, which can be variously conceived as we shall see, and fulfilling some function within it, but the framework itself precedes, or at least can be characterized independently of language.

The other type of theory I want to call "constitutive." As this word suggests, it is the antitype of the enframing sort. It gives us a picture of language as making possible new purposes, new levels of behaviour, new meanings, and hence as not explicable within a framework picture of human life conceived without language.

The classical case, and most influential first form of an enframing theory was the set of ideas developed from Hobbes through Locke to Condillac. I have discussed this in "Language and Human Nature."[1] Briefly, the Hobbes–Locke–Condillac (HLC) form of theory tried to understand language within the confines of the modern representational epistemology made dominant by Descartes. In

[1] In *Human agency and language*, Cambridge 1985.

16

the mind, there are "ideas." These are bits of putative representation of reality, much of it "external." Knowledge consists in having the representation actually square with the reality. This we can only hope to achieve if we put together our ideas according to a responsible procedure. Our beliefs about things are constructed, they result from a synthesis. The issue is whether the construction will be reliable and responsible or indulgent, slapdash, and delusory.

Language plays an important role in this construction. Words are given meaning by being attached to the things represented via the "ideas" which represent them. The introduction of words greatly facilitates the combination of ideas into a responsible picture. This facilitation is understood in different ways. For Hobbes and Locke, they allow us to grasp things in classes, and hence make possible synthesis wholesale where non-linguistic intuition would be confined to the painstaking association of particulars. Condillac thinks that the introduction of language gives us for the first time control over the whole process of association; it affords us "empire sur notre imagination."[2]

The constitutive theory finds its most energetic early expression in Herder, precisely in a criticism of Condillac. In a famous passage of the treatise on the *Ursprung der Sprache*, Herder repeats Condillac's fable – one might say "just so" story – of how language might have arisen between two children in a desert.[3] He professes to find something missing in this account. It seems to him to presuppose what it's meant to explain. What it's meant to explain is language, the passage from a condition in which the children emit just animal cries to the stage where they use words with meaning. The association between sign and some mental content is already there with the animal cry (what Condillac calls the "natural sign"). What is new with the "instituted sign" is that the children can now use it to focus on and manipulate the associated idea, and hence direct the whole play of their imagination. The transition just amounts to their tumbling to the notion that the association can be used in this way.

This is the classic case of an enframing theory. Language is understood in terms of certain elements: ideas, signs, and their association, which precede its arising. Before and after, the imagination is at work and association takes place. What's new is that now the mind is in control. This itself is, of course, something that didn't exist before. But the theory establishes the maximal possible continuity between before and after. The elements are the same, combination continues, only the direction changes. We can surmise that it is precisely this continuity which gives the theory its seeming clarity and explanatory power: language is robbed of its mysterious character, is related to elements that seem unproblematic.

---

[2] See *Leviathan*, ch. 4, Oakeshott edition, Oxford: Blackwell n.d., p. 20; *Essay concerning human understanding*, 3.3.2; *Essai sur l'origine des connaissances humaines*, 1.2.4.45–6.

[3] "Über den Ursprung der Sprache", in *Johann Gottfried Herder's Sprachphilosophie*, Hamburg: Felix Meiner 1960, pp. 12–14.

Herder starts from the intuition that language makes possible a different kind of consciousness, which he calls "reflective" (*besonnen*). That is why he finds a continuity explanation like Condillac's so frustrating and unsatisfying. The issue of what this new consciousness consists in and how it arises is not addressed, as far as Herder is concerned, by an account in terms of pre-existing elements. That's why he accuses Condillac of begging the question. "Der Abt Condillac [. . .] hat das ganze Ding Sprache schon vor der ersten Seite seines Buchs erfunden vorausgesetzt, [. . .]"[4]

What did Herder mean by "reflection" (*Besonnenheit*)? This is harder to explain. I have tried a reconstruction in *The Importance of Herder*.[5] We might try to formulate it this way: pre-linguistic beings can react to the things which surround them. But language enables us to grasp something *as* what it is. This explanation is hardly transparent, but it puts us on the track. To get a clearer idea we need to reflect on what is involved in using language.

You ask me what kind of shape this is, and I say "a triangle." Let's say it is a triangle. So I get it right. But what's involved in getting it right in this sort of case? Well, it involves something like knowing that "triangle" is the right descriptive term for this sort of thing. Perhaps I can even tell you why: "see, the thing is bounded by three straight sides." But sometimes I recognize something and I can't say very much if anything about why. I just *know* that that's a classical symphony we're hearing. Even in this case, however, I acknowledge that the question "why?" is quite in order; I can imagine working further on it and coming up with something, articulating what underlies my confidence that I've got it right.

What this brings out is that a certain understanding of the issue involved is inseparable from descriptive language, viz., that the word can be right or wrong, and that this turns on whether the described has certain characteristics. A being who uses descriptive language does so out of a sensitivity to issues of this range. This is a necessary proposition. Of a being, like a parrot, to whom we can attribute no such sensitivity, we would never say that it was describing anything, no matter how unerringly it squawked out the "right word." Of course, as we prattle on, we are rarely focusing on the issue of rightness; we only do so when we get uncertain and are plumbing unexplored depths of vocabulary. But we are being continuously responsive to rightness, and that is why we always recognize the relevance of a challenge that we have misspoken. It's this non-focal responsiveness which I'm trying to capture with the word "sensitivity."

So language involves sensitivity to the issue of rightness. The rightness in the descriptive case turns on the characteristics of the described. We might call this "intrinsic" rightness. To see what this amounts to let's look at a contrast case. There are other kinds of cases in which something we can roughly call a

---

[4] *Urprung* p. 12.
[5] "The importance of Herder", in *Philosophical arguments*, Harvard University Press 1995.

sign can be rightly or wrongly used. Suppose I train some rats to go through the door with the triangle when this is offered as an alternative to a door with a circle. The rats get to do the right thing. The right signal behaviour here is responding to the triangle positively. The rat responds to the triangle door by going through it, we might say, as I respond to the triangle by saying the word.

But now the disanalogy springs to light. What makes going through the door the right response to the triangle is that it's what brings the cheese in the end-chamber of the maze. The kind of rightness involved here is one which we can define by success in some task, here getting the cheese. Responding to the signal plays a role in completing the task, and that's why there's a "correct use" of the signal. But this is a different kind of rightness from the one involved in aligning a word with the characteristics of some described referent.

But, one might object, doesn't the rat do something analogous? Doesn't he recognize that the triangle "indicates cheese"? He is after all responding to a characteristic of the triangle door, even if an instrumental one. The rat, we might say, aligns his action with a characteristic of this door, viz., that it's the one behind which the cheese always is. So perhaps we might better "translate" his understanding by saying that the triangle indicates "rush through here." But this shift in translation alerts us to what is wrong with this assimilation. There are certainly characteristics of the situation in virtue of which "rush through here" is the right response to a triangle on a door. But getting the response right has nothing to do with identifying these characteristics or any others. That's why the question, under what precise description the rat gets it right – "that's where the cheese is," or "where reward is," or "where to jump," or whatever – is pointless and inapplicable.

What this example brings out is the difference between responding appropriately in other ways to features of the situation, on one hand, and actually identifying what these features are, on the other. The latter involves giving some definition, some explicit shape, to these features. This takes us beyond merely responding to them; or, otherwise put, it is a further response of its own special kind. This is the response we carry out in words. We characteristically define the feature in applying the word, which is why this application must be sensitive to issues of intrinsic rightness, to the fact that the word applies *because* of the defined features, else it is not properly a word.[6]

By contrast, let's call what the rat responds to a "signal," marking by this term that the response involves no definition of features, but rather rushing through to

---

[6] Nothing in our experience really corresponds to the wordless world of the rat. But we do have experiences which illustrate what it is to take the further step beyond inarticulate action. We are sometimes asked to articulate just what we have been responding to, for instance, what angers us in a person's demeanour, or why we find some scene pleasing. Being able to say gives an explicit shape to features which were, all undefined, moulding our feelings and behaviour. This alters our stance towards these features, and often opens up new possibilities for us. I repeat: this example is not intended to offer insight into the world of animals, because much of our world is *already* articulated, even when we are not focally aware of it. I will touch on this below.

reward. Otherwise put, where responding to a signal plays a role in some task, correct signal behaviour is defined by success in that task. Unless this success is itself defined in terms of getting something intrinsically right – which is not the case for winning through to cheese – correct response to the signal need involve no definition of any particular characteristics; it just involves reacting rightly, and this is compatible with recognizing a whole host of such characteristics, or none at all: the rat just knows to rush through here; he knows from nothing about descriptions and qua what he should rush it.

The rightness involved in description is crucially different. We can't just define it in terms of success in some task – unless we define this task itself in terms of what I called above intrinsic rightness. In other words, intrinsic rightness is irreducible to what we might call task rightness simpliciter: the account only works if we have already incorporated intrinsic rightness in our success criteria.[7]

This shows a possible ambiguity in the use of expressions like "knows that this is the proper door to rush through." Applied to the rat in the above example it can just mean that he knows how to respond to the signal. But in another context, we might mean something like: knows how to apply the description "the proper door to rush through" correctly. The point of the above discussion is to show that these are very different capacities. Having the first capacity doesn't need to involve aligning any signs with reality on grounds of the features this reality displays; having the second essentially consists in acting out of sensitivity to such grounds. In the second case a certain kind of issue must be at stake, animating the behaviour, and this may be quite absent in the first.

A confusion between these two bedevils a number of discussions about animal behaviour, most notably the controversy about chimp "language." We can prescind from all the arguments whether the chimps really always sign in the appropriate way, concede the case to their protagonists, and still ask what is going on here. That an animal gives the sign "banana" only in the presence of bananas, or "want banana" only when it desires one, doesn't by itself establish what is happening. Perhaps we're dealing with a capacity of the first kind: the animal knows how to move its paws to get bananas, or attention and praise from the trainer. In fact, the sign is aligned with an object with certain features, a curved, tubular, yellow fruit. But this doesn't show that that's the point of the exercise; that the animal is responding to this issue in signing.

But only in the latter case would the chimps have "language" in something like the sense we do. In the former, we would have to see their signing behaviour

---

[7] The above contrast between people describing and rats in mazes might be thought to be skewed by another obvious disanalogy between the two cases, that the person describing is emitting the signals, and the rat is only responding to them. But consider this case: certain birds are genetically constituted so that when one sights a predator he cries out, and all flee. There is a "right use" of this signal – one could imagine a case of a bird with damaged vocal chords who emitted the wrong sound, with disastrous consequences. But there is likewise no answer to the question, what precise "translation" to give to the cry: "hawk!", or "predator!", or "skedaddle!", or whatever.

as more of a piece with the clever instrumental performances that we know chimps can master, like manipulating sticks, and moving boxes around to get at things out of reach, which Köhler described.[8] The one kind of achievement need be considered no more properly "semantic" than the other.

Whereas to be sensitive to the issue of intrinsic rightness is to be operating, as it were, in another dimension. Let me call this the "semantic dimension." Then we can say that properly linguistic beings are functioning in the semantic dimension. And that can be our way of formulating Herder's point about "reflection." To be reflective is to operate in this dimension, which means acting out of sensitivity to issues of intrinsic rightness.

But we need to extend somewhat our notion of the semantic dimension. Above I was speaking of descriptive rightness. But we do more things in language than describe. There are other ways in which a word can be "*le mot juste.*" For instance, I come up with a word to articulate my feelings, and thus at the same time shape them in a certain manner. This is a function of language which cannot be reduced to simple description, at least not description of an independent object. Or else I say something which re-establishes the contact between us, puts us once again on a close and intimate footing. We need a broader concept of intrinsic rightness than just that involved in aligning words with objects.

We can get a more general description if we recur to a contrast I made above. The correct response to a signal for a rat trained in a maze was defined, I said, by success in some task. Let's use the word "sign" as a general term which can apply indiscriminately to this kind of case as well as to genuine uses of language. Then we can say that functioning with signs lies outside the semantic dimension wherever the right response is defined simply in terms of what leads to success in some non-semantically defined task. Where this account is not sufficient, the behaviour falls within the dimension.

Rats responding to triangles, and birds responding with cries to the presence of predators, meet this criterion. An account in terms of a simple task suffices. Where it fails to, we enter the semantic dimension. This can happen in two ways. First the task itself can be defined in terms of intrinsic rightness; for instance, where what we are trying to do is describe some scene correctly. Or else, where the end is something like: articulating my feelings, or re-establishing contact, the failure occurs at another point. As goals, these don't on the face of it seem to involve intrinsic rightness. But the way in which the correct sign-behaviour contributes to fulfilling them does.

Thus, when I hit on the right word to articulate my feelings, and acknowledge that I am motivated by envy, say, the term does its work because it is the right term. In other words, we can't explain the rightness of the word "envy" here simply in terms of the condition that using it produces; rather we have to account

[8] Wolfgang Köhler.

for its producing this condition – here, a successful articulation – in terms of its being the right word. A contrast case should make this clearer. Say that every time I get stressed out, tense and cross-pressured, I take a deep breath, and blow it explosively out of my mouth, "how!" I immediately feel calmer and more serene. This is plainly the "right sound" to make, as defined by this desirable goal of restored equilibrium. The rightness of "how!" admits of a simple task account. It's like the rat case and the bird case, except that it doesn't involve directing behaviour across different organisms, and therefore doesn't look like "communication." (But imagine that every time you feel cross-pressured, I go "how!," and that restores your serenity.) That's because we can explain the rightness simply in terms of its bringing about calm, and don't need to explain its bringing about calm in terms of rightness.

This last clause points up the contrast with "envy" as the term which articulates/clarifies my feelings. It brings about this clarification, to be sure, and that's essential to its being the right word here. But central to its clarifying is its being the right word. So we can't just explain its rightness by its de facto clarifying. You can't define its rightness by the de facto causal consequence of clarifying, in other words, make this outcome criterial for its rightness, because you don't know whether it's clarifying unless you know that it's the right term. Whereas in the case of "how!," all there was to its rightness was its having the desired outcome; the bare de facto consequence is criterial. That's why normally we wouldn't be tempted to treat this expletive as though it had a meaning.

Something similar can be said about my restoring the intimacy between us by saying "I'm sorry." This was "the right thing to say," because it restored contact. But at the same time, we can say that these words are efficacious in restoring contact because of what they mean. Intrinsic rightness enters into the account here, because what the words mean can't be defined by what they bring about. Again, we might imagine that I could also set off a loud explosion in the neighborhood, which would so alarm you that you would forget about our tiff and welcome my presence. This would then be, from a rather cold-blooded, strategic point of view, the "right move." But the explosion "means" nothing.

What this discussion is moving us towards is a definition of the semantic dimension in terms of the possibility of a reductive account of rightness. A simple task account of rightness for some sign reduces it to a matter of efficacy for some non-semantic purpose. We are in the semantic dimension when this kind of reduction cannot work, when a kind of rightness is at issue which can't be cashed out in this way. That's why the image of a new "dimension" seems to me apposite. To move from non-linguistic to linguistic agency is to move to a world in which a new kind of issue is at play, a right use of signs which is not reducible to task-rightness. The world of the agent has a new axis on which to respond; its behaviour can no longer be understood just as the purposive seeking of ends on the old plane. It is now responding to a new set of demands. Hence the image of a new dimension.[9]

If we interpret him in this way, we can understand Herder's impatience with Condillac. The latter's "natural signs" were things like cries of pain or distress. Their right use in communication could only be construed on the simple task model. Language arose supposedly when people learned to use the connection already established by the natural sign, between, say, the cry and what caused the distress, in a controlled way. The "instituted sign" is born, an element of language properly speaking. Herder cannot accept that the transition from pre-language to language consists simply in a taking control of a pre-existing process. What this leaves out is precisely that a new dimension of issues becomes relevant, that the agent is operating on a new plane. Hence in the same passage in which he declares Condillac's account circular, Herder reaches for a definition of this new dimension, with his term "reflection."

On my reconstruction, Herder's "reflection" is to be glossed as the semantic dimension, and his importance is that he made this central to any account of language. Moreover, Herder's conception of the semantic dimension was multi-faceted, along the lines of the broad conception of rightness above. It didn't just involve description. Herder saw that opening this dimension has to transform all aspects of the agent's life. It will also be the seat of new emotions. Linguistic beings are capable of new feelings which affectively reflect their richer sense of their world: not just anger, but indignation; not just desire, but love and admiration.

The semantic dimension also made the agent capable of new kinds of relations, new sorts of footings that agents can stand on with each other, of intimacy and distance, hierarchy and equality. Gregarious apes may have (what we call) a "dominant male," but only language beings can distinguish between leader, king, president, and the like. Animals mate and have children, but only language beings define kinship.

Underlying both emotions and relations is another crucial feature of the linguistic dimension, that it makes possible value in the strong sense. Pre-linguistic animals treat something as desirable or repugnant, by going after it or avoiding it. But only language beings can identify things as *worthy* of desire or aversion. For such identifications raise issues of intrinsic rightness. They involve a characterization of things which is not reducible simply to the ways we treat them as objects of desire or aversion. They involve a recognition beyond that, that they *ought* to be treated in one or another way.

This discussion brings us back to the central thesis that I want to draw out of Herder, the one that justifies the label "constitutive." I have been arguing

---

[9] Hence also my use of the word "intrinsic." This is a dangerous word, which triggers often unreflective reactions from pragmatists, non-realists, and other such idealists. Its point here is simply to serve as an antonym to "capable of reductive explanation."

above that operating in the semantic dimension is an essential condition of counting as a being which uses language in the full sense. No language without semantic dimension. But the crucial Herderian thesis also inverts this relation: no semantic dimension without language. This may seem a trivial consequence of the way I have set up this discussion. If we define the semantic dimension as sensitivity to certain issues concerning the right use of *signs*, then it follows tautologically that it requires language to be.

But a more substantive point follows from this way of seeing things. Being in the semantic dimension means that we can treat the things which surround us in new ways. We don't just respond to them in virtue of their relevance for our simple (i.e. non-semantic) purposes: as ways to get cheese, or trigger off serenity. We are also capable of dealing with them as the proper objects of certain descriptions; we might say: as the locus of certain features (or in more familiar language, as the bearers of certain properties), where recognizing them as such involves more than just treating them as functionally relevant to certain simple ends. As we saw above, such functionally relevant treatment need involve the recognition of no specific range of features: learning to rush through the triangle door doesn't involve attributing to this door the property: "way to food," or "good place for cheese," or gerundively "to be rushed through," or "to be approached." If we thus designate what is involved in description as the definition of features (or the attribution of properties), then we can say that being in the semantic dimension confers on the things which surround us meanings (in the familiar phenomenological sense of this term) of a new kind. They are not just paths or obstacles to simple tasks, but can also be loci of features. And similarly for the other facets of the semantic dimension.

The substantive point about language is an answer to the question, whether things can have this meaning for us without language. And the Herderian answer is "no." Contemporary philosophers are familiar with this thesis, and with arguments for it, most notoriously perhaps from Wittgenstein. These arguments are sometimes construed as deployed from an observer's perspective: how could you tell for any creature you were studying whether it was defining features or attributing properties, as against just treating things functionally in relation to simple ends, unless this being had language?[10] But Wittgenstein actually uses it at a more radical level. The issue is not: how would some observer know? but how would the agent itself know? And what sense would there be in talking of attributing properties, if the agent didn't know which? Wittgenstein makes us sensible of this more radical argument in *Philosophical Investigations* I.258 and following: the famous discussion about the sensation whose occurrences the subject wants to record in a diary. Wittgenstein pushes our intuitions to the following revelatory impasse: what would it be like to know what it is you're

---

[10] Mark Okrent offers an argument of this form in *Heidegger's pragmatism*, Cornell University Press, 1988, chapter 3.

attending to, and yet be able to say absolutely nothing about it? The answer is, that this supposition shows itself to be incoherent. The plausibility of the scenario comes from our having set it up as our attending to a *sensation*. But take even this description away, leave it absolutely without any characterization at all, and it dissolves into nothing.[11] Of course, something can defy description; it can have a *je ne sais quoi* quality. But this is only because it is placed somewhere by language. It is an indescribable *feeling*, or *experience*, or *virtue*, or whatever. The sense of being unable to say wouldn't be there without the surrounding sayable. Language is what constitutes the semantic dimension.

We could sum up the point in this way. Herder's analysis establishes a distinction between (Ro) the case where an agent's (non-semantic) response to an object is *conditional* on its having certain features, and/or *because* of certain features (the rat rushes the door when this has a triangle on it, because this has been paired with reward), and (Rs) the case where the agent's response consists (at least partly) in *identifying* the object as the locus of certain features. It is Rs that we want to call responding to a thing *as* that thing. Once these two are distinguished, it is intuitively clear that Rs is impossible without language. This is what Wittgenstein's example shows up. He chooses an exercise (identifying of each new occurrence whether it is the same as an original paradigm) which is inherently in the Rs range, and we can see straight off that there is no way this issue could even *arise* for a non-linguistic creature.

This in turn throws light on the other facets of the semantic dimension. Consider the case of strong value mentioned above. What would it be to have such a sense without language? It can't just consist in certain things being very strongly desired. There has to be the sense of their being worthy of this desire. The motivation has a different quality. But how would the distinction of quality stand out for the creature itself from differences of force of desire? We can't just say: because its reaction would be different. This is, of course, true as far as it goes. A difference of reaction may be at a certain stage the only way a moral distinction is marked. But then the distinction must be carried in the kind of reaction: e.g. one of shock, or horror, or awe and admiration. But consider what we mean by a reaction of horror. It doesn't just mean a negative one, even strongly negative. There is only horror when the reaction expresses a recognition that the act was heinous or gruesome. But how can a creature distinguish the heinous or gruesome from the merely (in a non-moral sense) repugnant, unless it can identify the act *as* heinous? How does it have a sense of *transgression*, unless it had language?

The impossibility of an external observer's knowing really turns on something more radical, the impossibility of the creature's being in the semantic

---

[11] *Philosophical investigations*, I para 261: "Und es hülfe auch nichts, zu sagen: es müsse keine *Empfindung* sein: wenn er "E" schreibe, habe er *Etwas* – und mehr könnten wir nicht sagen. Aber "haben" und "etwas" gehören auch zur allgemeinen Sprache. – So gelangt man beim Philosophieren am Ende dahin, wo man nur noch einen unartikulierten Laut ausstossen möchte".

dimension without language. This is the crux of Herder's thesis, that language is constitutive of reflection. And at the same time, this shows how a constitutive theory of language breaks out of the bounds of the enframing. We can't explain language by the function it plays within a pre- or extra-linguistically conceived framework of human life, because language through constituting the semantic dimension transforms any such framework, giving us new feelings, new desires, new goals, new relationships, and introducing a dimension of strong value. Language can only be explained through a radical discontinuity with the extra-linguistic.

Constitutive theory gave a creative role to expression. Views of the HLC type related linguistic expression to some pre-existing content. A word is introduced by being linked with an idea, and henceforth becomes capable of expressing it, for Locke.[12] The content precedes its external means of expression. Condillac develops a more sophisticated conception. He argues that introducing words ("instituted signs"), because it gives us greater control over the train of thoughts, allows us to discriminate more finely the nuances of our ideas. This means that we identify finer distinctions, which we in turn can name, which will again allow us to make still more subtle discriminations, and so on. In this way, language makes possible science and enlightenment. But at each stage of this process, the idea precedes its naming, albeit its discriminability results from a previous act of naming.

Condillac also gave emotional expression an important role in the genesis of language. His view was that the first instituted signs were framed from natural ones. But natural signs were just the in-built expressions of our emotional states, animal cries of joy or fear. That language originated from the expressive cry became the consensus in the learned world of the eighteenth century. But the conception of expression here was quite inert. What the expression conveyed was thought to exist independently of its utterance. Cries made fear or joy evident to others, but they didn't help constitute these feelings themselves.

Herder develops a quite different notion of expression. This is in the logic of a constitutive theory, as I have just described it. This tells us that language constitutes the semantic dimension, that is, that possessing language enables us to relate to things in new ways, e.g. as loci of features, and to have new emotions, goals, relationships, as well as being responsive to issues of strong value. We might say: language transforms our world, using this last word in a clearly Heidegger-derived sense. That is, we are talking not of the cosmos out there, which preceded us and is indifferent to us, but of the world of our involvements, including all the things they incorporate in their meaning for us. "Meaning" is being used in the phenomenologically derived sense introduced

---

[12] *Essay* 3.2.2.

above. Something has meaning for us in this sense when it has a certain significance or relevance in our lives. So much is standard English. The neologism will consist in using this as a count noun, so that we can speak of the different ways that things are significant as different "meanings," or speak of a new form of significance as "a new meaning."[13]

Then we can rephrase the constitutive view by saying that language introduces new meanings in our world: the things which surround us become potential bearers of properties; they can have new emotional significance for us, e.g. as objects of admiration or indignation; our links with others can count for us in new ways, as "lovers," "spouses," or "fellow citizens"; and they can have strong value.

But then this involves attributing a creative role to expression. Bringing things to speech can't mean just making externally available what is already there. There are many banal speech acts where this seems to be all that is involved. But language as a whole must involve more than this, because it is also opening possibilities for us which wouldn't be there in its absence.

The constitutive theory turns our attention toward the creative dimension of expression, in which, to speak paradoxically, it makes possible its own content. We can actually see this in familiar, everyday realities, but it tends to be screened out from the enframing perspective, and it took the development of constitutive theories to bring it to light.

A good example is the "body language" of personal style. We see the leather-jacketed motorbike-rider step away from his machine and swagger towards us with an exaggeratedly leisurely pace. This person is "saying something" in his way of moving, acting, speaking. He may have no words for it, though we might want to apply the hispanic word "macho" as at least a partial description. Here is an elaborate way of being in the world, of feeling and desiring and reacting, which involves great sensitivity to certain things (like slights to one's honour: we are now the object of his attention, because we unwittingly cut him off at the last intersection), and cultivated but supposedly spontaneous insensitivity to others (like the feelings of dudes and females), which involves certain prized pleasures (riding around at high speed with the gang) and others which are despised (listening to sentimental songs); and this way of being is coded as strongly valuable; that is, being this way is admired, and failing to be earns contempt.

But how coded? Not, presumably in descriptive terms, or at least not adequately. The person may not have a term like "macho" which articulates the

---

[13] Okrent, *Heidegger's pragmatism*, uses the happy expression "meaning-subscript-h" to carry this sense, contrasting it with "meaning-subscript-i" to carry the familiar sense where we want to talk about the meaning of a word. This is an excellent way to avoid confusion. But I don't know how to manipulate subscripts on this computer, and so I'm going to take a chance, a well-warranted risk considering the phenomenologically sophisticated audience I'm writing for here. I hope the context will always make clear which sense I mean.

value involved. What terms he does have may be woefully inadequate to capture what is specific to this way of being; the epithets of praise or opprobrium may only be revelatory in the whole context of this style of action; by themselves they may be too general. Knowing that X is "one of the boys" and Y is a "dude" may tell us little. The crucial coding is in the body expressive language.

The bike-rider's world incorporates the strong value of this way of being. Let's call it (somewhat inadequately, but we need a word) "machismo." But how does this meaning exist for him? Only through the expressive gesture and stance. It's not just that an outside observer would have no call to attribute machismo to him without this behaviour. It is more radically that a strong value like this can only exist for him articulated in some form. It is this expressive style that enables machismo to exist for him, and more widely this domain of expressive body language is the locus of a whole host of different value-coded ways of being for humans in general. The expression makes possible its content; the language opens us out to the domain of meaning it encodes. Expression is no longer simply inert.

But when we turn back from this rather obvious case to the original description case, which was central to HLC theories, we see it in a new light. Here too expression must be seen as creative, language opens us to the domain it encodes. What descriptive speech encodes is our attribution of properties to things. But possessing this descriptive language is the condition of our being sensitive to the issues of intrinsic rightness which must be guiding us if we are really to be attributing properties, as we saw above. So seeing expression as creative generates Herder's constitutive theory as applied to descriptive language.

This illustrates the inner connections, both historical and logical, between the constitutive theory and a strong view of expression. Either the espousal of the first can lead one to look for places where expression obviously opens us to its own content, which we will find in this domain of body language, and with emotional expression generally. Or else, the sense that expression is creative, which will likely strike us if we are attending closely to the life of the emotions, will lead us to revise our understanding of the much-discussed case of description. In the case of Herder, the connections probably go in both directions, but if anything the second is more important than the first. The major proponents of the HLC were all rationalists in some sense; one of their central goals was to establish reason on a sound basis, and their scrutiny of language had largely this end in view. The proto-Romantic move to dethrone reason, and to locate the specifically human capacities in feeling, naturally led to a richer concept of expression than was allowed for in Condillac's natural cries, which were quite inert modes of utterance. From the standpoint of this richer notion, even the landscape of descriptive speech begins to look very different. But whatever the direction of travel, a road links the constitutive insight with the strong view of expression, so that the alternative to the enframing theory might with equal justice be called the constitutive-expressive.[14]

Being constitutive means that language makes possible its own content, in a sense, or opens us to the domain it encodes. The two cases we have just looked at: bodily expression and ordinary description, seem to involve somewhat different forms of this. In the latter case, language gives us access in a new way to a range of pre-existing things. We identify them *as* what they are; they show up for us as loci of features. In the machismo case, we feel more tempted to say that something new comes into existence through expression, viz., this way of being which our bike rider values. Prior to the coinage of this range of expression, this life ideal didn't exist.

The parallel between the two cases is that in both language makes possible new meanings. In the descriptive case, the new meaning is just things showing up *as* something. This also involves a new way of being in the world for us. Reciprocally, the bodily gesture case involves more than a new way of being; machismo also makes pre-existing things show up in new ways, e.g. we show up as dudes. So each involves, as it were, two dimensions: (1) a new manner of disclosure of what in a sense already exists (that is, identity propositions hold between items under previously available descriptions and items described in newly accessible ways), and (2) a new manner of being, or a new human possibility. We might call these two dimensions respectively, the accessive (1) and the existential (2).

The difference between the two kinds of case lies in the balance of significance. Some new uses of language (e.g. a more rigorous scientific discourse) seem mainly significant because of their accessive dimension; others, like our bodily expression case above, seem important because of their existential innovations.

But it is not true, of course, that descriptive language invariably fits in the first category, while expressive gesture makes up the second. Many uses of descriptive language have primordially existential import.

This is already true of words identifying things of strong value, e.g. the terms "macho" and "dude" in the above example. Insofar as the bike-rider isn't totally inarticulate (and how could he be, being human?), terms like this will also, along with body language, help existentially constitute his way of being. But this is also true of the language of social positions and relations. Distinctions like friends/lovers, or king/president/leader, define a space of possibilities within a given culture. This space is not the same from culture to culture, which is why translation is often hazardous (Greek "philia" is only approximately rendered

---

[14] Charles Guignon has used the term "expressive" for this view on language, in specific application to Heidegger. See his *Heidegger and the problem of knowledge*, Hackett 1983. It follows from the above that this is just as legitimate a term as "constitutive," or the double-barreled combination.

by English "friendship"). These terms have helped constitute the existential possibilities for a given society.

Then there are the languages of the self. I have tried to show[15] how the language of inwardness, for instance, and the peculiar form of moral topography it lays out, is connected in the modern West with certain moral ideals and certain notions of identity. But such locations as "inner depths" wouldn't be immediately comprehensible to people in some other cultures. Language is helping to shape us here.

This can be made sense of in the light of the earlier account of descriptive language. It allows us to locate features, as I put it. New descriptive languages lay out new topographies, a new disposition of places. But humans as self-interpreting animals are partly constituted by their own self-descriptions. And so a new topography of the self cannot but have existential import.

So language is existentially constitutive in more than its expressive modes. But these are essential, as we shall see more clearly below, and that is what Herder picked up on. Now seeing the importance of expression does more than give us a new perspective on description. It also makes us place it in a context. Acts of description are speech acts, and our speech acts exist in an expressive dimension. I am not alluding here to the sense in which we can say that a speech act of description encodes or expresses the corresponding propositional thought. Rather I am thinking of a mode continuous with the body language invoked above: the way in which we present, enact, and thus make possible our way of being in the world and to others. Our way of speaking enacts a certain stance towards our interlocutor and the matter under view. Perhaps I am warm and open, inviting you to greater intimacy, perhaps I am cold and distant, warning you to keep your distance, or perhaps I am brusque and businesslike, implying that there is no question of any alteration in the footing we're on with each other. Again, I may be projecting excitement and interest in the matter, or bored indifference, or else my matter-of-fact manner circumscribes neatly its potential range of importance for either of us.

The media in which all this is encoded go beyond body language; as indeed, they did with the case of the bike-rider, but we down-played this aspect because we portrayed him (perhaps unjustly) as being rather inarticulate. But in the whole range of human interaction, these ways of being are carried as well in the language we use, the rhetorical style we permit ourselves, the modes of address we adopt, as well as in the language of the body *stricto sensu*. There is a language of strict factual report, related to and integrated into the various languages of science, which strives to cut out all "rhetoric," and in written form seems to strive to minimize its situation in any particular web of interlocutors. But this effect is only achieved by adopting its own style, a vocabulary "bleached" of

[15] See *Sources of the self*, Harvard University Press, 1989.

emotional meanings, and a severely impersonal mode of expression. It is of the nature of human speech that something must always be coming through on the level of expression, if it be only a studied impassivity.

What is dawning on us here is one of those context doctrines which have been much invoked in modern post-phenomenology (to coin an expression for Heidegger and those he's influenced). These are doctrines to the effect that X can only take place in the context of Y. Heidegger gives us an epoch-making one, where X is the contemplative grasp of things as *vorhanden* and Y is our being in the world as engaged agents, dealing with the *zuhanden*. The contemplative grasp is a "deficient mode," in the sense that it requires a certain retreat relative to our normal engaged stance. But what I am focusing on here is the facet of Heidegger's view whereby we can be said to be always engaged in some project in the world. When we set ourselves to describe things "disinterestedly," then this becomes our project. Being in the world always involves engagement at some level, even if the nature of the exercise requires a suspension of engagement at the level we normally inhabit.

Now this might be thought to be a terrible move, similar to the invalid turns frequently taken by metaphysicians or theists against anti-metaphysicians or atheists: declaring the anti-doctrine to be a kind of metaphysics, or atheism to be a proposition in theology. But these moves are only empty if carried out on their own. There can be a surrounding argument which shows them to be valid. I won't bother to rescue theism and metaphysics here (though I'm not sure they can't be). But in the case of Heidegger, the surrounding argument is the whole existential analytic. We are *"zunächst und zumeist"* engaged with the world in the ordinary sense, dealing with things in function of our purposes. This is how we begin, and how we are most of the time, and more important, how we are in the absence of a project of being otherwise. The contemplative is a stance you only reach by setting yourself to it. That is what makes engagement fundamental and always enframing. The context doctrine is based here on more than an arbitrary reclassification.

Now a somewhat similar context thesis holds where X is describing and Y is the expressive self-projection by means of body language and rhetoric. Like the *vorhanden/zuhanden* case, we are often engaged in the latter, even when not in the former; but the reverse is not the case: to be engaged in describing, or a speech act of any kind, is to be projecting. Impassivity is itself a form of projective expression. And this claim amounts to more than an arbitrary reclassification, because describing is something we do, and we project ourselves through what we do.

The expressive-constitutive outlook is leading us rather far afield from the old enframing doctrine. It is leading us to reconceive the scope of the phenomenon which needs explanation. The HLC tended to draw a circle around descriptive uses of language, and make these its explanandum. Of course, it also recognized other uses, what would later be called the "emotive" ones;[16] Hobbes ominously allowed that words could also be used to wound.[17] But these were parallel functions, they didn't need to be taken into account in explaining the mainline descriptive use.

But the message of the context thesis is that description can't be understood outside the context of the whole speech act, which incorporates an inescapable expressive-projective dimension. That's because description, or grasping things as bearers of properties, requires language, that is, (some degree of) formulation of this description in language. And formulating in language is inseparable from expression.

Put differently, the intellectual grasp of things involved in describing, i.e. the attribution of properties to things, cannot be attained outside of the activities of language use. These are sometimes covert, as when we think silently to ourselves. But they are often also overt. And this latter is more fundamental. A context doctrine holds here as well. We learn to speak aloud, in conversations or overt play, before we learn to speak to ourselves. A form of life in which there was overt speech without the silent variety is conceivable, but not the reverse. Covert speech builds on the capacities acquired in overt conversation.

So the attribution of properties arises only within the activities of speech, in the strong, overt sense. We have to understand it in this context, and can't take for granted that ignoring the context may not lead us to crippling misconceptions. In Humboldt's famous words, we have to think of language primarily as *energeia*, not just as *ergon*.[18]

But first, we should look a bit more at the activity. It has an inescapable expressive-projective dimension; that's what I've just been urging. But it has another feature as well. It is conversation. The first, and inescapable locus of language is in exchange between interlocutors. Language involves certain kinds of links with others. In particular, it involves the link of being a conversational partner with somebody; let's call this an "interlocutor." Standing to someone as an interlocutor is fundamentally different from standing to him/her as an object of observation, or manipulative interaction. Language marks this most fundamental distinction in the difference of persons. I address someone as "you", speak of them as "him" or "her."

What this corresponds to is the way in which we create a common space by opening a conversation. A conversation has the status of a common action. When I open up about the weather to you over the back fence, what this does

---

[16] See C. K. Ogden and I. A. Richards, *The meaning of meaning*, New York: Harcourt 1923. This is a classical example of the old enframing doctrine still marching on in the twentieth century, in blissful ignorance of the constitutive critique. This is what gives this work its rather quaint air.

[17] *Leviathan*, chapter 4, p. 19.

[18] Wilhelm von Humboldt, *On language*, translated by Peter Heath, Cambridge University Press 1988, p. 49.

is make the weather an object for *us*. It is no longer just for you, and for me, with perhaps the addition that I know it's for you and you know it's for me. Conversation transposes it into an object which we are considering together. The considering is common, in that the background understanding established is that the agency which is doing the considering is us together, rather than each of us on our own managing to dovetail his/her action with the other. I have discussed this phenomenon of common space in *Theories of Meaning*.[19]

An important issue for any theory of language is: what difference it makes, if any, for our understanding of descriptive speech that it is inescapably embedded in an activity which has at least the two other features I have mentioned here, that it has an expressive dimension, and that it is primarily the activity of interlocutors.[20] I would want to argue that it makes a huge difference. Not acknowledging this has been fatal to a number of contemporary theories, I believe.

But for the moment, let me just say that expressive-constitutive theories have generally thought that it did make a difference, and some of the reasons they did derive naturally from the considerations we've been examining. These theories, as we saw, recognize the creative role of expression. They recognize that expression can open us to the range of meanings it articulates. This is especially palpable in relation to what I have been calling projective expression, the presentation of our stance to others and to things through body language, style and rhetoric. But implicit in this is the recognition that the constitutive forms of expression, those which open us to a new range of meanings, go beyond descriptive language, and even beyond speech of any form, to such things as gesture and stance.

This suggests that the phenomenon which needs to be carved out for explanation is the whole range of expressive-constitutive forms, that we are unlikely to understand descriptive language unless we can place it in a broader theory of such forms, which must hence be our prior target. This view is strengthened when we reflect how closely connected the different forms are. Our projections are carried at once in linguistic (speech style and rhetoric) and in extra-linguistic (gesture, stance) form. And we saw that description is always embedded in acts which also projectively express. The idea that these could be treated as a single range was already pre-delineated in the definition I gave earlier of the semantic dimension. For even the projections of body language fit within its scope, as having their own kind of intrinsic rightness. The swagger of our bike-rider is right in relation to the way of being he values, in a way which cannot be accounted for in terms of a simple task.

---

[19] *Human agency and language*, Cambridge 1985.

[20] Of course, there is also monological speech. This is largely extensionally equivalent with covert speech. But a similar context doctrine obviously holds here. We converse before we soliloquize; we could only converse without soliloquizing, but not the reverse. We need to converse to acquire the capacity to soliloquize.

So constitutive theories go for the full range of expressive forms (what Cassirer called the "symbolic forms").[21] And within these falls another sub-range not mentioned so far, the work of art, something which is neither expressive projection nor description. In a sense, the work of art played an even more important role in the development of expressivism than what I have been calling projection. We can see this in the conception of the symbol, as opposed to the allegory, which played an important role in the aesthetic of the Romantic period, and indeed, since. As described, for instance, by Goethe, the symbol was a paradigm of what I have been calling constitutive expression.

A work of art which was "allegorical" presented us with some insight or truth which we could also have access to more directly. An allegory of virtue and vice as two animals, say, will tell us something which could also be formulated in propositions about virtue and vice. By contrast a work of art had the value of a symbol when it manifested something which could not be thus "translated." It opens access to meanings which cannot be made available any other way. Each truly great work is in this way sui generis. It is untranslatable.

This notion, which has its roots in Kant's Third Critique, was immensely influential. It was taken up by Schopenhauer and all those he influenced, in their understanding of the work of art as manifesting what can't be said in assertions in ordinary speech. And its importance for Heidegger in his own variant needs no stressing.

The work of art as symbol was perhaps the paradigm on which the early constitutive theories of language were built. In its very definition, there is an assertion of the plurality of expressive forms, in the notion that it is untranslatable into prose. From this standpoint, the human expressive-constitutive power – or alternatively, the semantic dimension – has to be seen as a complex and many-layered thing, in which the higher modes are embedded in the lower ones.

Outside of the attribution of properties, I mentioned above three other ranges of meanings which are opened to us by language: the properly human emotions, certain relations, and strong value. But each of these is carried on the three levels of expressive form that crystallized out of the above discussion: the projective, the symbolic (in works of art), and the descriptive. We express our emotions, and establish our relations, and body forth our values, in our body language, style, and rhetoric; but we can also articulate all of these in poetry, novels, dance, music; and we can also bring all of them to descriptive articulation, where we name the feelings, relations, values, and describe and argue about them.

We could think of these three levels as ranked in this way: each successive articulation allows us to take a freer stance to, and hence get a clearer articulation of the meanings involved. What we live unreflectingly on the level of projection, can be set out before us as something we can enjoy and contemplate in a work of art, and then made an object of description and possible analysis

---

[21] Ernst Cassirer, *The philosophy of symbolic forms*, Yale University Press 1953.

in prose. Of course, this ranking can also be reversed. It is possible to hold that certain meanings cannot be adequately captured at a freer, more analytical level. This has certainly been claimed against prose analysis on behalf of articulation in "symbol," as the above discussion intimated. But whatever our views of their potential scope, these three levels offer different kinds of articulation, progressively favouring a free stance to and clarity about the meanings concerned.

This multi-layered picture of the semantic dimension underlines afresh how our descriptions stand in a field of other articulations. Our macho bike-rider above doesn't have a word for what he values. He lives it in projecting it, and he relates to a certain kind of hard rock that presents it in "symbol"; but he hasn't yet tried to describe it, say what's good about it, and he is in no position to argue for it against critics. We think of him as maximally unreflecting, and yet he lives in a world of articulated meaning. Provided we take the word "language" in a broad sense, englobing all expressive forms, his world is as linguistically constituted as that of the philosopher. That is just to say that he lives in a human world. In its most unreflecting, just-lived-in, underdescribed, zuhanden form, this world is full of linguistic mediation, even taking "language" in a narrow sense. Descriptive language doesn't erupt in a world of pure animal purposes. This is important to bear in mind, both to understand the pre-objective world, and to grasp the conditions in which descriptive language operates.

Some of the issues which have arisen among linguistic anthropologists, and have been raised elsewhere in this volume, appear in a different light if we approach them with a constitutive theory of language. I'd like in conclusion to comment here briefly on one such issue, that around the Sapir–Whorf hypothesis about language–conceptual differences. The basic idea has been described as the thesis

that the semantic structures of different languages might be fundamentally incommensurable, with consequences for the way in which speakers of specific languages might think and act. On this view, language, thought, and culture are deeply interlocked, so that each language might be claimed to have associated with it a distinctive world-view.[22]

From a constitutive perspective, this hypothesis seems eminently plausible, but also one which will have greater force in certain domains of language than others. It is therefore surprising to see not only that a great deal of effort has been expended in trying to refute it, but also that some of this has concentrated on the case of color concepts.[23] The case made in much of this research is that even though there may be differences in color vocabularies, the color distinctions

---

[22] John J. Gumperz and Stephen C. Levinson (eds.), *Rethinking linguistic relativity*, Cambridge University Press 1996, p. 2; quoted in Penelope Brown, "Cognitive anthropology," this volume.

[23] See the discussion reported, and carried forward, in Paul Kay, "Methodological issues in cross-language color naming," this volume.

accessible to the speakers of these different languages seem to be more or less the same. Asked if they can discriminate, people seem to be responding to the same perceptual categories, even if the terms in current use seem rather divergent.

I am of course no expert on color perception (to put it mildly), but it seems to me entirely plausible that there should be some (perhaps physiologically grounded) constants in this area. This is not where a constitutive theorist would most readily expect to find incommensurabilities of language and thought. To conclude that constants discovered in this area refute or even seriously damage the Sapir–Whorf view seems odd to say the least.

Where then should one look for such differences? At one level, it falls out from the discussion in the previous section, that one should in no wise simply confine oneself to examining descriptive categories; that the expressive-constitutive force of language is also evident in the setting up and maintenance of conversations, of different rapports between interlocutors, and of different stances of these to their world. These may be encoded in such things as pronouns, deictics and tenses.[24]

But I shall leave this direction of thinking aside here, and concentrate after all on semantic categories. The obvious place to look among these for some backing for the Sapir–Whorf view is not among the everyday perceptual things which surround us in nature (what J. L. Austin called "middle-sized dry goods"), but rather in the human meanings which are constituted in language; in the terms I use above, our primary search should be not in the "accessive" but in the "existential" dimension. Because such things as emotions, virtues, and social positions and relations (the gamut of possible "footings" we can be on with each other) are constituted in language, because these peculiarly human meanings are impossible without language (whereas animals can discriminate colors), it would not be at all surprising to find that different languages constitute different such meanings, indeed, incommensurable ones.

And this is in fact what we find. If we follow Thomas Kuhn in defining "incommensurable" as "untranslatable," then the existence of such differences is an obvious fact of our world. I mentioned above such examples as the (ancient) Greek word "*philia*," which only roughly translates "friendship," but cases abound if we just remain on this cultural boundary: e.g. Aristotle's "magnanimous man" ("*megaloprepês*"), exhibiting a key virtue, seems odd and partly repellent to us.[25] The Greek concept "*isonomia*" has to be elaborately explained to today's students, and even then is hard to grasp.[26]

---

[24] The original impetus here comes from Wilhelm von Humboldt; but fresh and seminal new work has been done in our day by Émile Benveniste and Michael Silverstein,

[25] *Nicomachean ethics*, Book IV, 1122a18 and ff.

[26] I have discussed this in "Theories of meaning", in *Human agency and language*, Cambridge University Press 1985, pp. 248–292.

The reason why this is bound to be so is evident. Human beings in different societies constitute different ways of life. They recognize different emotions, different virtues, build different institutions, practices, and footings. Moreover, the ways of life, while never the harmonious, organic totalities often described in Romantic theory, while often racked by deep conflicts, have necessarily a high degree of internal consonance. A given emotion, a given virtue, a certain prized act, a certain kind of footing, may only make sense within the institutions and practices of that society, and in relation to its favoured ends. The meaning of words we might translate "equality" among the ancient Greeks (like the above "*isonomia*") has to be understood in the context of (male, warrior) citizenship in a Greek polis, of those political practices, and the ends sought in participation (like honour and glory). If we think of "equality" in its modern, post-Enlightenment, universalist, socially disembedded meaning, the ancients look inconsistent, even "hypocritical" to us.

That is why good ethnographic or historiographical work, intending to explain to us a society distant in time, space or culture, is faced with a familiar dilemma. It will either opt to translate key terms in the target vocabulary with familiar English words, as the great Victorian translators of Greek philosophy did when they rendered "*phronêsis*" as "prudence," and "*technai*" as "arts." But then one has to work really hard to explain that the ordinary English meanings are wildly off base, and keep the reader/student from sliding back into an assurance that he/she unproblematically understands. Or (as ethnographers often do), we keep key words in the original language; and then work terribly hard to supply some kind of context in which the reader/student can make (not too distortive) sense of them. So we say of Japanese samurai that they commit "*seppuku*," of Polynesians that they see certain acts as "*tabu*," of kshatriyas that they recognize a certain "*dharma*," of a certain force called "*mana*," and so on.

What this reflects is the basic untranslatability/incommensurability of these terms. I mean, of course, that they are untranslatable in the English of the time of their introduction. Languages are not static; they evolve, neologize, accept loan words. At a later phase, the originally alien can become naturalized. This has happened, for instance, with the word "*tabu*." But if the cultural distance is sufficiently great, this may just represent a further stage of a long-standing, lamentable cultural misunderstanding. We are assured by experts that the present current uses of "*tabu*" in European languages are seriously divergent from the original Polynesian expression. And how could it be otherwise? How could we ethnographically uneducated ordinary speakers of English or French ever grasp enough of that original context to feel the force of the original term?

But the evolution of living languages gives us fresh examples of incommensurability. New generations arise, with new practices, new ideals, new admired ways of being. Their parents even may find it hard to see what they're going on about; grandparents are often completely baffled. If one imagines going back farther, one can see that the communication would be almost impossible. Imagine explaining the contemporary word "cool" to Queen Victoria.

These kinds of Sapir–Whorf incommensurabilities are the very stuff of life in multicultural, "globalizing" societies. Make the following thought experiment. Some important issue of public policy hangs on your having an adequate understanding of a society with a very different culture and language. Would you be willing to take advice from people none of whom knew the language, and hence understood no more of what the people were saying than they could smoothly (i.e. without elaborate, context-providing explanations) translate into English? If you answer this question in the affirmative, I can only fervently hope that you are never asked to consult at the White House or the Pentagon, where the perception of the world's incommensurabilities is all too uncertain and intermittent.

In this dimension that I have dubbed "existential," where human meanings are constituted in language in the broad sense, englobing the whole range of "symbolic forms," some formulation of the Sapir–Whorf thesis approaches the status of truism. To seek to refute the thesis with evidence from constancy of color perception is to misunderstand its crucial thrust, and its relevance for our lives, both as social scientists and as citizens of today's world.

In closing I would like to touch on another area of constituted human meanings, which is raised in Elizabeth Povinelli's brilliant chapter in this volume,[27] that of the constitution of the self. Povinelli shows that the differences here go very deep, right down to the issue of how and where the self is bounded. We in the modern, secular, disenchanted West share a background "obvious" commonsense understanding of the self as bounded or buffered. We are so anchored in this understanding, that we find it hard to see that there are other terms in which people can live the human condition. But this makes it hard for us to understand even our own ancestors, in the former "enchanted" world, the world of spirits, demons, moral forces which our predecessors acknowledged. The process of disenchantment is the disappearance of this world, and the substitution of what we live today: a world in which the only locus of thoughts, feelings, spiritual élan is what we call minds; the only minds in the cosmos are those of humans (*grosso modo*, with apologies to possible Martians or extra-terrestrials); and minds are bounded, so that these thoughts, feelings, and so on, are situated "within" them.

This space within is constituted by the possibility of introspective self-awareness. This doesn't mean that everything within is capable of being brought to this awareness. The possibility remains that some things "in the mind"

---

[27] "Intimate grammars: anthropological and psychoanalytical accounts of language, gender, and desire."

are so deep, and perhaps hidden (repressed), that we can never bring them to consciousness. But these belong to this inner space, because they lie beyond and help shape the things we can grasp introspectively; as the things just beyond the horizon we see have their place in the world of the visible, even though we may never be able to go there to witness them. The "inward" in this sense is constituted by what I have called "radical reflexivity".[28]

What I am trying to describe here is not a theory. Rather my target is our contemporary lived understanding; that is, the way we naïvely take things to be. We might say: the construal we just live in, without ever being aware of it as a construal, or – for most of us – without ever even formulating it. This means that I am not taking on board the various philosophical theories which have been offered to explain and articulate the "mind" and its relation to the "body." I am not attributing to our lived understanding some kind of Cartesian dualism, or its monist materialist rivals, identity theory, or whatever; or even a more sophisticated and adequate theory of embodied agency. I am trying to capture the level of understanding prior to philosophical puzzlement. And while this modern understanding of the mind certainly opens itself to Cartesian type theories in a way that the earlier "enchanted" understanding does not, it isn't itself such a theory. Put another way, the modern idea of mind makes something like the "mind–body problem" conceivable, indeed, in a way inescapable, where on the earlier understanding it didn't really make sense. But by itself it doesn't offer an answer to that problem.

I started off explicating this understanding with the notion of mind. Thoughts, etc., occur in minds; minds are (*grosso modo*) only human; and they are bounded: they are inward spaces.

Let's start from the first principle. What am I gesturing at with the expression "thoughts," etc.? I mean, of course, the perceptions we have, as well as the beliefs or propositions which we hold or entertain about the world and ourselves. But I also mean our responses, the significance, importance, meaning, we find in things. I want to use for these the generic term "meaning" I introduced above, even though there is in principle a danger of confusion with linguistic meaning. I'm using it in the sense in which we talk about "the meaning of life," or of a relationship as having great "meaning" for us.

Now the crucial difference between the mind-centred view and the enchanted world emerges when we look at meanings in this sense. On the former view, meanings are "in the mind," in the sense that things only have the meaning they do in that they awaken a certain response in us, and this has to do with our nature as creatures who are thus capable of such responses, which means creatures with feelings, with desires, aversions, that is, beings endowed with minds, in the broadest sense.[29]

[28] See *Sources of the Self*, ch. 7.
[29] I must stress again that this is a way of understanding things which is prior to explication in different philosophical theories, materialist, idealist, monist, dualist. We can take a strict

But in the enchanted world, meanings are not in the mind in this sense, certainly not in the human mind. If we look at the lives of ordinary people – and even to a large degree of *élites* – five hundred years ago, we can see in a myriad ways how this was so. First, they lived in a world of spirits, both good and bad. The bad ones include Satan, of course, but beside him, the world was full of a host of demons, threatening from all sides: demons and spirits of the forest, and wilderness, but also those which can threaten us in our everyday lives.

Spirit agents were also numerous on the good side. Not just God, but also his saints, to whom one prayed, and whose shrines one visited in certain cases, in hopes of a cure, or in thanks for a cure already prayed for and granted, or for rescue from extreme danger, for instance, at sea.

These extra-human agencies are perhaps not so strange to us. They violate the second point of the modern outlook I mentioned above, viz., that (as we ordinarily tend to believe) the only minds in the cosmos are humans; but they nevertheless seem to offer a picture of minds, somewhat like ours, in which meanings, in the form of benevolent or malevolent intent can reside.

But seeing things this way understates the strangeness of the enchanted world. Thus precisely in this cult of the saints, we can see how the forces here were not all agents, subjectivities, who could decide to confer a favor. But power also resided in things. For the curative action of saints was often linked to centers where their relics resided; either some piece of their body (supposedly), or some object which had been connected with them in life, like (in the case of Christ) pieces of the true cross, or the sweat-cloth which Saint Veronica had used to wipe his face, and which was on display on certain occasions in Rome. And we can add to this other objects which had been endowed with sacramental power, like the Host, or candles which had been blessed at Candlemas, and the like. These objects were loci of spiritual power; which is why they had to be treated with care, and if abused could wreak terrible damage.

In fact, in the enchanted world, the line between personal agency and impersonal force was not at all clearly drawn. We see this again in the case of relics. The cures effected by them, or the curse laid on people who stole them or otherwise mishandled them, were seen both as emanating from them, as loci of power, and also as coming from the good will, or anger, of the saint they

---

materialist view, and hold that our responses are to be explained by the functions things have for us as organisms, and further by the kinds of neurophysiological responses which their perception triggers off. We are still explaining the meanings of things by our responses, and these responses are "within" us, in the sense that they depend on the way we have been "programmed" or "wired up" inside.

The materialist fantasy, that we could for all we know be brains in a vat, being manipulated by some mad scientist, depends for its sense on this view that the material sufficient condition for thoughts of all kinds is within the cranium. Hence convincing thoughts about a non-existent world could be produced by generating the right brain states. The inside/outside geography, and the boundary dividing them, which is crucial to the mind-outlook is reproduced in this materialist explication of it.

belonged to. Indeed, we can say that in this world, there is a whole gamut of forces, ranging from (to take the evil side for a moment) super-agents like Satan himself, forever plotting to encompass our damnation, down to minor demons, like spirits of the wood, which are almost indistinguishable from the loci they inhabit, and ending in magic potions which bring sickness or death. This illustrates a point which I want to bring out here, and to which I will recur shortly, that the enchanted world, in contrast to our universe of buffered selves and "minds," shows a perplexing absence of certain boundaries which seem to us essential.

So in the pre-modern world, meanings are not only in minds, but can reside in things, or in various kinds of extra-human but intra-cosmic subjects. We can bring out the contrast with today in two dimensions, by looking at two kinds of powers that these things/subjects possess.

The first is the power to impose a certain meaning on us. Now in a sense, something like this happens today all the time, in the sense that certain responses are involuntarily triggered in us by what happens in our world. Misfortunes befall us, and we are sad; great events befall and we rejoice. But the way in which things with power affected us in the enchanted world has no analogies in our understanding today.

For us, things in the world, those which are neither human beings, nor expressions of human beings, are "outside" of mind. They may in their own way impinge on mind – really, in two possible ways:

(1) We may observe these things, and therefore change our view of the world, or be stirred up in ways that we otherwise wouldn't be. (2) Since we are ourselves as bodies continuous with these external things, and in constant exchange with them, and since our mental condition is responsive causally to our bodily condition in a host of ways (something we are aware of without espousing any particular theory of what exactly causes what), our strength – moods, motivations, and so on – can be affected, and is continually being affected by what happens outside.

But in all these cases, that these responses arise in us, that things take on these meanings, is a function of how we as minds, or organisms secreting minds, operate. By contrast, in the enchanted world, the meaning is already there in the object/agent, it is there quite independently of us; it would be there even if we didn't exist. And this means that the object/agent can communicate this meaning to us, impose it on us, in a third way, by bringing us as it were into its field of force. It can in this way even impose quite alien meanings on us, ones that we would not normally have, given our nature; as well as, in positive cases, strengthening our endogenous good responses.

In other words, the world doesn't just affect us by presenting us with certain states of affairs, which we react to from out of our own nature, or by bringing about some chemical-organic condition in us, which in virtue of the way we operate produces, say, euphoria or depression. In all these cases, the meaning as it were only comes into existence as the world impinges on the mind/organism. It is in this sense endogenous. But in the enchanted world, the meaning exists already outside of us, prior to contact; it can take us over, we can fall into its field of force. It comes on us from the outside.

So we can explicate the idea that meaning is in things partly in terms of this power of exogenously inducing or imposing meaning. But in the enchanted world, the meaning in things also includes another power. These "charged" objects can affect not only us but other things in the world. They can effect cures, save ships from wreck, end hail and lightning, and so on. They have what we usually call "magic" powers. Blessed objects, such as relics of saints, the Host, candles, are full of God-power, and can do some of the good things which God's power does, like heal diseases, and fight off disasters. Sources of evil power correspondingly wreak malevolent ends, make us sick, weaken our cattle, blight our crops, and the like.

Once again, to point up the contrast with our world, we can say that in the enchanted world, charged things have a causal power which matches their incorporated meaning. The High Renaissance theory of the correspondences, which while more an elite than a popular belief, partakes of the same enchanted logic, is full of such causal links mediated by meaning. Why does mercury cure venereal disease? Because this is contracted in the market, and Hermes is the God of markets (Hacking). This way of thinking is totally different from our post-Galilean, mind-centred disenchantment. If thoughts and meanings are only in minds, then there can be no "charged" objects, and the causal relations between things cannot be in any way dependent on their meanings, which must be projected on them from our minds. In other words, the physical world, outside the mind, must proceed by causal laws which in no way turn on the moral meanings things have for us.

Thus in the enchanted world, charged things can impose meanings, and bring about physical outcomes proportionate to their meanings. Let me call these two respectively influence and causal power.

I want now to try to bring out how in this world, certain boundaries which are both familiar and crucial to us seem to fade. I have already spoken about the line between subjects and things among these charged beings. But more centrally, the clear boundary between mind and world which we mark was much hazier in this earlier understanding.

This follows from the fact of influence. Once meanings are not exclusively in the mind, once we can fall under the spell, enter the zone of power of exogenous meaning, then we think of this meaning as including us, or perhaps penetrating us. We are in as it were a kind of space defined by this influence. The meaning can no longer be placed simply within; but nor can it be located exclusively without. Rather it is in a kind of interspace which straddles what for us is a clear boundary. Or the boundary is, in an image I want to use here, porous.

This porousness is most clearly in evidence in the fear of possession. Demons can take us over. And indeed, five centuries ago, many of the more spectacular manifestations of mental illness, what we would class as psychotic behaviour, were laid at the door of possession, as in the New Testament times. One "cure" on offer for this condition was to beat the patient; the idea being that by making this site acutely uncomfortable for the demon, one would induce him to leave.

But the fuzziness is even greater than that. Even the line between ordinary cases of influence and full possession was not totally sharp. There is a gamut of cases. People spoke of possession when our higher faculties and powers seemed totally eclipsed; for instance, when people fell into delirium. But in a sense, any evil influence involves some eclipse of the highest capacities in us. Only in the case of good influence, for instance, when we are filled with grace, do we become one with the agent/force through what is best and highest in us. Demons may possess us, but God or the Holy Spirit enter us, or quicken us from within. Whether for good or evil, influence does away with sharp boundaries.

As a mode of experience, rather than as theory, this can be captured by saying that we feel ourselves vulnerable or "healable" (this is meant to be the favourable antonym to "vulnerable") to benevolence or malevolence which is more than human, which resides in the cosmos or even beyond it. This sense of vulnerability is one of the principal features which have gone with disenchantment. Any particular attribution of danger, e.g. to a witch, fits in that world into a generalized sense of vulnerability which this attribution specifies. This is what makes it credible. The enchanted world provides a framework in which these attributions make sense and can be fully believable. They are analogous in this way to an attribution of hostile intent to an armed person in one of those zones of urban lawlessness which exist in our world.

Of course, talk of gods and spirits can be grasped on the analogy of human amity/enmity. But this doesn't capture the whole of the pre-modern world view, as I pointed out above. This opens us to a universe which is much more alien than this. Cosmic forces which breach the boundary and can act within are not only personalized creatures like us. There is a whole gamut of them, which progressively depart from the personal, until we need a quite different model; that of cosmic realities which nevertheless incorporate certain meanings; and hence can affect us, make us live these meanings in certain circumstances.

Now all this has very important consequences for the whole way we live our experience. I'd like to try to spell out this crucial difference a bit more fully.

Let us take a well-known example of influence inhering in an inanimate substance; again like the correspondences above, this is drawn from elite theory rather than popular belief; but the principle is the same. Consider melancholy: black bile is not the cause of melancholy, it embodies, it is melancholy. The emotional life is porous here again; it doesn't simply exist in an inner, mental space. Our vulnerability to the evil, the inwardly destructive, extends to more than just spirits which are malevolent. It goes beyond them to things which have no wills, but are nevertheless redolent with the evil meanings.

See the contrast. A modern is feeling depressed, melancholic. He is told: it's just your body chemistry, you're hungry, or there is a hormone malfunction, or whatever. Straightway, he feels relieved. He can take a distance from this feeling, which is *ipso facto* declared not justified. Things don't really have this meaning; it just feels this way, which is the result of a causal action utterly unrelated to the meanings of things. This step of disengagement depends on our modern mind/body distinction, and the relegation of the physical to being "just" a contingent cause of the psychic.

But a pre-modern may not be helped by learning that his mood comes from black bile. Because this doesn't permit a distancing. Black bile is melancholy. Now he just knows that he's in the grips of the real thing.

Here is the contrast between the modern, bounded self – I want to say "buffered" self – and the "porous" self of the earlier enchanted world. What difference does this make?

A very different existential condition. The last example about melancholy and its causes illustrates this well. For the modern, buffered self, the possibility exists of taking a distance from, disengaging from everything outside the mind. My ultimate purposes are those which arise within me, the crucial meanings of things are those defined in my responses to them. These purposes and meanings may be vulnerable to manipulation in the two ways described above; but this can in principle be met with a counter-manipulation: I avoid distressing or tempting experiences, I don't shoot up the wrong substances, etc.

This is not to say that the buffered understanding necessitates your taking this stance. It is just that it allows it as a possibility, whereas the porous one does not. By definition for the porous self, the source of its most powerful and important emotions are outside the "mind"; or better put, the very notion that there is a clear boundary, allowing us to define an inner base area, grounded in which we can disengage from the rest, has no sense.

As a bounded self I can see the boundary as a buffer, such that the things beyond don't need to "get to me," to use the contemporary expression. That's the sense to my use of the term "buffered" here. This self can see itself as invulnerable, as master of the meanings of things for it.

These two descriptions get at, respectively, the two important facets of this contrast. First, the porous self is vulnerable, to spirits, demons, cosmic forces. And along with this go certain fears which can grip it in certain circumstances. The buffered self has been taken out of the world of this kind of fear: for instance, the kind of thing vividly portrayed in some of the paintings of Bosch.

True, something analogous can take its place. These images can also be seen as coded manifestations of inner depths, repressed thoughts and feelings. But the point is that in this quite transformed understanding of self and world, we define these as inner, and naturally, we deal with them very differently. And indeed, an important part of the treatment is designed to make disengagement possible.

Perhaps the clearest sign of the transformation in our world is that today many people look back to the world of the porous self with nostalgia. As though the creation of a thick emotional boundary between us and the cosmos were now lived as a loss. The aim is to try to recover some measure of this lost feeling. So people go to movies about the uncanny in order to experience a *frisson*. Our peasant ancestors would have thought us insane. You can't get a *frisson* from what is really in fact terrifying you.

The second facet is that the buffered self can form the ambition of disengaging from whatever is beyond the boundary, and of giving its own autonomous order to its life. The absence of fear can be not just enjoyed, but seen as an opportunity for self-control or self-direction.

And so the boundary between agents and forces is fuzzy in the enchanted world; and the boundary between mind and world is porous, as we see in the way that charged objects can influence us. Our modern way of being has rendered this condition weird and inconceivable for many of us.

And this "us" seems to have included Spencer and Gillen, to recur to Elizabeth Povinelli's paper. The buffered self has desires, and it can and is encouraged to classify them and understand them. One such classification is the sexual, which is connected to certain kinds of acts. And so the fateful indexical of Spencer and Gillen's question: the "that" that they were trying to get their native informants to give an account of. For the European observers, "that" seemed obviously to be classifiable as a sexual act. To have got closer to the aboriginal (Aranda) understanding of what was going on, they would have had to think outside the buffered identity, and explore the possibilities of a porous body/self.

Spencer and Gillen lifted out sex from a field-of-ritual-action defined by the penetrative, emissive, and encompassing actions necessary for the transsubstantiation of the initiate body and to effect a radical attachment of this body to the social and totemic landscape. [. . .] Aranda bodies were themselves the effects of spirits emerging from the ground at known conception centres and would sink back into it at death sites. During a variety of rituals Aranda men rubbed clay and sweat into human bodies and totemic sites. Men opened their veins and spilled blood onto the ground forming a hard clay surface on which totemic design would be painted through which totemic beings were induced to come out of/be. [. . .] Burning, burying, soaking, singing, rubbing, sweating, smoking, being born from a place and sinking back into it at death: during these ritual practices Aranda came to share a corporeal substance with the landscape, the social and totemic body. During initiation rites the collective and social body bore into the initiate's body. [. . .] Whose body? What body? Where? [. . .] You are not most intimately in your self, the skin, the surface does not separate you from the world, but rather provides a sensuous medium of contact with it. The bodily intensities laminated a *ritual grammar*, onto an *intimate grammar*. [. . .]

(Povinelli 1993:37–38)

Povinelli's ethnography brings us to a particularly deep and even unsettling incommensurability, which goes to the heart of what we tend to consider the most bedrock, unchallengeable features of the human condition, that each one of us is a bounded, buffered self – unless it be that we are prey to some shattering pathology. We are brought up short by an utterly puzzling, and alien way of being. We are incapable of understanding this, unless we find a way of letting go – at least in imagination – of this bedrock, and following the language, ritual, legends of the Aranda into the foreign world of human meanings which they constitute.

2

LINGUISTIC RELATIVITIES

JOHN LEAVITT

The principle of linguistic relativity, as put forward by linguists and anthropologists in the 1920s and 1930s, holds that the characteristics of one's language can affect other aspects of life and must be taken into account. While the implications of language specificities and differences have been argued for hundreds of years, little of this history has been considered in recent discussions. In the modern West, the overwhelming tendency has been either to deny or affirm the importance of language differences depending on one's philosophical preference for universalistic explanatory models that seek causes or pluralistic essentialist models that seek understanding. The linguistic relativity principle has usually been identified with the latter position; but I will be arguing first that the work of Sapir, Whorf, and their mutual guru Franz Boas represents an effort to rethink language difference in a more complex way, one that is pluralist but not essentialist and that has yet to yield its full theoretical effects; and second, that much of the more recent work on this question reproduces the very oppositions that the Boasians struggled to get beyond. This is particularly evident in the switch in the 1950s from a principle of linguistic relativity to a "hypothesis of linguistic relativism" or "determinism", often dubbed the "Sapir–Whorf hypothesis" that language determines thought, a classically essentialist position.

Universals, particulars, and relativity

Each of the six to ten thousand languages known (the number depends on how you define language versus dialect) is distinct at every level: in sound,

Thanks to Christine Jourdan and Kevin Tuite for thinking of me in this connection; and special thanks to Kevin Tuite for his constant discovering of useful and revelatory items in obscure places. I am grateful to Michel Izard for a first chance to present some of these ideas at the Ecole des Hautes Etudes en Sciences Sociales in 1996, to Gilles Bibeau for his invitation to speak on this topic in the PhD seminar in anthropology at the Université de Montréal, and to Francis Zimmermann for the invitation to present a new version at the EHESS in 2003. For tips and guidance I would like to thank, besides the aforementioned, Robert Crépeau, Jean DeBernardi, Alexandre Enkerli, Claude Faucheux, Michel de Fornel, Paul Friedrich, Michael Houseman, Konrad Koerner, David Leavitt, H. J. Leavitt, Penny Lee, Gérard Lenclud, John Lucy, Mark Mancall, Marie Mauzé, Jean-Claude Muller, Margaret Paxson, the late Jean Pouillon, Nicole Revel, Alice Shepherd, Michael Silverstein, Rajendra Singh, Dan Sperber, Pierrette Thibault, Jürgen Trabant, and András Zempléni.

lexicon, word order, grammatical categories, discourse patterns, and the culture of language. Language as a human faculty manifests itself in the form, and solely in the form, of specific systems, distinct languages. One of the most striking universals of language, then, is its diversity – not an unlimited diversity, but a tremendous diversity nonetheless. This contrasts with the much more limited physical variation of the species, which would, it has been proposed, lead a visiting Martian to expect to find something like half a dozen languages on earth (Steiner 1975: 50–51). Instead, there are thousands of them. It's a scandal, and has been felt to be one since the Tower of Babel.

What are the implications of this fact of linguistic diversity? Two opposed answers have been given to this question over the last several hundred years. To caricature, but only a little: for those who hold the universalist view that what is important about human beings is what is generally human and can be explained through natural-science-type laws, language differences are mere differences in surface expression of a single human experience and/or set of thought patterns. This has been the majority position in the West at least since Aristotle (*On Interpretation* 16a), and it characterizes the natural sciences and those who would like the human sciences to emulate them. On the other side has been the view that human experience and creation are fundamentally plural, each manifestation expressing an essence to be grasped and interpreted holistically, not causally explained. In this view, language differences signal differences among lived worlds: in any given case, language, culture, and thinking all express the same unique essence (see Althusser 1968 [1970]: 190–191).

Both law-seeking universalism and essence-seeking pluralism continue to be the evident choices in many disciplines (Leavitt 1991). The Boasians, while often adopting pluralist-essentialist language to argue against the institutionally more powerful universalist position, did not, in fact, promote an integral essentialism: while defending the importance of language specificity, they maintained that there was no necessary link between a people's language, their culture, and their cognitive processes. At the same time, they did hold that the language you speak is more than a mere means of conveying thoughts and perceptions that are everywhere the same; that the "cut" of the language itself has implications for the user's point of view on the world. The metaphor that Sapir came to in the 1920s was that of Einstein's principle of relativity: differences in the position and state of movement of an observer imply differences in his or her observations. Einstein himself proposed that an alternative name for his theory might be *Standpunktlehre*, the theory of point of view (Balibar 1984: 119). Such a theory cannot be reduced to any essentialism, determinism, or generalized relativism: it does not hold that there is no world outside our experience of the world, nor that there are no commonalities of human thought or experience, nor that there is no way to move in thought among different states or situations, and certainly not that "everything is relative," but that a difference in language, like one in position and velocity, implies a difference in point of view that must be taken into account.

Before Boas: a universe of laws or a multiverse of essences

The dominant philosophical view in the seventeenth and eighteenth centuries was that thought is everywhere either a more or less faithful reproduction of the reason that God had put in the human mind (Descartes and subsequent rationalisms) or a more or less faithful reflection of relations the mind picked up from the world (Bacon, Locke and subsequent empiricisms). Insofar as languages differ, they pose a problem. The rationalist solution was to propose a general grammar based on universal logic and to judge languages depending on how closely they stuck to this logic. The empiricist solution, proposed by John Locke (1632–1704), was to discipline language to correspond to the world itself (Bauman and Briggs 2000: 144–165).

A positive valorization of plurality was foreshadowed by Gottfried Wilhelm Leibniz (1648–1716), for whom language variety is "a wonderful thing for an understanding of the marvelous variety of [the] operations" of the human mind (cited in Trabant 2000: 37). This positive view of plurality took on importance in the late eighteenth century, primarily in Germany with the writings of Johann Gottfried Herder (1744–1803), and reached its apogee in the Romantic movement.

Herder

For Herder, each language, each people, expressed a *Volksgeist*, a national spirit; the diversity of language, custom, belief was an unambiguous good (Bauman and Briggs 2000: 166–194).

Every nation has its center of felicity in itself alone, as every sphere has its center of gravity . . . Is not the good distributed throughout the whole world? Simply because no one form of humanity and no one spot of earth could contain it all, it was divided into a thousand forms . . . and yet a plan of striving forward is always visible – my great theme.
(cited in Hendel 1955: 39)

As "the plan of striving forward" suggests, Herder presumed that some languages and nations are superior to others; at the same time, even inferior ones have something to offer.

Herder was a good essentialist in maintaining that the real nature of human understanding is not to follow out a line of reasoning but to grasp wholes, to seize the essence in its manifold expression. He shared this view with the philosopher Immanuel Kant (1724–1804), but broke with Kant precisely on the point of language difference. Kant held that while the human mind works from incoming data, it does so starting from a number of innate intuitions – on the order of space, time, causality – which serve as fundamental organizing principles. Herder criticized Kant's neglect of linguistic diversity and of the role language plays in conceiving the world. "In answer to Kant's positing of space and time as innate ideas, Herder offers language as the teacher of these ideas" (Penn 1972: 52).

Romanticism

Instead of a single mechanical world and a single linear order of thought, the Romantics supposed a multiplicity of worlds, each the expression of a distinct essence, the development of a distinct kernel. This held for individual personalities, great authors, historical periods, civilizations, landscapes. In the study of language, among the most important Romantic figures are the brothers August (1767–1845) and Friedrich (1772–1829) von Schlegel. Friedrich's book *On the Language and Wisdom of the Indians* (1808) championed two ideas that would remain fundamental in later linguistics. The first is that Sanskrit, the ancient language of India, is related historically to many languages of Europe, and more generally that it is possible to discover historical relationships among languages by comparing sounds and grammatical structures. This is the beginning of the field of historical linguistics. But Schlegel goes on to treat this whole family of languages, the family we now call Indo-European, as the exemplar of a single type whose key element, whose essence or inner structure (*innere Bau*), lies in the way it puts meaningful elements together to make words. This is what is now called word morphology. In a development of this idea, Friedrich's brother August (1818) came to distinguish the inflectional morphology typical of Indo-European languages from the isolating morphology of Chinese and the agglutinating morphology of many Old World languages, including Turkish. The whole presentation is the beginning of what is now called typological classification. The inflectional type is superior to the others because it is "organic," with words "growing" out of "roots," while in an isolating language meaningful elements simply bump up against each other, and in an agglutinating language they are stuck together mechanically.

Through the nineteenth century, genetic and typological ways of analyzing and classifying languages would diverge into two different schools. Historical linguistics would concentrate on the genetic relationships among languages of the Indo-European family, developing increasingly natural-science-style methods based on the establishment of laws, particularly of sound change. This would be the dominant linguistics of the nineteenth and early twentieth centuries (Tuite, this volume). At the same time, a minority linguistics, emerging out of the work of Wilhelm von Humboldt (1767–1835), would seek to analyze the greatest possible variety of language types in order to identify the specific essence of each.

Humboldt

Humboldt was a diplomat, philosopher, and student of many tongues who carried out descriptive analyses of languages as diverse as Basque, Sanskrit, Chinese, and Old Javanese.[1] Humboldt represents the very type of the glottophile. In a letter of 1803, he writes, "the sheer pleasure of entering with

---

[1] In citing Humboldt, I give the date of first publication or presentation of the text, followed by the volume and page in the *Gesammelte Schriften* (noted *GS*).

each new language into a new system of thinking and feeling bring[s] me unending delight" (cited in Swiggers 1985: 729; my translation).

While Humboldt's picture of language included an important universalist component, in its broad lines it draws out the implications of Romantic essentialism.[2] For Humboldt:

(a) Plurality and difference are inherently good.

we haven't done much if we do not [. . .] take account . . . of the many ways in which the world reflects itself in different (*verschiedenen*) individuals.

(1795 [1903]; *GS*1.286–287; my translation)

"Individuals" indicates not only individual people, but individual nations, historical periods, languages (Trabant 1989). This was, after all, the brother of Alexander von Humboldt (1769–1859), the founder of geography as a descriptive or cosmographic science, as opposed to a science seeking only universal laws (Bunzl 1996). Wilhelm was, if you like, a cosmographer of languages, a glottographer.

(b) One should therefore consider the largest possible number of maximally different languages.

(c) Each language possesses a unique inner form and should be understood as a system or a whole.

A language is a being (*Wesen*) determined everywhere by a single indwelling principle that cannot be classified into any general category, any more than can a human being or a human face.

(1829 [1907], *GS*6.356; my translation)

(d) Where is one to look for this indwelling principle? Humboldt, like the Schlegels, finds a key in morphology. Within linguistics, Humboldt will be remembered primarily as the great expositor of language typology. Yet Humboldt's goal was not classification in itself, but finding a way into the character of each language; "This is the keystone of linguistic research" (1820 [1905], *GS*4.13; my translation; cf. Trabant 1989).

(e) Each language operates on the basis of distinctive principles, and the grammarian must grasp these to provide an adequate description (Trabant 1986: 173–175), necessitating the development of "a method . . . adapted to the real genius of the language" (1825 [1906], *GS*5.238; my translation).

(f) Language is not only the means of expression of thought, but enters into its very constitution.

Language is the formative organ of thought . . . Thought and language are . . . one and inseparable from each other.

(1836 [1988]: 54; *GS*7.14)

---

[2] Aarsleff (e.g. 1988) maintains that the Idéologues, rather than Herder or Romanticism, were the primary source for Humboldt's view of language. Yet Humboldt's vocabulary and his basic ideas largely overlap with those of Herder and the Romantics.

The language-system stands between the subject and the world and orients his or her construction of this world.

(g) The fact of linguistic difference thus means that each language implies "a diversity of world views" (1820 [1905], *GS*4.27; my translation).

[E]very language draws about the people that possess it a circle whence it is possible to exit only by stepping over at once into the circle of another one. To learn a *foreign language* should therefore be to acquire a new standpoint (*Standpunkt*) in the world-view (*Weltansicht*) hitherto possessed.

(1836 [1988]: 60; *GS*7.60)

(h) Literature and poetry are the most developed expression of a linguistic essence (Trabant 2000: 33–34).

(i) Under normal circumstances, national character, language, race, world view all fit together. A language is of a people, of their blood, their bodies, all expressing the same essence. "One might wish to object" to this

that the children of any people, when displaced to an alien community before learning to speak, develop their linguistic abilities in the latter's tongue. This undeniable fact, we might say, is a clear proof that language is merely an echoing of what is heard, and depends entirely on social circumstances, without regard for any unity or diversity of the essence (*des Wesens*). In cases of this kind, however, it has hardly been possible to observe with sufficient accuracy how laboriously the native patttern has had to be overcome, or how perhaps in the finest nuances it has still kept its ground unvanquished . . . If language . . . did not also enter into true and authentic combination with physical descent, why otherwise . . . would the native tongue possess a strength and intimacy so much greater than any foreign one, that after long abstention it greets the ear with a sort of sudden magic, and awakens longing when far from home?

(1836 [1988]: 58–59; *GS*7.52)

To anticipate, this reluctance to give up a fully essentialist view of language, mind, and body explains why aspects of Humboldt's thinking, as of Herder's, were so attractive to the Third Reich, and why it seemed so important to the Boasians to keep insisting that there was *no* necessary connection between language, thought, and race.

(j) Humboldt maintains the superiority of inflectional Indo-European languages over others (Trabant 2000: 38).

After Humboldt

In the course of the nineteenth century, historical linguistics progressively lost interest in particular languages as systems or wholes. The object came to be not any language as it exists or existed, but a field of historical transformations of sounds and forms. Yet at the same time, the "Humboldtian stream" (Koerner 1977) continued to develop a systemic linguistics centering on the characterization of language types. The main representative of this current was Heymann Steinthal (1823–1899). Early on (1848), Steinthal attempted to ground Humboldt's linguistics in the philosophy of Hegel, and from the 1850s he sought to render linguistics more rigorous by defining its psychological foundations. Steinthal was interested in a wide variety of languages, producing manuals featuring grammatical sketches of representative languages for each of the major types (Steinthal 1860), again based on word morphology. While Steinthal maintained Humboldt's vocabulary of world view (*Weltanschauung*) and inner form, comparative typology seems to have replaced the project of characterizing particular languages.

Steinthal continued to rank languages, maintaining the superiority of Indo-European. He also followed Humboldt in his philological interest in literatures along with language structures, a model that directly inspired the Boasians (Bunzl 1996: 68–69); and he operationalized Humboldt's view that each language or language type deserves its own kind of description, not one based on Latin or Greek.

Steinthal's career parallels that of his contemporary Karl Marx (1818–1883). Both were of German Jewish background. Marx's father had converted to Lutheranism, and he himself was of course a devout atheist, but he was always identified as a Jew; Steinthal was a pillar of the Jewish community. Both were profoundly German in their training and tendencies. Both started out wanting to push the Hegelian envelope in new directions: Marx wrote his revolutionary revision of Hegel in 1844 at the age of twenty-six, Steinthal published his Hegelian rereading of Humboldt in 1848 (the year of the *Communist Manifesto*) at twenty-five. Both were fascinated by developments in natural science, and both spent much of their careers trying to develop scientific approaches in the human sciences. Both ended up with models that are both pluralist, requiring that given data be understood in the context of a particular historical "field" – Marx's modes of production, Steinthal's language types – and universalist, in that they proposed general ways of establishing the nature of these "fields".

Humboldt's influence extended beyond linguistics in the later nineteenth century, into the folk psychology of Wilhelm Wundt and the ethnology and geography of Adolf Bastian, two future mentors of the young Boas. It also marked a German philosophical movement that looked at real language and its role in thought (Cloeren 1988). These language philosophers seem to have been the first to use the term "linguistic relativity" (cf. Gumperz and Levinson 1996: 14, n. 2); the earliest appearance I have seen is Otto Friedrich Gruppe's "the necessary relativity of the whole of language" (*die notwendige Relativität der ganzen Sprache*) (Gruppe 1831 [1914]: 425; my translation). As this phrase suggests, however, the German language philosophers used the term to refer to language in general as a distorting factor in thought and perception, not to differences among particular languages.

Evolutionism
By the late nineteenth century, the most important universalist movement in the study of humanity was evolutionism, which ranked cultures and the people

who bore these cultures according to a single scale of development from most primitive to most highly organized. Apparently primitive institutions still existing among civilized peoples – superstitions and folk customs, for instance – could be understood as survivals from an earlier age. Peoples who live in a primitive way, such as those without agriculture and industry, were assumed not to have changed over the millennia. Since everywhere humanity was held to have passed or failed to pass through the same stages, this meant that information about hunting and gathering peoples could be used to reconstruct the early history of mankind; they *were* the early history of mankind, still available for consultation. And on any topic: their religion would still be close to the original religion, and their languages would be very much like the original languages.

But languages turned out to be hard nuts for the evolutionists to crack. People who had no agriculture or metallurgy also had no trouble talking with an adequacy that cannot be distinguished from that of speakers of any language. There just don't seem to be any primitive languages. While the evolutionists seem comfortable talking about animal husbandry or architecture, their chapters on language are nervous chapters. In *Primitive Culture* (1871), Sir Edward Burnett Tylor says that while there is no evidence for this, early language must have been dominated by gestures and onomatopoeias. He repeats anecdotes from travellers who say that tribes in Tasmania, Oregon, Brazil, and West Africa require gestures as a supplement to their "scanty sentences" (p. 164). In a note to *Ancient Society* (1877: 37), Lewis Henry Morgan writes, "As we descend through the gradations of language into its ruder forms, the gesture element increases in the quantity and variety of its forms until we find language so dependent upon gestures that without them they would be substantially unintelligible." He gives no references. In his book *First Steps in Human Progress*, the American anthropologist Frederick Starr has no chapter on language as such, but three on "Gesture and Speech". He says that there may be tribes whose languages are so dependent on gesture that their members cannot speak to each other at night. Certainly, he says, there are primitive groups whose meager languages depend on gestures to allow understanding. Overall, the level of civilization is in inverse proportion to the amount of gesture. The highly civilized Anglo-Saxons hardly gesture at all; it is "among peoples who, like the French and the Italians, speak in each of their movements and whose faces show all the thoughts that fly through their minds; it is among children, who have not yet learned duplicity; it is among the inferior races – the true children of nature – that one must go to find the best illustrations of our subject" (1901: 170).

The evolutionists also saw the fact that transcriptions of a word from a "primitive" language differ from author to author as indicating that these languages have poorly differentiated sounds. And they found evidence for progress in the greater elaboration of certain vocabulary domains in technologically more elaborate societies. Some languages, for instance, only have words for one, two, and many, and it is possible to make some correlation between a large-scale society, elaborate technology, and a large set of number terms. In the writings of the evolutionists, in fact, language is often virtually reduced to number terms.

Boas and Boasian linguistics

Boasian principles

As the Romantics created a pluralist linguistics in opposition to the universalism of the Enlightenment, Franz Boas (1858–1942) started his anthropological career and defined many of his positions in opposition to the evolutionists. Boas was the founder of the North American schools of cultural anthropology and linguistics. These vocations, made by him into academic disciplines, are radically new both in their practice and their theory. For the first time, there is a major school of linguistic analysis based on intensive field research with speakers of a range of largely non-Indo-European, in this case mainly Amerindian, languages, exhibiting enormous grammatical variety. Boasian linguistics was most often coupled with work on other aspects of culture. This new practice corresponded to a new theoretical stance. The Boasians rejected the evolutionist package on every level: they held that each language deserves to be treated on its own terms, that the specifics of each language are important, and that each linguistic system orients the habitual thought of its users. These positions parallel Humboldtian ones, and it is not surprising that Boas and his students are often presented as the theoretical heirs to Herder and Humboldt (e.g. Rossi-Landi 1973; Malkiel 1974; Steiner 1975). There is plenty of evidence of intellectual continuity from the Humboldtians of the nineteenth century to the American ethnolinguists: Boas was a German, trained in Germany, who acknowledged his debt to Steinthal; Sapir, his most important student in linguistics, was born in Germany, did a Master's in German literature and philosophy, wrote his Master's thesis on Herder, and was familiar with Humboldt.

At the same time, Boas and his students rejected some key Humboldtian tenets. First, while they sought coherent patterns in languages and cultures, they did not presume that such coherence was natural. On the contrary, a highly integrated culture or a pervasive linguistic pattern had to be a specific historical product, limited in time as in space. As apparently essentialist a book as Ruth Benedict's *Patterns of Culture* (1934), with its portraits of highly integrated and contrasting cultural styles, also presents societies whose various institutions seem to go off in different directions, and she points out that even some of the most integrated cultures have highly non-integrated pasts (pp. 223–227).

The Boasians also rejected the idea that language, culture, race, and thought are necessarily interlinked. On the contrary: speakers of very different languages can be very similar in economic activity, social structure, aesthetics, and/or religion, and speakers of the same language can differ drastically on these parameters. Any language is capable of expressing any content; the language one speaks does not limit what it is possible to think.

Yet these are the same people who argued through example and in doctrine that the specifics of one's language can be highly influential in the way one conceives the world and expresses experience. While this apparent contradiction, maintained throughout the production of Boas and his students, has sometimes been taken as an otherwise unaccountable incoherence, it could also be seen as the sign of a struggle to find language adequate for conveying a complex reality within a pre-existing discursive field massively oriented either to universalism or to essentialism.

The Boasians rejected any ranking of languages and cultures according to a fixed standard. This, I think, is a theory imposed on them by their practice. Any anthropologist or linguist of the Boasian school had to collaborate with sober, intelligent "primitive" adults who did not have childlike mentalities, whose languages were not incapable of abstraction, whose beliefs and religious practices did not seem any more superstitious or foolish than those of most Christians or Jews. In Boas's case, what he called his "scientific work" allowed what was already probably a strong democratic and radical tendency to reach a complete reorientation of thinking about human variation. And it is noteworthy that most of his most prominent students were institutionally marginal characters of one kind or another – relatively recent immigrants, members of minority ethnic groups, a disproportionate number of women for the period; and that in North America, anthropology was felt to be a discipline on the left side of the political spectrum.

A number of these points come together in Boas's own presentation of his predecessors in linguistics. Central is the idea that each language or language type deserves to be treated on its own terms. Boas writes in the *Handbook of American Indian Languages*,

No attempt has been made [here] to compare the forms of the Indian grammars with the grammars of English, Latin, or even among themselves; but in each case the psychological groupings which are given depend entirely upon the inner form of each language. In other words, the grammar has been treated as though an intelligent Indian was going to develop the forms of his own thoughts by an analysis of his own form of speech.

(1911: 70)

The terminology here comes straight out of Steinthal. Boas is said to have regretted not having been a student of Steinthal's, and in a letter he makes clear why: he writes that his goal was "a presentation of languages on Steinthal's principles, i.e., from their own, not an outsider's point of view" (cited in R. L. Brown 1967: 14–15).

But Boas's endorsement of Steinthal comes with a qualification which indicates the novelty of his overall conception of language. The source is a talk in Mexico City in 1910 announcing the publication of the *Handbook*.

The attempt to describe the psychological principles of various languages is not new. The works of Wilhelm von Humboldt and of Steinthal on the types of linguistic structure are the most important of this class. Steinthal's descriptions of [Nahuatl] and Eskimo are certainly the models of what I have tried to do. Naturally, the fundamental ideas are not the same. At the time of von Humboldt and Steinthal, the valuation of languages would have been one of the principal objects of investigation, while today this problem does not interest us; we are attracted, rather, to psychological problems.

(Boas 1910: 227; my translation)

Boas is both confirming and denying his filiation to the Humboldtian stream in linguistics. By continuing to value some types of language over others, the Humboldtians had managed to have a plurality that remained ordered on the basis of a single linguistic type, inflectional Indo-European. By abandoning this criterion, Boas precipitated a decentered linguistic world: not a chaos of relativism, at least not necessarily, but a world in which principles for ordering and for passing between situations had to be worked out from within a given perspective – there was no God's-eye-view – and by moving among perspectives, as much as possible without privileging any one of them. It is not surprising that Sapir and Whorf, weaned on this decentered way of thinking about language and culture, should have seized on Einstein's relativity as a way to conceptualize their new situation.

Boas, science, and linguistics

Boas himself was intensely aware of the tension, particularly in nineteenth-century German thought, between the positivist and universalist explanatory procedures and objectivist goals of the natural sciences and the particularist and essentialist interpretive procedures of what were called the spiritual sciences (*Geisteswissenschaft*). Boas's own early choices in training (Stocking 1965 [1968]; Liss 1996) show someone on the cusp of this antinomy. He started out in physics, but moved to the very distinctive German field of psychophysics, which sought to understand the relationship between natural phenomena as described scientifically and these phenomena as human beings perceive them. With his further move into geography, Boas became interested in how entire human societies perceive space; his first field research, with the Inuit (1882), compared maps drawn using scientific instruments with those drawn by the people who lived in the territory. Boas's journals show that the experience of living with the Inuit profoundly affected his attitude toward cultural difference, causing him to question the superiority of European civilization and to argue that the important thing was the *Herzenbildung*, the heart's construction, of each person, in any cultural setting (Stocking 1965 [1968]: 148). This is an interesting choice of word given the use of the term *Bildung* in Germany, notably by Humboldt, to mean the civilizational improvement of humanity as a whole, with modern European societies being the most *gebildet*.

In 1887 Boas joined in a debate with some senior American anthropologists on the proper way to organize museum exhibits (Stocking 1974). Boas argued against the then-current organization by institution, which sought to show the universal development of a single human civilization, in favor of a presentation by culture area, so that museums could reveal the multiplicity of cultures and the internal coherence of each. Boas even uses the word "relative": "It is my opinion that the main object of ethnological collections should be the dissemination of the fact that civilization is not something absolute, but that it is relative, and that our ideas and conceptions are true only so far as our civilization goes" (1887 [1974]: 64).

Boas's position raises the questions that relativist positions still raise. Are our ideas really just a product of our civilization? What does it mean then that Boas, by his own theory himself a product of his civilization, has the idea that our ideas are products of our civilization? Is he unfairly giving himself a privileged position, a point outside this circle, which allows him to look in on it?

A lecture given in German in 1888, "The aims of ethnology", suggests elements of answers to these questions. We may indeed be able to achieve a point of view outside that of our culture, precisely through the comparative critique of that culture, made possible by familiarity with others:

[E]thnology [. . .] alone opens to us the possibility of judging our own culture objectively, in that it permits us to strip off the presumably self-evident manner of thinking and feeling which determines even the fundamental part of our culture. Only in this way can our intellect, instructed and formed under the influences of our culture, attain a correct judgment of this same culture.

                                                                    (1889 [1940]: 71)

This reads like nothing so much as the Marx of the 1850s, whose critiques of political economy are critiques of the assumptions behind political economy, assumptions almost universally shared in the Western world of his time. Like Marx, Boas presumes that it is a good thing to take a critical distance on one's own unexamined ideas: his program is to attempt this through knowledge of human alternatives. The goal is not a place that is given or waiting outside all cultures, but a place to stand that must be constructed provisionally and largely negatively, through comparison and critique.

In his first major treatment of linguistic theory, the paper "On Alternating Sounds" (1889), Boas argues against the evolutionists' assertion that the clarity of speech sounds depends on the level of development of a language. If visitors to a given people transcribe the same local word differently, argues Boas, this is not because the word is being pronounced unclearly or inconsistently, but because the travelers, not equipped to hear the relevant distinctions, assimilate what they hear to sounds in their own languages. In an anticipation of phonological theory, Boas is holding that every language organizes the universe of sounds in its own way. True to his psychophysical training, Boas distinguishes between the way the ear perceives a sound and the way the linguistically preformed mind apperceives it (1889 [1974]: 74): "each apperceives the unknown sounds by the means of the sounds of his own language" (pp. 75–76).

Boas's theoretical linguistics culminated with the publication of the first volume of the *Handbook* in 1911. Boas wrote three and co-authored one of the grammatical sketches presented here, representing as many different language families, and closely supervised all of them. The introduction to the volume remains the major statement of his linguistics.

At the beginning Boas says that there is no necessary link among a people's language, biological inheritance, and culture. Near the end he says that there is no necessary correlation between language and thought in that one's language does not limit what one can think. As an example, Boas takes on the evolutionists' treatment of number. Counting one, two, many, writes Boas, tells us nothing about the cognitive capacities of the person doing the counting. All it tells us is that he or she lives in a society that does not require counting in the abstract (p. 66). A cowherd who does not have the vocabulary to say that he has twenty-seven cows can still tell when Bessie is missing.

Cradled between Boas's two negative affirmations, of the lack of necessary correlation between language, race, and culture and between language and thought, is the actual presentation of language. Here we have a picture of coherent structure at the levels of phonetics, lexicon, and grammar. In phonetics, Boas argues that the potential production of sounds by the human vocal apparatus is unlimited. A child who learns to speak is learning to suppress most of the sounds he or she is capable of making, thus allowing clear distinctions to arise among a limited number of sound-types.[3] The set of contrasting sounds used in any language forms a coherent system, and one different from other such systems. Boas repeats his argument that the apparent fluidity of sounds in exotic languages comes not from their lower level of evolution but from interference among systems.

When Boas turns to lexicon and grammar, his argument is the same: out of the potentially unlimited complexity of experience and ideation, each language must define and foreground certain configurations rather than others, whether by labeling (lexicon) or by turning the attention to some domains of experience rather than others through grammatical devices.

---

[3] This is the scenario Benedict will use to define the specifics of a culture (Benedict 1934) and that Lévi-Strauss will pick up and make the introductory argument of the *Elementary Structures of Kinship* (1949).

Since the total range of personal experience which language serves to express is infinitely varied, and its whole scope must be expressed by a limited number of phonetic groups, it is obvious that an extended classification of experience must underlie all articulate speech.

(1911: 24)

As with sounds, the limited and systemic nature of lexicon and grammar means that languages will differ

not only in the character of their constituent phonetic elements and sound-clusters, but also in the groups of ideas that find expression in fixed phonetic groups.

(1911: 24)

This section includes a manifold discussion of vocabulary examples meant to show the variety of ways different languages delimit fields of experience. Boas presents the various English words for different forms of water, then the famous example of Inuktitut words for snow: there are three, indicating what we call falling snow, snow lying on the ground, and drifting snow. This example was expanded by subsequent writers and in anthropological folklore to hundreds of words for snow (Martin 1986; uncharacteristically, Whorf appears to have been quite sloppy on this point), allowing subsequent revisionists to make hay with the "Eskimo vocabulary hoax" (Pullum 1989). But three words are plenty to illustrate Boas's point: their presence suggests, at least, that Inuktitut speakers conceive three different "things" where we conceive one, just as English-speakers conceive raindrops, rivers, and lakes as different "things" even though we know perfectly well that they're all water. On the other hand, does this tell us very much beyond this fact? One presumes that mariners will have lots of nautical terms, that serious skiers, like the Inuit, will have a pretty discriminating vocabulary of snow. Boas himself relativizes his lexical relativity:

[T]he selection of such simple terms must to a certain extent depend upon the chief interests of a people; and where it is necessary to distinguish a certain phenomenon in many aspects, which in the life of a people play each an entirely independent role, many independent words may develop, while in other cases modifications of a single term may suffice.

(p. 25)

Yet it remains that differences in such patterning, like the differences in the patterning of sound, imply shifts in what Boas will here call point of view:

[E]ach language, from the point of view of another language, may be arbitrary in its classifications . . . what appears as a single simple idea in one language may be characterized by a series of distinct phonetic groups in another.

(p. 25)

Besides these words, every language has "formal elements which determine the relations of the single phonetic groups." Such formal elements include, for instance, affixes such as the English /s/, which on its own indicates only the sound a snake makes, but indicates plurality when suffixed to certain nouns. How easy is it to distinguish between potentially independent words and these formal elements? For a hundred years, the difference had been held to be fundamental: it is what allows the distinction among isolating, agglutinating, and inflectional languages. For Boas, the difference between a word and a grammatical affix is not absolute, but involves a sliding scale of relative independence and abstraction. This effectively blows the earlier typological schemes out of the water, creating a much vaster field of structural variation. It also removes one of the bases for claiming the superiority of Indo-European languages.

One result of this shift is that formal affixes no longer look purely formal, but can be understood to convey meaning in themselves. Grammatical categories, in other words, have meaning too. In modern Western European languages, we are familiar with grammatical categories of tense, person, number, case, gender, each of which at least potentially is not only a formal indicator of word arrangement, but adds to or specifies meaning. Many of these categories are obligatory, as are the ones just listed: the speaker of the language does not have the choice not to use them. Boas's point here, which is probably his major single contribution to linguistic theory (Jakobson 1959 [1971]), is that the key difference among languages lies less in what they allow you to say – any language will allow you to say anything you want – than in what a given language *obliges* you to refer to. Different languages have different obligatory grammatical categories.

Boas goes systematically through the various parts of speech and shows how differently a wide variety of languages treat the relevant grammatical categories. English will not let you *not* refer constantly to time and number; Kwakiutl has no obligation to use tense or number, but requires specification of how you know what you are talking about (what would come to be called evidentiality); in a number of American languages, nouns have tense (Boas 1911: 35). After pages and pages of illustrations, Boas concludes

that in a discussion of the characteristics of various languages different fundamental categories will be found, and that in a comparison of different languages it will be necessary to compare as well the phonetic characteristics as the characteristics of the vocabulary and those of the grammatical concepts in order to give each language its proper place.

(1911: 43)

Here is something that we can call linguistic relativity. Note that Boas has not denied the existence of an objective world or of universal patterns of human thought, nor has he assumed that every language-culture-people is a seamless whole. On the contrary. But he does hold that the fact of distinctive phonetic patterning, lexical categorization, and obligatory grammatical categories in every language means that a shift from language to language is potentially a shift in point of view.

Boas continued to work on languages and linguistics until the end of his life, but he had made his main points in the 1911 introduction. Pushing the implications of language specificity farther would be up to several generations of students.

Sapir, Lee, Whorf

Edward Sapir (1884–1939), who was initially trained in literature, had a strong sense of the poetry of linguistic sound and patterning as well as an abiding concern for individual experience, for how languages were lived by human subjects. Under Boas's influence he became the master collector and analyst of languages in their own terms. In Sapir's manual *Language* (1921), particularly in the chapter on "Grammatical Meaning", he elaborates Boas's critique of typology, presenting a sliding scale of relative meaningfulness of grammatical forms and processes. Like Boas, Sapir denies any necessary connection among language, race, and culture. Yet throughout his work there emerges a sense of each language as a coherent whole, although not one that can be defined by one essential feature:

[I]t must be obvious to any one who has . . . felt something of the spirit of a foreign language that there is such a thing as a basic plan, a certain cut, to each language. This type or plan or structural "genius" of the language is something much more fundamental, much more pervasive, than any single feature of it that we can mention . . . When we pass from Latin to Russian we feel that it is approximately the same horizon that bounds our view, even though the near, familiar landmarks have changed. When we come to English, we seem to notice that the hills have dipped down a little, yet we recognize the general lay of the land. And when we have arrived at Chinese, it is an utterly different sky that is looking down upon us . . . Languages are more to us than systems of thought transference. They are invisible garments that drape themselves about our spirit and give a predetermined form to all its symbolic expression.

(1921: 120–121, 221)

It was Sapir who developed the concept of the phoneme; unlike Boas, Sapir was able to make a clear distinction between the sounds themselves as acoustic or articulatory entities and the phoneme as an element of a system. Sapir insisted on what he called "the psychological reality of phonemes" (Sapir 1933 [1949]): again, he was interested not only in the system as such, but in the system as perceived by human subjects. In phonology, Sapir writes of the "pattern feeling" which predisposes a speaker to perceive sounds in certain ways. Sapir held that the specifics of grammar, too, led the user of a given language into unconscious patterns of expectation, typical ways of putting things together (Erickson *et al.*

1997). In his general presentations of linguistics, Sapir states, sometimes in very strong terms, the dependence of the individual on conceptual patterning that is derived from the language that he or she speaks.

> Human beings do not live in the objective world alone, nor alone in the world of social activity as ordinarily understood, but are very much at the mercy of a particular language which has become the medium of expression for their society. It is quite an illusion to imagine that one adjusts to reality essentially without the use of language, and that language is merely an incidental means of solving specific problems of communication or reflection. The fact of the matter is that the "real world" is to a large extent unconsciously built up on the language habits of the group. No two languages are ever sufficiently similar to be considered as representing the same social reality. The worlds in which different societies live are different worlds, not merely the same world with different labels attached . . . We see and hear and otherwise experience very largely as we do because the language habits of our community predispose certain choices of interpretation.
>
> (Sapir 1929a [1949]: 162)

This is the passage most commonly quoted to demonstrate the supposed linguistic determinism of Sapir and of his student Whorf, who cites some of it at the beginning of one of his papers (1941a [1956]). Yet note that the passage does not say that it is not possible to translate between different languages, nor to convey the same referential content in both. Note also that there is a piece missing here, between "labels attached" and "We see and hear": the way I have presented it, with the three dots, is how this passage is almost always presented. If we look at what has been elided, we find the following, coming in a new paragraph immediately after "attached":

> The understanding of a simple poem, for instance, involves not merely an understanding of the single words in their average significance, but a full comprehension of the whole life of the community as it is mirrored in the words, or as it is suggested by the overtones . . .

So the apparent claim of linguistic determinism is to be illustrated by – a poem! In light of this missing piece of the passage, what Sapir seems to be saying is not that language determines thought, but that language is part of social reality, and so is thought, and to understand either a thought or "a green thought in a green shade" you need to consider the whole.

Sapir's theoretical claims were carried into an extended case study by Dorothy Demetracopoulou Lee (1905–1975) in her work on Wintu, a Penutian language of northern California, and the remembered traditional culture of its speakers. Lee published a series of articles (e.g. 1938, 1944) seeking to formulate the "unformulated philosophy" of the Wintu based on the grammar of their language. Lee looks at grammatical distinctions made in the Wintu noun, which has no obligatory gender or number, and in the verb, which has no obligatory tense. One of the most striking things about Wintu, not only in comparison with Western European languages but with other languages of the same family and the same geographical area, is an obligatory system of evidential markers that characterize different parts of speech. That is, it is quite impossible to speak anything like normal Wintu without at every point specifying how one knows what one is saying. Each Wintu verb has two forms, one for what is unknowable in a direct way, the other for what the speaker can access directly; each noun can take a generalized or a particularized form, the latter implying direct relevance for the speaking subject. Lee draws on this patterning to render explicit Wintu presuppositions about human agency and the nature of the world, presuppositions that contrast strongly with modern Western ones, which in turn they help to make explicit. For Lee, the Wintu have collectively developed a coherent unstated philosophy that has come to be crystallized in the grammar of their language. Lee's working assumption is that at least some obligatory categories carry meanings which become part of a speaker's orientation by virtue of their constant use; the method is contrastive comparison of Wintu categories with the author's own.

Like Lee, Sapir's student Benjamin Lee Whorf (1897–1941) actualized Sapir's views in extended analyses of a small number of languages, in his case primarily of Hopi, a Uto-Aztecan language spoken in Arizona. Thanks in part to his dynamic writing and his promotion of linguistic relativity, Whorf became the best-known proponent of the idea. After his death, his name became attached to the so-called "Sapir–Whorf hypothesis" that the specifics of a language influence or determine its speakers' thought, very often further read to mean that a language entirely determines thought processes and possibilities. To many who have read Whorf's published work, this seems like a misrepresentation; with some recent re-evaluations (Lucy 1992a, P. Lee 1996), we have a clearer idea of what Whorf was about.

Whorf was a chemical engineer and passionate amateur linguist – amateur only in the sense that he never took an academic degree in the subject: he became a highly accomplished descriptive linguist of Uto-Aztecan languages with an engineer's grasp of complex structures. Whorf studied with Sapir and ended up as part of the latter's research group while keeping his day job at Hartford Fire Insurance (Darnell, this volume). His work on Hopi was carried out primarily with a speaker living in New York City.

In his view of language and human conception, Whorf shares the basic Boasian tenets: that you can say anything in any language; that one cannot rank languages or judge them by a single yardstick of values; that languages are differently structured, at every level; that the constant use of certain forms rather than others predisposes the user to attend to certain domains rather than others. The metaphor here is not one of determinism, but of the laying down of easier rather than harder to follow grooves or paths. Sapir had written that particular grammatical patterns provide "grooves of expression which come to be felt as inevitable" (1921: 89). Whorf would write that in the study of an exotic language, "we are at long last pushed willy-nilly out of our ruts" (1941a [1956]: 138).

Whorf made a clear distinction between what is *possible* to think, which is in principle unlimited for speakers of any language, and what people habitually think, which may be strongly influenced by their language. In spite of sometimes deterministic phraseology, Whorf believed that much of human thinking and perception was non-linguistic and universal across languages. He was a fan of Gestalt psychology and its findings about presumably universal perceptual and conceptual processes (P. Lee 1996). He believed there was a real world out there, although, enchanted by quantum mechanics and relativity theory, he also believed that this was not the world as we conceive it, nor that everyone conceives it habitually in the same way.

Whorf also pushed the analysis of a language beyond that of explicitly marked parts of speech. He introduced the ideas of covert categories and cryptotypes, distinctions that are expressed across different parts of speech and are often only recognizable through comparing contexts (P. Lee 1996, ch. 4). And he moved between linguistic and non-linguistic data to talk more specifically than his predecessors about possible influences of language on thought and culture (Lucy 1992a). In one instance (1941a [1956]) he correlates Hopi grammar with Hopi religious practices, the grammar of Western European languages with work and timekeeping practices.

Whorf's most famous analyses are of the conceptual universe of the Hopi using Hopi grammar as a starting-point. Like Humboldt before him, he questions what we usually think of as basic orienting categories of the world on the level of the Kantian intuitions: substance and particular, space and time are, he writes, preconceived very differently by a traditional Hopi speaker and by the speaker of a modern Western European language. This is in part because the two live in different social, cultural, and material worlds; but it is also because the categories of their very different languages "point" their speakers toward different aspects of experience (an extension of Boas on grammatical categories) and make it easy to organize experience in some ways rather than others. Whorf is not proposing linguistic determinism, but something like powerful linguistic seduction.

Whorf also makes a moral and political pitch: he argues that to the extent that the language one speaks tends to guide one's thinking along certain lines, it is imperative to learn other languages, preferably very different ones, which offer different connective pathways. This is a lesson in humility and awe in a multilingual world.

We shall no longer be able to see a few recent dialects of the Indo-European family, and the rationalizing techniques elaborated from their patterns, as the apex of the evolution of the human mind, nor their present wide spread as due to any survival from fitness or to anything but a few events of history – events that could be called fortunate only from the parochial point of view of the favored parties. They, and our own thought processes with them, can no longer be envisioned as spanning the gamut of reason and knowledge but only as one constellation in a galactic expanse.

(1941a [1956]: 218)

The breathtaking sense of sudden vaster possibility, of the sky opening up to reveal a bigger sky beyond, may be what causes such strong reactions to Whorf. For some, he is simply enraging or ridiculous. For others, reading Whorf is a fundamental intellectual experience, and there are many stories of students coming to anthropology or linguistics largely because of Whorf (personal communications; Alford 2002).

Sapir, Whorf, and Einstein

Both Sapir and Whorf refer to Einstein's theory of relativity. Sapir (1924 [1949]: 159) cites

incommensurable analyses of experience in different languages. The upshot of it all would be to make very real to us a kind of relativity that is generally hidden from us by our naïve acceptance of fixed habits of speech as guides to an objective understanding of the nature of experience. This is the relativity of concepts or, as it might be called, the relativity of the form of thought. It is not so difficult to grasp as the physical relativity of Einstein . . . For its understanding the comparative data of linguistics are a *sine qua non*. It is the appreciation of the relativity of the form of thought which results from linguistic study that is perhaps the most liberalizing thing about it. What fetters the mind and benumbs the spirit is ever the dogged acceptance of absolutes.

To speak of incommensurable analyses may be to imply, as critics have claimed, that no passage is possible between two languages. This reading goes against one of the most fundamental tenets of Boasian thought, including Sapir's own. The rest of the passage makes clear that this is not at all what Sapir had in mind: on the contrary, whatever he means by "incommensurable" in no way precludes movement back and forth or the possibility of an "appreciation" of both analyses. But this is not something that happens automatically or easily; it takes work.

In one of his popularizing essays, Whorf (1940 [1956]: 213–214) lays out the relativity analogy in its canonical form:

We cut nature up, organize it into concepts, and ascribe significances as we do, largely because we are party to an agreement to organize it in this way – an agreement that holds throughout our speech community and is codified in the patterns of our language. The agreement is, of course, an implicit and unstated one, BUT ITS TERMS ARE ABSOLUTELY OBLIGATORY; we cannot talk at all except by subscribing to the organization and classification of data which the agreement decrees.

This . . . means that no individual is free to describe nature with absolute impartiality but is constrained to certain modes of interpretation even while he thinks himself most free. The person most nearly free in such respects would be a linguist familiar with very many widely different linguistic systems. As yet no linguist is in any such position. We are thus introduced to a new principle of relativity, which holds that all observers are not led by the same physical evidence to the same picture of the universe, unless their linguistic backgrounds are similar, or can in some way be calibrated.

Relativity was not a new idea; but Newtonian relativity still assumed an absolute space and a fixed passage of time giving coordinates by which events could ultimately be located. There remains a God's-eye view of the whole easily graspable in the terms of classical mechanics. Einstein makes this fixed frame vanish, so that all measurements become relative to the situation of the measuring entity. The principle of relativity becomes a general condition of observation, and the world thus disclosed is one that requires a new physics that is not easy for twentieth- or twenty-first-century Western humans – or maybe for any human – to conceptualize. Note that this is no relativism. Coherent relations continue to hold among different situations; they can, if you like, be calibrated. Similarly, for Sapir and Whorf languages represent frames of reference that orient the speaker, point him or her in certain directions rather than others. In neither case does this deny the possibility of getting an idea of other frames of reference, in astrophysics or linguistics (Alford 1981; Jakobson 1982 [1985]; Heynick 1983). On the contrary: that's the work that has to be done.

We have seen that the word relativity was already being used in reference to language in Humboldt-inspired philosophy in the nineteenth century. In a pleasing twist, it turns out that Einstein himself was likely influenced in his early thinking by none other than Humboldtian linguistics. The adolescent Einstein, having failed his college entrance exams, went in a sort of exile to Switzerland to continue his studies. He lodged with the family of one Jost Winteler (1846–1929), a local schoolmaster. This same Winteler had been trained in Humboldtian linguistics. His dissertation (Winteler 1876) was an analysis of the phonetics of his own dialect of Swiss German, an analysis that prefigured phonological theory (Jakobson 1960 [1971]: 414). Central to Winteler's conception was what he called "the relativity of relations" or "situational relativity" among sounds. By the time Einstein met him, Winteler was on the margins of scholarly life. Einstein had long talks with his landlord and continued to refer to him with respect and gratitude throughout his life (Jakobson 1982 [1985]: 258–260). There is no direct evidence that Winteler's linguistic ideas inspired Einstein's theory of relativity; yet, as Konrad Koerner once remarked in this regard (personal communication), *Se non è vero, è ben trovato.* It is not crazy to imagine that Winteler's far-reaching sense of relativistic relations among linguistic elements gave Einstein a model for a broader application of relativistic thinking in physics.

Relativity is not necessarily relativism. While Boas and his students did not consider some languages to be superior to others, and while they saw each language type as requiring terms appropriate to it, their own values were clear: they were democrats and progressives. Precisely because they had strong political values, Boas and his students felt that modern Western society should be pushed in certain directions rather than others – toward greater openness and greater equality – and that the greatest exposure to the widest range of ways of living, speaking, and interpreting the world would help to further this goal (Roth Pierpont 2004).

Beside Boas: structuralism and Neoromanticism

Other twentieth-century schools posed questions about linguistic difference. These included Russian formalism; the social-life-based psychology launched by L. S. Vygotsky in the Soviet Union; some strands of analytical philosophy and British social anthropology drawing on the work of Malinowski and the later Wittgenstein (Chatterjee 1985); the structuralism of Ferdinand de Saussure, with developments in the Prague school of the 1930s and the Paris-based structuralism of the 1960s and 1970s; and a neo-Humboldtian linguistics in Germany.

While structuralists have come up with some formulations that sound very much like determinism of thought by language (Saussure 1916 [1972]; Benveniste 1958), these have not attracted the ire often directed at Sapir and Whorf, perhaps because the argument to thought is marginal to the broad structuralist project. It is not at all marginal, however, to the school of Humboldtian linguistics that arose in the German-speaking world in the 1920s and that continues as a scholarly tradition today.

After Steinthal's death, his followers continued both descriptive typology (Finck 1910) and psychological readings of language and world view (Finck 1899). At the same time, Humboldtian ideas about the relationship between language and world view were being picked up by some literary historians and philologists. In the early 1920s the philosopher Ernst Cassirer (1874–1945) propounded the idea of a Herder–Humboldt stream in philosophy and linguistics (1923 [1955]). With his emigration to the United States, Cassirer's renewed pluralism and essentialism influenced American students and became a source of inspiration for the symbolic anthropology of the 1970s.

A parallel "return to Humboldt" was taking place in Germany in what would be called neo-Humboldtian or Neoromantic linguistics, which sought to make explicit patterns of meaning that are implicit in the vocabulary and to a degree in the grammar of given languages (Basilius 1952; Öhman 1953; Bynon 1966; Miller 1968). The main names in this movement, Jost Trier (1894–1970) and Leo Weisgerber (1899–1985), came out of literary history, not linguistics in the strict sense. The neo-Humboldtians speak of each language representing a world view, a world construction (*Weltbild*), and being characterized by an inner form. This form is carried primarily in the lexicon, in related and contrasting sets of words. To understand a language in its specificity, one must reconstruct not only its form, but the semantic fields, the word-fields, that make up its contents.

A central aspect of the neo-Humboldtian project has been the valorization of one's mother tongue, whose specificities are bound up with one's most profound values. In contrast to the Boasians, but perhaps in accord with some recent post-modernist arguments, the neo-Humboldtians hold that learning other languages cannot be of much help in expanding one's horizons, since one learns them through the mother tongue, and they remain marginal to it (Bynon 1966: 472). Their project will not be one of opening up possibilities of thought through exposure to non-familiar ways of organizing experience, but of deepening understanding of and implication in one's own linguistic and cultural milieu. The bulk of the work will be about German, with other languages cited primarily for contrast.

Leo Weisgerber, the best known of the neo-Humboldtians, worked on a series of sensory domains, arguing that one must distinguish among the physiochemical correspondents to an experience, the perceptual reception of the stimulus, and the conceptual construction of a lived field, the latter achieved largely through words (Miller 1968). In vocabulary, Weisgerber considers the high number of abstract color terms (what would later be called basic color terms) in German and other Western European languages a sign of their greater appropriateness for abstract thought. In syntax (Weisgerber 1954: 190–200; Miller 1968: 94–97), he proposes conceptual effects of the German trait of encompassing large amounts of material between the modifier and head of a given syntagm, a nesting of syntagms requiring the speaker to hold a complex pattern of relations in mind.

Its high valorization of German and its emphasis on the mother tongue as the loving matrix of normal human development made this view of language attractive to the Third Reich. In a review evidently in line with National Socialist thinking, Kurt Stegmann von Pritzwald (1936) sees Neoromanticism as representative of a new generation that rejects the cold science of the old historical linguistics and seeks to aid actively in the self-realization of the German nation. Weisgerber and other leading neo-Humboldtians were active participants in the regime and the war effort – not party members and, given the circumstances, not particularly murderous participants, but participants nonetheless (Hutton 1999). After the war, they maintained their respectability for the most part (Knobloch 2000). Weisgerber's magnum opus bears the characteristic title *The Powers of the German Language*.

The neo-Humboldtian school has sometimes (e.g. Miller 1968) been presented as a European twin of Boasian ethnolinguistics – or rather, it has been assumed that the latter represented an American version of Humboldtian essentialism. While this reading is understandable, it fails to recognize that the two schools took Humboldt's legacy in opposite directions. The neo-Humboldtians took one side of Humboldt, that of the normal unity of language, thought, and culture, and pushed it to its limits: valorization of a single language and abandonment of the equally Humboldtian project of large-scale comparison. While the

Boasian school hearkens back to *Geist*s and *Volk*s, it draws the opposite moral. Its commitment to contrastive comparison and to the critique of modern Western values forced the abandonment of the unity of language-thought-culture.

The neo-Humboldtians show what real twentieth-century linguistic essentialism looks like; by contrast, they show how different the Boasian project is. We might even be justified in speaking of a Right-Humboldtianism and a Left-Humboldtianism (cf. the Right-Hegelianism and Left-Hegelianism of the 1840s), except that the Boasian problematic represents a serious enough shift away from Humboldtian assumptions to put this into question.

After Boas: the near-death and rebirth of linguistic relativity

Sapir died in 1939, Whorf in 1941, Boas in 1942. Dorothy Lee published some papers on language and world view after this time, as did Harry Hoijer (1904–1976), who worked primarily on Athapaskan languages. But by the early 1950s the intellectual climate had changed. Social scientists were interested in experimentation and the testing of hypotheses on what was taken to be the model of the natural sciences. At a conference on language in culture, Hoijer (1954) first named a Sapir–Whorf *hypothesis* that language influences thought.

To call something a hypothesis is to propose to test it, presumably using experimental methods. This task was taken on primarily, in the 1950s, by psychologists (P. Brown, this volume). The terms were redefined to make them more amenable to experiment: the aspect of language chosen was lexicon, presumably the easiest to control; thought was interpreted to mean perceptual discrimination and cognitive processing, aspects of thinking which psychologists were comfortable testing for. Eric Lenneberg defined the problem as that of "the relationship that a particular language may have to its speakers' cognitive processes . . . Does the structure of a given language affect the thoughts (or thought potential), the memory, the perception, the learning ability of those who speak that language?" (1953: 463). If language influences thought, speakers of languages with lots of terms for a given domain should be able to make finer perceptual distinctions in that domain than speakers of languages with few terms. In the most influential studies, the domain chosen was that of color, one that had interested an essentialist tradition starting with Goethe, but that had not been treated by the Boasians. The decision was made to ignore any color terms that were derived from other aspects of the world and employ only those with the abstract color as their basic meaning. Red is a basic color term of this kind, but salmon is not. For the most part, these projects failed to show any influence of language on thought.

One can't help feeling that the Boasians would have predicted their failure. They had shifted the terms of reference from pervasive to very limited aspects of a given language and from thought as construal of the world to thought processes, potential, and ability, precisely those domains where the Boasians had rejected an influence of language on thought (Lucy 1992a). The choice of color is problematic in itself, since this is a domain that comes already highly structured for perception, regardless of the language you speak (Sahlins 1976; Lucy 1997a). And in addition to this, the choice of allowing only for basic color terms seems completely arbitrary.

By the late 1950s there had been a notable lack of breakthrough in the search for "Whorfian effects," and the psychologists who had been looking for them were now in the rising tide of cognitive science. Since the goal was to study the human mind as a single domain, the enthusiasm for the new cognitive sciences was antithetical to serious consideration of linguistic, or any, diversity, taken to be mere difference of surface structure, foam on the ocean of mind.

In the late 1960s, further studies on color seemed to drive more nails into the coffin of linguistic relativity. In a survey of languages with differing numbers of basic color terms, the linguists Brent Berlin and Paul Kay rephrased Sapir and Whorf as saying that the search for semantic universals was "fruitless in principle" because "each language is semantically arbitrary relative to every other language" (1969: 2, cited in Lucy 1992a: 177). If indeed, as Sapir and Whorf are here said to have said, languages categorize meanings in arbitrary ways, there should be an arbitrary distribution of basic color terms. What Berlin and Kay found was anything but. First, they found a confirmation of the saliency of certain focal colors across languages. Beyond this, they found unexpected support for the old models of cultural and linguistic evolution: languages spoken by people in small-scale, low-tech societies had few basic color terms, which gradually, in an apparent correlation with cultural evolution, increased to the seven or eight found in English. So not only was there no relativity effect; on the contrary, color terminology seemed to confirm our own feelings of cultural advancement.

This topic has been discussed extensively (Kay, this volume; Lucy 1997a). Let me just add a comment based on the historical material we have seen in this chapter. Replacing whole language systems with basic color terms is comparable to the replacement of whole languages with numerals, which we could just as easily call basic number terms: "like the fingers on one hand" is not a basic number term, while "five" is. With both numbers and colors we find an increase in the number of terms in societies whose members are required to handle more elaborate technologies. This says nothing about the sophistication of thought processes in general, but a lot about the necessity in some circumstances of having an array of easily transposable terms that can be abstracted from actual situations. To paraphrase Boas's reply to the evolutionists on numbers: The way people live in some societies means that they do not need very many basic color terms. If their way of living changes they pick up new ones. None of this tells us very much about cognition or about how different peoples construe the world.[4]

During this period some philosophers were discovering "the Whorfian hypothesis," and they did not like it. Lewis Feuer (1953) says that Whorf's theory is based on comparison of vocabularies: he gives the example of Inukti- tut words for snow. Feuer points out, as Boas had, but without citing him, that we must expect people to develop an elaborate vocabulary on a topic that is of great interest to them. Since Feuer says that linguistic relativity is entirely about vocabulary, this fact must completely disqualify linguistic relativity. Feuer goes on to say that linguistic relativity is the argument that each language is a completely sealed universe: "The 'principle of linguistic relativity' argues that there are incommensurable cultural universes. An incommensurable cultural universe would be an unknown one. The fact of linguistic communication, the fact of translation, belies the doctrine of relativity" (1953: 95). Similar argu- ments were put forward by Max Black (1962). Black says that Whorf believed that the "real world" was totally unstructured, and that all structure was imposed on it by language. If this were right, of course, translation would be impossible, and Whorf's very effort to render the Hopi world in English would be a non- sense. Again, Donald Davidson presents the Whorf hypothesis as "conceptual relativism" and linguistic determinism and as claiming that different languages cannot be calibrated: "Whorf, wanting to demonstrate that Hopi incorporates a metaphysics so alien to ours that Hopi and English cannot, as he puts it, 'be calibrated', uses English to convey the contents of sample Hopi sentences" (Davidson 1974 [1984]: 184). Davidson gives no page reference for his appar- ent citation, just the name of one of Whorf's papers – not, as it happens, one in which the word "calibrated" appears. In the place where Whorf does talk about calibration, the passage that we cited on a new principle of relativity (1940 [1956]: 214), he says exactly the opposite of this: that "speakers of different languages will not be led by the same physical evidence to the same picture of the universe *unless* their linguistic backgrounds are similar or can somehow be calibrated" (my italics). In other words, far from contradicting himself by writ- ing about Hopi in English to show that the two cannot be calibrated, Whorf's efforts are precisely attempts to calibrate them.

Davidson goes on to equate difference in world view or conceptual scheme with untranslatability: "We may identify conceptual schemes with languages,

---

[4] These arguments have come back to the fore in the recent flap over the Pirahã language of Amazonia, which is said to lack a number of what are generally taken to be universal features of human languages. While the scholarly debate (e.g. Everett 2005 with comments and reply) bears on phonology, prosody, vocabulary, and grammar, the initial semi-popular explosion of interest was based almost entirely on vocabulary. What piqued the interest of the media was the idea of a language without numbers, a discovery said to support Whorf's "hypothesis . . . that language is more a 'mold' into which thought is cast than it is a reflection of thought" (Holden 2004: 1093).

then, or better, allowing for the possibility that more than one language may express the same scheme, sets of intertranslatable languages" (1974 [1984]: 185). If it is possible to translate from one language to another, then their two conceptual schemes must be the same. Not surprisingly, given the universal possibility of translation, Davidson concludes that the very idea of conceptual scheme is of no use. It is interesting to set this claim that the very possibility of translation proves the irrelevance of language differences against the reverse neo-Humboldtian claim that *any* difficulty in translation proves that languages represent different worlds. "If in fact words in different languages were simply referring to 'the same objective reality' there would be no translation problems, no so-called untranslatable words, and the distribution of 'words and objects' . . . would form neat patterns" (Bynon 1966: 472). In fact, as translation theorists have noted for centuries, translation from any human language to any other is always possible but always problematic; it all depends on what aspects of the original you are trying to convey and how much you are willing to burden your translation in order to do so. A constant shift in point of view implying a kind of practical linguistic relativity seems to be a prerequisite for the very act of translation (Becker 1995). Translation is always possible, but it's never evident (Rossi-Landi 1973, ch. 11).

Robert L. Miller (1968: 114), drawing on these philosophical critiques, identifies Whorf with Trier's contention that speakers can't distinguish what their vocabulary doesn't tell them to. Miller writes: "The lack of a word expressing [a given] distinction probably merely indicates that the speakers . . . [do] not usually make the distinction." In other words, Miller is adopting Whorf's distinction between habitual thought and the potentialities of thought, but instead of crediting Whorf for this, he treats him as if he were Trier.

It is certainly unfair to present these discussions solely in terms of their misreadings (see Lucy 1992a; P. Lee 1996; de Fornel 2002). The point they want to make is fair enough: it is that thought and experience derive from more than language; that the brain, the world, and social life all influence thought in a way not directly dependent on language. These critiques – the questions of vocabulary, of sealed language-worlds, of translation, and of social influence on thought – would probably hit the mark if they were aimed at the neo-Humboldtians, but it is not at all clear that they touch the Boasians.

In an interesting twist, neo-Humboldtian linguistics itself has intervened in a way hostile to the idea of linguistic relativity. Helmut Gipper, a student of Weisgerber's and editor of his early papers, went to Arizona to study Hopi and judge Whorf's portrayal of the language for himself, particularly the claim that Hopi has no terms that refer specifically and primarily to the realm that we call time. Gipper (1972) offers a preliminary analysis and vocabulary of Hopi time-language, concluding that Whorf had misrepresented the data. Some years later, Gipper's student Ekkehart Malotki conducted long-term field research among the Hopi. His book *Hopi Time* (1983) documents time vocabulary in Hopi.

The first page of Malotki's book carries only two quotes, one from Whorf and one from Malotki's own Hopi field notes. The Whorf quote appears to say that Hopi has no words for time; the field note, a Hopi text with interlinear glosses and an English translation, appears to be about nothing but time. This ironic juxtaposition is evidently meant to show how totally off the mark Whorf is, something that will presumably be documented more fully in the succeeding almost 700 pages.

The only way to judge this juxtaposition is to take it philologically, first by looking at the context of the line from Whorf in the text from which it is extracted. Here the passage as Malotki presents it:

After long and careful study and analysis, the Hopi language is seen to contain no words, grammatical forms, constructions or expressions that refer directly to what we call "time". . . .

(from Whorf 1936 [1956]: 57)

Note (as does Lucy, 1992a: 286) that Whorf does not write time, but "what we call 'time'," in scare quotes. How important are quotation marks? Absolutely essential here, since a few lines above and a few lines down Whorf defines what he means by "what we call 'time'": it is the constructed, spatialized model of time typical of the modern West, with the past somehow behind us, the future in front of us. Whorf specifies in the same text that this very specific mental image is not to be confused with the universal experience of temporal change, of it "always getting later."

Here is the English translation of a Hopi sentence that follows on Malotki's page: "Then indeed, the following day, quite early in the morning at the hour when people pray to the sun, around that time then he woke up the girl again." See all the time words? In fact, this begs the question entirely. Whorf never said that the Hopi can't or don't talk about time; he said that they don't conceptualize time in the same way we do, and that language is a source of conceptualization. No one would deny that the most appropriate translation of a given Hopi sentence into normal English might involve English time words. The question is whether the words that convey this referential information and deictic temporal relation in Hopi work in the same way as do those in English, conveying the same background assumptions and, presumably, the same "metaphysic" of a spatialized past, present, and future. These are empirical questions which I cannot answer. But Gipper's lists of German translation glosses, Malotki's lists of English ones, do not answer them either.

The period of the 1950s through the 1980s, then, was one of the progressive triumph of universalist cognitive science. From the 1980s, one saw the concomitant rise of relativistic postmodernism. By the end of the 1980s there had been a massive return to the old split between universalizing natural sciences and their ancillary social sciences on the one hand, particularizing humanities and their ancillary cultural studies on the other. Some things, in the prevailing view, were universal, others so particular as to call for treatment as fiction or personal reflection. Nothing in between was of very much interest. In this climate, the idea of linguistic relativity was heresy, Whorf, in particular, a kind of stupid anti-Christ. Serious linguists (e.g. Pullum 1989) and psychologists (e.g. Pinker 1994: 59–64) continued to dismiss the idea of linguistic relativity with an alacrity suggesting alarm and, in particular, heaped vilification on Whorf, their favorite target, as an uncredentialed amateur, a lousy linguist, and/or a mystical loony.

Returns of relativity

Through all this there remained a stubborn little band of defenders of linguistic relativity (Hill and Mannheim 1992; Lucy 1997b). For many people, there continued to be something intuitively right about the proposition that the specifics of one's language were important for one's construction of the world. Paul Friedrich articulated this in terms reminiscent of Sapir: "I feel that American as against British English, and English of any major dialect as against Russian, and both languages as against the Tarascan language of Mexico constitute different worlds. I note that it is persons with experience of foreign languages and poetry who feel most acutely that a natural language is a different way not only of talking but of thinking and imagining and of emotional life" (1986: 16).

Continuing research on the implications of linguistic variation took a number of forms.

Ethnosemantics. The best known is probably the movement in North American anthropology variously known as ethnosemantics, ethnoscience, or cognitive anthropology (P. Brown, this volume), which had its heyday in the early 1960s. Ethnosemantics carried on the project of operationalizing a holistic view of language and thought, again by strictly limiting the data to what can be easily mapped. The famous studies in this field took vocabulary domains – animals, plants, skin diseases – and used the mutual delimitation of and relations among terms to construct models of speakers' classification systems (Tyler 1969). This remains a valid method, but, it was soon felt, cannot replace either full-scale participatory ethnography or consideration of all aspects of a language, not only lexical arrays.

Relativity of use. In the 1960s, Dell Hymes (1926–) sought to define distinctive cognitive styles implied in different language types (1961) and proposed what he called a second kind of linguistic relativity, a relativity of language use (1966) as distinct from the primarily referential interests of the Boasians. Not all societies use language in the same way. Mapping these specificities of use should be part of any ethnography. The field Hymes thus launched came to be

called the ethnography of speaking or communication. Besides strictly ethnographic analyses of language use and language attitudes, the field includes a
tradition of ethnolinguistics in the strict sense: a comparative study of theories
of language and language genres (Lucy 1992a: 91–93, 105–112). Major studies
were carried out on systems of classifying ways of speaking (e.g. Gossen 1974,
Sherzer 1983). There is a parallel to this tradition in the school of intensive
Africanist ethnography launched in France by Marcel Griaule (e.g. Calame-
Griaule 1987).

Grammatical nuance and ethnopoetics. Another new take on linguistic relativity has been proposed by Paul Friedrich (1927–). Friedrich had worked on
Tarascan, an isolate Mexican language with an obligatory system of shape-
marking (Friedrich 1969, 1972). For Friedrich, such categories represented
implicit metaphors, poetic figures inherent in the language itself and forming
an aesthetic force at least as powerful as the purely referential structuring usually
associated with the idea of linguistic relativity (Friedrich 1979, 1986). Friedrich
found inspiration in Sapir, and his efforts helped link questions of grammatical
structure and world view to the burgeoning ethnopoetics movement (Friedrich,
this volume; Hill and Mannheim 1992: 397–398).

Semiotic functionalism. Seeking to clarify the relationship between the structure of a language and the more or less explicit ideas about language held by
its speakers, Michael Silverstein (1976, 1977, 1979, 1981 [2001]) proposed
a hierarchy of aspects of language that would be more or less available to
speakers' awareness, thus giving a basis for some of the effects the Boasians
had noted: lexical items, for instance, are close to awareness and so easily
replaced or discarded, while pervasive grammatical categories are generally far
from awareness and less amenable to conscious manipulation. Silverstein has
reminded us that reference is only one of many functions involved in language
use. Of particular interest to him has been the way languages anchor the speaker
in a context through the use of indexicals or shifters, such as personal pronouns
or verb tenses, that both convey referential information and change depending
on who is talking, where, or when. Silverstein's shift to shifters offers a mech-
anism to link what is said into the situation of saying and so opens up linguistic
analysis to social analysis (Hill and Mannheim 1992: 395–397; Lucy 1992a:
115–126; Foley 1997: 211–213).

Relativitas rediviva
What has collapsed has not necessarily been superseded.
                                          (Trabant 1986: 206; my translation)

Meanwhile, however, things were shifting again. Since the 1980s, a small number of souls (e.g. Alford 1978, 1981; see also Lakoff 1987: chapter 18) had been
repeating that the prevailing interpretation of linguistic relativity was misplaced.
By the early 1990s, a critical mass seemed to have developed for rethinking the

concept. A conference on this theme was held in 1991 (Gumperz and Levinson 1996); new cognitive work began to be done based on more serious reading of Sapir and Whorf, and the relative success of these efforts gave the whole enterprise a new legitimacy. Just before this, Emily Schultz (1990) had proposed a Bakhtinian rereading of Whorf's text as largely ironic and fully engaged in the controversies of its time. In 1992, John Lucy offered a revised history of linguistic relativity that made it seem an interesting and provocative idea; some years later, Penny Lee produced the first monographic study of Whorf's thought as a whole, drawing largely on unpublished material (P. Lee 1996). Lee showed, in particular, how much of a universalist Whorf was on some issues. By 1997, the year of the Whorf centenary and of a number of symposia and conferences on the topic, research was rolling in multiple domains. Four seem particularly salient.

(1) There has been an explosion of studies in cognition (P. Brown, this volume). Lucy read Sapir and Whorf seriously and tried to use their ideas in designing cross-cultural psychological experiments, first on color, then in a study on noun classes and number in a Mayan language and in English, in this case working on the basis of obligatory grammatical categories and showing an influence of grammar on short-term memory (1992b). Combined ethnographic and experimental research is being carried out by scholars of the Max Planck Institute in the Netherlands, notably on the conception of space among speakers of Australian languages that have constantly used terms for the cardinal directions but none corresponding to our left and right (Levinson 1997; P. Brown, this volume). That there seem to be differences in spatial cognition between speakers of these languages and speakers of European languages is ironic, given that Whorf, following Gestalt psychology, believed that space was a domain that was likely to be conceptualized in the same way regardless of language (P. Lee 1996: 102 ff.).

(2) In linguistics proper, research on grammatical categories has been a growth area (e.g. Hopper 1982 on tense and aspect, Chafe and Nichols 1986 on evidentiality).

(3) Following the lead of sociolinguistics, a good deal of recent work has shown the relativity of linguistic ways of marking social and other kinds of situation (e.g. Duranti and Goodwin 1992). As William Hanks puts it, these are "approaches which push context dependency deeper into the language" (1996: 232).

(4) Ongoing work in ethnopoetics, performance theory, and the theory of translation (e.g. A. L. Becker's attempts to go "beyond translation," 1995) deals directly with the implications of linguistic specificity. This seems appropriate. If poetic language makes all levels of a language resonate (Jakobson 1960), then, as Humboldt believed, it is through poetic language that linguistic specificity is most intensely expressed. Phonetics and phonology represent unavoidable sound-worlds. Choice of words and their semantic fields, explicit or suggested,

becomes essential – think of all the uses of lake, river, stream, brook, rivulet, the sea in English poetry and song. The problem of grammatical categories and their translation becomes acute.

For the poetically awake ear, even just plain syntax, e.g. where you put the verb, becomes not just a key to deep structures or the sign of a language universal, but a source of rising suspense and falling relief. Here Weisgerber's observations on German nesting syntax are perfectly appropriate, not as an argument for the superiority of the intellectual architecture of German, but as elucidating a specific rhythm of ideas, an intellectual poetics. "Waiting for the German verb is surely the ultimate thrill" writes Flann O'Brien (1977) – a speaker and writer not only of English, but equally of Irish, a language that is verb-initial and that therefore usually gives the action away at the beginning of the sentence.

Conclusion

Language is the most massive and inclusive art we know.

(Sapir 1921: 220)

Human beings live in language; they speak and listen constantly to speech, and at least an important part of their silent thinking, imagining, and problem solving takes place in some transform of spoken language. Since there is no language in general, only particular languages, speaking, listening to speech, and thinking in words can take place only in the medium of a particular language and must bear the imprint of that language's peculiarities. If language specificities are important, each language may be seen as the expression of a unique essence. This is not the Boasian way of taking each language as a distinct "point of view" for the speaker/hearer. Its model is the relativity of Einstein; it is necessarily a more complex, off-center, and perhaps contradictory position than either the universalist or the essentialist alternative. Proponents of the non-importance of language differences have repeatedly taken the relativity model of the Boasians to be the essentialist model and have criticized it on that basis, as linguistic relativism or determinism.

Einstein's relativity was neither of these; it wasn't a doctrine or a moral philosophy, but a principle that allowed a more complex – but still coherent – way of thinking the world than did the earlier unstated principle of privileging a single fixed viewpoint. Similarly, linguistic relativity is no ism, but a principle meant to allow a more complex consideration of human conceptualization than the alternative, usually unstated, principles: (1) the way speakers of Western European languages conceive the world is right, everyone else is wrong; (2) everyone in the world conceives it in the same way; (3) each language is a unique universe that must be preserved in its purity. Linguistic relativity should not be identified with the last of these views; on the contrary, it problematizes all of them.

From the 1960s through the 1980s, the intellectual mood was one of hostility to the idea of linguistic relativity as antithetical to the universalist postulates of the prevailing schools. Since the 1990s, efforts are being made to recognize the possibility of the importance of linguistic difference, bringing a more sympathetic reading of linguistic relativity into already constituted paradigms: cognitive psychology, language philosophy, microsociology now seem ready to consider differences among languages while maintaining their own assumptions and methods. At the same time, we continue to see the dominance of cognitivist paradigms and the maintenance of cognitivist assumptions in thinking about language differences. In the words of *Rethinking Linguistic Relativity* (Gumperz and Levinson 1996), the book that as much as any other helped put linguistic relativity back on the intellectual map, "in the light of the much greater knowledge that we now have about both language and mental processing, it would be pointless to attempt to revive ideas about linguistic relativity in their original form" (p. 7).

Let us dwell on this for a moment. It is saying that what we now know about mental processing makes the original, Boasian, form of linguistic relativity pointless. But the Boasian version of linguistic relativity was quite explicitly not about thought in the sense of mental processing, but in the sense of conceptualization of the world. Testing the cognitive abilities or processes of speakers of different languages on different tasks, a worthy enough activity if carried out right, is in fact outside the Boasian project, which was also the Whorfian project. Yet the dream of such testing has dominated orthodox readings of linguistic relativity since the 1950s and, as the volume cited attests, remains well established today. Most of the great battles in the field have been fought on this terrain. It is not Boasian terrain.

On the Boasian terrain of the centrality of linguistic difference and a principle of linguistic relativity, both the dismissal of the "Whorfian hypothesis" for lack of experimental support and its recent rebirth as an experimental paradigm seem largely beside the point. Testing for "Whorf effects" in cognition may be like seeing whether people traveling at two different velocities are better or worse at cognitive tests; or, perhaps more fairly, and to use one of Whorf's own examples (1936 [1956]: 58), like testing someone who is used to Euclidean geometry against a hypothetical person who was raised using a non-Euclidean geometry. One might be better at solving some kinds of problems than others, and this difference might offer roundabout evidence confirming the fact that the two are using two different kinds of geometry. But we already knew that. The alternative non-relativity hypothesis here would have to be that both are secretly using Euclidean geometry to do the work, but that the ostensible (surface?) non-Euclidean is quietly adding an extra step and restating his or her findings in non-Euclidean terms. Similarly, we know already that Yucatec treats animate and inanimate count nouns differently for purposes of number where English makes no such distinction, that Guugu Yimithirr uses cardinal directions in most situations for which English uses left and right. That such pervasive and important aspects of these languages should have some incidence on the organization and remembering of experienced data is to be expected; confirming experimental results give roundabout support to the idea that speakers of Yucatec and Guugu Yimithirr are actually using the resources offered by their languages to help in cognitive and memory tasks. It would be more surprising if they weren't.

Cognitivist assumptions and methods are different from those of the Boasians, the people who started to draw the full effects of taking language specificities seriously. What, then, might be the tasks of a linguistic anthropology refounded on "the original form" of the idea of linguistic relativity? What might a Boasian or, hideous neologism, a neo-Boasian research program look like? Here I will offer only a couple of ideas.

It would have to take account of the evidence about cognition, development, and language universals that has been amassed by other disciplines.

It would have to pay attention to bilingual and multilingual situations and their implications and not assume monolingualism as the norm.

It would have to attend to the impossible reality of translation.

It would have to attend to all forms of speech without privileging the declarative sentence spoken in sober adult didactic mode. Poetry, empassioned speech, divine oracles and demonic ravings would be accepted as data just as much as a conversation, an extended monologue, or individual made-up sentences.

Instead of simply exemplifying them, it would have to try to understand the motivating phenomena of language love, language hate, language curiosity, and delight in language(s).

It would start with language as a whole, not with thought or meaning. The pervasive systematicity of non-semantic aspects of language, phonology and phonetics, would be treated with the same respect as its semantic aspects. Phonological systems are elaborate dances that every human speaker and listener has to master and which usually determine habitual ways of producing and receiving speech sounds. This level of language does not involve meaning directly, and so claims of its influence seem less threatening than those involving "thought." Yet the Boasians always seem to have treated the patterning of non-meaningful elements as comparable to that of meaningful ones: Boas attended to sound systems, Sapir invented phonology, and one of Whorf's illustrations is of restrictions on the phonology of English monosyllables (1941b [1956]: 223). Sound patterning certainly has effects on feeling, if not directly on ideation, which are valorized in poetic language (Sapir 1929b [1949]). If we could get past the valuing of thought over feeling, mind over body, and begin to think of habitual thought, like the habitual production of speech sounds, as a kind of habitus, we would give more mind to phonology's habitual choreography of speech organs and ear, bringing Winteler's "relational relativity" back into linguistic relativity.

At least as important is continuing work on grammatical categories, overt and covert. What does it mean to speak a language that requires you to specify time, or source of knowledge, or shape, hundreds or thousands of time a day? We still don't know. But putting the question like this suggests a clear and limited way of interpreting the idea that different languages represent different worlds.

And this whole idea of worlds . . . The work on deictics and context has opened up one of the central aspects of human language; yet it remains the case that one of language's important functions – a function it shares, to be sure, with other media – is to define a world and to project aspects of it on the mind's eye (and ear and nose . . .). This is the good old referential function, not as a propositional truth value, but as the definer of things and images: as the imagination. Not only do humans not live only in "the real world"; the perceived real world is, for any human being, only one piece of a much greater manifold of imagined or remembered virtual scenes. How these scenes are typically structured, how they are connected to each other and to the situation of speech, are likely to vary as much as any other aspect of language use and to depend to some degree on the specifics of the language being used.

The goal, then, might be to try to overcome essentialist weaknesses in the Boasian approach without once again throwing the baby out with the bath-water and returning to what are, in the end, equally limited rationalisms or empiricisms.

3

BENJAMIN LEE WHORF AND THE BOASIAN FOUNDATIONS OF CONTEMPORARY ETHNOLINGUISTICS

REGNA DARNELL

We dissect nature along lines laid down by our native languages. The categories and types that we isolate from the world of phenomena we do not find there because they stare every observer in the face; on the contrary, the world is presented in a kaleidoscopic flux of impressions which has to be organized by our minds – and this means largely by the linguistic systems of our minds.

Benjamin Lee Whorf (1956: 213)

The phenomena of language are background phenomena, of which the talkers are unaware or, at most, dimly aware . . . These automatic, involuntary patterns of language are not the same for all men but are specific for each language and constitute the formalized side of the language, or its "grammar."

From this fact proceeds what I have called the "linguistic relativity principle," which means, in informal terms, that users of markedly different grammars are pointed by their grammars toward different types of observations and different evaluations of externally similar acts of observation, and hence are not equivalent as observers, but must arrive at somewhat different views of the world.

Benjamin Lee Whorf (1956: 221)

The role of Benjamin Lee Whorf (1897–1941) in contemporary ethnolinguistics is an unusually complex one from the standpoint of the histories of anthropology, linguistics, and psychology, not to speak of philosophy.[1] It is arguable that Whorf has been misread more thoroughly than any other social scientist of his generation. And yet, his musings on the relationships among language, thought, and reality continue to be cited – largely under the interdisciplinary rubric of cognitive science – with the respect due to a pioneer whose work is foundational to that being done today.

Moreover, anthropologists and linguists remain curious about Whorf; they want to know whether he was right about linguistic relativity and the critical importance of grammatical categories to differences in the potential for the organization of the thought of individuals speaking a given language, relative

---

[1] I have been interested in Whorf from a number of standpoints (Darnell 1974, 1990, 1998a, 1998b, forthcoming). My thinking about his career and place in Americanist anthropology owes much to the following colleagues: Ray DeMallie, Peter Denny, Ray Fogelson, Dell Hymes, John Joseph, Konrad Koerner, Stephen Leavitt, Penny Lee, Stephen O. Murray, Doug Parks, and Samar Zebian. I am grateful to Christine Jourdan for the invitation to participate in this review of the state of the ethnolinguistic art.

to speakers of another language. The question, even stated in this simplistic form, continues to fascinate. That there would be no such relationship is counterintuitive; to demonstrate the precise nature of the relationship, however, remained an elusive prospect for Whorf's immediate successors. In my view, however, the kinds of experiments devised more recently by cognitive scientists have very little to do with Whorf's specific formulation of the problem of linguistic relativity. There is, therefore, a discontinuity – or at least an unacknowledged selectivity in contemporary readings of Whorf – which has received little historiographic notice and which calls for explanation.

Cognitive scientists have consistently acknowledged their debt to Whorf and his intellectual genealogy which stretches back through Whorf's mentor Edward Sapir to his teacher Franz Boas to the German Romanticism of Johann Herder, Wilhelm von Humboldt, and Hermann Steinthal. It is an honourable genealogy, deeply enmeshed in the moral imperative of North American anthropology which moved back and forth between the tolerance for diversity associated with the notions of cultural relativism or linguistic relativity and the obligation of the anthropologist as public intellectual to bring the fruits of cross-cultural investigation back to the critique of his/her own society. The tenor of the acknowledgments, however, has been to note that Whorf raised questions of contemporary concern but lacked sufficiently rigorous methodology to resolve them. Such pro forma acknowledgment of Whorf as predecessor often fails to re-examine the work he actually did or the specific claims he made about linguistic relativity. A re-examination of his contribution and its subsequent appropriation to quite different arguments is, therefore, long overdue.

In this paper, I would like to return Whorf to center stage and consider how his ideas are grounded in the general approach of Boasian anthropology to the study of North American aboriginal languages and cultures (Darnell 1998, 2001). This requires addressing a number of stereotypes about Whorf's position in the group around Edward Sapir at Yale in the 1930s and framing Whorf's formulation of what he called "the linguistic relativity principle" in relation to the larger body of his own linguistic work and that of his contemporaries.

Dell Hymes and John Fought, in their monumental discussion on American structuralism (1975: 997) identify a "first Yale school" around Sapir, discontinuous from the better-known school that emerged at Yale around Leonard Bloomfield in the 1940s and 1950s. The distinctive features of the first Yale school were:

(1) to develop methods of structural description and "to test their application in the analysis of both exotic and well-known languages";
(2) to develop the discipline of linguistics;
(3) to continue the urgent task of recording disappearing languages;
(4) to continue the work of demonstrating precise genetic relationship among American Indian languages;
(5) to link linguistics to other disciplines and to practical affairs.

Bloomfield accepted the importance of all of these tasks, although few of his students took up questions of genetic relationship, and although the balance among them was different from that of the Boasians. Moreover, Bloomfield's view of the relation of linguistics to other fields, particularly psychology and anthropology, was considerably narrower than Sapir's. Whorf's position was closely tied to the Boasian/Sapirian package summarized above; despite the overlap in questions and methods, his broad humanistic orientation to linguistics would have been alien to the ethos of the second Yale school under Bloomfield and his most ardent disciple, Bernard Bloch. That is, the post-Bloomfieldians moved even further from Boasian roots of Americanist linguistics than did Bloomfield himself. Post-war positivism further eclipsed the humanistic linguistics that neither Sapir nor Whorf were around to defend.

Our disciplinary oral traditions focus on the following reasons not to take Whorf seriously.

First, he is often dismissed as an amateur linguist because he never held an academic degree in anthropology or linguistics; moreover, his only teaching position was in 1937 to 1938 when he replaced Edward Sapir, who was on sabbatical, for a single course in American Indian linguistics. These indices of professional credentialization were indeed important by the 1930s; Whorf stood out among his contemporaries in not attempting to obtain formal credentialization from his apprenticeship with Sapir or to earn his living as a linguist.

Second, much of his writing appeared in unconventional journals, directed to engineers or Theosophists, and aimed to make technical linguistic material accessible to educated but non-professional audiences. North American linguistics was still becoming professional, its disciplinary autonomy dating back only to the founding of the Linguistic Society of America and its journal *Language* in 1925. Whorf's publication outlets challenged these new-found respectabilities and disciplinary specializations. Linguists based in anthropology, indeed, no longer seemed so central to mainstream North American linguistics (an increasing isolation which would be accelerated during and after the Second World War). This increasing hiatus culminates in the contemporary marginalization of linguistic anthropology within the four-field structure of the North American discipline.

Third, Whorf's Theosophical Society leanings and fascination with Asian philosophies have inspired charges of mentalism, already highly suspect, degenerating into mysticism. Such religious preoccupations were readily dismissed in an intellectual climate that emphasized the superficial appearance of science. Science was understood to be self-consciously and unequivocally secular.

Fourth, there has been some question of how much Whorf actually knew about Hopi. He worked extensively with the language in New York City with Ernest Naquayouma, a native speaker of Hopi who, obviously, was bilingual. Thus, Whorf's access to the Hopi language in its proper cultural context and among monolingual speakers was extremely limited. And if grammatical categories highly influenced or even determined thought, as Whorf suggested, then a bilingual informant could hardly be taken to represent unproblematically the thought-world of his natal community. Whorf was not able to carry out conventional fieldwork except on an occasional vacation from his non-academic employment, although he did receive prestigious and highly competitive funding from the Social Science Research Council for fieldwork. His contemporaries, however, spent much more time "in the field," which was considered part of the mystique of being a "real" anthropologist.

Although all of these things are true, they do not add up to an accurate picture of Whorf's professional stature as it was perceived by his contemporaries. Whorf's career was indeed anomalous, but it is curious that such issues arise in the context of assessing his ideas about linguistic relativity, with virtually no attention to the structure of his ideas as a whole (what Penny Lee [1996] has called "the Whorf theory complex"), his reputation among his contemporaries, or the degree of complicity of Sapir in his mystical or mentalist formulations about the relationship of language and culture.

Whorf was a well educated man, albeit not within the disciplines in which we remember his work today. A generation earlier, virtually everyone was trained in something else. But by Whorf's professional generation, doctoral credentials in anthropology were becoming *de rigueur*. Although contemporaries and successors judged him by the emerging standards, Whorf's university degree in chemical engineering from MIT served him well in his lifelong employment as a fire insurance claims adjustor. He did not separate his scientific training in engineering from his work in linguistics. Indeed, he was wont to employ examples from his work about the relationship between linguistic categories and real-world experience. There was nothing mystical about his belief in the real world.

Best known is his cautionary tale of the empty gasoline drum, treated as no longer dangerous because of a linguistic label but still containing sufficient fumes to cause an explosion. Although the story arises from his personal experience, and has consequences of particular interest to a fire insurance company employee, Whorf makes no claim that the explosion of an empty gasoline drum caused him to arrive at what his predecessors have called "the Whorf hypothesis." Rather, the story serves as a representative anecdote, illustrating how what he called "habitual thought" relies on unexamined linguistic categories. Whorf took for granted that it was possible for any speaker of a given language to bring such categories to conscious awareness and articulate them in words. This insight arose from his long-term work on Hopi and the "multilingual consciousness" it inculcated in him (as well, presumably, as in his key consultant).

Employment was a problem not just for Whorf but for his entire generation. They came of age professionally in the midst of the Great Depression when there were few academic jobs available in any field, even less in so new and apparently insignificant a discipline as linguistics. Whorf was one of the few to hold steady employment.[2] Linguistics in North America did not come into its own until the Second World War demonstrated its practical utility in dealing with unfamiliar but suddenly politically significant cultures and languages, particularly in Asia and the Pacific.

The turn of the 1940s was a time of loss for the kind of linguistics in which Whorf's ideas developed. The world was girding itself for war. Edward Sapir had his first heart attack in the summer of 1935 and died early in 1939 at the age of fifty-five. Whorf learned that he had cancer late in 1938; he underwent surgery and continued to write until his death in 1941 at the age of forty-four (Lee 1996: 13). Almost certainly, had he lived to a normal life span, he would have elaborated the ideas for which he is remembered today as having provided little empirical evidence. Instead, he was forced to concentrate on getting his ideas on how to approach linguistic questions into print, with the hope that others would choose to follow it up (as indeed they did).

Sapir's version of process grammar and his concern with the relations of language, thought, and reality were not followed up at Yale after his death; the students, mostly what we would now call post-docs, were not senior enough to succeed him and the Department of Anthropology turned away from linguistics almost totally (Darnell 1998a). Boas and Bloomfield both tried, in anthropology and linguistics respectively, to mentor Sapir's former students, but the unity and sense of purpose of the group dissipated without Sapir. In the period after Whorf's death, under the leadership of Leonard Bloomfield, North American linguistics veered sharply toward behaviourism and experimentalism, explicitly striving for the status of science and equating science with the exclusion of meaning from the purview of linguistics. This is not a definition of science that would have made sense to Whorf.

Ironically, Whorf himself knew more about science that any of his fellow Boasian linguists, because of his training in engineering. He read widely in the physical sciences and frequently applied scientific metaphors in his linguistic work. Albert Einstein's theory of relativity was the most significant scientific discovery of Whorf's lifetime and he followed its technical elaboration as well as extending it metaphorically to the at least superficially incommensurable thought-worlds associated with different languages. His comment in the MIT *Technology Review* in 1940 (1956: 214) suggests that Whorf expected this audience to follow the process by which his own train of thought had moved from Einstein's physics to questions of linguistic form:

---

[2] Mary Haas, in an interview with Stephen O. Murray published in *Anthropological Linguistics* in 1998, recalled that Sapir did his best to find short-term positions on research projects or in the field for his students. But there were few academic opportunities until well after Sapir's death in 1939. Stanley Newman (Darnell 1989) wanted to pursue Sapir's interests in "linguistic psychology" but moved into American Indian linguistics because he could find no other way to support himself and his family.

We are thus introduced to a new principle of relativity, which holds that all observers are not led by the same physical evidence to the same picture of the universe, unless their linguistic backgrounds are similar, or can in some way be calibrated.

The reference to calibration invokes a method of scientific experiment which Whorf found highly congenial. He too wanted linguistics to be a science.

Whorf was not alone in his fascination with the physics of relativity. As early as 1924, Sapir had explicitly compared "the relativity of the form of thought" grounded in the "incommensurable analyses of experience in different languages" (1949: 158). It was "not so difficult to grasp as the physical relativity of Einstein" in spite of the blinders imposed by "our naive acceptance of fixed habits of thought" (1949: 159). Yet Sapir's flirtations with linguistic relativity were not received with the same skepticism as Whorf's. The sheer magnitude and quality of his other work allowed him to be taken seriously in ways that Whorf never was.

In the eyes of linguists in the 1940s and 1950s, however, what was not scientific about Whorf's work was primarily the methodology underlying his comparisons of Hopi and what he called "Standard Average European." Whorf almost certainly did not intend his pronouncements to be interpreted literally as having resulted from controlled scientific comparison of the two languages. Robin Ridington (1991) has glossed some of Whorf's most lyrical theoretical statements in poetic lines to indicate the assemblage of his argument in terms to which scientific experiment in the narrow sense is irrelevant. Rather, Whorf's work was exploratory and suggestive of directions for further investigation of meaning and its expression in language.

In spite of their skepticism toward anything that talked about "mind," the Bloomfieldians and neo-Bloomfieldians, who dominated Yale linguistics after the deaths of Sapir and Whorf, expended considerable energy in attempting to formulate the Whorf hypothesis (sometimes called the Sapir–Whorf hypothesis) in terms amenable to unambiguous testing. Harry Hoijer, himself a former Sapir student from the latter's pre-Yale days, edited an influential collection of conference papers in 1954 which concluded that the experimental results were inconclusive. After that, linguistic relativity retreated as a topic for serious investigation, although lip service to its underlying insight was retained.

Whorf as a linguist among his peers

In his own time, "Ben" Whorf was acknowledged as one among a group of peers, most of whom had followed Edward Sapir when he moved from Chicago to Yale in 1931. In addition to Whorf, the cohort included: Morris Swadesh, Stanley Newman, Mary Haas, George Trager, George Herzog, Zellig Harris, and later Carl Voegelin, Charles Hockett, and indirectly Joseph Greenberg. Whorf, who joined the group only after Sapir arrived in New Haven, could not have been singled out then for the crucial idea now identified as the "Whorf hypothesis" because it did not yet exist. His dramatic formulation of the relationship of language, thought, and reality came only at the end of his lifetime. Whorf's best-known paper on linguistic relativity, "The Relation of Habitual Thought and Behavior to Language", appeared in the year of his death, 1941, in a memorial volume for Sapir. Its influence, of necessity, was subsequent to that publication and proceeded without further input from the author.

Whorf, in his own lifetime, was acknowledged for his work as an American Indian linguist in the Sapirian vein. He was the only one of the former Sapir students to contribute two grammatical sketches (on Milpa Aztec and Hopi) to the linguistic memorial volume edited by Harry Hoijer (1946). He worked on problems of historical linguistics; with George Trager, he succeeded in linking Sapir's Uto-Aztecan stock to Tanoan. Mary Haas wrote to Whorf (16 February 1937: YU)[3] that the Tanoan connection followed up well on "Sapir's intuitions." Both Whorf's synchronic and diachronic work were respected among his peers.

Ironically, however, Sapir's students were more interested in linguistic classification during the 1930s than was Sapir himself; he seems to have turned to other problems after presenting his six-unit classification in 1921 (revised to its more familiar form in 1929). The students saw themselves as taking over where Sapir had left off, linking linguistic stocks to produce a culture history of the continent that could be read in broad strokes (Darnell 1990; Haas 1998). Sapir was apparently not much involved in the collective revised synthesis. His own professional identity evolved toward linguistics as an autonomous discipline, whereas his students embraced the Boasian view of his own early career.

There is no question that Sapir thought highly of Whorf. He wrote to Alfred Kroeber (30 April 1936: UCB):

Whorf is an awfully good man, largely self-made, and with a dash of genius. He is sometimes inclined to get off the central problem and indulge in marginal speculations but that merely shows the originality and adventuresome quality of his mind [. . .] [He] is one of the most valuable American Indian linguists that we have at the present time.

For Sapir, if not for all of his contemporaries, imagination was a desirable quality. Especially after the onset of Sapir's illness, Whorf increasingly became the focal point of the Yale cohort as they dispersed for fieldwork and employment. Whorf's personal papers at Yale University contain round robin letters which he appears to have been responsible for keeping in circulation. He was often left to decide what Sapir, given his precarious health, should be bothered with and what not. All of the students were protective of Sapir's time and energy.

During Sapir's sabbatical in 1937 to 1938, which he spent mostly in New York City attempting to recover his health, Whorf was hired to teach the required

[3] I have cited archival documents from the Alfred Kroeber papers at the University of California, Berkeley (UCB), the Yale University Archives (YU), and the Yale University Department of Anthropology administrative files (YUDA).

course on "Problems of American Indian Linguistics" to anthropology graduate students, many of whom were dubious about the relevance of such technical material to their ethnological interests. Whorf was elated by the opportunity to share his enthusiasm for linguistics in general and American Indian languages in particular. He wrote to Yale anthropology department chair Leslie Spier, a Boas-trained Americanist ethnologist (4 August 1937: YUDA):

I realize that [. . .] the students will have, for the most part, only the haziest notions of linguistics, and my idea would be to excite them in the linguistic approach as a way of developing understanding of the ideology of other peoples.

That is, Whorf realized he would have to appeal to ethnological reasoning to hold the attention of his students. He had neither the status nor the charisma of Sapir, and he knew it. Tolerance for cultural diversity, i.e. cultural relativism, was at the core of the Boasian program, and Whorf aspired to demonstrate it in terms of American Indian linguistic data. Spier apparently agreed with this strategy, writing to Dean Edgar Furniss (6 August 1937: YU) that Whorf

has a very stimulating way . . . and I would like to take advantage of his interest in hooking up language and ethnology, for I think it would take with many of our students. They might thus be encouraged to give serious attention to linguistics, when a "straight" linguistics course might leave them cold.

To John Carroll, Whorf envisioned (August 1937: YU) "a psychological direction" to the examination of "the organization of raw experience into a consistent and readily communicable universe of ideas through a medium of linguistic patterns." This, in my view (Darnell 1990: 381), is the moment of origin of the Whorf hypothesis. It was not a new theory or methodology but a pedagogical effort to translate the linguistic work of Sapir and his students so that it would be comprehensible to non-linguists. The other members of Whorf's cohort would have shared most of his logic in this construction of their common agenda.

On the other hand, Whorf's background was somewhat different from that of others in the cohort, in ways which perhaps explain why he was the one to take up this particular pedagogical mission. John B. Carroll, editor of the volume of Whorf's selected writings which appeared in 1956, emphasizes Whorf's "contact with a small but earnest band of Sapir's students" as the watershed in his recognition as a professional linguist. Whorf was accepted into the doctoral program in linguistics at Yale, but he chose to follow Sapir's courses rather than to pursue the degree as such. Whorf already had considerable experience in several languages, including Hebrew, Nahuatl and Mayan, as well as a broad professional network in anthropology.

Whorf was introduced to Sapir as a protégé of several prominent Harvard archaeologists who worked in Mexico (Alfred Tozzer, Herbert Spinden, and Sylvanus Morley). These mentors had some stake in providing Whorf with credentials in the cutting-edge linguistics of the day. He had already done considerable work on Mayan and Aztec cryptography and iconography. They wanted Whorf, or someone like him, to help them interpret their archaeological data. Most of Boas's students were engrossed by the more acutely endangered languages of the Americas north of Mexico. Moreover, there was some tension between Columbia and Harvard, with an effective division of the discipline between cultural anthropology and linguistics under Boas in New York, on the one hand, and archaeology and physical anthropology in Cambridge in the naturalist, scientific tradition initiated by Frederick Ward Putnam in the late nineteenth century, on the other hand.

The Harvard archaeologists, however, failed to recognize that American linguistics itself was changing, with an increasing division between Boas and Sapir over phonetic vs. phonemic transcription (Darnell 1990). Boas held that the ethnologist as linguist was responsible for recording the greatest possible detail of languages which were rapidly disappearing, while it was still possible to do so. Sapir held that the interesting facts about languages were to be found in their underlying relational patterns rather than in their surface details. His formulation of the concept of the phoneme, which appeared in 1925 in the first volume of *Language*, constituted a turning point in the affiliation of Sapir and his students with the discipline of linguistics rather than with its roots in anthropology. Boas, although he served as an early president of the Linguistic Society of America and was honoured within it as an elder statesman, never became a linguist in this sense of primary professional identity. Linguistics was for him, as for most of the cultural anthropologists he trained, a handmaiden to ethnology rather than an end in itself.[4]

Sapir's emphasis on phonemic patterning fed into his growing fascination with the relationship of culture and the individual. In language, this became "the psychological reality" of the phoneme. In ethnology, it drew on the long-established Boasian search, through the collection of native language texts, for "the native point of view." Whorf found this tradition of attention to linguistic creativity at the level of the individual, different in realization across languages and cultures, remarkably congenial. What might seem to have been trivial technical details in the grammars (including sound systems) of particular

---

[4] The situation is ironically parallel to the reception of Sapir's *Time perspective in Aboriginal American culture: A study in method* in 1916. Sapir's most powerful examples of how to reconstruct the past history of peoples without written history were linguistic. In language, as opposed to the rest of culture, Sapir argued that sound changes made it possible to distinguish the results of genetic diversification from a common ancestor and borrowing or diffusion. Sapir's colleagues in Boasian ethnology adopted this perspective, which culminated in his reduction of the linguistic families of Native North America to only six, as a framework for their studies of culture. They did not care about the linguistic evidence as such, trusting Sapir, the linguist among them, to have gotten it right. Americanist ethnologists applied the linguistic relativity principle in similarly unreflective ways, in the service of other questions and in the absence of serious linguistic analysis. The reception of glottochronology as a dating technique for unwritten languages as posed by Whorf's Yale colleague Morris Swadesh can be read in similar terms.

American Indian languages provided entrée into the multiple thought-worlds of the speakers of those languages.

Whorf came to argue that the linguist could transcend the patterns of habitual thought characteristic of his/her first language by virtue of its contrastive pattern relative to languages learned in the field and described in their own unique terms. "Multilingual awareness" – what his Yale colleague George Trager would later call "metalinguistic" awareness – was the proper goal of linguistic science. It allowed the linguist to return to his/her own society and see it more clearly.

I have argued elsewhere (Darnell 2001) that Whorf's formulation of the linguistic relativity principle owes much to Ruth Benedict's *Patterns of Culture* (1934), whose goal was for the anthropologist to become "culture-conscious." The moral imperative toward critique of then-contemporary North America is pervasive in Benedict, albeit geared to the humanities, and is echoed repeatedly in Whorf in expectation of an audience among fellow scientists. Ironically, these Benedictine passages are the very ones in which Whorf is accused of mysticism by linguists (most of whom do not read Benedict). Again, Whorf's most contentious positions are deeply grounded in Boasian anthropology, in the intersection of linguistics and ethnology around the study of the American Indian. Again, this is the context which has been obscured in recent readings of Whorf.

Whorf and cognitive science

Whorf's characteristic phrase "linguistic relativity" is retained by Gumperz and Levinson, albeit their edited collection on the state of the art in cognitive science simultaneously proposes that the concept needs "rethinking" (1996: 2): "Readers will find that the original idea of linguistic relativity still live[s], but functioning in a way that differs from how it was originally conceived." The tone of papers and introductory discussions is firmly revisionist.

Stephen Levinson is the most articulate advocate of a new synthesis provided by cognitive science. He emphasizes that the differences from Whorf's position are substantial. Whorf was interested in cultural and linguistic differences rather than in universals; cognitive science assumes a species-wide, wired-in explanation for cross-culturally attested similarities in the processing of linguistic and other communicative forms. Levinson characterizes the contemporary search for psychologically and biologically grounded universals as rationalist, with Whorf's position relegated to the status of mere empiricism. Whorf was unwilling or unable to arrive at the kind of generalizations Levinson is interested in. Levinson further opposes the realism of cognitive science to the idealism of Whorf, that is, the mentalist concern with what was going on in people's heads, presumably to the exclusion of attention to the real world outside linguistically-conditioned human minds.[5] "In this light, the Sapir–Whorf hypothesis [in its original form] seems uninteresting" (Gumperz and Levinson 1996: 177). Levinson further suggests (1996: 134) that anthropology

[. . .] remains largely outside this current of thought: viewed from cognitive science it is a reactionary output of empiricist ideas with an outmoded stress on human ideational difference and the importance of environmental learning [i.e., socialization into a particular culture and language].

That is, Levinson apparently is willing to dismiss the Boasian historical particularist emphasis on the unique grammatical categories of each human language, arguing by implication that organization of the discipline of anthropology around the concept of culture is an unproductive strategy, given what we know today about universal cognitive structures. The emphasis on particular ethnographies as a result of participant observation fieldwork and extensive work with particular "informants" to produce native language texts seems rather a waste of time from this extreme (if only because of its explicitness about what is at stake) formulation of the cognitive science perspective.

Whorf, in contrast, took for granted a Boasian ethnographic particularity. For him, the universals of linguistic form were of considerable interest, but they would be arrived at by a different strategy, one of adding up and comparing the commonalities among many languages. Levinson's strategy would certainly have appeared to him as a case of the premature generalization which Franz Boas habitually deplored in all fields of anthropology, not just in his critique of evolution.

When Levinson calls for "a sophisticated theory of the co-evolution of mind and culture" (1996: 141) in approaching the pragmatic inseparability of language and culture, his language is directly counter to the thrust of Boasian speculations on similar issues. For Sapir, for example, the binary opposition of interest was culture and the individual (or culture and personality) which he understood as "sides of the same coin." Agency and creativity were at the core of Sapir's theory of culture

Even more fundamentally, Boas's critique of the theory of evolution as applied to culture was essentially complete by 1894; he would not have wanted to talk about evolution in the same breath as diversity of linguistic or cultural forms. The biological overtones of Levinson's desiderata also were unacceptable in an Americanist anthropology which separated culture from biology and centered the discipline around the former. I have argued elsewhere (2001), for example, that Boas's work on race was foundational to the move from arbitrary typological classification to plasticity and population adaptation. But Boas moved on, after about 1912, to concern himself far more with racism than with race per se. Racism, for him, was a question of culture rather than of

---

[5] This is emphatically not Whorf's position. "Reality" formed the third term of his position, summarized by Carroll in the title "language, thought, and reality."

biology. And yet, when Levinson turns to his own data on spatial expression in Tzeltal, a Mayan language, his negative assessment of the Boasian agenda is mitigated. He deplores the unintentional ethnocentrism of semantic analysis based on unproblematized Indo-European categories. This formulation would have made perfectly good sense to both Boas and Whorf, as a way to characterize the uniqueness of a particular set of categories. Clearly, when Levinson is not carving out an intellectual space for cognitive science among the disciplines and in relation to its arguable home base within Americanist anthropology (as understood by Whorf), he is still very much interested in cross-linguistic variation of the sort that so fascinated Whorf. This is the "intermediate position" identified in the introduction to the collected volume, in which the cognitive synthesis results in "such diversity being viewed within the context of what we have learned about universals" (1996: 3). Fair enough.

A more nuanced version of the rejection of Whorf's methods and conclusions alongside praise for his intuitive genius is found in John Lucy's insistence that Whorf did his best to test his ideas empirically (indeed they have yet to be tested formally in the ways Whorf himself understood the empirical problem). Whorf, in Lucy's view, successfully produced "the nucleus of a procedure for establishing a neutral basis for the comparison of language-reality relationships" by playing off Hopi and SAE against one another without privileging either of them (in Gumperz and Levinson (eds.) 1996: 43; see also Lucy 1992). Moreover, Whorf adopted a moral framework for linguistics "which placed the science of language at the centre of all efforts to advance human understanding" (1996: 64). This is what John Joseph (1996: 372), in comparing Whorf's position to that of general semantics, identifies as the "magic key" view of language associated with Wilhelm von Humboldt.

It is possible to arrive at cognitive science by routes alternative to the Boasian one associated with Whorf, some of which may rely less on a rhetoric of discontinuity (Murray 1994) to justify their own innovativeness. For example, Maurice Bloch, a British social anthropologist with strong ties to French structuralism, argues (1998: 40) that contemporary anthropology is being torn apart by a dichotomy between, on the one hand, "the hermeneutic and literary dimensions of ethnography" and, on the other hand, an "aggressively naturalist" insistence on the realism of the world as the grounding for mental constructs. Bloch (1998: 40) views these too frequently opposed strains of anthropological theory as "two fundamentalisms" which have

[...] developed in the work of anthropologists who identify with only one side of this dual heritage and who consequently wish to "purify" anthropology of the other orientation. We are therefore faced with two movements which have in common their rejection of the hybrid character of the discipline.

He suggests that anthropologists, especially in North America, have permitted their quest for "scientific credibility" to erode the discipline's traditional reliance on the ever-continuing cross-checking of theory against data emerging from participant observation fieldwork; they have, he argues, simply accepted what their informants tell them about their worlds as authoritative and ceded their own obligation to analyze and compare (1998: 41).

Bloch argues persuasively that cognitive science provides a way out of the respective fundamentalist impasses because it informs ethnographic practice with some hope of objectivity in dealing with the traditional core subject matters of [social] anthropology; in his view, these are social structure, political organization, and ritual (1998: 43). Unlike Levinson, at least in his rhetorical mode, Bloch insists that the particularism of ethnography is crucial to testing cognitive schemas in cross-cultural contexts. It is, in his view, inevitable that anthropologists will employ psychological theories in their efforts to interpret the behavioural patterns of other societies. Cognitive psychology offers more valid and replicable ways of interpreting alterity than does an unreflexive folk psychology (which, in any case, is usually applied naïvely) (1998: 43–44). Although Bloch's position provides a plausible rationale for the ethnographic application of cognitive science, its internal concerns have been less with discovery procedures for fieldwork and more with universal constraints on human thought across cultural and linguistic communities. His argument may persuade anthropologists to attend to cognitive science, but it is less clear that the reverse is true.

The collection edited by Gumperz and Levinson provides a useful overview of the contemporary status of linguistic relativity debates because it includes contributors from a wide variety of disciplinary and theoretical backgrounds. There is a considerable range of opinion among the contributors, although not all address directly the continuities or discontinuities from cognitive science back to Whorf. It is perhaps not surprising that the contributors most sympathetic to the Whorfian position are the fieldworking anthropologists, whose work is mostly subsumed under the rubric of ethnography of speaking.

Indeed, the most powerful reformulation of Whorf's position has been Dell Hymes's "Two Types of Linguistic Relativity" (1966) which suggested that Whorf's emphasis on variations in linguistic structure among languages went along with a glossing over of variability in favour of an assumed uniformity of such structures within each speech community. Reversing Whorf's argument but retaining his consideration of non-trivial relativity, Hymes called for attention to a second kind of linguistic relativity, in the uses of language. Language functions, he argued, would prove to be universal, although they would take dramatically different surface forms in particular societies. Moreover, Hymes has referred almost interchangeably to "the ethnography of speaking" and "the ethnography of communication" reflecting a commitment to explore ethnographically modalities other than language and their relative positions in a given communicative economy. The object lesson here is that the Whorfian tradition within Americanist anthropology is not necessarily incompatible with the rationalist and universalist agendas of cognitive science. Whorf, like Sapir, explored the foundations of what today is called ethnolinguistics as a critical part of his linguistic relativity principle.

Nevertheless, the Whorf who is cited as an ancestor or precursor to cognitive science is not a Whorf who would have been recognized in his own time. As Levinson astutely observes, the intellectual climate changed in the 1960s, allowing for the reworking of the Boas–Sapir–Whorf position in ways that our erstwhile ancestors could not have imagined.

4

COGNITIVE ANTHROPOLOGY

PENELOPE BROWN

Cognitive anthropology across four decades

What is the relationship between language and thought? How do language and other cultural semiotic systems influence the way humans think? How is knowledge organized in the mind, and what is the role of language in constraining this organization? Such questions have stirred an enormous amount of speculation, controversy, and research across a number of fields: especially philosophy, logic, linguistics, anthropology, and psychology. Cognitive anthropology arose as a specific approach to these questions, with well-defined aims and a methodology that focused on exploring systems of concepts through their linguistic labels and comparing them across languages in different cultural settings in order to find their underlying principles of organization.[1] The field has diversified so that today there are a number of different schools within self-styled 'cognitive anthropology' as well as much work in related disciplines which speaks directly to the same issues. There are certain chronic tensions among adherents of different approaches, especially between (i) those who emphasize universals of human cognition vs. those who stress the importance of cultural differences, and (ii) those who treat cognition as 'in the head' vs. others who insist on its embodied, interactional, and contextually dependent nature. What they all share, however, is an anthropological, comparative approach to the study of human cognition in its cultural context and an insistence on the interaction of mind and culture. This contrasts with the predominant zeitgeist in cognitive science, with its emphasis on universal properties of human cognition presumed to be innate and very largely insensitive to cultural variability.

There are forerunners to cognitive anthropology, major theorists who formulated anthropological approaches to language and thought and considered them comparatively (especially the American anthropological linguists Boas, Sapir and Whorf, and the French structuralists Hertz, Mauss, Lévi-Bruhl, and Lévi-Strauss). But cognitive anthropology is today a loose coalition of researchers in several distinct subdisciplines, where developments are converging on a

---

[1] For contrasting reviews of the intellectual background and origins of cognitive anthropology, see Casson 1981: General Introduction; Dougherty 1985: Introduction; Levinson 1995; D'Andrade 1995: ch. 1; Foley 1997: 106ff; Duranti 1997: chs. 2 and 3.

96

renewed interest in cognition in its cultural setting. Cognitive anthropology arose in North America in the late 1950s as a movement within linguistic anthropology, one of the four subfields of American anthropology. There was (and increasingly, is) some overlap with research in the related field of psychological anthropology,[2] which historically has focused on the comparative study of affect and the expression of emotion but increasingly is broadening to include studies of cognition (Stigler *et al.* 1990), including neo-Vygotskian studies of practical knowledge (Lave 1988; Suchman 1987; Rogoff and Lave 1984) and the related cultural psychology studies of Cole and Scribner (1974, 1977; Scribner and Cole 1981). There is also some overlap with work in cognitive linguistics (the branch of linguistics emphasizing the cognitive representations underlying language and the encyclopedic nature of meaning), and in developmental psychology (where studies of child development and language acquisition are concentrated). All of this research is heavily influenced by the cross-disciplinary program of cognitive science (the study of how knowledge is represented in the brain/mind); as a result there is increasing exchange of methods and theory across disciplinary boundaries. Indeed, in recent years cognitive anthropologists have looked more to other disciplines than to other branches of anthropology for their primary interlocutors, with especially close links being developed to work in psychology, cognitive linguistics, and artificial intelligence (AI).[3]

There are parallel developments in French anthropology coming out of a longstanding emphasis on cognition. (See e.g. Sperber 1985, 1987, 1996; Boyer 1993.) Another new development is a re-vitalization of the linguistic relativity issues, sparked in part by strong universalist claims from cognitive scientists blissfully unaware of the extent of linguistic and cultural variation around the world, and in part by cross-linguistic studies of child language acquisition which have shown that languages can vary fundamentally in the semantic parameters that organize a semantic domain and that children show very early sensitivity to such language specificity.[4] Now many of the same questions are being

---

[2] Or the related field of "cultural psychology" (see Shweder 1990 for discussion of the intellectual distinctions among these disciplines). See Bock 1994 for a survey of psychological anthropology that includes cognitive anthropology within it.

[3] After a hiatus of ten years (since Dougherty 1985), there suddenly appeared four excellent new textbooks on linguistic/cognitive anthropology. These survey historical links and current trends from four quite different perspectives, illustrating my theme of increasing diversity in the field. In writing this review I have relied heavily on these textbooks (D'Andrade 1995; Hanks 1995; Foley 1997; Duranti 1997). The first two of these take a narrow view of cognitive anthropology, the latter two take a broader view, consonant with my own, as do four new edited volumes addressing linguistic relativity (Gumperz and Levinson 1996) and linguistic anthropology (Blount 1995; Brenneis and Macaulay 1996; Duranti 2001a). For more interdisciplinary perspectives on language and thought, see, for example, Levinson 1995, Carruthers and Boucher 1998.

[4] The most abundant evidence for this early sensitivity is in the domain of spatial language and cognition (e.g. Bowerman 1985, 1996a,b; Bowerman and Choi 2001, 2003; Choi *et al.* 1999, McDonough *et al.* 2003; Casasola 2005; de León 2001; Brown 2001).

approached from a variety of subdisciplines. The issues in common include the nature of cultural knowledge, how mental processes affect the organization of knowledge, how different forms of knowledge – including language – affect mental processes (for example, memory and reasoning), how knowledge is used in everyday life, and how it is acquired by children.

In this review I take a broad but selective view, treating as "cognitive anthropologists" those who directly address issues of how cognition relates to language and culture. In what follows I first summarize the approach and aims of cognitive anthropology as originally conceived, and its demise in the early 1970s. Then I review two distinct lines of research, one on cultural models, centered in the United States, the other, new approaches to the question of linguistic relativity focusing especially on recent work on spatial language and cognition, centered in Europe. Finally, I assess the overarching program of these diverse approaches and offer a proposal for future directions in cognitive anthropology.

Classic ethnoscience and its direct heirs

Ethnoscience and "the new ethnography"

Cognitive anthropology originated in the movement within American anthropology, beginning in the 1950s, to revise both the notion of "culture" anthropologists work with and the methods of ethnography. Cognitive anthropology (also originally known as "the new ethnography," "ethnographic semantics," or "ethnoscience") proposed that anthropology should move away from "culture" conceived in terms of behavior or artifacts to "culture" as systems of knowledge, or mental dispositions. The job of the anthropologist was to reconstruct a society's culture, which (in a famous passage by Goodenough [1964:36]) is taken to be:

whatever it is one has to know or believe in order to operate in a manner acceptable to its members, and do so in any role that they accept for any one of themselves. Culture, being what people have to learn as distinct from their biological heritage, must consist of the end product of learning: knowledge, in a most general, if relative, sense of the term.

The preferred method for investigating such knowledge was through language, especially formal structural semantics (with parallel investigations of cognition often recommended but not usually instantiated). The presumption was that rigorous formal methods would revolutionize the study of human categorization and thereby of mind. The basic strategy was to focus on the taxonomic and paradigmatic structure of categorization systems as revealed through semantic feature analysis, later expanded to prototype semantics. Knowledge was seen as essentially a set of propositions, relatable to each other; the goals were to find the principles that organize culture in the mind and establish to what extent these are universal. The focus was on the system of rules, with a relative neglect of how these were connected to the environment.

This cognitive anthropological agenda, set initially by Goodenough, Lounsbury, Frake, Wallace, Conklin, Romney, and D'Andrade,[5] lost its impact on mainstream anthropology in the early 1970s, due in part to the contrast between the hybris of its sweeping goals and the limited nature of the studies (lexical semantics of particular domains, predominantly kinship, biological, and color terminologies), and partly to the impoverished view of cultural knowledge. Even within the group of practitioners there was some puzzlement as to the ontological status of the categories being discovered – as to their "psychological reality," and to their degree of sharedness across individuals – as well as a sense that problems were being artificially simplified, "deflect[ing] attention from the deep complexities of meaning and context and deep questions about the rule-governedness of social behavior" (Keesing 1987: 369, see also Keesing 1972). Cognitive anthropology was also attacked by those (e.g. Harris 1968) who objected to the linguistic definition of culture, arguing that anthropology should stick to classic economic and political issues. Another basis for rejection arose in the anti-scientistic trend toward interpretive approaches to the study of culture (e.g. Geertz 1973: 12). Ironically, with the rise of cognitive science, cognitive anthropology – which initially had been taken to be part of the interdisciplinary coalition (Gardner 1989) – became for a while a minority interest.

There are some enduring achievements of the early period, for example, the work on kinship terminologies by Lounsbury, Conklin, Goodenough, and others (see Tyler 1969; Casson 1981), as well as the discovery by Berlin and Kay (1969) of significant universals in color terminology and the work of Berlin and his associates on ethnobiological classification (Berlin *et al.* 1973, 1974; Berlin 1992). The latter two lines of research continue today, retaining the original ethnoscience interest in thought as revealed in the structure of linguistic categories but with a new emphasis on function and use rather than solely on innate principles of human minds. Work in ethnobiology has moved beyond the study of biological taxonomies per se to their relation to ecology and cultural use (Hunn 1985, 1995; Atran 1990); that on color terminology has become more broadly comparative.[6] More recent additions to the ethnosemantic repertoire are to be found in the study of terms for emotions (D'Andrade 1995), and interpersonal terms (G. White 1980), leading to the use of multidimensional scaling techniques to show that universal evaluative factors underlie such terms in unrelated languages and cultures. (See D'Andrade 1995.)

---

[5] See papers in the edited volumes by Hymes 1964; Romney and D'Andrade 1964; Tyler 1969; Spradley 1972; Goodenough 1981 for classic statements of this agenda.

[6] For surveys of recent work on ethnobiological systems see Berlin 1992; Foley 1997; for color see Kay, this volume.

I will focus here on a third "direct heir of ethnoscience" (Quinn 1997), research on cultural models, which has been particularly responsive to critiques of the language-based approach to cultural knowledge and eager to accommodate insights from cognitive science.

Cultural models

Work in the "cultural models" paradigm has attempted to counter the presumptions that cognition is necessarily or only interestingly revealed through linguistic analysis, and that cultural knowledge is essentially a set of propositions. The shift is to thinking of meaning in terms that go beyond semantic features and taxonomic relations, to try to capture the cultural knowledge that underlies the understanding of meaning in a domain, knowledge in the form of "models of culturally constituted common sense." Such knowledge is organized as "schemas," a term borrowed from psychology, cognitive linguistics, and AI.[7] "A cognitive *schema* is a generic version of (some part of) the world learned from experience and stored in memory" (Quinn 1997: 4). Casson (1983: 430) is more explicit: "schemata are conceptual abstractions that mediate between stimuli received by the sense organs and behavioural responses, . . . [and] that serve as the basis for all human information processing . . ."[8] Quinn adds that a "cultural model" (or, equivalently, "folk model," or "ideational system"), a system of connected ideas about a domain, is such a schema which is shared with other members of one's cultural group. By the early 1980s, models in terms of such schemas were being formulated in conjunction with a connectionist theory of mental processing, with schemata being seen as constructed by association networks built up from repeated experiences without any necessary reference to language. The method for studying these, however, does involve linguistic analysis, principally discourse analysis of interviews and how people talk about a domain. The domains most thoroughly examined have been in American society where native-speaker intuitions can also be drawn upon; these include Quinn's analysis of the American "ideational systems" concerning marriage and love and Strauss's on work and success (see Strauss and Quinn 1997).

Taking cultural models to be "internal representations" of sets of ideas that transform and facilitate complex cognitive tasks has prompted the study of the role of such ideas in the mental processing of reasoning and memory (see D'Andrade 1995: ch. 8), as well as of motivation and of learning (D'Andrade and Strauss 1992). The aim is to include outer world, not just inner mind – the outer world of use, function, and motivation to action; the claim is that looking at the psychological properties of shared cultural ideas allows us to focus on the intersection of outer and inner views.

---

[7] See, for example, Schank and Abelson 1977.

[8] "Schemata" joins a catalogue of labels for mental entities that includes "representations," "prototypes," "frames," "cognitive maps" (Casson 1983).

With this emphasis on cognitive schemas, and culture as a process of meaning-making that is not necessarily linguistic, work in this area has close links with cognitive linguistic studies of metaphor (Lakoff and Johnson 1980; Lakoff 1987; Quinn 1991; Dirven *et al.* 2003), treating metaphor – a means of viewing one kind of experience in terms of another, of finding coherence across unrelated events – as providing conceptual schemata (or "folk theories") through which humans understand the world. The cultural models perspective also links with that of a number of European anthropologists (cf. Boyer 1993; Bloch 1994, 1998) who argue that culture cannot be equated with what is explicitly statable in language. The emphasis here is away from universals, to the significance of particular cultural models for particular forms of thinking. In a similar vein there are also anthropological studies of child development, for example, the work by Harkness and Super (Harkness 1992; Harkness and Super 1996), showing that cultural beliefs about parenting play a role in how children develop. This relates to earlier work on language socialization by Ochs and Schieffelin (Ochs 1988; Ochs and Schieffelin 1990; Schieffelin 1990) which has showed that, from the earliest stages of language acquisition, the deep differences across speech communities in how people use language socializes children to think about and use language in culture-specific ways. Similarly, work on reasoning in different cultural and linguistic settings (Scribner 1977; Hutchins 1980; Bloom 1981; D'Andrade 1989; Hamill 1990) links the logic of patterns of reasoning to particular sets of cultural values and beliefs.

In response to critiques from the "cultural practice" school there is now concern with how cultural models function in "practice," how they are "good to think with," and help humans to perform cognitive tasks like navigating (Hutchins 1983, 1995; Frake 1985) or reasoning (Hutchins 1980; D'Andrade 1989; Quinn 1996). More ambitiously, attention has turned to motivation in human behavior, as influenced by cultural models, and to the investigation of "master schemas" which motivate a wide range of behavior (cf. D'Andrade and Strauss 1992; Quinn 1997; Strauss and Quinn 1997).

This school of cognitive anthropology today, like the founders of ethnoscience, retains the view of culture as knowledge and takes the main question of cognitive anthropology to be "how cultural knowledge is organized in the mind" (D'Andrade 1995: 248). To this they have added, however, awareness that not all knowledge is linguistic, that practice as well as codified knowledge is an important part of culture, and that what is most different across cultures is perhaps linguistically expressed, what is more universal is the nature of schemas forming the underlying bases for behavior and practice (Quinn 1997). All these culture theorists concerned with the relationship between culture and language, as Hill (1988: 23) points out, "share a 'cognitive' paradigm, in which culture is seen as a set of 'complexly rational' mental phenomena (Dougherty 1985: 3)." Many of them concur in taking these mental phenomena to have the form of hierarchical rules for constructing propositions, some of which are taken-for-granted and relatively inaccessible to introspection ("constitutive rules"), others are more articulatably normative ("regulatory rules") (D'Andrade 1984).

One important critique of this view of cultural knowledge comes out of work on "cultural practice" by anthropologists and cultural psychologists on how people think in actual situations (for example, Lave 1988; Suchman 1987). This work casts serious doubt on the *internalness* of thought and the idea that knowledge can be represented by a set of propositions or a set of schemas. Knowledge, in this view, is not just something in an individual's mind. As instantiated in action, in everyday practices, cognition is "distributed – stretched over, not divided – among mind, body, activity and culturally organized settings (which include other actors)" (Lave 1988: 1). Much cognition occurs between individuals and is distributed across them (Hutchins 1995), emerging from their interaction. Furthermore, knowledge resides not only in individual minds, but also in the tools people use (Dougherty and Keller 1985; Keller and Keller 1996); therefore "the proper unit of analysis for talking about how cognition takes place must include the human and material resources that make problem-solving possible" (Duranti 1997: 31). Duranti also points out (1997: 31) that "the most common way of reproducing knowledge in the world is apprenticeship," learning by doing, a perspective also emphasized in Vygotskian approaches to learning and cognitive development (Wertsch 1985; Rogoff and Morelli 1994).

Another complaint about the cultural models approach may be levelled: The unmotivated basis for *what* one studies the cultural models of, and *whose* models they are. As with the original ethnoscience program, issues of interviewing, sampling, and the social significance of the cultural models they explore are often under-theorized.

Much of the work on cultural models (e.g. in Holland and Quinn 1987) is really addressing the *content* of mind, not *process*. It appears to be little more than old "cultural beliefs," dressed up in new language opportunistically borrowed from cognitive science. A real advance, however, is made in the recent attempts to add process to the structures, to construct (via connectionism) psychological models of how cultural models are tied to emotion (memories associated with feelings), and thereby to motivation, reasoning, and other cognitive processes, and how they are learned. This is very much a cognitive science inspired development, with connectionism the preferred theoretical link and the goal an abstract psychological theory of mental representations. This move has broken the complete dependence of thought on language, as the main things in the mind are no longer taken to be symbols and features, but schemata.[9] The view of the mind, however, is rather hodge-podge, as these units of culture in the mind are not necessarily integrated; in fact "[t]he overall view is one in which culture is seen to be particulate, socially distributed, variably internalized, and variably embodied in external forms" (D'Andrade 1995: 248). Indeed,

---

[9] See D'Andrade 1995: 143–149, 246; Strauss and Quinn 1997: 48–84.

D'Andrade, in an argument recalling modularity assumptions in cognitive science, disputes Geertz's view of culture as an octopus (1995: 249):

The empirical fact is that culture looks more like the collected denizens of a tide pool than a single octopus.... Each cultural model is "thing-like," but all the models together do not form any kind of thing.

However, this insistence on the heterogeneity and non-integration of different aspects of cultural knowledge ignores the fact that some fundamental aspects of cognition, while demonstrably culturally conditioned, *cross-cut* different mental domains. A prime example of these is how humans think, reason, and talk about space, which forms another focus of investigation in modern cognitive anthropology, to which we now turn. This approach has developed out of the original linguistic relativity debate, and doggedly retains the central focus on language as central to mental life and thought. But language is reconstrued, informed by new views of meaning: culture is brought back into meaning and seen as instantiated in communication rather than located in individual minds, with meaning seen as arising in situated interactional contexts (Duranti 1997; Gumperz and Levinson 1991, 1996; Hanks 1995). These modern studies of linguistic relativity with an explicitly comparative methodology are now tied to cross-linguistic studies of language acquisition (Bowerman and Levinson 2001). These have formed a distinct line of research which converges in one respect with that described earlier: in serious attention to findings in cognitive science about how the human mind/brain works and a desire to contribute an anthropological, comparative perspective to the cognitive science enterprise.

Linguistic relativity

This second modern school of cognitive anthropology addresses a somewhat different set of questions: does language – or rather, the grammatical and lexical categories in language – constrain thought? How? How can this be studied? What does it reveal about universals vs. culture-specifics in the nature of the human mind?

The core idea of linguistic relativity, sometimes known as the Sapir–Whorf hypothesis after its two most articulate adherents, is that "culture, *through* language, affects the way we think, especially perhaps our classification of the experienced world." (Gumperz and Levinson 1996: 1) This idea has both entranced and infuriated scholars off and on for centuries. In its non-extreme form (not language *determines* thought, but rather habitual language patterns and ways of categorizing experience *influence* thought) it was at the heart of the ethnoscience program (though not always acknowledged as such), and it went out of fashion in the 1970s with the latter's demise. After a couple of decades of disrepute (see Rosch 1977), it is now "in" again, its rehabilitation due in large part to the articulate championing of John Lucy (1985, 1992a,b, 1996, 1997b; Lucy and Wertsh 1987; Lucy and Gaskins 2001, 2003). Lucy has reassessed the notion of linguistic relativity, clarified what Sapir and Whorf actually did and did not claim about it, and formulated a rigorous program for empirical investigation to which he himself has made major contributions. In addition, around the year 1997 (the centenary of Whorf's birth), many workshops and conference sessions were devoted to reconsidering linguistic relativity.[10]

The rehabilitation of Sapir and Whorf[11]

Sapir and Whorf are the names most closely associated with the central issue at the heart of cognitive anthropology, the relation between language and thought, and particularly with the claim that the language we speak structures our thought.[12] The original idea – differently articulated by Humboldt, Boas, Sapir, and Whorf –

> was that the semantic structures of different languages might be fundamentally incommensurable, with consequences for the way in which speakers of specific languages might think and act. On this view, language, thought, and culture are deeply interlocked, so that each language might be claimed to have associated with it a distinctive worldview.
>
> (Gumperz and Levinson 1996: 2)

In this sweeping version which makes claims to a grandiose "world view" from the observation of particular semantic patterns in a language, the idea was abandoned in the 1970s, with the rise of the cognitive sciences and the associated emphasis on cognitive universals based in human genes. It was also discredited by the discovery of significant semantic universals in color, ethnobotanical, and kinship terminologies (Gumperz and Levinson 1996: 3; see

---

[10] This resurgence of interest spans a number of subdisciplines within anthropology, linguistics, and psychology. In addition to a 1991 Wenner–Gren conference, attended mostly by anthropologists and developmental psychologists and published as Gumperz and Levinson 1996, there was a 1994 conference at the Max Planck Institute for Psycholinguistics attended by developmental psychologists and cognitive anthropologists (entitled "Language acquisition and conceptual development," published as Bowerman and Levinson 2001). There were also at least two sessions at the American Anthropological Association meetings in November 1997 (one entitled "The Implications of Linguistic Relativity," and one "Whorf and the Politics of Relativism"), as well as a 1998 conference in Duisberg, Germany (the 26th LAUD Symposium, on "Humboldt and Whorf revisited: universal and culture-specific conceptualizations in grammar and lexis," published as Pütz and Verspoor 2000 and Niemeier and Dirven 2000), and a conference organized by psychologist Dedre Gentner called "Whither Whorf?" at the University of Chicago in May 1998, published as Gentner and Goldin-Meadow 2003. To quote from a comment by John Leavitt, organizer of one of the AAA panels (LingAnth list, Feb 1998): "The sheer variety of approaches represented this Whorfday suggests that after forty years of controversy over and dismissal of Whorf's ideas by philosophers, linguists, and some anthropologists, the Whorfian legacy seems to be not only solid, but growing in a number of diverse directions." See also Lee 1996.

[11] See Lucy 1992a,b, 1997b; Hill and Mannheim 1992; Gumperz and Levinson 1996; Foley 1997.

[12] See Sapir 1921; Whorf 1956 for their statements.

also Hill 1988; Hill and Manheim 1992). But there has been a recent swing back in psychology, linguistics, and linguistic anthropology toward a position that views diversity in linguistic and cultural practice *within* what has been learned about universals. The new intellectual climate – and greatly increased knowledge about language and about mental functioning – is demonstrated in the interdisciplinary book of Gumperz and Levinson (1996), which explores evidence that different languages code the world with distinct semantic concepts, that these influence cognitive processes, and that a wider definition of meaning – one that incorporates contextual influences on interpretation – provides the basis for a new view of linguistic relativity based in cultural practices, social interaction, and the social distribution of knowledge and understanding (Gumperz and Levinson 1996: 8). There is a shift from theories of context-free lexical and grammatical meaning, which were at the heart of the classic Whorfian studies, to theories of situated language use, distinguishing universal principles from culture-specific characteristics of language use in context. Such universal principles (arguably) may include Gricean conversational "maxims", or the principles governing the systematics of conversational turn-taking, or the underlying principles of interactional politeness.[13] But much more seems to be culture-specific, and worthy of investigation as to its effects on cognition. One central focus of study here is indexicality, which anchors meaning to contexts of use; this appears to be a prime site for Whorfian effects. Another is cognition in practice (Lave 1988; Scribner 1992). Another is social interaction, seen as a way of externalizing thought, allowing joint solutions to problems. Gumperz and Levinson (1996: 9–10) summarize it as follows:

Viewed in these ways, the issue of linguistic relativity shifts significantly. From an "inner circle" of links between grammar, categories, and culture as internalized by the individual, the focus shifts to include an "outer circle" of communication and its relation on the one hand to interaction in social settings and on the other hand to individual patterns of cognition which are partly contextually attuned, and even perhaps acquired primarily through patterns of communication, in turn enabling it.

This work on linguistic relativity is thus another attempt to build a bridge between psychology and anthropology, distinct from the school described earlier.

Lucy (1985, 1992b, 1996, 1997b) has provided a sustained critique of the universals bias in cognitive and psychological anthropology on the Whorfian grounds that many universal claims reflect methodological and conceptual presumptions deriving from our own language. He also argues that misconstruals of Whorf invalidated early attempts to test the hypothesis, pointing out that Whorf didn't claim that the world is *perceived* in infinite variety ("kaleidoscopic flux"), rather that it *presents* itself as such and language organizes the

---

[13] For examples of each of these, see Grice 1975; Sacks, Schegloff and Jefferson 1974; Brown and Levinson 1987, respectively.

flux. Linguistic relativity in Whorf's terms does not rule out semantic universals. To operationalize Whorf's hypothesis, we have to recognize habitual ways
of speaking, linguistic patterning on a large scale across different grammatical
forms, both covert and overt (as for example, in Whorf's treatment of "time"),
and our analysis must be explicitly comparative across at least two languages
and cultures. It also requires an articulated theory of nonlinguistic thinking.
With such a resuscitated Whorfian program, there have been new attempts to
test Whorf's hypothesis that "grammatical categories, to the extent that they
are obligatory and habitual, and relatively inaccessible to the average speaker's
consciousness, will form a privileged location for transmitting and reproducing cultural and social categories" (Hill and Mannheim 1992: 387).[14] Lucy's
own contribution to this program is a study of relativity in number, shown in
a careful comparison of the grammar of number in Yukatek and English, and
its effect on non-linguistic thinking (Lucy 1992a). Yukatek and English differ
in the grammatical marking of number with nouns. Yukatek does not require
pluralization of noun phrases, but does require unitization by means of numeral
classifiers when they are counted (as in "two long-thin-thing banana," meaning
"two banana leaves"). Speakers of English, in contrast, must mark plural for
nouns that refer to animate entities and physical objects (boys, rocks, etc.), but
not for amorphous substances (sugar, dirt, etc.), which have to be quantified
using a classifier-like word (one cube of sugar, one lump of dirt, etc.). Lucy
argues that there is a fundamental semantic difference between Yukatek and
English nouns: Yukatek common nouns are semantically unspecified for quan-
tificational unit, as if they all referred to substances. He therefore predicted that
in *non*-linguistic tasks (e.g. sorting, memory tasks) Yukatek speakers would
attend more to the material composition of objects (the "substance" which in
speech has to be unitized with a numeral classifier), while English speakers
should attend more to their shape (since shape provides the major basis for unitization in English count nouns). Hill and Mannheim (1992:392) summarize
Lucy's work as follows:

Analyzing descriptions of line drawings by speakers of the two languages, Lucy confirmed that the grammatical patterns are in fact reflected in ways of speaking, at
least in the experimental context. Experiments using recall and sorting showed that
English speakers were more likely to be sensitive to number than to substance, while
Yukatek speakers were the opposite. Lucy argued that this result was related to linguistic patterning: English speakers presuppose unity centering on form, and find number
changes interesting and noticeable, while Yukatek speakers presuppose substance and
are thus somewhat indifferent to number; this is consistent with their characteristic
grammatical strategy, which is not pluralization of units, but unitization of substances.

Recently Lucy and Gaskins (2001, 2003) have extended this work to establish
the point at which children acquire these different mental propensities. In a

---

[14] See Hill and Mannheim 1992; Koerner 1992; Lucy 1992a, for surveys of this work.

comparison of the sorting strategies that English and Yukatek children use when confronted with the task of sorting objects of different kinds and materials into "like" and "unlike" categories, they found the two groups behaving the same (both sorting on the basis of shape) up to age seven, but clearly differentiating (English children sorting on shape, Yukatek on material) by the relatively late age of nine. The implication is that children learn to speak their native language fluently and use it for a number of years before a cognitive reorganization takes place where the effects of linguistic patterning on non-linguistic thinking can be demonstrated.

Recent work in related disciplines has taken up the Whorfian flag in certain respects. In developmental psychology the work of Slobin as the major proponent of cross-linguistic studies of language acquisition has been influential.[15] Slobin (1996) argues for a developmental perspective that abandons notions of "language" and "thought" as static wholes, thinking instead in terms of the relation between grammatical categories and the on-line process of converting thoughts into words – a limited Whorfian perspective he calls "thinking for speaking." Grammatical categories may force speakers to encode features that have to be constructed – resulting in cross-linguistic differences, for example, of narrative style, which children gradually acquire by learning to selectively attend (or disattend) to aspects of a scene that their language forces them (or doesn't make them) attend to (Berman and Slobin 1994; Strömquist and Verhoeven 2004). The work of Bowerman and her colleagues (Bowerman 1985, 1996a,b, 2000; Choi and Bowerman 1991; Bowerman and Choi 2001, 2003) has also been important in demonstrating that, cross-linguistically, children do not necessarily make the same initial assumptions about meanings as one would expect if a universal set of semantic parameters provides the basis from which all linguistic meanings are constructed.

Whorfianism, and its limitations, are often illustrated with color.[16] I'll use space, another domain fundamental to human cognition, and equally often thought to be universal.

Spatial language and spatial thinking across cultures

Space is fundamental to human life, involving everyday reckoning of where one is, one's internalized geographical map, navigating and route finding, giving route directions, indicating where to find things one is looking for, how to track locations and travels in a narrative, spatial reasoning, and much more. There has been a great deal of work on space in linguistics and psychology,

---

[15] See especially his five edited volumes containing detailed theoretical and empirical studies of child language acquisition across about twenty different languages and cultures (Slobin 1985, 1992, 1997).

[16] See e.g. D'Andrade 1995; but see Lucy and Shweder 1979, 1988 for a critique.

so that much is known about how it is expressed in different languages and
how it is represented in the brain (see Bloom *et al.* 1996; Hart and Moore
1973; Pick and Acredolo 1983). The symbolic uses of space have also been
a focus of anthropological enquiry (e.g. Hugh-Jones 1988; Keating 1998). In
the spatial domain, languages have fundamentally different linguistic systems
for representing spatial relations, reflecting different construals of the same
bit of "reality."[17] Now, do these divergent cultural distinctions influence their
cognitive characterizations in a way that shows up in non-linguistic tasks of
memory and reasoning?

The standard line in philosophy, psychology, and cognitive science presumes that the *universal basis* for spatial cognition resides in the biological
structures that come from our mammalian inheritance. The dominant view is
that an egocentric perspective is fundamental to human spatial thinking: three
planes through the body provide the basis for thinking in terms of space "in
front/behind," to the "left/right," and "above/below."[18] This view seems to be
supported by (i) modularity in the brain (distinct "what" vs. "where" systems)
and (ii) certain linguistic evidence, for example of how children acquire spatial
prepositions in Indo-European languages. The conclusion has perhaps over-
hastily been drawn from these kinds of evidence that the universal basis for
spatial language resides in our common human egocentric visual system and
constrains how we can think about space.

However, findings from a large comparative study of spatial language and
cognition carried out at the Max Planck Institute for Psycholinguistics have
cast doubt on the universality of egocentric space as the basis for linguistic
systems of spatial description. It turns out that spatial linguistic systems around
the world are much more variable than had been presumed (Levinson 1996a,
b, c, 1998, 2003a; Levinson and Wilkins, in press). In particular, they differ
systematically in their underlying *frames of reference* (their coordinate systems
for reckoning spatial relations). There are at least three major frames of reference, only one of which is egocentric. The three basic frames of reference are
"*Relative*" (using the speaker's viewpoint to calculate spatial relations, like the
familiar "left"/"right"/"front"/"back" systems of European languages), "*Absolute*" (using fixed angles extrinsic to the objects whose spatial relation is being
described, like the cardinal direction systems of many Australian Aboriginal
languages), and "*Intrinsic*," relying on intrinsic properties of objects being
spatially related (e.g. parts and shapes of the Ground object, positions of the

---

[17] See Haviland and Levinson 1994; England 1978 for evidence of this variability within just one
language family, the Mayan. See Friedrich 1970, 1971; and de León and Levinson 1992, for
other Mesoamerican languages; Pinxten *et al.* 1983 for Navajo.

[18] See eg. Clark 1973; Miller and Johnson-Laird 1976. For the philosophical basis, see Kant 1991.
Whorf himself seems to have agreed with the mainstream cognitive science view that space was
probably universal (Foley 1997: 215).

Figure object)[19] to reckon spatial relations, as in the bodypart systems of many languages.

These three frames of reference are made use of differently in different societies. First, there are different default systems for spatial language across cultures. For example, western speakers of English use mainly Relative and Intrinsic systems, using Absolute only for large-scale geographic reckoning (between, e.g., two cities). But in the Australian Aboriginal language Guugu Yimithirr speakers use only one frame of reference, an Absolute North/South/East/West system which is used both for long-distance and small scale spatial reckoning. (Thus people talk not only of heading "north" or A being located "north" of B; they also routinely say things like "There's a fly on your northern knee" [Levinson 1997b].) Secondly, there are different distributions of systems across functions. Spatial description in different languages and cultural settings may emphasize different frames of reference for small-scale spatial relations, or have different defaults for particular purposes (small-scale vs. long-distance, for example). Thirdly, cognition is related to the default systems. Note that these different frames of reference are not conceptually equivalent: they have distinct conceptual bases (egocentric, object-centered, or geographically centered), resulting in different implications for spatial memory and reasoning (e.g. rotation differences, cognitive maps). They also differ in cognitive complexity.[20] And the second important finding from the Max Planck project is that there is a clear link between what linguistic system is used and non-linguistic spatial cognition. Results on a range of non-linguistic tasks carried out in over ten unrelated languages and cultures show that people think, remember, and reason in the system they use most for speaking with (Levinson 1997a, 2003a; Pederson *et al.* 1998). This is then a prime example of a Whorfian link between language and non-linguistic cognition.[21]

As an example, take the case of the Mayan language Tzeltal, spoken in the peasant community of Tenejapa in southern Mexico. In this community set in precipitous mountain terrain, the main frame of reference is in terms of "uphill" and "downhill." This Absolute frame of reference, based on the overall slope of the land downwards from south to north, is used for both large-scale and small-scale spatial description.[22] Using this abstract conceptual slope, Tzeltal

---

[19] The terms Figure and Ground in discussions of spatial language derive from the gestalt psychology terms; they refer to the object being located (the Figure) and the object or region in relation to which it is located (the Ground). See Talmy 1983.

[20] Complexity clearly is different for the two-place topological relations of an Intrinsic system (e.g. "at the house's face"), three-place egocentric relations for a Relative system (e.g. "left of the house"), three- or four-place Euclidean grid for an Absolute system (e.g. "north of the house"). See Levinson 1996b, 2003a.

[21] This conclusion, unsurprisingly, has been resisted by some cognitive scientists, due in part to misconstrual of the evidence; see Levinson *et al.* 2002; Levinson 2003b; Majid *et al.* 2004.

[22] See Brown and Levinson 1993a,b, 2000; Levinson 2003a; Brown 2001; and Levinson and Brown 1994, for details.

people routinely describe motion as "ascending"/"descending"/"going across," and objects as being "uphill" or "downhill" or "acrossways" in relation to a Ground object, both on sloping and on completely flat terrain. Correlated with this Absolute linguistic system is the fact that on non-linguistic tasks of memory and reasoning Tzeltal speakers have a strong tendency to code in Absolute terms, in contrast to Dutch speakers who code in Relative "left/right/front/back" terms (Brown and Levinson 1993a; Levinson 1996b, 2003a). Other cultural features of this Tzeltal society reflect the absence of left/right distinctions and reinforce the cognitive effects of this Absolute frame of reference: there is a strong preference for left–right symmetry in cultural artifacts (weaving, architecture, ritual), and there is evidence that people are to some degree "mirror-image blind." For example, on a task requiring discrimination between two otherwise identical but mirror-image reversed photographs, Tzeltal speakers routinely say "They are exactly the same" (Levinson and Brown 1994), a result consonant with the fact that these are people who speak a language with no projective left/right distinction and have not been forced by literacy to attend to left/right distinctions.

Given such findings of Whorfian effects in spatial language and cognition, the question leaps to mind: how do children learn to think differently depending on what spatial reference system they learn to use? The mainstream (Piagetian) view is that cognitive development proceeds through universal stages, uninfluenced by the linguistic categories of a particular language; cognitive development precedes, and lays the basis for, linguistic development (Piaget and Inhelder 1967; Laurendeau and Pinard 1970). This view seems to be supported by the order in which children learn spatial prepositions – across a number of European languages, simple (*topological*) ones like "in" and "on" are learned before more complex (*projective*) ones like "in front of"/"behind" (Johnston and Slobin 1979). But a third finding from work at the Max Planck Institute for Psycholinguistics is that children are very early attuned to the semantic spatial categories that their language uses (Bowerman 1996a,b; Bowerman and Choi 2001, 2003), and in line with this finding, there appears to be cultural variation in how children learn their spatial linguistic system. Evidence from a longitudinal study of Tzeltal children indicates that they learn the Absolute system relatively early, having productive mastery of the complex sets of semantic oppositions by age four, and the ability to use the system in novel situations on table-top space by between age $5\frac{1}{2}$ to $7\frac{1}{2}$. In addition, children seem to learn the Absolute system – the "projective" and therefore cognitively more difficult one – as soon as, or possibly even before, they master their Intrinsic "topological" system, at least as suggested by their linguistic production (Brown 2001; Brown and Levinson 2000).[23]

---

[23] See also de León 1994 for Tzotzil (Mayan). Related work in Bali (Wassman and Dasan 1998) has also shown early learning of an Absolute system and in India and Nepal (Mishra *et al.* 2003).

These findings show that important Whorfian effects can be demonstrated not only at the grammatical level (as emphasized by Whorf, and shown by Lucy) but at the lexical level. Lexical distinctions that require speakers to notice and remember particular aspects of their experience may pervade thinking and memory about, for example, spatial relations. A second point is that, in such an important domain, we may expect to find relations between linguistic concepts and other cultural ideas and practices. In Tzeltal, for example, the language of spatial description in terms of uphill/downhill matches concepts in Tzeltal cosmology, aesthetics, weaving style, agricultural practices, and literacy (Levinson and Brown 1994; Brown 2002b).

It is now clear that three streams of investigation should form part of a serious study of the relation between language and conception in a given linguistic/cultural setting:

(i) Do a linguistic and semantic analysis of a particular conceptual domain (e.g. space) (what are the semantic concepts in the domain, what are their grammatical properties, how are they used in everyday life, how do they relate to other cultural practices?).

(ii) Carry out "experiments" on non-linguistic thinking processes (memory, reasoning, in the domain) and correlate these with the linguistic patterns.

(iii) Look at how children learn the language of the relevant domain: for example, do they go through universal stages in learning the semantics of words in their language? Is their cognitive development – how they develop more complex ways of processing information, and higher-order forms of understanding and reasoning – influenced by their language? Since the limits to cultural variability are in large part dictated by what children can learn, evidence of how they learn semantic and cultural concepts speaks directly to what is and isn't universal about human thinking.

If you want to explore the Whorfian issue there is a fourth essential step: to compare these three-strand investigations across different linguistic and cultural settings. Whorfian effects must be studied comparatively, and non-linguistically as well as linguistically.

Within the modern climate of thinking about mind as made up of separate modules specialized for specific tasks, it no longer makes sense to ask if language influences thought across the board. We must ask the question for specific domains, being precise about our predictions and being sure to test these non-linguistically. There will not necessarily be any effect in realms where, for example, imagistic thought rather than propositional thought dominates (Keller and Keller 1996). In some realms, language is crucially relevant to cognition; these are the ones where cross-linguistic, cross-cultural studies can reveal important ways in which language influences human cognition. In others, perhaps not (but one must not prejudge which is which; Danziger 2001).

A final methodological point is clear: investigating Whorfian effects requires a strict methodology, with careful design of linguistic and cognitive tasks so that they are tightly linked. Only then may we infer from their connection a model of the mental representation of the particular domain (e.g. space) in the relevant language and culture. Since the object of investigation is not just the content of thought (what people can say about what they think about, e.g. space), but the structure of the mind in a particular domain, an interdisciplinary approach and an eclectic tool-kit is required, including, for any domain studied, serious attention to ethnography and to the context of use and interpretation, interactional evidence of use and contextual variability, non-linguistic tasks to check cognitive effects. Since knowledge has aspects that are both universal (e.g. spatial modules) and culturally particular (e.g. frames of reference), methods for exploring both are required.

Conclusions: The coming of age of cognitive anthropology

Despite methodological quarrels and theoretical diversity, there are clearly common themes in recent cognitive anthropological work. The current trend is toward more integrated theories of mind and culture, along with an insistence on the role of culture (and thereby, of cultural difference) in cognition (cf. e.g. Bloch 1994; Shore 1996; Levinson 1997a, 1998; Brown 2002). The role of culture is being explored not just in the content and structure of mental entities (meanings), but in cognitive processes such as memory, motivation, and reasoning. Work is increasingly interdisciplinary, with attention to the accumulating knowledge about human mental processes within the cognitive sciences (especially cognitive linguistics, developmental psychology, AI, neurophysiology, and evolution). At the same time there is some (healthy) skepticism about exorbitant claims for universals based almost exclusively on work in English-speaking societies, a skepticism that is modulated by enthusiasm for understanding the universal underlying bases for human behavior and cognition. A further trend is attention to how children learn cultural knowledge, and how it affects their cognitive development.

The trends I have described in cognitive anthropology are clearly connected to trends in the broader traditions of anthropology and linguistics, which also have not remained untouched by the cognitive revolution.[24] These include changing views of "language" and "culture," away from monolithic entities to cultural practices located and learned in interaction with others in one's social networks, as well as the deconstruction of culture, with different bases for "common ground," more fragmented, partially shared, ideologically based

---

[24] There is, for example, work in sociocultural anthropology on literacy, (J. Goody 1977, 1989), on non-language-based cultural knowledge (Bloch 1998; Shore 1996), and even on religion (Boyer 1993) which has been directly influenced by the dominant paradigm of the past half century.

(see Fox and King 2002, for a review). There is also a broadened view of language as social interaction, and a perspective on interpretation rather than on language production, including levels of linguistic patterning invoked by "contextualization cues" (Gumperz 1992), complex transpositions, markers of stance, the cueing of context through subtle, subliminal cues reminiscent of Whorf's view of the subliminal nature of grammatical patterning. These can vary significantly across languages, networks, and cultural groups. It is now taken for granted that the object of study is precisely the complex interplay between inner and outer, individual and environment, between language as resource and language as historical product and process. And finally, these trends include attention to speculations in evolutionary anthropology concerning the evolution of human cognition via social interaction (Byrne and Whiten 1988; E. Goody 1995), the evolution of language (Lieberman 1984; Bickerton 1990a) and the coevolution of mind and culture (Durham 1991). All of these have important implications for how we think about the human mind. I would concur with D'Andrade (1995: 251–252) that: "[O]ne of the main accomplishments of cognitive anthropology has been to provide detailed and reliable descriptions of cultural representations" – one of the original goals of ethnoscience, he comments, that continues today. "Another . . . has been to provide a bridge between culture and the functioning of the psyche." Cognitive anthropology has demonstrated that human thought is influenced by cultural representations, and also that the cultural heritage itself is constrained by our biological capacities and limitations.

I would, however, add that the main challenge confronting cognitive anthropology today is this: what kind of *theory of mind* should anthropologists be developing and contributing to? Whatever its form, it must be more sophisticated and more detailed than theories now on offer in cognitive science (connectionism, modularity, etc.). Furthermore, it must (i) be informed by the new knowledge of universal constraints, (ii) incorporate the range of diversity in human languages and cultural ideas, and (iii) put humans into evolutionary relationship with other animals. Humans have long been preoccupied with the question of what is different about us – a question which up to a century ago would be answered in terms of "the spark of God," the soul. Now the emphasis is on the human mind in relation to the demands of social interaction, especially interactive reflexive reasoning, the pragmatics of meaning in interaction, the externalization of thought in social products and activities. Directly relevant to this emphasis are the new developments in our understanding of the evolution of language, of communicative abilities, culture, and the human mind.[25]

In the eternal tension between universals vs. particulars in language, cognition, and culture we have come to a new cross-road. We are finally moving

---

[25] See Byrne and Whiten 1988; E. Goody 1995; Durham 1991 for recent evolutionary arguments; see Barkow 1994 for a sketch of related ideas and their importance to psychological anthropology.

away from universals vs. particulars as poles in an argument to the awareness
that these must coexist. Even if there are very extensive universal properties
of human cognition (as appears to be the case in, for example, the domain of
space), these may be accompanied by cognition-penetrating cultural specifics
(like the frame of reference used for calculating spatial relations on the hori-
zontal). The human mind is both what we as humans share, which makes us
able to interact, understand and communicate across cultural boundaries, and
also what separates us, makes us sometimes not understand one another. It is
the study of the structures and processes which create and manifest these two
sides of the same coin that will take cognitive anthropology forward into the
future.

5

METHODOLOGICAL ISSUES IN CROSS-LANGUAGE COLOR NAMING

PAUL KAY

In the period from roughly 1940 to 1965, linguistics and anthropology in North America and much of the world were dominated by Whorfian radical linguistic relativity. The challenge from Chomskian innateness was on the horizon, but not yet the dominant force it was to become. The main tenets of the linguistic relativity doctrine were, and in many quarters remain, that (1) the categories that each language imposes on the world are the categories in which its speakers are constrained to experience the world and (2) the linguistic – hence cognitive and perceptual – categories of each language are arbitrary, conventional stipulations. In what is probably his most frequently cited passage, Whorf wrote:

> The categories and types that we isolate from the world of phenomena we do not find there because they stare every observer in the face; on the contrary, the world is presented in a kaleidoscopic flux of impressions which has to be organized by our minds – and this means largely by the linguistic systems in our minds. We cut nature up, organize it into concepts, and ascribe significances as we do, largely because we are parties to an agreement to organize it in this way . . .
>
> (1956 [1940])

In this and many other passages, Whorf appeared to endorse both tenets: (1) linguistic categories structure experience and (2) linguistic categories are arbitrary social conventions – although in other places he more or less explicitly disavowed (2).[1] In any case, linguistic relativists following Whorf have assumed tacitly that there are no interesting universal constraints on the substance of linguistic categories. Following upon the small cross-language color-naming study of Ray (1952) and the intensive ethnographic investigation of Hanunóo color terms by Conklin (1955), color naming quickly became the

I would like to express my appreciation to David Wilkins for his comments and for the use of his data and analysis regarding Arrernte word associations; these are presented in Figure 5.1. I would also like to thank Luisa Maffi for comments on an earlier draft.

[1] For example, in contrasting Hopi concepts of time, as encoded in that language, with those of "Standard Average European," Whorf nonetheless asserts that there is a kind of rock bottom experience of the passage of time that precedes linguistic categorization and is shared by Hopi and English speakers: "Our *awareness* of time and cyclicity does contain something immediate and subjective – the basic sense of 'becoming later and later.' But in the habitual thought of us SAE people, this is covered under something quite different . . ." (1965 [1941]: 139, italics in original). For further discussion see Kay and Kempton (1984: 76f).

empirical *locus classicus* of the linguistic relativity doctrine. Ray claimed his data established that, ". . . there is no such thing as a natural division of the spectrum. Each culture has taken the spectral continuum and has divided it upon a basis which is quite arbitrary" (1952: 252). This view was echoed in H. A. Gleason's influential linguistics text of 1961: "There is a continuous gradation of color from one end of the spectrum to the other. Yet an American describing it will list the hues as red, orange, yellow, green, blue, purple, or something of the like. There is nothing in the spectrum *or the human perception of it* which would compel its division in this way" (Gleason 1961: 4, italics added). Eugene Nida, who was perhaps the leading United States authority on translation of the period, wrote, "*The segmentation of experience by speech symbols is essentially arbitrary.* The different sets of words for color in various languages are perhaps the best ready evidence for such essential arbitrariness . . ." (1959: 13, italics in original). Why the mid twentieth-century relativists chose color terminology as the parade example of semantic arbitrariness we can now only guess. It was known at the time that humans possess specialized peripheral neurochemical structures, the cones and the retinal and geniculate cells they feed, devoted to color perception, rendering color terminology a lexical domain unique, or nearly so, in its close relation to biologically specific perceptual structures. *A priori*, one might have considered color the least likely lexical domain in which arbitrary linguistic conventions could determine perception. Perhaps the relativists reasoned that if they could demonstrate semantic arbitrariness in the color domain they could sweep the board in one bold move: if color categories are arbitrary, then all linguistic categories must be arbitrary.

The independence of tenets (1) and (2) of the linguistic relativity doctrine is frequently overlooked, especially by advocates. For example Roberson, Davies, and Davidoff (2000) mistakenly take their experimental findings supporting (1) to support (2) as well.[2] This conclusion is unjustified because their experiments deal, not with comparative color naming, but with the influence of lexical color boundaries on various non-naming, cognitive tasks involving color

---

[2] These authors conclude ". . . *that color categories are formed from boundary demarcation based predominantly on language* . . ." (Roberson, Davies, and Davidoff, 2000: 394; italics added), and that foci are then derived from these boundaries, rather than the boundaries from the foci: "*Once a category has been delineated at the boundaries, exposure to exemplars may lead to the abstraction of a central tendency so that observers behave as if their categories have prototypes* . . ." (p. 395; italics added). These authors propose moreover that across languages, color term boundaries are constrained only loosely, by very general principles: "*[t]he most important constraint would be that similar items . . . are universally grouped together. Thus, no language would exhibit categories that include two areas of color space but excludes* [sic] *an area between them*" (p. 395; italics added); by implication, the actual location in color space of these contiguous color categories is not considered to be substantially constrained, but rather determined arbitrarily in a language-specific manner. Roberson *et al.* claim to "*present evidence in favor of linguistic relativity*" (p. 394; italics added), but it should be realized that they present evidence only for tenet (1).

judgments. They test speakers of only two languages: Berinmo, an otherwise undocumented language of Papua New Guinea, and English. Roberson *et al.* test speakers of Berinmo and English on several memory and similarity tasks involving stimuli close to the yellow/green boundary in English and the comparable lexical boundary in Berinmo; they find that indeed differences in the precise placement of the lexical boundary differentially affect the performance of speakers of the two languages on these non-naming, cognitive tasks. However, the color *terminology* system of Berinmo, as they report it, is quite similar to that of many other languages with five major color terms. Berinmo has major terms for black, white, red, yellow-orange-brown, and green-blue-purple. The boundary between the yellow-orange-brown term and the green-blue-purple term includes some yellowish greens that would be called green, rather than yellow, in English. The focal (best example) choices for Berinmo color terms agree well with (English and) universal focal choices (Kay in press). The experiments of Roberson *et al.* show that a difference in the precise placement of the green/yellow boundary of English and the comparable boundary in Berinmo affects memory and similarity judgments of speakers of the two languages – supporting tenet (1), but they present no data that show the *terminology system* of Berinmo to be arranged other than around the basic universal focal colors black, white, red, yellow, green and blue; hence, their data do not support tenet (2).

The universals and evolution (UE) tradition of research on cross-language color naming to be discussed in this paper is concerned only with tenet (2) of the linguistic relativity doctrine. In the domain of color, this aspect of the linguistic relativity doctrine has been largely discredited by research on comparative color naming. It appears that on the whole tenet (1) of linguistic relativity has considerable support, while tenet (2) is without foundation with respect to color.[3] The independence of claims (1) and (2), both logically and empirically, bears emphasis.

The investigations of Berlin and Kay (1969) were conducted in the era of dominance of the undifferentiated linguistic relativity doctrine and cast into question tenet (2) of that doctrine. Applying the color naming procedures of Lenneberg and Roberts (1956) to speakers of twenty languages in the San Francisco area and supplementing these data with additional reports on the basic color lexicons of seventy-eight languages from the literature, that study advanced the following two hypotheses:

In sum, our two major findings indicate that [1] the referents for the basic color terms of all languages appear to be drawn from a set of eleven universal perceptual categories,

---

[3] In recent years there has been impressive empirical research supporting tenet (1) of linguistic relativity, both in the color domain, e.g. Davidoff (2001); Davidoff, Davies, and Roberson (1999); Roberson Davies, and Davidoff (2000); Witthoft *et al.* (2003); and in other domains, e.g. Boroditsky (2001); Bowerman and Choi (2001); Lucy (1992a); Levinson (1997); Majid *et al.* (2004); Slobin (2003); and many others.

and [2] these categories become encoded in the history of a given language in a partially fixed order.

(Berlin and Kay 1969: 4f)

Following the appearance of these hypotheses, a number of field studies were undertaken to subject them to field tests on monolingual speakers in their native surroundings (insofar as possible).[4] Based on the results of these and other studies, there have been a number of revisions of the original UE model presented in Berlin and Kay (1969). The principle points of revision have been (1) addition of the idea of successively refined partitions of the perceptual color space to the original proposal of successive encodings of focal colors, (2) replacement of the idea of exactly eleven universal perceptual categories with the idea of the six Hering primaries (black, white, red, green, yellow, blue) along with a restricted subset of their possible unions and intersections,[5] (3) recognition that some languages have terms spanning hue and achromatic categories – e.g. a term naming the union of black, green, and blue, or of white, red, and yellow, (4) recognition that there are really two – occasionally overlapping but mostly successive – evolutionary sequences: (i) the division of the disjunctive categories, including those discussed under point (3), into the six Hering primaries and (ii) subsequent naming of the intersective categories, like pink, purple, brown, orange and gray, (5) full acceptance of the fact, entertained tentatively in Berlin and Kay (1969), that there is probably nothing magic about the number eleven as an upper limit on the number of basic color terms a language may possess, and (6) recognition of the "Emergence Hypothesis" according to which not all languages have a complete set of basic color terms, i.e. a set of lexemes of abstract color denotation whose denotata jointly exhaust the perceptual color space.[6]

---

[4] For example, Berlin and Berlin (1975); Dougherty (1975, 1977); Hage and Hawkes (1975); Harkness (1973); Heider (1972a, 1972b); Heider and Olivier (1972); Heinrich (1972); Kuschel and Monberg (1974); MacLaury (1986, 1987, 1997); Maffi (1990b); Monberg (1971); Senft (1987); Snow (1971); Turton (1978, 1980).

[5] (Kay and McDaniel 1978). In the Kay and McDaniel model, the binary categories (orange, purple, etc.) are modeled as psychological mixtures (formally, scaled fuzzy set intersections) of the neighboring primaries. For example orange is said to be based on the fuzzy intersection of red and yellow, purple on the fuzzy intersection of red and blue. This hypothesis is refuted by the recent finding that English speakers' locations of 'focal' examples of binary terms (orange, purple, etc.) in a cone-opponent space do not correlate with their corresponding locations of unique primary hues (red, yellow, blue, etc.) (Malkoc 2003; Malkoc, Kay, and Webster 2002; Malkoc, Webster, and Kay 2002).

[6] The principal works embodying these revisions are Berlin and Berlin (1975); Kay (1975); Kay and McDaniel (1978); Kay, Berlin, and Merrifield (1991); Kay, Berlin, Maffi, and Merrifield (1997); and Kay and Maffi (1999). As pointed out in Kay and Maffi (1999); Kay and McDaniel (1978) helped disseminate an error in interpreting the individual cell responses recorded by De Valois *et al.* (1966) in the lateral geniculate nucleus (LGN) of macaque monkeys as providing the physiological locus for the Hering opponent hue responses. Accordingly, Kay and McDaniel misleadingly referred to the red, green, yellow and blue sensations as "fundamental neural response categories." The two main reasons for the rejection of the early interpretation of the

The World Color Survey (wcs) was begun in the late 1970s to respond to legit-imate criticisms of Berlin and Kay (1969), among which were the facts that (1) experimental data were collected on only twenty languages, (2) there was often no more than one native speaker per language, (3) the experimental data were collected in the San Francisco Bay area, (4) all the native language collaborators spoke English and (5) seventeen of the twenty languages assessed experimen-tally were written languages, mostly of technologically advanced societies. The wcs collected data comparable to the Berlin and Kay data[7] from 110 unwritten languages, with a mean of twenty-four and a mode of twenty-five speakers per language, *in situ*, employing native collaborators as monolingual as could be found.[8] There have appeared recently some objections to the methodology of the wcs and related studies in the UE tradition. I will review here what I consider to be the most important of these objections, attempting to sort out useful from invalid criticisms. The principle authors of these critiques are John Lucy, John Lyons, the team of B. Saunders and J. van Brakel, Anna Wierzbicka, and the team of Debi Roberson, Jules Davidoff and Ian Davies. I have dealt above with the critique of Roberson *et al.* and elsewhere with the arguments of Lyons (Kay 1999). Berlin and I have replied to Saunders and van Brakel's most detailed criticisms (Saunders and van Brakel 1997; Kay and Berlin 1997). Since there is considerable overlap between the further criticisms of Saunders and van Brakel and those of Lucy, I will deal here with the former mostly through my replies to the latter.[9]

---

macaque LGN data as providing the physiology of red, green, yellow, blue are, first, that the cross-over points of the wavelength oppponent cells were found to be in the wrong places to produce the R, G, Y, B sensations (Derrington *et al.* 1984) and, secondly, that the firing patterns observed by De Valois *et al.* provide no support for the psychophysically established short-wavelength red response (for further discussion, see Abramov 1997: 107).

[7] Except that naming data were obtained by presenting one chip at a time in a fixed random order rather than, as in the Berlin and Kay study, presenting the entire array and asking the collaborator to indicate all chips bearing a given native language name.

[8] The 110 wcs languages represent forty-five families: Kwa, Trans-New Guinea, Austronesian, Mayan, Arawakan, Angan, Oto-Manguean, Macro-Ge, Zaparoan, Sepik Hill, East Geelvink Bay, Kru, Indo-European, Chibchan, Jivaroan, Tacanan, Barbacoan-Paezan, Panoan, Chiquito, Niger-Congo, Algonquian, Arauan, Nilo-Saharan, Gur, Bantoid, Taracahitic, Huavean, Upper Sepik, Karajá, Nimborean, Pama-Nyungan, Dani-Kwerba, Algic, Muskogean, Adama-Ubangi, Non-Pama-Nynungan (Australian), Uto-Aztecan, Wintoan, Hokan, Shipibo-Konibo, Tupi, Athabaskan, Talamanca, Tuscaroan, Eskimo-Aleut, and Múra-Pirahã. In addition, among the 110 wcs languages are five creoles: Chavacano [Zamboangueño], Djuka, Garífuna [Black Carib], Kriol and Saramacan; four isolates: Jicaque, Kuna, Camsa and Ticuna; and two unclassified, possibly isolate, languages: Tlapanec and Waorani. The wcs sample is thus not excessively concentrated in a small number of families. I gratefully acknowledge the assistance of Mathew Dryer in establishing the genetic affiliations of the wcs languages.

[9] Apart from their flamboyant contention that current psychophysical and physiological vision theory is in total disarray as regards color perception, Saunders and van Brakel complain that Berlin and Kay (1969) *assumed* a vision-language correlation at the outset and set up their investigation so that it would produce the false appearance of having *discovered* one. Examination of the Saunders and van Brakel text uncovers no evidence supporting this allegation. In fact, Berlin and Kay employed both the stimuli and the elicitation methods of Lenneberg and Roberts, who

Lucy's principal and most extensive exposition of his objections to the methodology of the WCS, and to the whole UE tradition of research, are contained in Lucy (1997a). In that paper, Lucy makes three main points:

Lucy's point 1: *In many or all languages, words that denote color properties also denote non-color properties.* (One of Wierzbicka's [1990] two main criticisms will be treated under this point as well.)[10]

Lucy's point 2: *In many or all languages, words that serve to express color properties do not constitute a morphosyntactic class.*

Lucy's point 3: *The UE findings are a methodological artifact.*

Response to Lucy's point 1

Lucy's prime example of the encoding of non-color information along with color information is taken from Conklin's classic description of Hanunóo color

conducted their investigation in an attempt to establish Whorfian effects in color vocabulary. Saunders and van Brakel, after claiming that the UE empirical findings are merely a methodological artifact, nevertheless go on to provide an alternative explanation for these findings! That is the explanation offered by Tornay (1978: xxxi), according to which universals in color term semantics are really the result of "the progressive domination of the West" (Saunders and van Brakel 1997: 198). Berlin and Kay (1969) explicitly pointed out nine cases in which expansion of a color vocabulary involved borrowing a term from a major written language or a language influenced by a major written language and detailed studies in the UE tradition have documented such influence in detail (e.g. Dougherty 1975, 1977). While acknowledging the frequent influence of colonial languages on the unwritten languages with which they come in contact, Kay and Berlin (1997) point out that the widespread existence in unwritten languages of terms spanning green and blue and of terms spanning red and yellow cannot possibly reflect anything existing in European languages as recently as the colonial era. This point is discussed further below.

[10] Wierzbicka's other major criticism is that she believes that ". . . color PERCEPTION has very little to do with the question of color CONCEPTUALIZATION . . . Whatever happens in the retina, and in the brain, it is not directly reflected in language" (1990: 102–103, emphasis in original). I suppose we must interpret this passage generously to mean that whatever happens in the retina and the *visual areas* of the brain is not reflected in language. Presumably, Wierzbicka does not intend to claim that language is nowhere represented in the brain. Rather, we must interpret her intent to be that, physiologically speaking, higher, cognitive brain centers or processes mediate between visual inputs and the color categories expressed in languages. But if this is so, then these higher, cognitive centers governing linguistic categorization appear to be operative in some closely related species. Wierzbicka does not discuss the literature showing not only human-like color discrimination but also human-like color categorization to be closely approximated by Old World primates and prelinguistic human infants, but not by New World primates, e.g. Bornstein *et al.* (1976); DeValois *et al.* (1974); Essock (1977); Grether (1939); Matsuzawa (1985); Sandell *et al.* (1979); Franklin and Davies (2004); Franklin *et al.* (2005). This literature suggests, for example, that Old World monkeys, chimpanzees, and young human infants may have the *categories* red, yellow, green and blue, while New World monkeys do not. Wierzbicka does not explain the distinction she makes emphatically between perception and "conceptualization," but if the categories named by the English words *red, yellow, green* and *blue* reflect Wierzbickian conceptualization, then chimpanzees, old world monkeys and human infants may also be capable of Wierzbickian conceptualization. Wierzbicka's claim that the color categories found in human languages reflect conceptualization rather than perception would seem to predict that categories such as red, yellow, green and blue are absent in species not possessing language, but the facts appear to be otherwise.

words (Conklin 1955). That description made it clear that the word *(ma)rara'*, covering "maroon, red, orange, yellow and mixtures in which these qualities are seen to predominate" may also express the property of "dryness or desiccation" and the word *(ma)latuy*, covering "light green and mixtures of green, yellow, and light brown" may also express the property of "wetness or freshness." Lucy quotes a favorite sentence of critics of the UE approach: "A shiny, wet, brown-colored section of newly cut bamboo is *malatuy* not *marara'* " (Conklin 1955; 190 quoted in Lucy 1997a: 324). Thus, *(ma)latuy* can mean something like English *green* in the sense of "colored green" and it can mean something like English *green* in the sense of "unripe, immature." In English, a green twig may be brown in color and an apple that is green in color may or may not be ripe.[11] We don't suppose that these facts constitute a problem for the claim that English contains a basic color term *green*, because we take for granted that the color sense and the "unripe" sense are just that, two distinct senses. But how do we know that this isn't also the case in Hanunóo? Conklin tells us that *latuy* can be used to predicate a color property and that it can also be used to predicate the property of succulence. He does not consider the question whether *latuy* is vague with regard to the notions "green color" and "succulent" or polysemous. Lucy assumes the former tacitly. Interestingly, Lyons (1999) in making the same argument contra the UE approach as Lucy about Hanunóo *latuy*, and extending it to Ancient Greek *khlôros* as well, is aware of the vagueness versus polysemy problem and states flatly that, in contrast to the English word *green*, "the colour-term sense of *khlôros* is inseparable from its more general sense" (1999: 22–23). It is clear in context that Lyons intends this statement to cover Hanunóo *latuy* as well. Lyons, however, provides no support for his assertion of the monosemy of *latuy* and *khlôros*. Wierzbicka takes a variant of the same line, as follows:

Of course one could say the "wetness" implied by *latuy* is a separate semantic feature, which can be A D D E D to a description in terms of hue, brightness and saturation. But the evidence presented by Conklin suggests that in the speakers' mind [sic] this "wetness" or "juiceness" IS N O T an independent semantic feature: rather, it is an integral part of the same prototype which accounts for the kind of greenness associated with this word . . .

(1990: 119 emphasis in original)

What Conklin actually writes about the theoretical status of the relation of the color meaning of *latuy*, and other Hanunóo color words, to their non-color meanings is restricted to the following:

---

[11] A recently attested kitchen conversation:

SHE (*cutting into* a lemon) This is the greenest lemon I've ever seen.
HE (*craning his neck*) Do you mean green-colored or unripe?
SHE Unripe.

The basis of this Level ı classification [i.e., the color significata of the four Hanunóo basic color terms, including *latuy*] appears to have certain correlates beyond what is usually considered the range of chromatic differentiation, and which are associated with non-linguistic phenomena in the external environment.

(1955: 191)

This statement is silent on the issue of irreducible prototype versus separate features and similarly silent on the more general issue of vagueness versus polysemy. It is the only statement Conklin makes regarding the theoretical relation of the color significata of Hanunóo color words to their non-color significata. A metonymic or metaphorical relation between the meaning green (or grue) color and the notions of immaturity and/or succulence is widespread in the languages of the world, including, close to home, the Germanic, Romance and Celtic languages (Kay 1999: 84–85) as well numerous unwritten languages like Hanunóo. In the thoroughly documented European languages, the relation is clearly one of distinct senses rather than an irreducible prototype or some other sort of vagueness. The question needs to be investigated in the less well-documented cases, not simply asserted to be the reverse of the known cases.

Lucy's interpretation of Conklin's "newly cut bamboo" example is as follows:

... the terms have other meaning values, meaning values which are not, despite assertions of others to the contrary,[12] merely connotational colorings, but which have to do with other typical referential values . . . [This is] *not* "mere"[13] connotation . . . , it is direct reference pure and simple.

(Lucy 1997a: 324, 326)

Lucy, thus, considers just two possibilities for the relation between the color and non-color meaning elements of color words: (1) the color meanings constitute the denotation, and the non-color meanings the connotations, of a single sense (wrong) and (2) both color and non-color meanings go to make up the denotation of a single sense (right). Lucy does not consider the possibility that *latuy*, for example, has more than one sense.

Lucy discusses a second example from a non-Western language in which color words embody non-color information. This example, involving the Zuni words for yellow (including orange), is instructive for two reasons. First Lucy's discussion, based on that of Hickerson (1975), inadvertently reveals how superficial analysis can obscure semantic similarities between languages. Secondly, the juxtaposition of this example with that of Hanunóo *latuy*, etc. illustrates the useful distinction between conjunctive and disjunctive cases of association of color and non-color meaning elements in a single word.

---

[12] Lucy does not say who these others are.

[13] The source of the quotation is again not revealed. Lucy (1997a) contains several other direct attributions of foolish or offensive usages to unidentified adversaries, for example those who have putatively advanced "premature judgments about 'deficient' color systems, or evolutionarily 'primitive' ones" (Lucy 1997a: 341).

After concluding his discussion of Hanunóo, Lucy continues as follows:

Let us take a second example. In an early study of color terms in the Zuni language, Lenneberg and Roberts (1956: 24) claimed that Zuni speakers do not differentiate the colors "orange" and "yellow", but have a common lexical category *lhupz/inna* referring to the two. The Zuni terms used to refer to color seem to differ from ours in more than the ways just indicated, that is, in their general culture and linguistic-systemic values as well. The linguist Stanley Newman (1954: 87–88), provided the following information concerning Zuni terms referring to the "color 'yellow'":

Zuni has two lexemes expressing the literal notion of the color "yellow." Lexeme A would be used in contexts such as "yellow shirt" and "yellow paint." Lexeme B is employed in combinations such as "yellow skin" and "yellow leaves." The difference is not one of hue. Rather, lexeme A covers many shades of yellow characterizing an object while lexeme B refers only to an object that has become yellow (or a related hue . . .), as a result of ripening or aging . . . [S]uch a distinction . . . suggest[s] that an investigation of color terms must recognize that such terms may express discriminations other than those involved in the color spectrum. [. . .]

In a comparison of the morphological status of the various Zuni terms referring to color, Hickerson (1975) reached a similar, although more general, conclusion about Zuni color terminology, namely that there are two basic kinds of terms with color reference, broad, abstract terms deriving from verbs, and specific terms deriving from substantives (nouns, and particles). She says, "The verbs [referring to color] deal, ultimately, with processes of change or 'becoming': most of the actual forms indicate an apprehended verbal state. Nouns and particles refer to intrinsic color, specific to a substance or object, and are unchanging. In other words, these two types of terms, verbals and substantives, seem to reflect two basically different types of experience" (Hickerson 1975: 228). Thus, the cultural and systemic meanings of the Zuni terms differ substantially from our own . . .

(Lucy 1997a: 337–338)

The Lucy–Hickerson interpretation of Newman's report makes Zuni color terms sound exotic: "two basically different types of experience," and so on. But English morphology expresses a similar, if not identical, semantic contrast. The basic form class for color words in English is adjectival, while apparently it is nominal in Zuni. We should not be surprised at this; in Somali, for example, some basic color terms are intransitive (stative) verbs, others are adjectives and one is a noun (Maffi 1990b). In both Zuni and English there are verbal forms denoting events in which something becomes a certain color. In English these are derived from the color adjectives by processes of limited productivity: *to whiten, to redden, to yellow*, etc. The past participles of these derived causative and inchoative verbs serve in turn as the sources of secondarily derived resultative adjectives, *whitened, yellowed*, etc., which denote the state of having become a certain color. Recall Newman's example of becoming yellow via a process of ripening or aging, perhaps the kind of thing Hickerson has in mind when she talks of "an apprehended verbal state." Zuni may well contain distinct sets of color words "which reflect two basically different types of experience." If so, English does too, and, so far as we can tell, pretty much the same two types

of experience: colors as inherent properties versus colors as resultant properties. Morphologically speaking, while in English the inchoative and resultative
color forms are derived, in Zuni the corresponding words appear, in at least some
cases, to represent distinct root morphemes. Since the derivational processes
involved in the English resultative color words include some that are minimally
productive, the distinction between the distinct root morphemes of Zuni resultative color words and the derived status of English resultative color words does
not amount to a distinction between the rote-learned and the compositionally
generated parts of the two languages. In short, Newman's report on the grammar
and denotations of Zuni yellow words does not indicate that they differ in any
theoretically significant way from the corresponding English words. A single
semantic contrast (inherent color versus resultant color) is expressed in the two
languages by slightly different morphological means.[14]

The second observation suggested by the Zuni yellow example is of the
widely overlooked contrast between conjunctive and disjunctive encodings of
color and non-color information in a single word. Lucy is not alone among the
critics of the UE tradition in citing examples such as the Zuni words for yellow
and English words like *blond* and *palomino* as examples on a par with Hanunóo
latuy (Lucy 1997a: 343–344). But while the Zuni yellow words and words
like English *blond* have meanings of the form "yellow" AND "result" or "light-
colored" A N D "hair (or furniture)," a word like English *green* or Hanunóo *latuy*
has the meaning "green-colored" OR "unripe/succulent."[15] To be aptly called
blond or *palomino*, something has to have *both* a color property *and* a non-color
property. But with *latuy*, as with English *green*, a thing may be aptly characterized by the word if it possesses *only* the color property or *only* the non-color
property. We recall that in Conklin's famous example, the brown-colored piece
of freshly cut bamboo is *latuy* only in that it is wet and, of course, a green-colored
piece of dyed thread or a green color card are *latuy* only in that they are green in
color.

The disjunctive character of *latuy* strongly suggests that *latuy* may be ambiguous, like English *green*, rather than vague, as Lyons and Wierzbicka claim and
Lucy tacitly assumes. Future studies of color vocabulary should, in any case,
attend to the distinction between conjunctive and disjunctive combinations of
color and non-color information. Critics of past and current research efforts
might also benefit from a recognition of this distinction, especially as Conklin's Hanunóo observations, published thirty years ago, play such a prominent
role in contemporary critiques of the UE approach.

---

[14] The superficiality of Lucy's linguistic analysis in the two counterexamples he proposes to the UE
approach, Hanunóo and Zuni color words, should not be taken to impeach his valid admonition
that the U E tradition could benefit from greater attention to linguistic structure.

[15] OR here denotes logical or. Something can, of course, aptly be called *green* if it is both unripe
and colored green.

These problems aside, what can we retain of value in the observation that many languages contain words that denote both color and non-color properties, sometimes within a single sense? Berlin and Kay (1969) tacitly assumed that each language contains a small set of words (more carefully, word senses) whose significata jointly partition the perceptual color space. All the major critics of the UE view have proposed, with varying degrees of clarity, that although this is true for English and familiar European and Asian languages (and surely also of many carefully documented languages of the Americas, Africa, Australia and Oceania), it may not be true of all languages. It is possible that some languages do not have any set of word senses whose significata jointly exhaust the perceptual color space. This proposal has been dubbed the Emergence Hypothesis (EH) (Kay 1999; for an earlier statement of essentially the same idea, see Maffi 1990a, who speaks of evolution *toward* basic color terms). It is possible that preceding – or accompanying – the familiar evolution *of* basic color term systems, there may be an evolution toward basic color term systems. Only detailed field investigations by workers familiar with the language(s) they are studying will be capable of making this kind of determination. A full assessment of the place of color words in the grammar (as properly urged by Lucy) and extensive observations on natural usage – as well as mappings to standard color stimuli – must all be part of an investigation capable of evaluating whether a language is an "EH language."[16]

---

[16] Levinson's report on the language of Rossel Island (1999) satisfies many of these criteria. This language appears to be an EH language more by virtue of simply not naming all the color percepts than by naming some of them only with words of the *blond* type. Kay and Maffi (1999) review the data available on the 110 languages of the World Color Survey for evidence of the EH. Acknowledging that these data were not gathered with the EH in view, Kay and Maffi find four languages that appear to provide direct evidence for the EH and three more languages which may provide indirect evidence for the EH. (The latter possibility depends on the correctness of Kay and Maffi's speculation that the EH plays a role in the genesis of yellow/green categories.) An anonymous referee for *Anthropologie et Sociétés* [where the original version of this paper appeared] voiced what is probably a widespread concern: that the methods of the World Color Survey, like those of the original Berlin and Kay (1969) study, militate against the discovery of EH languages. This is probably correct, despite the mitigating findings of Kay and Maffi and it is why Kay (1999), comparing the Berlin and Kay (1969) and WCS findings to those of Levinson (1999), urges, "the WCS data . . . were not systematically gathered with the EH in mind and only data gathered *in situ* with the EH specifically in mind are likely to shed more than pallid light on this hypothesis." If one distinguishes data from analytical method, the problem may be somewhat less grave than the quoted warning suggests. To be sure, "data gathered *in situ* with the EH specifically in mind" are greatly to be desired. But once the analyst entertains the EH, existing data can sometimes be newly appraised. For example Berlin and Kay (1969: 57) classify Pomo as a Stage II language with terms for BLACK, WHITE, and RED. (No designation more precise than "Pomo" is furnished for this language.) This was one of the twenty languages treated experimentally by Berlin and Kay. In the data section of Berlin and Kay (1969: 127) one observes that the (single) Pomo collaborator assigned two of the 329 color chips to the term glossed BLACK, one chip to the term glossed WHITE and six chips to the term glossed RED, leaving 320 chips unnamed. In retrospect, it seems that glosses of "black," "white" and "red" would have been more justified than "BLACK," "WHITE," and "RED," the capital letters of the latter implying that these three words partition the entire perceptual color space. Knowing what we do now about EH languages, we would not jump from these data to the conclusion that

Response to Lucy's point 2

Lucy finds the fact that the basic color terms of a language do not always constitute a natural class on morphological or syntactic grounds to constitute a
devastating critique of the UE program. He stresses repeatedly that some work
in the UE tradition, a tradition going back to Lenneberg and Roberts (1956),
is based on a correlation of word denotations with a set of color stimuli and is
not embedded in a thorough morphosyntactic analysis of the words in question.
Methodologically speaking, any task of mapping word denotations to color
stimuli should ideally be pursued within a complete description of the relevant
morphology and syntax. Lucy is entirely correct in this. It is for this reason that in
the original *Basic Color Terms* study, we did extensive interviewing to discover
which were the basic terms, relying on a mixture of morphological, syntactic and semantic observations, before assessing the denotations of any terms.

In analyzing the WCS results, our ability to control the relevant grammatical
facts is perforce more limited. Our instructions to field workers have urged
sensitivity to morphological and syntactic issues and we have sometimes been
able to correspond with the field workers in the course of interpreting their
records in order to obtain greater grammatical detail. Using internal evidence
from the forms themselves along with consultations with the original field
workers, and sometimes with other workers on the target languages or closely
related ones, the WCS staff believes it has done a competent job of assessing
the grammatical issues that go into deciding which are the basic color terms of
the languages under study. It is of course likely that we have ended up making
some mistakes and it is certain that even with full grammatical knowledge there
are terms in some languages whose basic status is marginal. I believe that the
overall results of our study will nonetheless be found grammatically sound. In
any case, the data and the inferences from them will all be made available in a
forthcoming monograph (Kay *et al.* to appear) for those who prefer to withhold
judgment until they know the facts.

At the methodological level, Lucy's insistence on maximum possible knowledge of the grammatical status of color terms when assessing their semantic
value is a valuable contribution. At the theoretical level, however, Lucy appears
to suffer from a view of language according to which there is a one-to-one mapping between grammatical and semantic categories. For example, Lucy notes
that several English color adjectives like *red* form verbs in *-en* while others
like *yellow* don't, that we have nouns like *yellowing* but no analogous nouns
*bluing, **orang(e)ing*, etc. and a number of similar facts regarding partially
overlapping morphological sub-groupings of English color terms. Lucy states,
without supporting argument, that:

Pomo is simply a Stage II language, with three basic color terms covering the perceptual color
space. Clearly, more collaborators and a wider range of tasks would be necessary to decide
the issue definitely, but it is clear that the data presented in Berlin and Kay (1969: 127) do not
justify their assignment (1969: 57) of this language to Stage II.

These differences in [morphological] potential both contribute to and arise from the meanings of the terms. In particular, what accounts for the absence of the *-en* forms . . . or the absence of the *-ing* forms . . .? There is clearly some difference in lexical meaning here which prompts the differential treatment.

(Lucy 1997a: 328)

There could, of course, be a semantic basis for the morphological distribution observed, although one is obliged to view with suspicion Lucy's confident claim that such a semantic basis exists since he is either unwilling or unable to reveal its nature. Lucy simply assumes, here and elsewhere, that *every* semantic category corresponds to a morphosyntactic category and conversely. That is the basis on which he concludes that if the basic color terms of a language don't form a morphosyntactic class they can't form a semantic class.[17] Contrary to Lucy's belief, grammars are full of semantic arbitrariness. There is, for example, no plausible semantic reason why English should allow all the sentences in (1) a–c but not (1) d or allow the complex pattern seen in (2).

(1) a. The motor began to vibrate.
    b. The motor continued to vibrate.
    c. The motor ceased to vibrate.
    d. *The motor stopped to vibrate.

All English aspectual verbs take gerundial complements *(began vibrating)*, none take bare infinitive complements *(*began vibrate)*, and all except *stop*, take marked infinitive complements. It is doubtful that this can be explained semantically.

English adjectives of probability show similar vagaries of syntactic valence that resist semantic explanation.

---

[17] In the assumption that every semantic class corresponds to a formal class, Lucy falls into the same trap Whorf (1956 [1941]) did in inferring a difference in Hopi and so-called Standard Average European *weltanschauung* from the fact that the grammar of Hopi does not yield a past/present/future semantic contrast – while not noticing that the grammar of English contains no such contrast either. It appears that Whorf was so sure *a priori* that the grammar of English *must* contain a grammatical contrast corresponding to the notional contrast past/present/future that he didn't bother to look. Had he done so, he could not have failed to notice that past and present in English are expressed by inflections of the finite verb stem while future is expressed either by the modal auxiliary *will*, which precedes the main verb stem and may be separated from it by other auxiliaries and adverbs, or by a raising version of the present participle of the main verb *go*. (Chomsky has made this point in lectures.) Neither French nor German (presumably also 'Standard Average European' languages) conform to Whorf's S A E tense picture, either. Briefly, while English has finite inflections for present and past and an auxiliary for future, French has finite inflections for present and future and an auxiliary for (non-progressive) past. Older and formal German has a system essentially like that of English, while modern colloquial German expresses future with the traditional present tense inflection, relying on adverbs or context to convey the notional distinction between present and future time. Incidentally, these grammatical differences among Whorf's so-called Standard Average European languages not only show no correlation with the past/present/future notional opposition, but also cast doubt on Whorf's notion of Standard Average European grammar. The most ardent exponents of the power of linguistic form to mold thought have not always been among the most careful analysts of linguistic form.

(2) a. It is likely/unlikely that Pat will win.
    b. Pat is likely/unlikely to win.
    c. It is certain that Pat will win.
    d. Pat is certain to win.
    e. *It is uncertain that Pat will win.
    f. *Pat is uncertain to win.
    g. It is probable/improbable that Pat will win.
    h. *Pat is probable/improbable to win.

Among adjectives of probability, *likely* and *unlikely* permit both extraposed sentential complements (2a) and raised N P subjects (2b). Both Extraposition and Raising structures occur with *certain* (2c, 2d), but neither occurs with *uncertain* (2e, 2f).[18] Extraposition is possible with both *probable* and *improbable* (2g) while Raising structures are compatible with neither *probable* nor *improbable* (2h). Distributional facts like these defy semantic explanation. These, and many analogous observations, show that distributional classes need not correspond to notional classes.[19] Just as, *contra* Lucy, every distributional class need not correspond to a notional class, so every notional class need not correspond to a distributional class. We will see below an example from Wilkins' work on Arrernte word associations of a notional class, color, that fails to match any distributional class.

Lucy holds that the UE enterprise is invalid because the basic color terms of a language do not always constitute a morphosyntactic class and only sets of items that form a morphosyntactic class are valid subjects of semantic investigation: "To repeat," he writes, "meaning is not reducible to denotation but is also a function of and a determinant of structural position. Yet in this attempt to probe the semantics of language, attention to linguistic structure is virtually lacking . . . A content-based collection of lexical items does not constitute a linguistic system" (Lucy 1997a: 328, 330). It is this belief which allows Lucy to discount reports like that of Maffi (1990b) on Somali, which after careful evaluation of all factors, morphological, syntactic, historical and denotational concludes that the language does contain a set of basic color terms and that they do not constitute a homogenous morphosyntactic category. Maffi goes on to point out, as several others have done for other languages – and as even Berlin and Kay noted for several languages in 1969 – that morphological subsets within the color terms may coincide with the basic–non-basic cut and also with evolutionary stage sets, such as black-white-red, within the basic terms. In

---

[18] An anonymous referee for *Anthropologie et Sociétés* found (2)e acceptable. Interpersonal variation in this set of judgments serves only to reinforce the point that the syntax doesn't correlate
in any uncomplicated way with the semantics, since disagreements about the acceptability of
these sentences do not appear to be accompanied by corresponding disagreements about what
they mean (or would mean if grammatical).

[19] See Hudson *et al.* (1996) for a collection of examples of this type.

Somali the terms for black, white and red belong to one morphosyntactic class, those for yellow and green to a second and the term for blue to a third.

Some recent unpublished work by David Wilkins on Arrernte color-word associations demonstrates that a set of words isolated, not by distributional criteria but only by the fact that they all denote colors, apparently forms a cognitively real unit.[20] The results of Wilkins's elicitation of free associations of six Arrernte speakers to 125 lexical items of mixed form class are shown in Figure 5.1. Figure 5.1 is abridged from a handout prepared by Wilkins and all the text that appears on figure 5.1 is Wilkins's. The figure is self-explanatory. Figure 5.1 shows that although the four basic color terms of Arrernte are "on formal grounds . . . part of a much larger set of terms," these four terms elicit each other almost exclusively in a free association elicitation paradigm (21 out of 24 responses) and never occur as responses to any of the other 121 terms used in the test.

Response to Lucy's point 3

Lucy is aware of the cross-language findings of the U E tradition and is at pains to discredit them.

what about the success of the [UE] approach? After all, as apologists for this tradition often note, it works! These color systems are there! Surely that is an interesting and important fact in its own right. Well I agree that something is there, but exactly what? I would argue that *what is there is a view of the world's languages through the lens of our own category*, namely, a systematic sorting of each language's vocabulary by reference to how, and how well, it matches our own.

(Lucy 1997a: 331 italics in original)

Lucy says that starting with the color space and looking at how different languages lexicalize it guarantees findings of the UE type. But if this were the case it would be very hard to understand how all the mid-century relativists assumed the contrary. As noted above and repeated just below, H. A. Gleason summarized a dominant anthropological and linguistic consensus or the 1940s, 1950s and 1960s in his influential *Introduction to Descriptive Linguistics*:

There is a continuous gradation of color from one end of the spectrum, to the other. Yet an American describing it will list the hues as red, orange, yellow, green, blue, purple, or something of the kind. There is nothing inherent either in the spectrum or the human perception of it which would compel its division in this way.

(1961: 4)

Gleason is saying, "If you examine the way the words of another language split up the perceptual color space, you will find no reflection of the distinctions you find in English." I want to focus first, not on the consequent of this conditional statement but on the method implied by its antecedent, which is:

---

[20] Arrernte is the language known in the older literature as Arunta, Arranda, etc.

- Four "color" terms embedded in a word association tests of 125 Arrernte terms
- Other terms in list are a mixed bag of nominals, adverbs, verbs, etc.
- List randomly ordered
- Task done with 6 adult Arrernte speakers
- Arrows go to responses, and number on arrows indicate how many people gave that response.

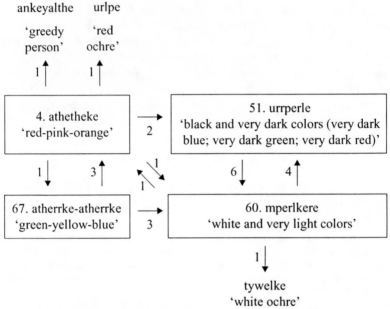

- The words identified as 'basic color terms' overwhelmingly call up other 'basic color terms' [There are 66% to 100% intrafield responses to stimulus]
- There appears to be a particularly strong association between *urrperle* 'black and very dark colors' and *mperlkere* 'white and very light colors' – for all 6 respondents, *urrperle* calls up *mperlkere*, and for 4 respondents *mperlkere* calls up *urrperle*.
- Of the three responses outside the semantic field (interfield choices), two were given by the oldest respondent (a man), were the names for ochre types which exemplify the color term given as the stimulus terms. The remaining term, *ankeyalthe* 'greedy person', was given in response to *athetheke* 'pink-red-orange'. This color is associated with 'greed', and several idioms referring to greed include the color term.
- NONE of the other 121 stimulus terms was responded to with one of these four terms. [Further consolidating the view that this may be a close-knit semantic set.]
- On formal grounds these four terms are actually part of a much larger set of terms to do with the visible surface (reflective) properties of objects.

Figure 5.1   *Arrente Word Associations, from a handout by David Wilkins*

start with the perceptual color space and see how the lexicons of different languages segment it. Gleason and his fellows assumed, just as Berlin and Kay did, that every language contains a set of words which jointly denote all the colors. This assumption may be slightly wrong. But it doesn't follow from this possibility that examining color denotation cross-linguistically *ipso facto* guarantees a universalistic result. Gleason (and Ray 1952, 1953; Bohannon 1963; Nida 1959; Krauss 1968, and many others) in effect predicted that research conducted in the U E manner would find no universals. It was and remains *logically* possible that every language cut up the color space in a way unrelated to that of every other language, as Gleason and Co. thought.[21] If an arbitrarily selected language were as likely to have a color category spanning, say, orange, yellow and chartreuse as to have one spanning green, turquoise and blue, then that is what the U E tradition would have found. Lucy says, "The universalist conclusions are built into the methodology and conceptualization of language employed in this research . . . the universal finding is packed into . . . the use of the Munsell array . . . (1997a: 338)." We could have used a Munsell array and found what the mid-century Whorfians said we would find (and what Ray thought he *had* found) if the color nomenclatures of the languages of the world were the way the Whorfians thought they were.[22]

Lucy declares that he is going to tell us how the UE methodology locks in universal results from the outset: "To see how the universal result is guaranteed, let us look at the procedure in its most usual form" (1997a: 332). But he does not do this.

Lucy's first argument is that many languages don't have a word meaning "color." He says without such a word, "we have a conceptual or cognitive category, but not a linguistic one"(1997a: 332). If true, this statement might fit into an argument that the UE findings are not about language but about something else. But this assertion has no discernible connection with the claim that the UE results are guaranteed by their method.

Lucy's next argument is that the basic color term concept ignores the morphology and syntax of the language. "The actual grammar of the language plays almost no role in the analysis, . . ." (1997a: 333).[23] Again, this could conceivably contribute to an argument that the UE results are about something other than language, but it has no relation to the claim that the method guarantees the results.

The remainder of Lucy's argument that UE methods guarantee UE results consists in the following assessment of the scientific probity of current research in the UE tradition. Lucy writes:

---

[21] And as strongly suggested by the citations from Roberson *et al.* in note 3.

[22] This point has been made before, e.g. by Maffi and Hardin (1997: 350).

[23] Unaccountably, Lucy completes this sentence "yet our own grammatical pattern is applied as the standard for identifying appropriate color forms," although he has been at considerable pains five pages earlier to argue that English color terms do not form a grammatical class.

when a category is identified now, it is really the investigator who decides which "color" (or "composite color") it will count as. What are the odds that an investigator would ever report a system with terms corresponding to dark, white, purple, and brown? My suspicion is that it would be coded either as a two-term system of dark/cool versus light/warm with two other non-basic terms, or perhaps as a four-term system of black, white, red, and yellow. Either way purple and brown simply will not emerge.

(1997a: 334)

It is not clear what sort of hypothetical data Lucy has in mind. If the term he calls "dark" includes the denotata of the terms he calls "brown" and "purple," the brown and purple terms are, by definition, not basic. If, on the other hand, the denotata of the brown and purple terms are not included in those of the dark term, then "dark" is an incoherent gloss. This problem aside, it is unclear from this description whether or not Lucy intends in this hypothetical color lexicon that large regions of the color space are unnamed, and if so just what regions these are. Lucy's description of these hypothetical data does not add up to any clear picture. The remaining element of the argument consists in Lucy's suspicions about what a UE analyst would say about this murky hypothetical case. Even if the made-up data were clear, Lucy's suspicions regarding the conclusions an unidentified UE analyst would draw from them would still not constitute a scientific argument.

The current (unpublished) WCS analyses contain numerous cases of both brown and purple basic terms that occur in relatively early systems, not to mention several cases of terms that cover just brown and purple, others that cover just brown and gray, many that include brown or purple or both in the black term, and even a few that cover just brown, purple and gray. WCS analysts can and do recognize data sets that challenge the theory. Many details of the theory have changed since 1969 in response to new data as they have been encountered.

Lucy's allegations that statements of universality across languages in color naming rested on the subjective judgments of investigators rather than on objective test bore a certain credence when he made them (1997a) because these judgments were ordinarily made on the basis of visual inspection of charts showing what *appeared* to be obviously non-chance coincidence of the focal points of color terms across languages. Recently, however, objective tests have been applied to the WCS naming data which validate the impression that the vast majority of color terms in the world's languages are built around a small number of salient points in the color space. Kay and Regier (2003) performed two Monte Carlo simulations on the full corpus of WCS naming data which establish that (1) the centroids (centers of mass) of the color terms of the WCS cluster more than would expected by chance, with chance likelihood less than 0.001 and (2) the centroids of the WCS color terms fall closer than expected by chance to those of the original twenty Berlin and Kay languages, with chance likelihood again less than 0.001.[24]

To summarize point 3, Lucy states repeatedly that the UE method is not scientifically rigorous and has the UE results built into it. Two of the three observations he presents as arguments for this claim do not address the claim and the one argument that does address the claim is based on Lucy's suspicions regarding a hypothetical analyst's classification of ill-defined hypothetical data. The recent work of Kay and Regier (2003) shows that the centroids of WCS naming responses cluster to a degree much greater than that expected by chance and, further, that they are quite close to the corresponding points in the Berlin and Kay (1969) data. Lucy claimed that analyses of the WCS materials were based on intuitive judgments that were biased to fit the UE models. Although this claim was not directly controvertible at the time it was made, it can now be definitively rejected on the basis of statistical analyses the WCS naming data – which involved no intermediate stage of interpretation (Kay and Regier 2003).[25]

Saunders and van Brakel (1997 and many earlier papers separately and jointly) echo Lucy's claim that UE methods guarantee UE results. In replying to Saunders and van Brakel, Berlin and I have made the point that the repeated occurrence of only a few of the logically possible composite categories in the world's languages, demonstrates an order in the cross-language data that cannot be a projection from English (or other languages of industrial societies). Suppose for purposes of argument, that red, green, yellow and blue were pure creations of English, not evidenced, for example, in the behavior of macaques (Sandell *et al.* 1979) and chimpanzees (Matsuzawa 1985). Even so, there is nothing in English which suggests that green-or-blue and red-or-yellow should be popular composite categories in the world's languages, that green-or-yellow should be an unpopular one and that a red-or-blue composite should not exist in any language (despite the subjective shading of red into purple and purple into blue). Lucy alleges (1997a: 334) that diagnosis of composite categories is unconstrained by the data and strictly at the whim of the investigator. But the myriad reports in the literature of green-or-blue categories, for example, antedating Berlin and Kay (1969) show that this claim cannot be correct (e.g. Franciscan Fathers 1910; Cuervo Marquez 1924; Prost 1956; Voegelin and Voegelin 1957; Gudschinsky 1967 – not to mention numerous personal

---

[24] Since each simulation was based on 1,000 random trials, 0.001 was the smallest significance level that could logically result. In fact, in both simulations the test statistic fell well below the lower limit of the Monte Carlo distribution. The two statistics tested measured (1) the dispersion of naming centroids (translated into CIEL*a*b* color space) of all WCS color terms and (2) the total distance in CIEL*a*b* space of each color term centroid in WCS to the closest term centroid in Berlin and Kay (1969). For further details, see Kay and Regier (2003).

[25] Regier, Kay, and Cook (2005) present a statistical analysis of WCS *focal* choices that demonstrates universal tendencies in color naming which are even stronger than those shown by Kay and Regier (2003) for naming responses.

communications cited in Berlin and Kay 1969, whose authors could only have been influenced by U E theory if they were able to foresee the future).

Conclusion

Regarding Lucy's first point, that color words may also signify non-color properties, this fact about Hanunóo color words was discussed in the first paragraph of *Basic Color Terms*. In light of the facts touching conjunctive and disjunctive combinations of color and non-color meanings considered above it appears likely that the four Hanunóo basic color terms are each ambiguous between a color and a non-color sense, according to one or more systematic metonymies. But even if Hanunóo color words are monosemous, the fact that their color meanings neatly fit the UE classification has yet to be successfully explained away. More fieldwork, and less textual exegesis, needs to be done on color systems like Hanunóo, where major color words appear to conflate color and non-color information.

Lucy's second point, that basic color terms do not always form a unified morphosyntactic class, is also frequently recognized in the UE literature. It has been pointed out that morphological subsets of the basic color terms of a language may correlate with UE evolutionary stages and also that a morphological distinction sometimes obtains between the basic and the non-basic terms. Lucy is simply wrong that semantic classes in general always correlate with morphosyntactic classes, as shown both by numerous English non-color examples and Wilkins's free association work on Arrernte color terms. But Lucy is right that close attention needs to be paid to the grammar of color words in future studies, particularly those attempting to evaluate the Emergence Hypothesis, according to which there are languages which do not have full-fledged basic color term systems in the UE sense.

Lucy's third point (echoed by Saunders and van Brakel), that the U E results are methodological artifacts, is supported by no sound argument. On the other hand, the confidence of the mid-century relativists in an approach of precisely the U E type, the non-English character of the U E findings on composite categories, and the statistical results of Kay and Regier (2003) and Regier, Kay, and Cook (2005) establish that the proposed universal tendencies in cross-language color naming are not methodological artifacts but real, if so far unexplained, empirical findings.

6

PIDGINS AND CREOLES GENESIS: AN ANTHROPOLOGICAL OFFERING

CHRISTINE JOURDAN

... speaking so as not to die is a task undoubtedly as old as the word.

(Foucault 1977: 53)

Among the various fields of contemporary linguistics that anthropologists recognize as potentially relevant for their own discipline, pidgin and creole studies figure prominently. Why? For three essential reasons. First, pidgins and creoles have arisen in sociocultural situations that have proved to be of great interest to anthropologists since the 1950s, namely situations of cultural contacts often fostered, but not necessarily so, by European colonization. Second, pidgins and creoles have developed concomitantly with new cultural worlds, thus comforting anthropologists in their understanding of language as part of culture and of language as culture. Part of this approach has its intellectual roots in the works of the German philosopher Herder, and has been instrumental in shaping much of North American cultural anthropology (see Leavitt, this volume). Third, the cultural processes linked to pidginization and creolization show that "enlanguagement," defined here as the process by which sociocultural groups create for themselves the language that becomes the medium of their new cultural life, is a cultural process as much as it is a cognitive one. But overall, the question of the birth conditions of these new languages is what has caught the attention of anthropologists. And the stories are fascinating, not only because of the human drama that has set the stage for the birthing process (colonization, slavery, indentured labour), but because of what this birth reveals about human agency.

For their part, pidgin and creole (PCs for short) studies remained for a long time peripheral to the questions that were central to modern linguistics particularly in its generative incarnation. Once considered the backwater of linguistics, PCs studies have come a long way and have been transformed into a very

Research for this chapter was made possible by a grant from the Social Sciences and Humanities Research Council of Canada. I am grateful to Kevin Tuite and Jeff Siegel for comments and suggestions, and to Alexandrine Boudreault-Fournier and Catherine Bélair for her help in editing and formatting it. The sections entitled "Pidgins and creoles: the state of play" and "Cognition, substrates, and universals" are updated and modified versions of some sections of Jourdan (1991) Pidgins and creoles: the blurring of the categories. *Annual Review of Anthropology*. 20: 197–209, where they are explored in a different way.

dynamic and theoretically challenging field of contemporary linguistics. Due to the short history of these languages (some of them, such as the Melanesian pidgins, are barely 200 years old) PCs have shed light on the interaction of cognition and culture in the process of language genesis. An important question remains: can the study of creoles reveal the exact role played by the universal faculty of language in language formation and interlingual communication?

Pidgins and creoles are "new" languages and scholars had hoped that if they could "crack the code"of their development, they might have a glimpse of the emergence and biological basis of human language and of the development of the world's languages. Of course, these were false hopes, rooted in epistemological flaws. For one thing, human language itself evolved in a linguistic vacuum. This is not true of pidgins and creoles; their makers did not start with a linguistic *tabula rasa* as did *Homo erectus* (see Foley 1997), but rather with a repertoire of languages (substrate and superstrate languages) that they used to create the new languages they needed. Thus the processes that give rise to proto-language (Bickerton, 1981) and to pidgins and creoles are not, ontologically, of the same kind. Second, in historical terms, and if only by the dramatic conditions in which PCs appeared, the early development and diversification of the world's languages followed pathways different from the processes that allowed for the emergence of pidgins and creoles.

Focusing on the place of social relationships in PC genesis, this article is constructed around four sections. The first one will serve as a general introduction to the current axes of research in the field of PC studies. The second section will pay a special attention to the most common cultural settings that have served as matrix (Alleyne 1971) for pidgin genesis, namely that of the plantation societies. I will propose that *work* and *work-related* activities can be identified as the cultural and cognitive locus of pidgin genesis. Given that the bulk of pidgins and creoles studied in the literature have emerged on plantations during the European colonial period, the analysis I present here focuses directly on, and is limited to, these types of socio-economic settings. Yet it is probably relevant, with some variants and caveats, to other loci of PC genesis where work, trading, and other types of economic exchanges represented the core of cultural contacts. In the third section of this article, the genesis of PC will be analyzed with regard to a theory of power. Far be it from me to offer the idea of a universal explanation for the birth of pidgins and creoles: if we have learned something in the course of the last forty years of research on these languages it is that it would be foolish to assume that all of them have had the same type of origin, or the same developmental path. Yet, we cannot ignore that they are the products of particular forms of social conditions and cultural contacts. The fourth section will revisit the place of cognition in the genesis of pidgins and creoles. The sets of remarks I present below seek to contribute to a further understanding of the link between these conditions and forms of contact and PC genesis.

Pidgins and creoles: the state of play

Contemporary debates in PC studies are centered around four main axes. First, serious efforts have been made to understand the social and historical contexts that have served as matrix to the linguistic genesis of pidgins and creoles (Arends 1993, 2001; Baker and Corne 1982; Crowley 1990; Dutton 1983; Goodman 1987; Keesing 1988; McWhorter 1992; Samarin 1982a, 1989; Siegel 1987; Singler 1993b, 1993d; Troy 1985; Woolford and Washabaugh 1983). As if an answer to the call of Gillian Sankoff (1979), PC scholars have become better historians. At last, the sociocultural history of the speakers who "created" these languages has become relevant in the linguistic analyses and theories that seek to explain their genesis. Attention to history is not special to PC studies but has developed in parallel to the more "general historic turn in the human sciences" (McDonald, 1996) that took place around the 1970s. Careful study of social relations in which speakers were immersed at the time when pidginization (and creolization) took place has contributed to changing significantly our understanding of how that process took place. For instance, in Baker and Corne's work (1982) on the origin of Ile de France, creole presents an image dramatically different from the one drawn by Chaudenson (1974). Similarly, Keesing's historical study of the development of Pacific pidgins (1988) alters in no small way the picture of the history of these languages presented by Mühlhäusler (1978), and is in turn revisited by Baker (1993) who proposes a different reading of the origin of Melanesian pidgins. Arends's (1993, 1995) careful analysis of the history and demography of Surinam at the time of the genesis of Sranan, the creole of what is now Dutch Guyana, allows him to propose a very slow developmental cycle that has countervened established truths and enlivened the debate. These are only a few examples of a rich lineage. One wonders why it took so long for sociolinguistic historiography to take off and become important in this field of study. It is probable that this development had to await the efflorescence of sociolinguistics and ethnography of communication within linguistics – that is, wait for a conception of language studies that puts the speakers, real and not idealized, at the center of theories. Moreover, the emergence of history in creole studies is linked undoubtedly to the growing consensus that "creolization cannot be understood fully without reference to history and to the anthropological data relevant to the emergence and jelling of creole languages" (Stoller 1985: 1–2). After all, is not language a social phenomenon as much as a linguistic one? Whereas there had been "a tendency for research in this area to become lost in the rarefied outer limits of formalism and for scholars to lose touch with the specifically human, i.e. social component" (Hancock 1986: 73), the sociohistorical and sociolinguistic approaches to pidgins and creoles, which had been introduced by D. Hymes, M. Goodman, W. Labov, G. Sankoff, A. Valdman, and D. Winford, remind us that linguistic agency and praxis, individual and collective, are generated and shaped by the nature and extent of social interactions. It would seem rather obvious that one would want to understand the nature and essence of the cultural worlds that fostered the birth of the new languages.

Third, the interest of PC scholars in the linguistic praxis of pidgin and creole speakers has rendered manifest the diversity of pidgins and creoles. Readily observable facts that had been obliterated by formal theories and rich data are now available showing dialectal diversity within particular pidgins and creoles (Escure, 1997; Garrett 2000; Jourdan 1985; Meyerhoff 2000; Patrick 1999; Rickford 1987; Smith 2002). They show also that pidgins and creoles emerged in very diverse social conditions (even though the vast majority of them arose in association with European colonization), and did not necessarily follow the same developmental path. The respective history of Melanesian pidgins (Troy 1985; Keesing 1988; Crowley 1990; Siegel 1987; Tryon and Charpentier 2004), African pidgins, Caribbean creoles (Lefebvre 1998; Singler 1995), and of Guyana creoles (Rickford 1987; Arends 1993) are cases in point.

Fourth, researchers are progressively, and sometimes painfully, realizing that the theoretical tools and the dominant working definitions of concepts central to the field of inquiry have become inadequate in view of the complexity revealed by recent data. As a result, many of the most important concepts in the field, e.g. universals, bioprogram, substrate influences, relexification, pidginization, colonization, nativization, the creole continuum and its series of "lects"[1] have been more intensively scrutinized and refined. But if the tools are proving inadequate to an understanding of the processes through which pidgins and creoles have emerged, is it not because the historical scenarios that are now emerging are proving to have been much more complex, fluid, and diverse than we had thought them to be? The field of pidgin and creole studies has done its homework and sought to revisit the central concepts of the discipline in light of the new data and theories that have emerged in the last twenty years. One of the obvious shortcomings of excessive formalism has been the reification of pidgins and creoles and their lumping into a special group of languages, impervious to the effect of culture, and set aside from the rest of the human languages, those that are "natural" (refer to Jourdan 1991; DeGraff 1999, 2003; McWhorter 1998). Historical and sociolinguistic pidgin and creole studies are helping to correct and refine the globalizing tools and categories that have dominated the field. The result is the development of an ever richer school of pidgin and creole ethno- and sociolinguistics that focuses on linguistic

---

[1] Some scholars have favoured the use of a so-called creole continuum (Bickerton 1977; Rickford 1987; Escure 1997; Patrick 1999) to analyze the sociolects, dialects, and other varieties that comprise the world's pidgins and creoles. Each creole is likely to be divided into three discrete varieties that differ in phonology, syntax, and lexicon. All varieties are established with regard to the standard language that coexists with the creole and served as its lexifier: the basilect is the variety most distinct from the standard; the acrolect is the variety closest to the standard; and the mesolect are all intermediary varieties.

variation (more specifically Escure 1997; Garrett 1999, 2000; Jourdan 1985; Meyerhoff 2000; Patrick 1999; Rickford 1987; Siddell 1998, 1999, 2001); on socialization (Garrett 2000; Smith 2002); on the cultural rooting of pidgins and creoles (Jourdan 1985, 1994; Jourdan and Keesing 1997; Samarin 1982a and b, 1989). This new trend in pidgin and creole studies, pioneered by Sankoff and Laberge (1973) parallels similar changes elsewhere in the social sciences: History, literary criticism, anthropology, and sociology have been affected by a new conception of social formations that puts the individual at the center of social relations, thus stressing the dialogic, contextual, and fluid nature of individual and collective praxis and agency.

Culture in pidgin and creole genesis

In the past twenty years, hypotheses and theories on the genesis of various pidgins and creoles have been hotly debated, and the controversy continues – for instance, in the debate between Naro (1978, 1988) and Goodman (1987, 1988) with regards to the origins of pidgin Portuguese in the fifteenth century; in the reactions to Bickerton's bioprogram hypothesis (1984) (Goodman 1984; Keil 1984; Marantz 1984; Mufwene 1984; Muysken 1984; Seuren, 1984, and more recently Mufwene 1999); in the exchange between Chaudenson (1983, 1988) and Baker (1983) and Corne (1983) on Ile de France creole; in the exchange between Bickerton (1990) and Mufwene (1989) apropos of Keesing's book on the origin of Melanesian pidgins (1988); in the debate between Lefebvre (1998) and DeGraff (2001) a propos the origin of Haitian creole; on the arguments between McWhorter (1998) and De Graff (2003) on the typology of pidgins and creole languages. These are partial examples among many. Looking back at their history, one can observe that these heated debates/controversies are fuelled by our inability to explain, in a way acceptable to us all, how these languages appeared and evolved. Not that it was supposed to be easy.

Leaving aside all the hypotheses and theories of pidgin and creole genesis that are currently generating the most debate and stimulating the most research in linguistics, I am focusing on the role of culture in pidgin genesis, proposing that work and work related activities were the essential cultural matrix in which these new languages developed.

Anthropologists have defined culture in different ways, and quite a number of them seem to disagree on how best to talk about it. Over the years, new perspectives have replaced earlier ones, rallying some scholars and alienating others. However, there seems to be a consensus on understanding culture as a knowledge system that renders meaningful the world in which we live: no one among us is a perfect exemplar of the cultural group in which we live, but rather each of us is a repository of a small part of the knowledge system of that group. The product of that knowledge system – that some say is made transparent through cultural behaviour – is often taken as the visible dimension of culture, or rather, as the proof that culture exists. Whether culture is a knowledge system that is essentially cognitive as Goodenough (1971) and Keesing (1981) insist it is, or whether it is known only through its public manifestations, as Geertz (1973) puts it, culture is produced by social relations that are in turn, produced by it, and as Bourdieu (1977:72) puts it, by "structuring structures." In other words, by social institutions and established social practices. Central to the definition I am using here is the role of human agency in the creation of culture. In this perspective, culture is not a prepackaged immutable whole inherited from parents and peers, but the product of social relationship in which individuals are both actors and participants, *and* also recipients and transmitters. Human agency is what makes it possible for people to engage with culture and to make it change (Jourdan 1994). Culture is never pristine, it is always changing (at times more than at others), and because of individual agency, enculturation (the process by which adults transmit their culture to their children) is never totally successful: each generation makes culture its own with the material at hand: that of their parents, that of their friends, that which they imagine and create, in the constant dialogue of social relationships.

It is with this conception of culture that I am approaching the genesis of PCs. The pidgin and creole languages that have become the focus of much of the specialized literature are the ones that developed in association with the plantation societies of the Atlantic, the Indian Ocean and the Pacific.[2] For this reason I will focus here on these types of social organizations, aware as I am that the model I am suggesting here is not necessarily applicable to all situations of PC genesis. If the concept of culture is going to be heuristic in our understanding how these languages came to be, one must therefore ask: what were the cultures of these plantation societies? What kinds of social worlds were they? Historical, demographic and economic research by Alleyne (1971); Hancock (1986); Arends (1995); Mintz (1974); Moitt (2001); Price (1983); and Singler (1993b, 1995) for the Atlantic and the Caribbean; by Galenson (1986); Thompson (1975) for English America; by Corris (1973); Saunders (1974); Moore (1985); and Siegel (1987) for the Pacific, shows that they shared many characteristics: the labour force was in most cases taken away from their home place, either forcibly or through a system of harsh indentured labour; the ratio of men to women in the initial period was rather unequal on the Pacific plantations (see Corris 1973), but was more equal in other places as new research by Singler (1995) for Haiti and Martinique; by Arends (1995) for Surinam; by Moitt (2001) for Guadeloupe show; contact with the home country and the home language was maintained by a succession of cohorts of workers, so that part of the culture of home was kept alive for some time; most of the social

---

[2] Hancock cited by Stoller (1985) has suggested that *lançado* English may have served as a basis for some Caribbean creoles: "In the slaving forts the traders attempted to teach the slaves 'English', and so the English-derived pidgin came into being, a pidgin which was later creolized in the Caribbean" (Stoller 1985: 11).

activities were essentially work related activities (Mintz, 1982); and finally, not all members of the home society were represented: elders were absent, and so were collaterals. In addition, and as is typical of other confined societies such as prisons, institutions, hospitals, boarding schools, etc . . . , social life was limited and organized and structured from above (Foucault 1975). Rigid timetables, physical constraints and at times physical violence, psychological trauma, lack of privacy, all this was negating the individual needs of the workers while seeking to transform them into pliable, if not well adapted, members of the work community.[3] In addition, as Thompson (1975: 38) remarks, isolation from the outside world was essential, and its effects pervasive.

To isolate is normally to continue previously formed habits and customs. But when a new settlement begins as a collection of individuals drawn from widely diverse backgrounds, as is generally true of plantation settlement, it becomes necessary to destroy in order to re-create. To break the wills and habits of others in the formation of a new institution, to redirect and maintain a new direction, requires a situation of isolation.

We can take the view that plantations functioned essentially as bounded social worlds, with a world view that was predominantly local. That was true for many of them. But we can also, as Arends (2001) does for Surinam for the period 1700–1775, take the view that there existed contact and network relations between plantations. And that was also true for many plantation settings. To what degree workers interacted with workers of neighboring plantations is still a matter of speculation for many plantation settings, particularly for the early period of the plantation system, about which much historical work still needs to be done. But there were certainly situations where workers had opportunities to establish links with workers from other places through work-related activities for instance. Arends lists a few: work, trade, leisure, the first two being particularly relevant to arguments I am presenting here. We can surmise, though, that the nature and the intensity of contact probably varied through time. And of course, there was marronage, itself an extreme type of channel of exchange and diffusion of information between workers of different plantations.[4] We can also surmise that the long work hours typical of slavery and indentured labor (Moitt 2001; Moore 1985; Morissey 1989) did not leave much room or much opportunity for the development of other types of group-based cultural relationships to be established among the laborers on the plantation initially. In short, plantations societies seem to have been truncated cultural units, linked and focused as they were to the economic exploitation of the land, in which workers found themselves locked into power relationships with overseers and

---

[3] See Thompson (1975) for a thorough analysis of social and race relations of the plantations of the South of the United States. See Morissey (1989) and Moitt (2001) for a study of gender stratifications in Caribbean plantations.

[4] I am grateful to J. Singler for reminding me of the importance of marronage for contact between workers from different plantations, and also a channel for exchange and diffusion of knowledge.

owners on the one hand, and with fellow workers on the other. There was also limited time or opportunity for individual and collective symbolic expression, even though one expects (as will be shown below) that laborers retained their original cultural knowledge and kept whatever practices from home that they could keep in the new setting. At any rate, these workers were in no position to bring about changes to the structure of the system, and whatever form of locally produced culture emerged, did so within the confines of that system. It is important to make a distinction between hegemonic structural conditions that serve as the locus of social life, and modes of life within these hegemonic structures that leave interstitial spaces, or "loopholes," where people engage with each other and are able to build on these exchanges.

Importantly, and in addition to the trauma of slavery and/or indentured labor and isolation from the home place, the social world that the newly arrived workers once knew seem to have had no immediate direct relevance for the new world they were thrown into. On the surface of things, it seems that their knowledge systems, including the organizing categories of their languages, could not help them make sense of the new social world they experienced. Their cultural models (such as for instance religious beliefs, clan ideologies, social organization, gender relations, etc . . .) were now at odds with the world they encountered. Yet it is through the prism of their cultural knowledge that workers understood the new life they were thrown into, and were able to assess, understand, interpret it and engage with it. Culture is one of the frames through which we experience the world. For instance, in their article on the expectations that African slaves had of slave life in the Americas, Lovejoy and Trotman (2002) show that plantation workers in the Caribbean knew what slavery was back in Africa, and had expectations about this practice.[5] However, they argue, the type of slavery workers encountered in the Americas, based as it was on racial categories, was very different from the African slavery they were aware of. Newly arrived workers reacted culturally: whatever interpretations and meanings they were going to give to the new social world they encountered was done from the perspective of their own cultural experience, comparatively speaking, and from tapping their own cultural and individual skills. Individual and collective cultural interpretations probably took place quickly. On the one hand plantation societies were social worlds where various knowledge systems, those of the workers[6] and those of the Europeans, met and confronted each other. On the other, it was also a space where they engaged each other: each group assessed and understood the other from their own cultural vantage point.

---

[5] Thanks to John Singler for pointing out to me the book "Questionning Creole" edited by Verene Shepherd and Glen Richards.

[6] We need to recall that the knowledge systems of the slaves, either in the Atlantic or in the Pacific, were heterogeneous. The slaves came from different cultural backgrounds, and, even though generalities could be established, these backgrounds were different, thereby creating de facto multiculturalism in single plantations. See also Mintz and Price (1992: 14–15).

Clearly, the new cultures that were progressively developing on the plantations were not starting in a vacuum. Even in the cases of dramatic displacement
of people typical of the slave trade of the Atlantic or the system of indentureship
of the Pacific, the ancestral cultures of the workers were not totally lost, just
as their ancestral languages were not totally lost. They remained alive through
the continual arrival of new slaves or laborers, but most importantly, through
peoples' individual and sometimes collective memories. This made it possible
for the more symbolic dimensions of culture to keep existing. Following on
Herskovitz's work, Alleyne (1971) claims that the more symbolic dimensions
of African social life such as religion, music, magic and forms of amusement
endured on plantations, while the more structural, such as technology and forms
of political organization did not. Singler (1993b: 210) talks about "continued
Africanness." Historical work done in Queensland by Corris (1973); Moore
(1985);[7] and Saunders (1974), shows clearly that in the initial period of their
arrival on the Queensland plantations, starting around 1860, workers sought to
keep alive some cultural dimensions of their home islands. The environment
and the social context dictated what they could keep, of course, and what they
could not. As much as was possible, they planted small vegetable gardens the
way they did at home, they propitiated ancestors and practiced divinations the
way they did at home, and cooked food the way they did at home, roasted on
the fire, or wrapped in banana leaves (Fatnowna, 1989). Some men even kept
men's houses. But they could not uphold the rules of marriage (the preferred
form was clan exogamy) for the good reason that not all members of their
societies were there and that membership in clans and lineages was difficult to
reckon when clans and lineages themselves had ceased to be meaningful social
units. Writing about African slaves in the New World, Mintz and Price ([1976]
1992) make it clear that if ideas about institutions could be maintained, the
institutions themselves could not. Their analysis also holds for the Pacific.

All these efforts made to maintain a link with the culture of the past, and to
find a niche for it in the cultural world in which the slaves and laborers found
themselves, are at the basis of many syncretic aspects of Caribbean and South
American cultures today. Whatever new culture was likely to evolve among the
labor force was bound to be a construct of the old cultural world the workers
knew, truncated and transformed as it were by displacement and reanalyzed in
the light of the new reality. Again, in view of the cultural heterogeneity that
often characterized many plantations, it is appropriate to think of new cultural
worlds, in the plural, rather than as a totalizing cultural world.[8] But if these new
cultural worlds drew part of their meanings from, and were shaped by the racial

---

[7] In his analysis of the history of Solomon Islands indentured laborers in the town of Mackay in
the state of Queensland (Australia), Moore writes about "Melanesian Mackay" and describes the
coexistence of purely Melanesian religious rituals and Christian beliefs.

[8] Current debates about the cultural make up of plantation worlds challenge the view that profound
cultural heterogeneity was the rule (see Kouwenberg 2004).

ideology that sustained slavery and often sustained indentured labor, they were also limited by the social practices of the plantation economy.

Whether plantations developed their own particular culture to the extent that Thompson (1975) claims is a point of debate best left to historians. Whatever new cultures were emerging out of the cultural encounter – however limited in scope the result was initially, given the nature of the social space that served as its matrix – were the product of a group of workers who were no longer a crowd of individuals but had become a community (Mintz and Price [1976] 1992: 14–18). Not that it was a simple process: in many cases, multiculturalism (and attendant multilingualism among the workers) along with the structural organization of plantation life hindered for some time the transformation of such a group of individuals (and their individual responses to the new conditions of life) into a social community. One should be careful not to argue for a purely creativist approach to culture genesis, given that the resulting cultural formations owed much to reactive processes than to purely creative ones.

Keeping the above in mind, we can identify four characteristics shared by plantation cultures in the early plantation period: (1) the cultures that were emerging were essentially centered around work or work-related activities; the control established over the laborers' timetable and whereabouts ensured that hardly any time, or hardly any space, was left for socializing; (2) the cultures that were emerging were constrained by the lack of vernacular cultural depth in situ,[9] by the structure of the plantation system, and by lack of access to European cultural depth, so that true acculturation did not take place; (3) the cultures that were emerging developed initially in relative isolation, in self-contained social and economic world, even though some measure of contact between plantations and plantation workers, around sugar processing mills for instance, clearly existed; (4) the cultures could emerge as such only when a crowd of individual workers became a community of workers (Mintz and Price [ibid.]).

With these new cultural worlds appeared also new cultural subjectivities and identities that were grounded in specific practices workers had not experienced before. Writing about the role agency and cultural logics in the transformation of subjectivity, Holland *et al.* (1998:7) propose: "This is our objective here: to respect humans as social and cultural creatures and therefore bounded, yet to recognize the processes by which human collectives and individuals often move themselves – led by hope, desperation, or even playfulness, but certainly by no rational plan – from one set of socially and culturally formed subjectivities to another."

What is the relationship between these new cultural formations and the emergence of PCs? A look at work and work-related activities is crucial to the answer to this question. In addition to being the economic "raison d'être" of plantations

---

[9] Cultural depth refers to the body of cultural rooting over at least a few generations of practices and ideologies. It is through cultural depth that languages acquire social legitimacy.

(or mines, trading posts, etc . . .), work and work-related activities also provided the only social context where regular, repeated, and sometimes prolonged communication could take place between workers and plantation overseers and owners (be they "petits blancs" in Haiti and Martinique, or "mulatto" intermediaries), on the one hand, and between laborers themselves. This is true also of other types of social contexts that fostered the development of PCs elsewhere or the restructuring of some languages such as Sango (Samarin, 1982a) and Swahili (Fabian, 1986).

Part of the argument I am making here involves paying more attention to cultures as barriers to, and facilitators of communication. If a local culture is likely to develop, it will be out of a cultural space shared by workers on a regular basis. As we have seen above, workers shared some measure of expectations of their new circumstances, their experience of cultural and spatial dislocation. But they shared also their experience of work conditions in a plantation setting: the same pressures from a rigid timetable and the long hours of work;[10] the same hardship on the body; the same relationship, or lack thereof, with Europeans; etc. Work was the common space, the common denominator that opened the door for exchange, cultural and linguistic, in other words for pidginicity to appear.

The culture of work became the locus for the exploration of meaning, through trial and error. Be it in the fields or in the sugar mills, it was also the cognitive center of the plantation community around which much of the meaningful daily social life initially revolved. From its very nature (physical activities, gestures, movements, planning), work is an ideal locus for the birth of vocabulary. Regular and sustained contact between peoples, including workers and overseers, made transfer of technical and practical vocabulary possible and easy, whatever the occupations of the laborers in the plantation economy. By its very nature, work fostered the development of communicative collaboration: without collaboration, how could one interpret an order, learn to execute what was expected, explain to others how to perform tasks, coordinate actions so that the work could be done in a speedier (or slower?) fashion? Work provided the social space where individual identity could be reshaped and group consciousness could develop initially: all workers were defined in relation to it, and the hierarchical nature of the plantation social world came to the fore in those moments and activities. Keeping the above in mind, one can propose that it is around work-related activities that the PC varieties initially developed in a given plantation and, that from that cultural sphere it then spread to the other cultural spheres of plantation social life, however limited they may have been. This process does not mean that there existed a long lag between the

[10] Moore (1985: 123) notes that Melanesians in Mackay (Queensland) worked "under supervision in open fields for twelve hours a day, six and a half days a week." Moitt notes that in the French Caribbean the Code Noir of 1685 placed no limits on a slave's workday, but prohibited work on Sundays and other Christian holidays.

time of PC creation in work-related settings, and its expansion/application to other settings. Nor does it mean that no other collective activities outside of work eventually developed that would also foster the development of new languages (such as cooking for instance, sharing meals, the practice of daily life, establishing friendship links, seeking support, etc.). It means that the incipient PC progressively became central to the social life of work, where most intergroup social interactions took place, while the ancestral languages remained all the while rooted in the cultural depth associated with the places of origin. Thus, while the PC developed in response to or in association with local sociolinguistic conditions and demands (multilingualism, necessity, pragmatism, group consciousness, among others), the ancestral languages were central to the cultural memory of the workers, to those cultural practices that they were able to maintain, and to the individual and personal contact workers may have had with members of their ethnic groups. They remained vital to any cultural consciousness anchored in the past and certainly facilitated the psychological and emotional transition into the present. By virtue of the coexistence of these cultural worlds, the incipient PCs and the ancestral languages also coexisted.

To sum up, in accordance with historical evidence at the time of PC genesis, plantations were the loci of several coexisting cultural worlds: (1) truncated European cultures and social worlds sustained by the superstrate language as manifested by local social dialects; (2) truncated vernacular cultures of the workers, sustained by their respective languages, and lived and experienced by individuals who became progressively removed from them; and (3) a culture of plantation work sustained by an incipient PC, which was progressively developing and stabilizing, adopting structural features and interpreting symbolic dimensions from the European culture(s), transferring features from their original cultures, and building on both.[11]

But what about the new languages that appeared in such a setting? To conclude, and this is only an educated guess, but arguably a very reasonable one, I propose that work offered the unifying leveling cultural context that made it possible for PCs to develop (or to stabilize in cases where workers had picked up some smattering of pidgin on board recruitment ships, as Keesing (1988) reports for the Pacific for instance), despite the coexistence of partial cultures of origin. Just as these cultures shaped the cultural worlds that were developing within the plantation's social structure,[12] the ancestral languages shaped the incipient PC varieties that were developing on each plantation.

---

[11] However, as Fabian (1986) argues, and as the PC literature has established, this model of some pidginization is not universal. It certainly does not apply to the development of some pidgins in Central Africa, particularly with regard to the ratio of Europeans to Africans.

[12] In his article on family structure and plantation systems in the Western hemisphere, Smith also makes a distinction between the social relationships linked to the production process (work, here), and the others: "I therefore assume that the involvement of the plantation population in systems of social relationships other than those involved in the process of production must be considered capable of variation from one plantation to another in a way that the relations involved in the process of production are not" (1959:149).

Power, knowledge, and resistance

Scholars of language ideology have shown that language is not a socially neutral and functional tool of communication equally accessible to all, but is rather, and with all other dimensions of culture, open to symbolic appropriation (Bourdieu, 1975 and more recently Woolard and Schieffelin, 1994, and Schieffelin, Woolard and Kroskrity, 1998). The key to that statement lies in the difference one establishes between language as a system of rules, and language as cultural practice. When studied as a system of rules, irrespectively of the speakers who create and use them, language is simply the product of the human mind. But the conditions of production of language are central to its constitution and use: they cannot be ignored. Discourse, defined as the social practice of language, is itself power producing in that it is reality producing. It anchors language in a socially controlled space of enunciation where speakers are agents: they state, enact, engage the world and other members of their social group.

As Foucault (1979) reminds us, power exists in terms of relationships between individuals, families, groups, corporations, states, and other units of social life: "Power must be understood in the first instance as the multiplicity of force relations immanent in the sphere in which they operate and which constitute their own organization" (Foucault 1979: 92). But power is also linked to the contexts in which these relationships develop: factors such as time, place, and motives alter the nature of the relationships and often alter the "power game." Thus power is both relational and situational. It is also multifaceted: the sheer power of number, the power of knowledge (and of its constituents, acquisition, secrecy and transmission), the power of birth right, the power of money. Building on the insights of Foucault (1979), anthropology has recognized that culture, as an ideological system resting on the meaning of symbols, is the locus *par excellence* of power relationships, as much as it is the focus of power relationships. The practice and politics of everyday life, as was made clear in the previous section of this article, pervades one's social group, and is expressed through opposition, resistance, conformity, symbolic posturing, identity building, in the home and outside. In short, "the constitution of social reality is itself considered a central form of power" (Philips 2001: 190).

Just as the production of language is marked by the conditions of its enunciation, so is the birth of a new language; it cannot be separated from the forces that produce it. In the case that concerns us here, clearly the context involves power relationships typical of the colonial worlds: between cultural worlds and ideologies that meet and confront each other on the plantation; between the workers and their masters; among workers themselves, in the course of daily interactions, particularly during work. To this picture, one must add race as a pivotal element of the power equation: within colonial relationships, the discourse on race is inscribed in power relationships that are themselves central to the cultural matrix of pidgin genesis; it is central to the discourse on language.

As Thompson (1975: 38) reminds us: "The plantation represents one type of situation in which the labor problem and the race problem meet." It should not come as a surprise that the languages created in these circumstances be gathered into, and confined by a label such as pidgin, the meaning of which being associated by observers (and sometimes by speakers as well) with simplicity and inadequacy.

In the attention they paid to the conditions of multilingualism and to the limited access to the superstrate obtained by vernacular speakers on plantations, PC scholars have shown that they have taken seriously the argument about power. As was seen earlier, creolists have paid particular attention to the power of numbers: a focus on the number of people involved at the time of genesis, on the types of languages that were spoken, and careful demographic analyses of gender ratio, age pyramids and size of cohorts of slaves have proved essential to our understanding of pidgin genesis, and in some cases have corrected tenets on the topic (see Arends 1993; Baker and Corne 1982; Singler 1993b and 1993d).

Shifting our attention away from numbers and towards the speech communities in which pidgins develop, it becomes clear that the plantation daily regimen of life left little room to the laborer for changing the system:

More over, in most cases there is still the rather rigid social order of the plantation hierarchy, and the sharply limited opportunities it offers those at the bottom to change their relative position in the social order.

(Mintz 1974: 52)

In such situations of social liminality, and plantation workers certainly were at the periphery of the social order, performance of identity through symbolic expression of the traditions that were left behind was hardly possible. In addition, the continual presence of cultural others required that forms of cultural engagement be enacted among the workers themselves in fashion that would require negotiation of meaning and an acceptance of the Other. These moments of awareness of the Other, together with the consciousness that one is caught up in radical historical transformations, force the development of "a complex, on going negociation that seeks to authorize cultural hybridities . . ." as Bhabha puts it (1994: 2). Discussing the articulation of power and difference from a minority position, read here from marginal and liminal positions, Bhabha suggests that the only space left to the minority resides in the creation of new cultural forms. As I have shown elsewhere, hybridization and cultural creolization are often the outcome of an engagement with cultural liminality (Jourdan 1994). On plantations, workers grabbed whatever power space they could, usually in the form of covert resistance, even in the form of language.

Can we construe the emergence of pidgins as a form of resistance to hegemony? In some ways, certainly. For beyond the real and practical advantages that pidgins offered (they made it possible for communication to take place among workers and caused the breaking down of their linguistic isolation), the new languages also allowed for the crystallization of a nascent cultural identity, different from, and yet in relative continuity with that of the Europeans and that of the vernacular cultures. PCs as an avenue to empowerment? Without any doubt. Whether they wanted it or not, whether pidgin "makers" were conscious of it or not, the creation of pidgins proved to be one of the most important symbolic and pragmatic actions that the workers could undertake. It was the first step towards empowerment, the first step towards a subversion of hegemony, the true product of cultural agency. I am not suggesting here that pidgins developed out of a deliberate desire on the part of the workers to challenge the hegemonical conditions that controlled their life. But to speak is to create; it is to represent; it is to establish a link between one's self and the world. To speak a word is to appropriate its meaning, and its power. To speak a word is also to create the world. By virtue of having a new language at their disposal that was in continuity with the vernaculars and made use of the significant elements of the superstrate, pidgin makers set themselves on a course of linguistic independence that changed their relationship to the world.

In the process of linguistic and cultural reanalysis that is at the basis of the genesis of PCs, the dimension of the superstrate culture to which the workers where most often exposed, albeit in a rather summary manner, was its language: the words linked to work were spoken to and around the workers regularly by overseers and plantation managers. Their meaning progressively became transparent and served as a common linguistic denominator among the workers. If a language was likely to develop in these circumstances, it seems rather obvious that the superstrate would play a part in it.

Scholars of PCs languages have proposed different scenarios to explain the role of the superstrate in creole genesis and I will not go over them here. What interests me is the question of the intentionality behind the genesis of pidgin. Some scholars have proposed that the superstrate was the target language of the workers and that pidgins are the results of failed second language acquisition. I do not deny that this might have been the case for a number of workers, particularly for the domestic servants, as opposed to the fieldworkers. One can expect that the more sustained the contacts with the superstrate were, the more likely workers were to learn it, or the more acrolectal their variety of pidgin would be. For these people, the superstrate language may have come to be associated with power and may truly have been the language that they wanted to learn. At a more symbolic level, its words were there to be taken, as if by taking them one controlled their power, and the power they seem to be giving to their original speakers. But this represented a minority of people. As the PC literature has shown, the great majority of workers did not have regular access to the superstrate, and were never in a position to be able to learn it, or to want to learn it. The scenario I prefer is one whereby workers made use of the resources that are offered to them, identifying those linguistic elements that are likely to be operational, i.e a lexicon that is the common lexical denominator for all. In my mind, pidgin makers saw early how useful the superstrate lexicon was to overcome linguistic diversity; but the lexicon only does not a language make.

With regard to a theory of power, what do we have? On the one hand, a very small minority of workers who probably had the possibility of having the superstrate as a target language, succeeding or not in learning it. And a very large majority of workers who did not think of the superstrate as the language that they needed or could learn. By imprinting their own reading on the language of the other, by making use of their own languages to impart a special shape to the new language, whether they were aware of it or not, an incipient language was born. I am reminded here of Baker's argument (1995) on motivation in creole genesis: it squares with the analysis I am presenting here, even though I am not prepared to go as far as he does on the degree of deliberate social consciousness that he attributes to pidgin makers in the process of pidgin genesis. Resistance to cultural hegemony has often to do with seizing whatever space is devoid of control and claiming it. In this case, the void was linguistic. Symbolic and practical reasons mutually reinforced each other to lead to the development of PCs. Whatever the motivation, and languages are not only the products of sheer acts of volitions on the part of their makers, the result was an opening towards a new identity that could, from then on, be expressed in words. This was a distinct improvement in the life condition of the workers: it was not likely to lead to structural changes, but it was likely to lead to the crystallization of group consciousness and thus lead to a sense of empowerment; how limited it was. PCs as a form of counter culture? Why not? PCs makers were certainly creating a language that existed in parallel to others sustained by developing social relations. They were shaping this new language in the image of their own, while possibly giving to the authority the impression that they were trying hard to learn the superstrate, or – and given the racial stereotypes that were prevalent – that they would never be able to do so.[13]

If symbolic power seems to have been neglected from our studies of pidgin genesis, so has the power derived from knowledge. Yet one can easily imagine the prestige obtained by the first workers who were able to decode some of the meanings of the world they were thrown into, and could interpret it for others. The prestige derived from this knowledge was invaluable: whether it was derived from regular and sustained access to this world;[14] whether it was inferred from observation, or from direct and regular contact with the superstrate culture, knowledge probably gave some individuals a degree of prestige that conferred on them some measure of power. And the smaller the workers'

---

[13] See Thomason and Kaufman (1988) for a discussion of creativity in pidgin genesis, and Baker (1990, 1995) for a discussion on the superstrate as target language, and on directionality in pidgin genesis.

[14] Compare for instance the situation of house laborers to that of fieldworkers.

speech community, the more the importance of such individuals, or groups of individuals, in the shaping of some varieties of pidgin.

In the scenarios that have been proposed to account for the genesis of PCs, it may be the case that too much attention has been paid to conflicting power relationships and not enough to the types of collaborative behaviors that may have also existed alongside the conflictual ones. Collaborative behaviors were probably just as important; and in many cases they were the key to physical survival and psychological health. One place where collaborative behavior is needed is certainly the development of a new language. This collaboration must have taken different forms, and probably worked at various levels. A basic question concerns the various loci where collaboration is needed in any situation of communication: collaboration in the interpretation of meanings, in letting people talk, in proposing words for ideas, in understanding the intention of the interlocutors, in allowing phonological and syntactical variations, in conceding that one's choice of word could become secondary or even eliminated, and so forth. Communication is also a story of concessions and collaboration, just as it is the story of turn taking, stealing the floor, and shouting matches. And certainly communication is what made it possible for social and linguistic accommodation (such as dialect leveling) to take place. Along these lines, we can consider foreigner talk as a form of sociolinguistic collaboration, as much as an expression of power on the part of speakers. We can also look at the social principles guiding language mixing or koineization (see Siegel 1997) as another form of cooperation: if efficient communication is what guides the selection and use of linguistic features, then, *mutatis mutandis* those factors that promote efficiency are more likely to appear in the new language. In his brilliant article on the principles that guide language mixing and leveling, Siegel (1997) shows that the most important factors are unmarkedness, transparency, regularity, frequency, economy of linguistic forms. Only one of them, symbolic salience, is probably due not to collaborative behavior but to the effect of symbolic power or to the power obtained by group of speakers because of its numerical importance.

Of the many phases involved in pidgin genesis, dialect leveling is certainly one of those that are the result of a combination of collaborative and non collaborative behaviors between pidgin makers. If we conceive of dialect leveling as a step towards efficient communication, it follows that some measure of collaboration must have played a role in it, alongside the more conflictual and less consensual leveling. The latter is usually the product of social forces at play, such as the progressive adoption of a linguistic form over another by the linguistic community because of the sheer number of speakers using this form or because of hegemonic forces that shape the direction of linguistic change. And what is dialect leveling if not a form of linguistic change: a harmonization of linguistic forms in relation to the social pressures and cultural values at play.

Cognition, substrates, and universals

The argument that pidgins and creoles reflect elements of the grammatical structures of indigenous languages dates back at least to the work of Schuchardt in the
nineteenth century ([1883]1980). It was further developed, partially in relation
to Caribbean creoles, through the citing of parallels between particular West
African languages and Caribbean creoles (Alleyne 1980; Bentolila 1971), and
required that linguists start to pay close attention to the indigenous languages
from which models could have been drawn. The most systematic comparisons
are found in the work of Keesing (1988) and Lefebvre (1998). Yet, the emerging
picture seems to be of an interaction among substrate influences, superstrate
influences, and universal structures and faculties of language simplification. As
Goodman (1984); Mufwene (1986); and Keesing (1988) argue, these forces
are not mutually exclusive but complementary and interactive; their relative
weights vary from case to case. Strong substratum positions, such as that argued
by Lefebvre (1986, 1998) and her colleagues (Lefebvre and Lumsden 1989)
for Haitian creole, are crucial to our reflection in that they force us to address
important questions: Why is Haitian creole not, then, a dialect of Fon? What
about the many other African languages, typologically quite different, spoken
by the slaves in Haiti? How do we account for the many features Haitian creole shares with creoles that do not have Fon as substratum (Mufwene 1986)?
Demographic and historic data presented for the Pacific and for Liberian English
(Singler, 1988) make it clear that the more homogeneous the substrate languages
(i.e. as part of the same language family), the greater the chances that the substrate will significantly shape the pidgin or the creole created by their speakers.
This seems obviously the situation in the case of Haitian creole. In the Solomon
Islands and in Vanuatu, the relationship between substrate languages and Pijin
and Bislama, respectively, is likewise obvious. As I have shown elsewhere,
Solomon Islanders speaking Southeast Solomonic languages who do not know
Pijin upon arriving in town need barely three to four weeks of daily immersion
in Pijin to master it (Jourdan 1985, 1988). I argue that they can do so precisely because they realize intuitively how much of Pijin grammar is mapped
onto the vernaculars they speak natively – the languages that have shaped it
historically, as Keesing (1988) shows. However, urbanization and concomitant
language change are altering very quickly the intensity of substrate influence
for urban speakers for whom it is a primary language, not one acquired in young
adulthood. Obviously, some cases of substrate influences are more difficult than
others to argue.

With his Language Bioprogram Hypothesis seeking to explain the process
of creolization, Bickerton (1984) shook the hereto gentle world of pidgin and
creole studies (see Fournier 1987). Comparing Hawaiian creole English with its
immediate ancestor Hawaiian pidgin English, Bickerton found that the differences between the two could not be attributed to any languages available to the
speakers at the time, and hence must be due to more general cognitive abilities

of these creole makers. These cognitive abilities, he proposed, are part of the human language bioprogram. Being universal, these faculties explain why linguistic features distinctive of creoles are so widely distributed in historically unrelated creoles. The anthropological implications of such strong innatist and universalist claims deserve closer examination. If, as Bickerton asserted, "the human child would have in his mind all possible grammars, although different weighting attached to the various settings would mean that certain types of grammar would have a preferred status" (1984: 178), and if, as Chomsky (1981) posited, language rested primarily on innate linguistic structures and faculties, then social anthropologists would have a limited interest in language. Historical and sociological processes, and cultural embedding of languages, would be relatively superficial phenomena. Languages as socially created, established, acknowledged, and controlled forms of knowledge would be surface elaborations – mere variations of deep designs innate to our species.

Such a strong innatist and universalist position seems increasingly problematic, particularly in view of new developments in cognitive approaches to language structure: while they are unearthing universals, the researchers find them much more heavily based on experiential commonalities and functional constraints, and much more directly related to general cognitive capacities, than Chomsky's and Bickerton's models propose (see Brown, this volume). These approaches to universals, showing how they arise partly from common experiential orientation and thought processes and partly from the interaction situation and its functional constraints on communication of information and affect, leave ample room for the analysis of linguistic knowledge as socially constituted. What is particularly fascinating with pidgin and creole languages is that despite our still rather patchy data concerning their genesis, their history lies in a social world of communicated knowledge, of negotiations of meanings and of linguistic forms. If communication is the key to social interaction, then intelligibility of competing forms will result in speakers making the "right" guesses about meaning: "Those guesses that promote intelligibility will be the right guesses" (Thomason and Kaufman 1988: 153). Such guesses are the ones likely to be incorporated into the pidgin or the creole. This is where substrate and universal influences on pidgin and creole genesis can happily meet. Even the staunchest proponents of the influence of substrates in the genesis of pidgins and creoles will acknowledge the role of universals; but they may not acknowledge their influence in their Bickertonian bioprogrammatic form. It is our intuitions about what allows communication in the language we know, our abilities to simplify and strip off inessential surface marking, that allow us to negotiate meanings in intercultural communication. These are the guesses Thomason and Kaufman are talking about, that promote the incorporation of the less marked features into a pidgin.

The similarity of pidgins and creoles, if we insist that they represent special kinds of languages, would be due not to special faculties accessible to children and disappearing in adulthood, but to a more general human ability to read through and eliminate surface representations as noise, thereby allowing us to reach core meaning (see Jourdan 2000). The structural differences between pidgins would be due to the differences between their various source languages. As a result, at the time when a pidgin jells, its grammar will include (a) some marked features common to its source languages, and (b) the unmarked features reached through language universals.

As was explained in section above, not all aspects of vernacular cultural domains, and not all aspects of European cultural domains, were present on plantations (and in the other social contexts that fostered the development of PCs, even though we are not talking about these explicitly here). If we assume that the workers came to the cultural encounter with the European plantation world from the perspective of their vernacular cultures, they progressively came to realize that many of their semantic categories were inapplicable. This, in my view, explains why, despite calquing and relexification, PCs are not totally similar to their substrate languages. This explains why Solomon Islands Pijin is not a copy of Kwaio (Keesing 1988), and why Haitian creole is not a copy of Fon (Lefebvre 1998). Not that these authors imagine these new languages to be exact copies of the old ones. They, too, are aware that in the transition between the home world of the workers, and the world of the plantations, too many cultural changes have taken place that make it impossible for whole semantic domains, lexical categories, or syntactic structures to be systematically transposed from vernaculars to the incipient pidgins. In addition, new cultural phenomena have developed locally that warranted the creation in pidgin of new lexical items that were not present in the vernaculars.

The perspective on culture that I am using here allows me to propose that PCs are also, and foremost, the results of a process of cultural translation inherent to all instances of contact situations (see Jourdan 2001), and of a process of language creation. In these types of translations, cultural reanalysis and inter-pretation is just as important to the language that is being created as is linguistic reanalysis. This is the case even when the social groups in contact do not share the same type of cultural categories and reference (a situation typical of the colo-nial encounter). Cultural interpretations, and cultural translations also involve recreation: the result of these interpretations and translations is not a copy, but an appropriation of meaning, and a re-casting of meaning in different terms, and with different labels.

Conclusion

Poiesis, rather than mimesis: making not faking. (Turner)

In this chapter I have tried to show the relevance of anthropological concepts to our understanding of PCs genesis. Focusing on plantations settings, and starting with culture, I showed that the development of pidgins appeared concomitantly with the development of local cultures. In doing so, I showed also that individual agency drives cultural reanalysis and cultural creation: faced with a situation over which they had no control, and using the tools they had, while negotiating the hegemonic conditions of the plantation worlds, the workers engaged the social and structural world that controlled their lives and put their imprint, linguistic and cultural, on it. The departure point of these new linguistic cultures are the cultures of work that developed on the various plantations.

Just as the new cultures are the results of negotiations of meaning that start with the individual, so do the new pidgins. Using the concept of meaning as a reference point, I proposed that when cultural worlds are in contact, as they were on plantation, it requires on the part of individuals and groups an accommodation to the difference, to what we now call in anthropology "otherness." Cultural and linguistic contacts imply the existence of states of intersubjectivity that also involve the interpretation of the "other": this takes place in the light of one's own personal experience, and within the ideological regimes produced by cultural life and social relationships. It often results in different outlooks that individuals have on their new cultural world.

A discussion on the dialogical nature of power allows for different analyses of the social relationships likely to foster the genesis of PCs. In addition to the conflictual relationships archetypal of colonial worlds, more consensual relationships are also necessary for new languages, or new ways of speaking for that matter, to appear. In situations of cultural alienation or cultural liminality, the creation of a new medium of communication can be seen as a form of resistance to hegemonic social conditions, as much as an expression of identity. In this light, the birth of PCs is as much the result of the pragmatic need to break cultural and linguistic isolation, as it is a form of empowerment on the part of their makers. Given the nature of human agency and of the sociocultural conditions that served as the matrix of these languages, I come to the conclusion that the genesis of pidgin and creole languages was inevitable.

7

BILINGUALISM

MONICA HELLER

Why worry about bilingualism?

The first question that needs to be asked in a book like this is why this chapter is here at all. How did it come to pass that a concept like "bilingualism" got constituted as an area of enquiry for ethnolinguistics? I will begin here with a consideration of that question as one that is fundamentally about language ideologies, and then go on in the rest of the chapter to explore some of the specific questions that flowed, in my view necessarily, from an understanding of languages as being whole, bounded objects tied to whole bounded social and political units like ethnic groups, nations or states. Bilingualism (a term I will use here to cover multilingualism as well) is an affront to this idea, or at best a puzzle needing to be solved. As a result, academic work on the subject has tended to focus on explorations of the way bilingualism tests our ideas either of language or of social and political categories. One set of questions addresses whether or not bilingualism challenges linguistic theories linked to the idea of language as autonomous and whole; another examines the relationship between bilingualism and the construction of categories like ethnicity, or the nation (or the nation-State), understood as homogeneous and bounded entities, as well as with related categories or concepts, such as community or identity, all of which are central to ethnolinguistic enquiry.

The rest of this chapter will then deal with the major areas of each line of enquiry. The first is mainly constructed around the idea of codeswitching, that is, the use of more than one language by a single speaker, and approaches to it stemming from linguistic theory, neurolinguistics, social psychology, conversation analysis, sociolinguistics and linguistic anthropology. What we will find here is an unresolved set of issues regarding the tenability of the very concept of "code," that is, the foundational concept of autonomous linguistic systems.

The second area of enquiry has more to do with the ways in which bilingualism calls into question the idea of the homogeneous group, usually understood as a nation, and normatively organized as a nation-State. Here work has clustered around various ways in which bilingualism is lived, either by individuals as members of social groups, by groups collectively, or by the State and its institutions. Thus, bilingualism has raised questions about individual

156

and collective identity, about the social organization of linguistic resources, about inequality, and about how language is linked to social, political and economic resources. Here we will see how enquiry into the social, political and economic side of bilingualism has necessitated understanding ways in which ideologies of homogeneity have been historically linked to relations of power. We will look at the unfolding of thinking about social aspects of bilingualism, from structural–functional approaches uncritical of the foundational ideologies of homogeneity, to critical approaches linking bilingual language practices in everyday life to structural processes of social categorization and social stratification (or, the production of social difference and social inequality). We will see how structural–functional approaches revealed patterns of complexity, multiplicity and change which the approach itself could not adequately describe or explain, necessitating a re-thinking of the relations between language-in-(inter)action and the social organization of language choice. Here we will be concerned with domains and diglossia, interaction and interpretation, and difference and inequality. The major question arising here joins that which emerges from more language-focused explorations, that is, what, in the end, counts as a language, and who gets to decide the content of such definitions? The two sets of questions converge in the area of enquiry about the role of language in the construction of the categories which serve as principles of social organization.

Let me begin, then, with a brief consideration of why we have been asking questions about bilingualism at all. The answer seems fairly straightforward: to the extent that nineteenth-century nationalism, especially of the Romantic variety, posited the naturalness and desirability of the existence of nations understood as organic and culturally and linguistically homogeneous units (Hobsbawm 1990), bilingualism necessarily stood as a potential problem for the maintenance or reproduction of such nations, or as a threat to their boundaries. At the same time, relations among nation-States required some kind of negotiation of power, and such negotiations could be conducted through the management of linguistic differences as well as through discussions of geographical boundaries, disputes over shared resources, or other areas of mutual interest.

Thus we have France debating already at the time of the Revolution how best to construct a unified France in which all could equally benefit from the values of the Revolution, that is, through bringing the message to the people through their own language varieties (whether Breton or Gascon, Picard or Occitan) or by assuring that everyone spoke the same language (Grillo 1989; Higonnet 1980). The result of the debate, as we well know, was the promotion of monolingualism in the name of *liberté, égalité et fraternité*. This was institutionalized, largely through education and the military, and decades and even centuries of work were undertaken to establish the homogeneity which was only ever partially realized on the ground (cf. e.g. Weber 1976; MacDonald 1990; Jaffe 1999; Lafont 1997; Boyer 1991). Similar struggles, each with its own specificities, could be found across Western Europe around the same period and exported to the colonies.

Similar issues also arose, perhaps even with greater urgency, in the polyglot empires of Central and Eastern Europe. This has been most extensively examined with respect to the Habsburg Empire, which encountered in the nineteenth and early twentieth centuries the limits of the possibility of reproducing an imperial régime, and for which the discourses of nineteenth-century Romantic nationalism proved especially difficult challenges (cf. e.g. Rindler-Schjerve in press; Gal 1995). Attempts to balance the reproduction of central imperial power with the demands of diverse regions through policies of multilingualism (including some forms of bilingual education) seem not to have been able to withstand the difficulties of asserting such control in the face of a powerful alternative model (that is, of nation-Statehood), one which had to appeal to local élites.

Disciplines such as ethnology or anthropology, demography and sociology, and of course, linguistics, were all drawn into the scientific exploration (and legitimation) of what is fundamentally a politically and economically informed set of converging ideologies, whether regarding the management of diversity internal to an empire or a nation-State (whether established or posited), or regarding the management of relations between such entities. Bilingualism would have to be explained, its consequences for the health of "normal" individuals, groups and political entities evaluated, positions taken as to what, if anything, needed to be done about it.

It is difficult here to trace in detail the extent to which the emerging disciplines of the social sciences addressed bilingualism in the nineteenth and early twentieth centuries. Demography certainly became involved in the management of bilingualism through censuses in the mid nineteenth century (Gal 1993); dialectology and historical linguistics can also be seen as ways to make homogeneity out of diversity. Attention to the properties of the messiness of bilingualism may have emerged more strongly in the period following the Second World War, perhaps as empires crumbled, and imaginations turned to liberation. Not surprisingly, discourses of resistance to centralizing states take up the legitimizing discourse of the state for their own purposes, and so, while attention to bilingualism increased, the grounds for understanding it have only very recently begun to shift.

As I mentioned earlier, such attention can be understood as coming from two directions; the first concerns approaches fundamentally focused on understanding the linguistic system, and the second concerns approaches fundamentally focused on the role of language in the organization of social and political life. Both are relevant to the story, insofar as our disciplines produce knowledge of value to broader, historically and socially contingent ways of understanding the world.

In the following section, I will turn to some of the ways these issues have been taken up in linguistics, as well as by connected disciplines. These will include concerns for what bilingualism makes us ask about linguistic systems, and for what it makes us ask about the relationship between putatively autonomous linguistic systems and other aspects of cognitive and social activity.

Bilingualism as a test for linguistic theory

Linguistic theory has approached bilingualism in a number of ways, including by ignoring it. But the fundamental question posed has had to do with whether existing global theories of language can account for bilingual forms and practices. An early and influential study, by Weinreich (1953), took a descriptive, almost taxonomic, approach, which we find in many studies to this day. Drawing on empirical data from a bilingual community in Switzerland, Weinreich sought to classify types of bilingual forms, and hence types of bilingualism, with central concerns forming around to what extent one or more grammars could be said to be involved, how aspects of one grammar might influence another, and what kinds of conditions (mainly social, but also psychological) might explain why things look one way or another. In some sense, Weinreich's approach was an extension of descriptive linguistic methods to the phenomenon of bilingualism, and an attempt to maintain a tradition which sought simultaneously to discern universal patterns of linguistic order, and to discover the links among language, cognition and society.

Each one of these questions has led to separate, albeit interrelated, streams of research. Some of the more socially oriented streams will be taken up in the next section. Here I want to focus on current versions of the linguistic issues, by focusing on one area of bilingualism which has long been held to be potentially particularly fruitful as an avenue for exploring them, namely code-switching. The term itself is vexed, with authors varying in what they mean by it; some today, as we shall see, wish to distance themselves from it altogether. The term was largely meant to capture a form of bilingual behavior which has been thought to allow for particularly fine-grained empirical analysis of the relationship between bilingualism and linguistic theory, that is, the intersections of codes in bilingual performance. The concept of code is clearly related to that of language, insofar as both refer to autonomous and bounded linguistic systems; it has been preferred in the literature largely to make a distinction between large-scale moves from one language to another (say from one set of activities or group of speakers to the next), and the kind of close relations within utterances or conversations that analysts have wished to understand. However, the boundaries between such phenomena are usually fuzzy, and so it is no surprise that definitions of codeswitching have been bountiful, and arriving at watertight taxonomies difficult.

Codeswitching data have been used to test linguistic theories, largely in order to explore what kinds of global theories of language can account for such data, on the assumption that such an accounting will help develop theories which represent, in some way, the nature of an underlying universal linguistic system which is common to all linguistic form and performance (Heller and Pfaff 1996). Muysken (e.g. 1995) has actively pursued the development of generative theory from this perspective.

However, the field has perhaps been most influenced by ongoing debates between Poplack and Myers-Scotton (cf. e.g. Poplack 1988; Myers-Scotton 1993a, b). Both have sought universal descriptions for codeswitching data, but from different angles. Poplack has sought to use the tools of variationist sociolinguistics and descriptive grammar, aiming at a grammar which embeds the notion of variability in its core, and seeking explanations purely within the realm of grammatical structure and process. Myers-Scotton has aimed at an account which presupposes relations among grammars and a means of explaining their interrelationships. She seeks explanations, moreover, which tie linguistic phenomena to cognitive and social ones.

These approaches have in common that they privilege a notion of universal grammar. They have all been controversial in the details of their accounts, but the greatest controversy has concerned the relationship between linguistic and other phenomena. This problem has been addressed by analysts who question the basis of the enterprise itself, arguing for a radically different view of language as social practice (cf. notably, Meeuwis and Blommaert 1994), but that view will be treated in greater detail in the following section of this paper. For the moment, I want to focus on a different critique, one which remains focused on linguistic performance, but worries about the relations between utterance-level grammar and other forms of linguistic structure.

Here, the central critique has been formulated by Peter Auer (1984, 1998), who argues that much codeswitching data can best be accounted for by understanding it as embedded in interaction. The argument is that the nature of codeswitching is linked to (possibly also universal) dimensions of the regulation of conversation, the nature of which is best captured by some form of ethnomethodologically inspired conversation analysis. This theoretical move is much more than an extension of linguistic theories to the level of discourse or conversation, however. What it does is to posit a radical rethinking of the grounds of linguistic theory, by placing language as performance at the center of how we think about language generally. In a collection of articles on this theme edited by Auer (1998), Alvarez-Cáccamo pushes this line of thought to its logical outcome; he argues that if we think of language as practice, and put the speakers, not the system, at the center of our analysis, we have then to wonder why we need a concept of autonomous linguistic system at all. Instead, Alvarez-Cáccamo suggests, what if we replaced the idea of code with the idea of linguistic resources which are socially distributed, organized certainly by speakers individually and collectively, but which do not necessarily ever have to correspond to some closed and wholly describable system? What if language were part of a set of practices which had varying manifestations (both for individuals and sets or networks of people), but which could not be firmly distinguished from other kinds of behavior? What if grammar were the order speakers impose, more or less successfully, on their linguistic resources?

From the perspective of linguistic analysis, then, we are left with a set of questions which are foundational; bilingualism has brought us to question the nature of the concept of language itself. As we will see in the next section, approaches to bilingualism which have taken a more socially or culturally informed angle have led to much the same set of questions.

Bilingualism, culture and society

Descriptive typologies and structural–functionalism in the development of studies of bilingualism in culture and society

From an ethnolinguistic perspective, earlier ideas about the boundedness of cultures were accompanied by ideas about the boundedness of the languages that were supposed to go with them. Bilingualism was an obvious affront to this idea, and one that was going to require explanation. Initial explanations, as per the dominant explanatory frameworks of the time, were primarily structural–functional.

The most influential approaches came on the one hand from Weinreich (1953), Mackey (1968), Ferguson (1964), and Fishman (1968); and on the other from Gumperz (1964, 1971, 1982) (the work of the latter will be discussed in greater detail in the section below). The first set of authors approached bilingualism from the perspective of an analysis of the ways in which different languages, or language varieties, might correspond to different social functions. Weinreich was among the first to examine bilingualism in terms of a related set of forms and functions, in an attempt to describe the different linguistic manifestations of bilingualism as they might relate to different structural and functional distributions of linguistic varieties in a community. Mackey's work on typologies of bilingualism followed in this vein. Both were concerned with what might be termed a "languages in contact" approach, in which the focus remained on relations between or among linguistic systems, albeit in connection with their social distribution.

Ferguson's concept of *diglossia* famously pointed to the ways in which even different varieties of one language could be assigned different functions within a hierarchy of prestige and status, with the "high" language conventionally involving more institutionalized functions connected to the distribution and definition of valued resources, and the "low" language connected to everyday life and relations of solidarity among marginalized segments of the population. The concept seemed applicable to situations where the linguistic varieties in question were conventionally thought of as different languages altogether.

Fishman extended this concept to broader ways of conceptualizing functional differentiation across *domains*, with an understanding that domains were primarily connected to social activities (often institutionalized: religion, work, education, the family, and so on) which might or might not be equally prestigious or otherwise connected to power and status differences. Fishman's work laid the foundations for much subsequent work concerned with the measurement, statistically or through other means, of the scope of functions associated with specific language varieties, understood as a reflection of the extent to which a language had a social basis for reproduction.

Put differently, a structural–functional approach is based on the notion that the normative condition is one language, understood as a whole, bounded system, and which corresponds to a community, also understood as a whole, bounded system (Heller 2002a). This monolingual norm, associated with ideologies of the nation, and eventually of the nation-State, has been the dominant one influencing studies of bilingualism. Many of these over the past forty years or so have been devoted to measuring deviation from the norm as an index of assimilation, or of language loss or endangerment, whether seen from a linguistic, demographic, sociological or social psychological perspective. Many of these have also been inscribed, explicitly or implicitly, in political movements for linguistic minority autonomy (and hence we tend to have the greatest number of these emerging in areas such as Canada, Belgium, Catalunya, or Corsica), or more recently in movements for the protection of minority languages within a concept of linguistic ecology, which defends linguistic diversity as an inherently positive thing (cf. Skutnabb-Kangas 2000; and, for a critique, Blommaert 2001).

There are more examples of such studies than I could possibly do justice to. For our purposes here, let me mention a few categories: (1) studies of the "linguistic vitality" of minority communities, designed to measure the extent to which the community is likely to be able to reproduce itself as a bounded community in which bilingualism is possible as long as it is kept in clear functional distribution with the minority language (cf. Landry and Allard 1996); (2) studies of assimilation based on census returns measuring shifts of numbers of minority language speakers over time (cf. Castonguay 1996); (3) survey-based studies of functional distribution of languages by domain in specific communities, where the lack of a "full" range is understood as a deficit to be repaired (in the parlance of Catalan sociolinguistics, the concept of a "full range" of domains is associated with *normalizació* or "normalization," that is, extending the range of uses of a minority language, in this case Catalan, to cover the full range of functions existing in Catalan society; Aracil 1982; and see Boix and Vila 1998 for a discussion of such work, especially as it applies to the Catalan case); and (4) studies of the linguistic manifestations of language contact as associated with structural analyses of the social conditions of that contact, as a means of discovering what kinds of social structures are linked to what effects on linguistic structure (cf. Poplack 1988; Mougeon and Beniak 1991).

Within this range of types of study, particular attention has been paid to the role of legal institutions in providing an infrastructure for the production or reproduction of specific visions of bilingualism and bilingual communities (cf. Woehrling 1996), and to the role of education in actually engaging in the process of production and reproduction of bilinguals (cf. Baker 2001; Heller and Martin-Jones 2001; de Mejía 2002). Some attention has been paid to language practices and socialization in bilingual families (Varro 1984; Heller and Lévy 1994; Deprez 1994), to bilingualism in the workplace (Heller 1989; Goldstein 1997) and to the link between bilingualism and income-earning (that is, to the value of bilingualism on the job market; Vaillancourt 1996; Grin 1999), but very little to institutions such as religion or health. (Note, however, that some of the studies mentioned above fall outside the scope of structural-functionalism, taking a critical ethnographic perspective on the arguments developed in that paradigm.)

The structural–functional paradigm has been extremely productive, allowing in particular the development of a discourse regarding the relative advantages or disadvantages of specific forms of bilingualism for specific groups. It has, however, remained resolutely committed to a paradigm in which languages are understood as whole, bounded systems, associated, moreover, with whole, bounded communities. This set of assumptions have been increasingly challenged, in part by the very studies they inspired: so often what is found is a set of bilingual practices or ambiguous affiliations which persist over time, contrary to efforts to stamp them out, which emerge where they have in principle no business emerging, or which seem simply not amenable to structural–functional analysis and explanation (for a general critique of structural–functionalism in the sociology of language, see Williams 1992). The constant emergence of traces of different languages in the speech of individual bilinguals goes against the expectation that languages will neatly correspond to separate domains, and stay put where they are meant to stay put. In the following section, I will examine first an interpretive approach to bilingualism anchored in a focus on bilingual practice in social interaction, the role of bilingualism in the construction of cultural meaning, and their ties and challenges to a structural-functional approach, and then outline some of the ways in which both structural-functional and interpretive approaches are giving way currently to critical analyses concerned with ideologies of bilingualism, and their involvement in the production and reproduction of relations of social difference and social inequality.

Bilingualism in social interaction

Unlike structural–functional approaches which were concerned with large-scale social patterns, interactionists have been concerned with the manifestations of bilingualism in social interaction. Now, some of this work has been functionalist in inspiration, insofar as it gave rise to a long series of studies aimed at typologies of functions of bilingual practices, notably of codeswitching, in interaction (cf. Gumperz 1982; Zentella 1981; McClure 1981; Auer 1984). Blom and Gumperz (1972) formulated an initial, influential, distinction, between *situational* and *metaphorical codeswitching*, which attempted to capture not only the ways that domain analysis could account for distribution of languages, but also the messy ways in which bilinguals imported linguistic resources across domain boundaries. The assumption was that domain-based distribution was central to the attribution of meaning to linguistic varieties, and that conventional situational or domain distribution could then serve as a meaning-making resource for bilingual speakers across domains. Cultural meaning, in terms of the substantive understanding of identities and social relations (what it means to belong to specific groups, to engage in specific language practices), is understood to flow from political economic relations.

While in the long run the distinction between situational and metaphorical codeswitching proved to be inadequate as a full account, it did introduce into the debate some essential ideas, notably those concerned with looking at bilingual speakers as social actors engaged in the practice of making meaning, and those concerned with conversation, or discourse, itself, as a site for meaning-making. What the distinction failed to account for were forms of codeswitching whose meaning could not be said to be metaphorical in the strict sense, that is, they did not refer in any way to any substantive meaning which might be linked to activities or domains with which they were putatively conventionally associated. Instead, they tended to cluster around the management of the conversation or the contextualization of content, that is, in Auer's (1984) terms, to be *participant-oriented*, or oriented towards management of the unfolding of talk, that is, of the participation of conversational partners, or *discourse-oriented*, that is, oriented towards the framing of what was being said. In many ways, the contrast between linguistic resources understood as belonging to distinct codes itself served as the relevant resource, a long way away from any direct relationship between a language and a domain (or, even less, a community of speakers).

Interactionist approaches to bilingualism began, then, to explore more directly the ways in which bilingual resources could be involved in the construction of social meaning, both in terms of the construction of social categories (primarily those connected to ethnolinguistic identity, but also those connected to local social roles, such as speaker and addressee), and in terms of the contextualization of talk (see for example papers in Heller 1988). Bilingual resources in interaction or performance (see, for example, an emerging body of work on multilingual rap and rai in France; cf. Billiez 1998) are particularly rich sources for the exploration of voicing and footing, that is, ways in which speakers signal stances and perspectives on their own utterances as well as on those of others, and are available as windows onto interactional processes of learning (especially, of course, learning language). Beyond such general sociolinguistic concerns, though, such phenomena illustrate the permeability of boundaries, whether between languages or sociolinguistic domains. They also point to the impossibility of direct associations between language and identity, and rather to the complex, often ambiguous and multiple nature of all these concepts. They also raise the question of the creative use of linguistic resources for aesthetic purposes, or more broadly in the construction of cultural meanings which may lie far afield from the political economic bases of the distribution of linguistic resources (Rampton 2002).

The question then arises of what link there might be, if any, between structural aspects of distribution of linguistic resources and the uses speakers make of them in interaction, whether in terms of the organization of interaction or in terms of cultural meaning of categories and of practices, or more simply of the making of meaning in the broadest sense. Structural accounts have to take into consideration the messiness of actual usage, and interactional accounts, in order to arrive at useful explanations, have to take into consideration the situation of speakers in space and time. The following section addresses some of the ways those links have been attempted.

Critical approaches to the study of bilingualism and society: community, identity, language

Recent approaches have attempted to make linkages by appealing to four sets of concepts. The first set has to do with calling into question the nature of some of the foundational concepts in ethnolinguistics, namely community, identity, and language; rather than treating these concepts as natural, and bounded, phenomena, it has become more common to see them as heuristic devices which capture some elements of how we organize ourselves, but which have to be understood as social constructs (in the definition of which ethnolinguists participate as much as anyone else; cf. Gal 1995; Blommaert 1999; Heller 2002b). Since we are discussing social constructs (that is, since that is the ontological position we take regarding the nature of the phenomenon under investigation), it becomes possible to investigate some of the fuzziness and complexity that persistently emerge in data. Social constructs by definition have to get constructed, and processes of construction can be long and complicated. People do not necessarily agree on what to construct or how to construct it, and even if they do, it can take time to find the way there. In many areas long associated with linguistic minority movements, for example, it is increasingly difficult to find consensus on who counts as a Catalan, or a francophone, and people are increasingly loath to identify primarily with one superordinate category (say, an ethnolinguistic one) over others equally relevant to their lives (say, gender), if they are willing to participate in the game of categorization at all.

In addition (this is the second set), such a perspective requires asking questions about who is doing what, and with what resources. This entails looking at language as a set of resources which are socially distributed, but not necessarily evenly, and so speakers have to act within certain kinds of structural constraints (cf. Giddens 1984). For example, working-class speakers far from the sites of definition of what counts as "good" language, or prestigious performance, are placed at a disadvantage in situations where their linguistic performance is judged by members of classes other than their own; they have to do what they can with what they have, given the structural relations of inequality in which they find themselves (and this of course can include resistance as well as collaboration).

The third set of concepts further investigates these questions, this time by seeking to explain why people do what they do, not just in terms of what kinds of resources they can muster, but also in terms of what they do with what they can gain access to, and why they act in certain ways with them. If the uneven distribution is understood as not random, but rather the product of a history of political economic processes, then the question of the relationship between power, social organization and ecology comes to the fore (cf. Barth 1969). Further, as Gumperz (1982) pointed out, linguistic resources are understood as conventionally having certain value and as connected to certain frames of interpretation; however, it is always someone's notion of what counts, and someone's ability to control access both to resources and to the definition of their value, which ultimately make a difference to people's lives. Processes of social selection are centered around interactions and performances which are evaluated, not as indices of mastery of conventions, but as indices of other kinds of competence (intelligence, work skills, personality, and so on). So the question here is, what resources are assigned what value, by whom, how, why and with what consequences? How are these issues manifested in education, in legal institutions, in the field of health care, in the reproduction of State structures? How do speakers draw on their linguistic resources in the situations they find themselves in, to accomplish what, or with what perverse or unintended consequences?

The final set of concepts involves the ways in which people make sense of their engagement in these processes. Generally understood as a matter of *language ideology* (cf. Schieffelin *et al.* 1998; Blommaert 1999; Kroskrity 2000), this area of enquiry investigates the discourses in which processes of attribution of value to linguistic forms and practices are inscribed, along with the processes of construction of social difference and social inequality with which they are associated. Our ideas about language(s) are, in other words, not neutral; we believe what we believe for reasons which have to do with the many other ways in which we make sense of our world, and make our way in it. Why are so many governments in North America and Europe now concerned with "literacy"? Why does it matter whether or not there is a policy regarding official languages, or languages of education? Why do languages get taught the way they do?

All these concepts provide a means for reorienting studies of language, community and identity, and hence of bilingualism, away from autonomous structure and towards process and practice. What emerges now is a sense of bilingualism as only one perspective on a more complex set of practices which draw on linguistic resources which have been conventionally thought of as belonging to separate linguistic systems, because of our own dominant ideologies of language, but which may more fruitfully be understood as sets of resources called into play by social actors, under social and historical conditions which both constrain and make possible the social reproduction of existing conventions and relations, as well as the production of new ones.

8

THE IMPACT OF LANGUAGE SOCIALIZATION ON GRAMMATICAL DEVELOPMENT

ELINOR OCHS AND BAMBI SCHIEFFELIN

An offer[1]

The architecture of grammatical development in the talk of young children is the central concern of language acquisition research. The critical task of language acquisition scholarship over the last several decades has been to account for when, how, and why children use and understand grammatical forms over the course of the early period of their lives. Language socialization – the process in which children are socialized both through language and to use language within a community (Ochs and Schieffelin 1984; Schieffelin and Ochs 1986a, b) – has been largely examined without regard to the dynamics of grammatical development, focusing, rather, on culturally relevant communicative practices and activities.[2] In this discussion, we reverse this orientation and focus directly on the role of language socialization in the acquisition of grammatical competence.

What can a language socialization perspective offer to scholarship on grammatical development? A language socialization perspective yields a more sophisticated model of grammatical development, that is, one tuned into certain cultural realities that influence when, how, and why young children use and understand grammatical forms. Such a model of grammatical development takes an informed look at ideology and social order as forces that organize children's use and comprehension of grammatical forms. A language socialization enriched model decries reductionistic visions that view the sociocultural context as "input" to be quantified and correlated with children's grammatical patterns. Rather than reducing the context of grammatical development to frequencies of grammatical forms in the child's linguistic environment, our socialization enriched model accounts for children's grammatical development in terms of the indexical meanings of grammatical forms. This approach rests on the assumption that, in every community, grammatical forms are inextricably tied to, and hence index, culturally organized situations of use and that the

[1] Our thanks to Lois Bloom, Patrick Gonzalez and Brian MacWhinney for comments on an earlier draft of this chapter. An earlier version of this paper was published under the title "The Impact of Language Socialization on Grammatical Development," in P. Fletcher and B. MacWhinney (eds.), *The Handbook of Child Language*. Oxford: Blackwell, 1995, 73–94.

[2] For reviews of recent trends in language socialization research see Garrett and Baquedano-Lopez (2002) and Kulick and Schieffelin (2004).

indexical meanings of grammatical forms influence children's production and understanding of these forms.[3] In this approach, the frequency with which a grammatical form is used in the child's environment may or may not have very much to do with a child's handling of grammatical forms. As we will discuss later, a grammatical construction may be ubiquitous in the child's hearing environment and yet the child may not use the construction until quite late in his or her development. And conversely, a form may be used relatively rarely by adults and others in the child's surroundings and yet be ubiquitous in the child's speech.

In a language socialization enriched model of grammatical development, children are viewed as tuned into certain indexical meanings of grammatical forms that link those forms to, for example, social identities of interlocutors; they may not use a form they frequently hear because it is indexically inappropriate for them to do so, and they may use a form they don't often hear because it is indexically appropriate for them to do so. Children's nonuse of grammatical forms may be a reflection of their indexical sensitivities (Ochs 1988; Peirce 1931–58; Silverstein 1993) and not a reflection of their lack of grammatical competence or awareness. Counting and correlations can't differentiate between nonuse that is socially and culturally competent and nonuse that is incompetent. Only an informed understanding of the indexical scope of grammatical forms can provide this information.

What makes a language socialization approach different from existing functionalist approaches to grammatical development? Functionalist approaches to grammatical development tend to end their enquiry at the level of the immediate informational or actional context of grammatical forms, relating children's use and understanding of grammatical forms to, for example, foregrounding and backgrounding of information on the one hand, and/or to speech acts on the other. A language socialization approach relates children's use and understanding of grammatical forms to complex yet orderly and recurrent dispositions, preferences, beliefs, and bodies of knowledge that organize how information is linguistically packaged and how speech acts are performed within and across socially recognized situations.

A language socialization approach promotes an updated version of linguistic relativity and asserts that children's use and understanding of grammatical forms is culturally reflexive – tied in manifold ways to local views of how to think, feel, know, (inter)act, or otherwise project a social persona or construct a relationship. At the same time, a language socialization approach promotes the notion that certain relations between grammatical forms and sociocultural order have universal scope (Ochs 1990, 1993). Language socialization involves children in language and cultural competencies that span the boundaries of

---

[3] Research on children's understanding of word meanings in terms of event structures (Nelson 1986; Sell 1992) indicates that early in their lives, young children develop conceptual structures that link language systematically to situational contexts.

local communities. That is, children are being socialized the world over to draw on similar grammatical resources to index thoughts, feelings, knowledge, identities, acts, and activities not only because of biological and cognitive patterning but also because of universal characteristics of culture as a common artifact of humankind.

In the remainder of this discussion, we articulate ways in which a language socialization approach can enrich existing accounts of the phenomena of child language acquisition. Although this approach is orthogonal to the controversies surrounding learnability and innateness mechanisms underlying grammatical competence (in the sense that it does not take sides), it is highly relevant to all theories relating grammatical development to mind, brain, and experience. Our discussion opens the discourse of grammatical development to a domain of orderliness that exists beyond the person, indeed, that exists between persons who interact on a regular basis and who belong to a community with a history and a future.

The language socialization approach advocated in this chapter integrates universal and local properties of language-in-culture. In particular, it provides *a culturally organized means–ends model* of grammatical development. Informally, this model provides for the possibility that across many cultures, members rely on certain similar linguistic means to accomplish certain similar social ends, such as the use of quantifiers to index affective intensity (e.g. "He spilled it all over the place," Labov 1984; Ochs and Schieffelin 1989). However, at the same time these ends are culturally organized in terms of their situational scope – who appropriately attempts to accomplish this end, when, where, how often, etc. – and their significance *vis-à-vis* local ideologies about emotion, person, language, and the like. Communities thus are both alike and different in the ways in which they rely on grammatical resources, and as such, children's understandings of grammatical forms are accordingly both alike and different as one traverses the boundaries of language communities. Similar linguistic realizations of social goals across communities enable communication within our species; different cultural organizations of social goals, however, throw a monkey wrench into cross-cultural exchanges and make the task of acquiring second languages in different communities all the more difficult.[4]

This culturally organized means–ends perspective will be applied to three questions relevant to accounting for grammatical development in early childhood:

1. Does grammatical development depend upon children's participation in a simplified speech environment?
2. Can cultural systems of belief, knowledge, and social order partially account for young children's acquisition of particular grammatical constructions?

---

[4] The work of John Gumperz (1982a, 1982b) and his collaborators investigating interethnic communication, or "cross-talk," amply demonstrates many of these difficulties.

3. Can cultural systems of belief, knowledge, and social order partially account for young children's acquisition (and nonacquisition) of particular languages in linguistically heterogeneous communities?

We turn now to address each of these questions.

The cultural milieu of language acquirers

A critical question addressed in acquisition research is whether or not children's grammatical competence is an outcome of children's participation in simplified communicative exchanges designed to facilitate language use and comprehension. Our response to this question is a qualified "no." This conclusion is based on the observation that all normal children acquire a measured degree of competence in producing and understanding grammatical constructions in the early years of their lives, yet the ways in which cultures organize communicative exchanges with children varies widely from community to community (see, for example, Brown 1998, 2002; Clancy 1985, 1986, 1999; Cook 1996; Crago 1988; de León 1998; Heath 1982; Miller 1982; Ochs 1985, 1988; Ochs and Schieffelin 1984; Philips 1983; Schieffelin and Ochs 1986a, 1986b; Schieffelin 1985, 1990; Scollon 1982; Sperry and Sperry 2000). To explore this phenomenon in a culturally illuminative fashion, we focus on how cultures organize communication directed to children (children as addressees) and by children (children as speakers).

Cultural organizations of talk to children (addressees)

In all societies, members want to get their intentions across to children. This is a universal propensity of human culture, a prerequisite for the transmission of cultural orientations from one generation to the next. Furthermore, when members set the goal of getting their intentions across to children, they tend to modify their language in similar ways across the world's communities. Adults, older siblings, and others wanting to communicate to infants and small children in many cultures tend to simplify the form and content of their talk to achieve that end. Common simplifications characteristic of speech addressed to children include consonant cluster reduction, reduplication, exaggerated prosodic contours, slowed pace, shorter sentences, syntactically less complex sentences, temporal and spatial orientation to the here-and-now, and repetition and paraphrasing of sentences (Ferguson 1964, 1977, 1982).

If we are promoting the notion that communicating intentions to children as addressees is a universal end and that simplification is a widespread if not universal means to achieve that end, how do we justify the conclusion that grammatical development does not depend on children's exposure to simplified speech? A culturally organized means–ends approach to the question of simplified speech urges us to examine further the goal of communicating intentions to children and the kinds of simplifications made once this goal is set in motion within particular communities. Ethnographic observations suggest that cultures differ widely in the contextual pervasiveness of setting this goal and in the extensiveness of simplification processes when speakers do set this goal, and that these differences are integrally linked to cultural views of children, social order, and the path to grammatical competence.

How, then, is the goal of communicating intentions to children realized across different communities? While in all communities, children participate as addressees in interactions with others, the developmental point at which they take on this role varies from community to community. In some communities, such as white middle-class communities in the United States and Canada, children are given this role starting at birth, when mothers begin to greet and otherwise attempt to converse with their infants (Bates, Camaioni and Volterra 1979; Bloom, K. 1990; Ochs and Schieffelin 1984; Stern 1977). Once the goal of communicating intentions to small infants is put into effect, speakers have quite a job on their hands if they hope to be understood and responded to (see Brown 1977). Indeed, in the case of communicating intentions to newly born infants, caregivers may not only go to great lengths to gain and sustain their attention (e.g. via high pitch, exaggerated intonation), they also may have to voice or do the child's response themselves (Lock 1981; Stern 1977; Trevarthen 1979). In other communities, members do not generally set the goal of communicating intentions to children (i.e. wanting children to understand and respond) at quite such an early point in their lives. In a number of societies, infants are not engaged as addressees until they evidence that they can produce recognizable words in the language. For example, among the K'iche' Mayan, "vocal interaction between infants and parents is minimal, although there is some variation between parents in this regard, particularly among different economic classes [. . .] K'iche' parents treat their toddlers as conversational partners after they learn to speak" (Pye 1992: 242–243). Similarly, African-American working-class families in the town of "Trackton" in the Piedmont South Carolina region of the United States "do not see babies or young children as suitable partners for regular conversations. For an adult to choose a preverbal infant over an adult as a conversational partner would be considered an affront and a strange behavior as well" (Heath 1983: 86). In rural and urban Javanese communities, adults also address babies infrequently. Smith-Hefner (1988: 172–173) notes:

Javanese children are clearly the objects of great pride and affection, and yet what is striking to the western observer is that Javanese do not talk to babies very much. In response to my initial questions concerning talking to babies, Javanese caregivers frequently commented that little babies (and even young children for that matter) *durung ngerti* or "do not yet understand" [. . .] the most common way of holding young babies is on the hip with the child naturally facing outwards or half hidden under the mother's arm. We never recorded in all of our observations a mother holding her young baby in the face-to-face position facilitating dialogue.

These descriptions are also paralleled in accounts of talking to infants in traditional Western Samoan communities (Ochs and Schieffelin 1984; Ochs 1982, 1988) and among the Kaluli of Papua New Guinea (Ochs and Schieffelin 1984; Schieffelin 1990).

In societies such as these, infants are not singled out as preferred addressees. Rather, they tend to participate in communicative interactions in the role of overhearers of nonsimplified conversations between others. This assumes that small children are being socialized in the context of multiparty interactions, the unmarked condition in traditional and many other societies. In many upper-middle-class households of the United States and Europe, however, small children may pass the day primarily in the presence of a single adult (e.g. mother) and thus may not have the situational opportunity to take on the role of over-hearers of nonsimplified conversations. Indeed, the communicative ecology of upper-middle-class households may be an important factor in organizing young children in the role of addressees. The sole adult in the household is not likely to talk to herself/himself all day long and thus may be situationally predisposed to attempt to recruit a child of whatever age as a communicative partner in meaningful, albeit highly simplified, exchanges.

In those communities where infants and small children are generally not recruited as conversational partners, they still become grammatically competent speakers–hearers, developing linguistic knowledge in a communicative environment full of grammatical complexity and oriented towards competent interlocutors. Some communities have an explicit ideology of language acquisition centered on precisely the idea that children need to hear linguistically complex and not simplified speech to become grammatically competent. Kaluli adults were surprised that American parents produced baby talk in the presence of young children and wondered how the children learned to speak proper language (Schieffelin 1990).

In addition to differences in goal setting, cultures also differ in the extent to which they simplify when they do address children. In some communities, such as among the Tamil (Williamson, 1979), Inuit (Crago 1988), and working and middle-class Americans and Europeans (Cross 1977; Newport, Gleitman and Gleitman 1977), simplification involves phonological, morphosyntactic, and discourse modifications. In other communities, such as among Samoans (Ochs 1988), working-class African-Americans of Trackton (Heath 1983) and Louisiana (Ward 1971), Javanese (Smith-Hefner 1988) and Kaluli (Schieffelin 1990), simplification may be primarily restricted to the domain of discourse, and in particular, to self-repetition of an earlier utterance. An important difference between simplification through repetition and simplification through phonological and grammatical adjustments is that the former tends to preserve the integrity of the adult form of the utterance whereas the latter does not. To understand this difference, think of setting the goal of getting a young child to participate in a traditional dance. One way of getting the child to understand what she or he is supposed to do is to let the child see repeated uninterrupted performances of the dance. In this way, the integrity of the dance is preserved, and the simplification primarily consists of showing it over and over again. Another way of achieving competence is to break down the dance into components and to repeatedly present one component at a time until the child evidences that she or he understands the steps. This simplification strategy deforms the conventional shape and execution of the dance in an effort to guide children's participation in the dance (Rogoff 1990).[5]

An interesting possibility is that cultures that simplify at all levels of linguistic structure in talking to children may put children in the role of conversational partners, i.e. as addressees expected to actively and centrally participate in communicative exchanges, more often than in cultures that simplify primarily through repetition. A similar point was made by Brown (1977: 12) when he argued that baby talk is not used by caregivers to teach their children how to speak but rather to communicate with them: "What I think adults are chiefly trying to do, when they use BT with children, is to communicate, to understand and to be understood, to keep two minds focused on the same topic." Brown's conclusion was influenced by the research of Cross (1977: 166–167), which captures the effects of 62 parameters of mothers' speech on children's language in the comment

Few researchers in the area of mothers' speech would argue that the provision of language lessons to the language-learning child is the primary motivation for mothers' speech adjustments. Rather, they appear to be the incidental outcome of trying to converse with a listener capable of expressing and receiving meaning in verbal form, but with very undeveloped linguistic skills.

A corollary of the possibility that cultures with a highly simplified baby talk register may treat children as conversational partners relatively often is that cultures that rely on such widespread simplification may expect children to be active and central participants in conversational exchanges at an earlier age than children growing up in cultures where simplification is primarily through repetition. More empirical evidence is needed to substantiate these possibilities; however, in cultures where speakers addressing children simplify infrequently and primarily through repetition, there appears to be little interest in engaging young infants in extended conversational exchanges. For example, Heath (1983) and Ward (1971) describe working-class African-American adult family members in rural South Carolina and Louisiana not only as dispreferring infants as conversational partners but also as hardly simplifying their speech

---

[5] We are not suggesting that these are the only strategies for simplifying the dance to novices. As the work of Lave and Wenger (1991) and Rogoff (1990) suggest, the child could, for example, be assigned a limited role in the dance and not have to master the entire routine. In language, this might correspond to expecting the child to understand and respond to/display only a portion of a message.

to young children. And the same is true for traditional Samoan (Ochs 1988); Kaluli (Schieffelin 1990); and Javanese (Smith-Hefner 1988) family members. From the perspective of the working-class African-American, Samoans, Kaluli, and Javanese communities studied, members of cultures that rely on widespread simplification are more eager (or perhaps even anxious) for children early in their lives to take on central communicative roles. In these African-American communities and among the Samoans, Javanese, and Kaluli, however, there seems to be less pressure for very young children to assume an active, central role in the social exchanges at hand, but rather a preference for children at this early stage to stay on the sidelines – on the backs of caregivers, or nestled on their laps or hips or alongside – as observers and overhearers.[6]

In summary, if we look across cultures, children who are expected to be active communicators early in life are often likely to be addressed with highly simplified speech and put in the position of conversational partner. On the other hand, children who are expected to participate actively in communicative exchanges somewhat later in their childhood hear predominantly unsimplified speech and are treated as conversational partners less frequently. The upshot of this discussion, however, is that while these children are socialized into different expectations concerning their social role *vis-à-vis* other participants in a social situation and perhaps as well into different cognitive skills (e.g. the role of overhearer may enhance observational skills), *the outcome in terms of the ultimate acquisition of grammatical competence is not substantially different across these two cultural strategies.* In both cases, most children growing up in these cultures are producing and understanding grammatical constructions before their second birthday. In Western Samoa, for example, a child of nineteen months was not only producing multimorphemic utterances but using with some skill two phonological registers (Ochs 1985). Kaluli children between twenty and twenty-four months use imperative and declarative verb forms, first and second-person pronouns, locatives, possessives, several forms of negation, and discourse particles (Schieffelin 1985).

Cultural organizations of talk by children (speakers)

An important focus in the controversy over effects of the communicative environment on language acquisition is the extent to which grammatical competence is facilitated by the practice of caregivers verbally reformulating a child's intended message in grammatically correct adult form. This practice is known as expansion (Brown *et al.* 1968). Typically expansions are caregivers' responses to a young child's relatively ambiguous message and function as

---

[6] Rogoff (1990) presents the interesting hypothesis that children and caregivers who are in body contact with one another for most of the day have the opportunity to communicate nonvocally through body movements. Infants can signal discomfort and caregivers can manipulate the infant entirely through somatic means.

requests for confirmation or repair initiations (Schegloff, Jefferson, and Sacks 1977). The facilitating effect of expansions is posited on the assumption that children will match an intention that is currently in their consciousness with the adult formulation of the intended message (Brown *et al.* 1968; McNeill 1970).

The effects of expansions on the acquisition of particular grammatical constructions have been widely discussed in the psycholinguistic literature, and the results are at best mixed (see, for example, Cazden 1965; Cross 1977; Newport *et al.* 1977; Shatz 1983). Our focus here is on the cultural organization and import of expansions, a discussion that situates expansions in cultural ideologies and systems of social order which organize how members of societies respond to ambiguous or partially unintelligible utterances of interlocutors, whether adult or child. Within a culturally organized means–ends approach, we explore the extent to which the goal of trying to formulate the ambiguous intentions of others is culturally viable. We also explore how cultures organize children of different ages as speakers, particularly as authors of utterances.

Infants and small children universally produce utterances whose sense is not transparent to those present, and universally those copresent respond using one or more of the following strategies: (1) ignore the utterance; (2) indicate to the child that the utterance is unclear (e.g. by claiming nonunderstanding, by directing the child to repeat the utterance, by teasing the child for being unclear); (3) present to the child a candidate understanding or reformulation of the utterance (i.e. make a guess). However, while children's unintelligibility and responses to it are universal, the preference for strategy (1), (2), or (3) varies across communities for reasons of ideology and social order. Specifically, communities organize the goal of decoding the intentions of children in different ways. In some communities, members are keen to disambiguate aloud what infants and young children might be intending across a wide range of situations, and in other communities the situations in which members take on this goal are highly restricted.

To pursue the cultural organization of decoding the intentions of children it is necessary to unpack some of the assumptions of this end. One assumption that underlies this end is that children are indeed acting intentionally, the children are the authors of their utterances. One variable of cross-cultural import is the developmental point at which children are treated as intentional beings who not only vocalize and gesture but do so to make a communicative point. Another way of considering this aspect of cross-cultural variation is to see cultures as varying in their view of children as authors of messages. In some communities, children are treated as if their gestures and vocalizations are meaningful and communicative from a very early point in their infancy (see especially Trevarthen's [1979] analysis of middle-class British caregivers interpreting small infants in this manner). Caregivers in these communities will respond to the actions of tiny infants as if they were intentionally directed towards them, and in this way establish the child as an interlocutor (Lock 1981). In middle-class American and European communities, this practice of treating the infant as an author is the counterpart to treating the infant as addressee in that both roles combined constitute the infant as conversational partner.

Many of us may take for granted that caregivers and infants interact in this manner and may find it surprising that in many communities infants are not considered as authors. Their gestures and vocalizations are not considered by others as intentional communicative acts. For example, among the Warlpiri, before the age of two, "'talk' by the child is not interpreted as language, and there are no expansions and recasts of the child's early words" (Bavin 1992: 327). Similarly, among the Inuit, caregivers rarely responded to the vocal and nonvocal actions of very young children. Crago (1988: 210–211) describes Inuit interactions with two children under the age of two years:

Suusi and Jini were the youngest of the four children at the outset of the videotaping. In several of the tapes that were made of them, they frequently made unintelligible vocalizations. The majority of these vocalizations went unheeded. Many times their parents did not respond, not even by looking up at the children. [. . .] Clarification of unintelligible vocalizations did not take place on any of the videotapes. Intentions, then, were not imputed to these early unintelligible utterances nor did they elicit a communicative response from the caregivers in most instances.

Even if, within a community, an infant's or young child's vocalizations are constructed as intentional by a copresent adult or older sibling, there may still be a strong dispreference for attempting to clarify intentions through candidate expansions of the child's intended message. In both Kaluli (Schieffelin 1990) and Western Samoan communities (Ochs 1988), for example, caregivers rarely clarify children's utterances because there is a strong dispreference generally towards guessing at the unarticulated psychological states of others. Kaluli say that one cannot know what is in another's head. Samoans not only rarely expand an unclear utterance of a child, they also rarely conjecture about possible motivations for an action undertaken, or disambiguate riddles, or try to figure out test questions, where there is some notion in the mind of another that has to be discovered (Ochs 1982).

In traditional Western Samoan communities, issues of social order also impact the dispreference for expanding children's ambiguous vocalizations and gestures. In particular, if we compare the three alternative responses to a child's unclear action – ignore, indicate unclarity, and provide candidate understanding of child's intended meaning (expansion/guess) – the responses differ in the extent to which they require an interlocutor to take the perspective of the child. Ignoring requires almost no perspective-taking whatsoever, and the various means of indicating unclarity (e.g. by requesting a repetition, teasing) also demand little decentering by others. Preferring a candidate understanding of the child's message through an expansion, on the other hand, involves other interlocutors in searching for clues as to what the child could be intending – looking at what the child is doing, where the child is gazing, what the child was just doing or saying, and other situational leads to arriving at intentionality. The extensiveness of this cognitive accommodation runs counter to Samoan notions of the caregiver-child relationship, which is grounded in social asymmetry. As in other societies, sibling and adult caregivers in traditional Samoan communities expect and socialize the children in their charge to accommodate to them. Both siblings and adult family members are keen to socialize children at a very early age to decenter and take the perspective of more mature interlocutors in their presence. For these reasons and others, Samoan caregivers tend to respond to children's unclear messages in ways that force children to make a greater effort to meet the communicative needs of those around them. They are far more likely to ignore or say "What?" or tease than to attempt to formulate what the child could be intending and offer it up to the child to confirm or disconfirm.

Finally, in some communities, members allow for the possibility that children are speaking intentionally but rather than trying to establish what these intentions might be, members assign a socially normative meaning to the child's utterance. As noted earlier, a psycholinguistic argument is that expansions facilitate language acquisition because they build on a child's personal intentions, matching the child's meaning to adult message form. In contrast, there is evidence that, in certain communities, children's personal intentions sometimes take second place to the members' notions of what is socially appropriate to a situation at hand. For example, Scollon (1982) reports that Athapaskan adults provide a cultural "gloss" for the child's unclear utterance, that is, a socially appropriate rendering that is situationally sensitive, disregarding what the child might be intending to express.

The use of cultural glosses is far more widespread than might be assumed, in that adults may impose a cultural gloss on children's gestures and utterances without recognizing that they are doing so. First words, for example, may reflect and construct cultural expectations concerning what children want to communicate. In many communities, first words are highly conventionalized. For example, among the Kaluli, the words for "mother" and "breast" are recognized as everyone's first words. In traditional Samoan communities, the child's first word is part of the curse "Eat shit!" Among the Gapun people of Papua New Guinea,

a child's very first word is generally held to be *ki* (go+IRREAL STATUS). This is a Taiap vernacular word meaning, approximately, "I'm getting out of here". Attributed to infants as young as two months, this word encapsulates the adult belief that babies will "do what they want" [. . .] and go where they will regardless of the wishes of others.
(Kulick 1992: 101–102)

It can also be argued that although caregivers in white middle class American, European, and Japanese households are acting on the belief that their expansions capture the intended meaning of the child's utterance, their expansions may similarly reflect their cultural understandings of what children want. Clancy (1986, 1997, 1999) and Cook (1988, 1996), for example, argue that middle-class Japanese mothers often reformulate children's utterances to be culturally acceptable.

These practices from diverse communities suggest that a primary goal of members is to socialize infants into culturally appropriate persons and this goal may override any goal relating to drawing out and validating the child as an author of a unique personal message. In these situations, other members actively participate in the authorship of messages. Other-authorship of children's utterances is also manifest in prompting practices, wherein members author a culturally appropriate message for the child to repeat back to the author (dyadic interaction) or to a third party (triadic interactions). Extended prompting of this sort is practiced in a wide range of societies, including Kaluli (Schieffelin 1990); Samoan (Ochs 1988); Mexican-American (Eisenberg 1986); white working-class American (Miller, 1982); Basotho (Demuth 1986); Javanese (Smith-Hefner 1988); and Kwara'ae (Watson-Gegeo and Gegeo 1986). A more extreme version of cultural prevoicing is found in the practice of ventriloquating for preverbal infants, wherein a member speaks as if the infant were speaking and others respond as if this were the case. Kaluli caregivers, for example, hold small infants facing a third party addressee and speak to that addressee in a high pitch nasalized register (without grammatically simplifying utterances). Here the infant is presented as a speaker without being presented as an author.

The many practices that are alternatives to expansions of personalized messages – either ignoring the utterance, indicating unclarity, providing a cultural gloss, prompting, or ventriloquating – socialize the child to accommodate to the social situation at hand. In contrast, attempts to expand the child's intended meaning evidence an accommodation by others to the child. That is, expansions of the sort discussed by psycholinguists reflect a child centered style of socialization (characteristic of the communities of the psycholinguists), whereas the alternative practices reflect a situation centered style of socialization (Ochs and Schieffelin 1984; Schieffelin and Ochs 1986a). Similarly, pervasive use of grammatically simplified speech directed to children as addressees reflects a child centered orientation, whereas more restricted use of simplification reflects a situation centered orientation. Because children living in communities falling along the continuum of child and situation centered communicative practices acquire grammar, grammatical development per se cannot be accounted for in terms of any single set of speech practices involving children.

The cultural milieu of children's grammatical forms

While the achievement of grammatical competence in itself cannot be said to depend on any particular cultural circumstances, the acquisition of specific grammatical constructions can be profoundly impacted by the cultural organization of language. Children produce certain constructions and not others and come to an understanding of constructions in part because of their cultural significance. As noted earlier, grammatical constructions are intricately linked to norms, preferences, and expectations that organize how members are to act, think, and feel in social situations. Children's acquisition of grammatical constructions in this sense is partly the acquisition of language competence and partly the acquisition of cultural competence. Further, because grammatical constructions are systematically and profoundly associated with social order and cultural beliefs, values, and knowledge, they carry sociocultural meanings, which are acquired along with their formal features. In the following discussion, we consider three circumstances in which sociocultural organization impacts the production and comprehension of particular grammatical forms:

(1) Where a grammatical form is widely used in the child's verbal environment, but is not produced by the child in the early stages of language acquisition because it is socially inappropriate.

(2) Where a grammatical form is infrequently used in the child's verbal environment, but nonetheless becomes part of the child's earliest linguistic repertoire because it is socially appropriate.

(3) Where a grammatical form used to express specific stances and speech acts in the child's verbal environment is acquired early as part of the acquisition of those stances and speech acts.

Grammatical form as frequent but inappropriate for child use

While perceptual salience, frequency, and conceptual complexity of forms in the verbal environment of the child can affect when children acquire particular grammatical constructions, these variables need to be evaluated vis-à-vis the social and cultural matrix of each construction. It may well be the case, for example, that a form that is perceptually salient, highly frequent, and conceptually relatively simple may not appear in the child's linguistic repertoire until rather late. In these cases, children's nonproduction of a particular form may reflect their understanding of that form as a sociocultural resource for displaying social statuses, social relationships, stances, actions, and other situational dimensions, and in particular, reflect their understandings of that form as inappropriate for child use.

An example of a widely used, relatively simple grammatical form that is not produced by children early in their language development is the Samoan deictic verb *sau* "come." Among the set of deictic verbs in a language, "come" is considered to be conceptually less complex than verbs such as "give" and "bring" (Clark and Garnica 1974) and tends to be produced and understood by young children before these more complex forms. While Samoan children evidence understanding of the verb *sau*, "come," early in their development (by nineteen months), they tend to produce the deictic verb *'aumai* before they produce *sau*, and they produce *'aumai* far more frequently than *sau* (Platt 1986). What can account for this acquisition order? Why don't Samoan children produce a form that they routinely hear and appropriately respond to? In traditional Samoan communities, physical movement is associated with relatively lower status persons; higher status persons tend to position themselves and direct lower status persons to carry out actions that require movement. Young children, for example, are bombarded with imperative forms of *sau*. When these children begin to use language, they appear to be aware of the social indexicality of this verb. As they are usually the lowest status persons in the household, there are few opportunities to use the verb appropriately. When the children do use *sau*, they use it in the imperative form to direct the movements of lower ranking entities, such as animals and younger infant siblings. In some cases, the children will use the form at the prompting of an older person to call out to an older child to come to that still older person (e.g. Mother: *Vala'au Iuliaga e sau*, "Call Iuliana to come" [. . .] Child: *Ana sau*, "Iuliana come!"). In contrast, children are widely encouraged to beg for food and other items. The verb *'aumai*, "give/bring," is the conventional grammatical structure (imperative form) for carrying out the act of begging. This imperative form of the verb appeared prevalently in children's speech from nineteen months of age on (Platt 1986; Ochs 1988). Another example of a construction that is widely used by adults in the child's verbal environment and is relatively simple is the Kaluli imperative verb of saying, *a:la:ma*, "say (like that)." While pervasive in the verbal environment of all children, this construction is produced only by a subset of young, language acquiring Kaluli children (Schieffelin 1990). *A:la:ma* is used in prompting sequences in which an older child caregiver or adult tells the young language learning child what to say to a third party, followed by the imperative *a:la:ma*. As noted earlier, all Kaluli children actively participate in extensive prompting sequences. When we look at children's own use of *a:la:ma*, there is a marked gender difference: only young girls (two to four years) produce this form to direct even younger children to "say like that." When they do so, it is with the appropriate demeanor of an assertive voice, and an appropriate message form, followed by the imperative verb of saying. Furthermore, young girls will also engage their mothers in playful routines, getting them to respond (dyadically) to their requests to "say like that." Boys, who were also addressees and respondents repeatedly in such socializing interactions, never produced *a:la:ma*. They associated this form with the talk of women and older sisters, who were responsible for all of the caregiving. Indeed, fathers very rarely used *a:lama* with children. The absence of *a:la:ma* in boys' verbal repertoires in this sense is a reflection of their understanding of gender appropriate behavior, a form of social knowledge never made explicit. It should be noted that adult men do use *a:la:ma* in social activities in which young children are not participants. Hence, boys eventually come to use *a:la:ma* in these activity settings.

It should also be noted that young children's understandings of the relation between gender and *a:la:ma* is finely tuned, in the sense that it is only the imperative form of the verb "to say like that" that is gender associated. Other forms of this verb are used widely by both men and women in the verbal environment of the child, and both boys and girls use the verb in a variety of inflections and moods – for example, to report others' speech as well as their own. Children's understandings of gender and other social roles are clearly indexed in a language like Kaluli where each verb stem is morphologically differentiated for tense and mood and where specific morphological forms such as the imperative (*a:la:ma*) may carry social meanings, e.g. gender-marked language instruction. The point that we are trying to make is that children are sensitized to the social and cultural indexicality of particular morphosyntactic encodings of verbal forms. The social and cultural contexts of imperative forms seem especially salient as they are exploited in a variety of speech acts, such as requesting, begging, and prompting. This may be because these acts involve issues of desire, control, and most importantly, require some type of action uptake on the part of another member of the community. These action uptakes provide immediate and salient social and cultural validation or sanctioning of the child's and other's use of that form. This degree of fine-tuned sensitivity to how different forms of the same verb encode social information is also evident in Kaluli children's acquisition of the compound verb *o:mina*, "having chewed, give." Children hear this verb often and in a variety of inflected forms, such as first person present interrogative, "Having chewed it, do I give it to you?" (*ge o:miyo:lo?*). The children themselves, however, use the compound verb only in its present imperative form *(ge) o:mina*, "You, having chewed, give," as a request to a parent or older sibling to chew food (for the child) and then give it to the child (Schieffelin 1985). In so doing, young Kaluli children are acting in a role-appropriate manner. They are expected to ask for food to be chewed and given to them but are not expected to chew and give food to others.

Grammatical form as infrequent but appropriate for child use

A language socialization approach to grammatical development can also help to account for why young children produce forms that are relatively rare in their verbal environment. For example, as noted above, young Kaluli children produce the imperative form of the Kaluli compound verb "having chewed, give." What was not noted, however, is that this form of the verb is almost never used by others in the child's environment, as adults and older children have no need to request that someone else chew food for them. This phenomenon should sensitize us to the fact that children's linguistic repertoires are not a simple reflection of what they do or do not hear in their surroundings[7] but rather that children are taking an active role in constructing language that is most useful to their needs and appropriate to their social status.

Another interesting example of children's productive use of a grammatical form that appears relatively infrequently in their verbal environment is Samoan children's use of the first person affect-marked pronoun *ta ita*, "poor I/poor me." This form is morphologically productive and can appear in a variety of cases and be inflected for number and specific/nonspecific as well as for alienable/inalienable possession when used as a genitive constituent. That is to say, this form is not a frozen or idiomatic lexical form. It appears far less often in household interactions involving children (as overhearers, and perhaps in other roles) than the more neutral first person pronoun *a'u*, "I," yet young children produce the affective pronoun earlier (19 months) and more often than the neutral form (Ochs 1988). In particular, young children use the affective pronoun as a benefactive (*ia te ita* "for poor me"). This form is the linguistic core of the speech act of begging, which, as noted in section 2, is expected of and appropriate for young children. Samoan children, thus, appear to pull from their linguistic environment and deploy strategically those linguistic structures that help them to satisfy their desire for food and other objects. We have seen earlier that relatively marked circumstances in which children's grammatical repertoire cannot be easily predicted from either the rate of use or relative complexity of grammatical forms in the child's verbal environment. Rather, children's use of particular grammatical forms at particular moments of their language development is profoundly linked to social and cultural norms, expectations, and preferences which may not be explicit and are not easily detected or counted. Children acquire grammatical forms as part of becoming a person in society; they use grammatical forms as communicative resources to participate in social situations, express their ideas and feelings, and otherwise accomplish social and individual goals. Language socialization theory provides a framework for how children use such forms for sociocultural ends. One notion within language socialization research is that members of communities (including language acquiring children) use grammatical forms to build speech acts and express stances which, in turn, are part of more complex social identities and social activities (Ochs 1993). Thus, in Kaluli a grammatical form such as *a:la:ma* "say like that" is used to build the speech act of prompting and this act in turn is used to help establish the gender identity of girls; and *o:mina* "having chewed, give" is used to build the speech act of requesting and this act in turn is used to help establish the generational identity of young children.

---

[7] This point was emphatically made by Bloom (1970) regarding the absence of the instrumental and dative in children's early utterances in spite of their pervasiveness in adult speech.

Similarly, in Samoan *sau* is used to build the directive to come and this act in turn helps to establish the identity of the speaker as relatively higher status than the addressee. Other examples of the interface of culture and the acquisition of particular grammatical forms remain to be described by other researchers.

The cultural milieu of children's code of choice

Thus far we have focused on the impact of culture on the acquisition of one particular language and have not attended to acquisition of more than one language in linguistically heterogeneous communities. A language socialization perspective can account for code acquisition in such communities by examining the social distribution and social meanings of code choice within communities and households and constructing a model of language ideology that informs patterns of code selection and acquisition. Just as children's acquisition of a particular grammatical form cannot be accounted for simply in terms of rate of that form in the child's verbal environment, so children's acquisition of a particular code cannot be accounted for simply in terms of the presence of that code in the child's intimate environment. A language socialization perspective can account for why and how children may not be acquiring the languages in their multilingual environment in spite of the fact that their parents say that they want their children to speak these languages. What is missing from the majority of psycholinguistic studies of simultaneous bilingual acquisition is in-depth ethnographic analysis of the complex language ideologies, i.e. the values attached to the different codes, that are characteristic of multilingual communities and their relation to language practices in those communities (see essays in Kroskrity, 2000; Schieffelin, Woolard, and Kroskrity 1998).

Psycholinguistic studies of the simultaneous acquisition of two languages (i.e. bilingualism under the age of five years) have focused on the question of whether young children develop a unitary, undifferentiated language system (integrating features of both languages) or whether they develop two differentiated systems used in contextually sensitive ways (see reviews in Genesee 1989; Romaine 1989; De Houwer 1990). In pursuing this question, many psycholinguists have assumed a notion of bilingualism similar to that articulated by Weinrich (1953: 73): "The ideal bilingual switches from one language to the other, according to appropriate changes in the speech situation, but not in unchanged speech situations and certainly not in a single sentence." It is widely assumed that the "ideal" bilingual situation (wherein the speaker associates particular codes with particular situations) facilitates bilingual acquisition, whereas code mixing in a single situation, especially by a single speaker, inhibits bilingual acquisition (McLaughlin 1984).

Two types of studies address the issue of code differentiation in the course of bilingual acquisition. The first set of studies examines bilingual acquisition among children from bilingual Spanish–English-speaking communities in the

United States (e.g. the Southwest). Most used an experimental design where child speakers were told that an investigator only understood one language, thus inhibiting the use of the other language. The second set of studies examines bilingual acquisition among children who have at least one bilingual parent but who resided otherwise in a monolingual community (e.g. children with a German–Italian bilingual parent residing in Italy (Volterra and Taeschner 1978). Investigators tape-recorded adult–child speech in the home. To ascertain the norms of bilingual code use in particular households, most researchers rely exclusively on parental reports of their speech practices with young children.[8] In parental reports from both sets of studies, parents insisted that they followed the one person-one language rule ("rule of Grammont" [Ronjat 1913]), that is, they did not mix languages when speaking to the child. From a language socialization perspective, this response reflects a widespread belief across many societies that mixing two languages lexically and/or grammatically is indicative of confusion and lack of education, and is generally stigmatized as impure language. When researchers employed more ethnographic methods of investigating bilingualism by looking at naturalistic speech to and in the hearing environment of the child, they found that, despite parental reports of "one person-one language", their language practices showed a significant amount of code switching (Goodz 1989; De Houwer 1990). Because these naturalistic studies do not analyze the effects of code mixing on bilingual acquisition and because other psycholinguistic studies do not examine bilingual practices in the home, the question of what type of bilingual language practices (one person–one language versus language mixing) facilitates the acquisition of separate codes cannot be adequately answered at this time.

One consequence of pursuing the question of unitary or differentiated bilingual acquisition is that researchers have neglected a very important acquisition phenomenon, namely the acquisition of code switching itself in early childhood. While there are numerous sociolinguistic studies of school-age children's code switching behavior (Auer 1988; Genishi 1981; McClure, 1977; Zentella 1990, 1997), there are no studies of the acquisition processes that lead to this competence in later life. Questions that might illuminate grammatical development include: how does code switching change over developmental time? Do young children's code switching practicing follow the same lexical and grammatical constraints as that of the adults in their speech communities? How do young children use code switching to achieve pragmatic ends?

In many bi or multilingual communities, not all languages are valued equally; some may be viewed as prestige forms whereas others may be disvalued or even stigmatized by the community and/or by members of a child's family. The prestige forms are often associated with educational achievement and social

---

[8] Two exceptions are De Houwer (1990) and Goodz (1989), both of whom relied not only on parental report but also examined speech practices in the home.

and economic mobility, while the nonprestigious forms are often associated with traditional values. These ideologies surrounding particular languages are socialized along with the codes themselves, sometimes in extremely subtle ways. Where there is high value placed on a particular code over another, the highly valued code has a better chance of survival as part of a young child's individual linguistic repertoire as well as part of the community's repertoire over historical time.

A dramatic example of the role of ideology in causing a shift from multilingual to monolingual acquisition is found in Kulick's language socialization study of the Gapun community of Papua New Guinea, where Taiap and the lingua franca Tok Pisin as well as the vernaculars of other villages are actively used (Kulick, 1992). In this community, the local vernacular Taiap is rapidly disappearing from the linguistic repertoire of language acquiring children, not because of an explicit devaluation of Taiap but because of implicit devaluation through language socialization practices. Taiap adults insist that they want children to acquire the local vernacular, and place the blame for its loss on the will of the children to reject Taiap in favor of Tok Pisin. However, their language socialization practices indicate that caregivers code switch into Tok Pisin far more than they realize and that they socialize young children into associating Tok Pisin with modernity, Christianity, and education and Taiap with backwardness and paganism. The result is that "although no village child under ten actively commands the vernacular language, most children between five and ten possess a good passive understanding of Taiap" (Kulick 1992: 217).

Another example of how ideology affects bilingual acquisition comes from Schieffelin's language socialization study of Haitian families in New York City (Schieffelin 1994). Young children in these families participate in Haitian creole, English, and sometimes French conversational exchanges, but for the most part are using English. Adults assume that all Haitian children learn to speak creole; it is integral with their Haitian identity. English, on the other hand, is seen as essential for success in school and for successful participation in American society. In contrast to creole, English is viewed as requiring attention and explicit instruction. This ideology can be seen in language socialization practices with children, wherein adults will themselves use creole to praise children when the children speak in English. In addition, adults convey this ideology through recurrent code switching in which they paraphrase their own and children's creole utterances in English. As a result of these practices, children growing up in Haitian diaspora communities are no longer acquiring creole.[9]

These studies were among the first to point out the centrality of language socialization activities for theorizing patterns of language acquisition, choice, maintenance and shift in language contact situations. Subsequently, language

---

[9] Focusing on young adults and children, Schmidt (1985) and Bavin (1989) have related language ideology to language shift among the Djirbal and Warlpiri peoples of Australia respectively. For studies of language shift more generally, see Dorian (1989); Gal (1979); and Hill and Hill (1986).

socialization researchers have increasingly turned their attention to investigating connections among language ideology, language socialization and language acquisition in bi and multilingual communities. This is evident, for example, in the research of Garrett (1999) and Paugh (2001) in Caribbean communities; Field (1999) and Meek (2001) in Native North American communities; Riley (2001) in French Polynesia and Fader (2001) in New York City.

Steps to a cultural ecology of grammatical development

A consistent message throughout this chapter is that grammatical development cannot be adequately accounted for without serious analysis of the social and cultural milieu of the language acquiring child. We have seen that grammatical development is an outcome of two primary sociocultural contexts: (1) where children participate regularly in socially and culturally organized activities, and (2) where the language(s) being acquired is/are highly valued and children are encouraged to learn it/them.

The first point implies that no special form of language, such as simplified grammar, is necessary for children's grammatical development; the only requirement is that children are involved routinely in a community's social network and in the everyday activities that hold that community together. We have suggested that certain linguistic accommodations may be an outcome of cultural conceptions of the child, including expectations about the communicative roles of young children from birth onward. In communities where infants and young children are frequently expected to take on central communicative roles such as addressee or speaker, members provide a great deal of social, cognitive, and linguistic support. For example, in selecting an infant or young child as addressee, members may simplify their grammar, as a means of getting the child to respond. Or, in selecting a child as speaker, members may simplify the child's task by, for example, ventriloquating, prompting, or expanding the message. On the other hand, in communities where infants and young children are often assigned the more peripheral role (Lave and Wenger 1991) of overhearers, they are participants in linguistically complex activities. In all communities, children take on a range of communicative roles but when in their development, in which social situations, and how often they do so varies from community to community. A culturally organized means–ends model accounts for this pattern in that it allows for cross-cultural similarity in the linguistic means employed to accomplish social ends (such as talking to a child), but allows for the possibility that there will be cultural variation in the situational manifestation of a particular social end (e.g. the developmental point at which members start treating children as addressees who are to respond in culturally appropriate ways.)

The second point implies that mere exposure to a language is not sufficient to account for its acquisition. Analyses of grammatical development in linguistically heterogeneous communities need to be culturally contextualized by including the language ideologies prevalent in those communities. Further, as noted earlier, analysts cannot rely exclusively on members' reports of their own and others' speech behavior to assess these ideologies; ideologies are often below the level of awareness and must be investigated through the systematic analysis of speech practices. For example, in multilingual communities, the practice of codeswitching reveals values attached to each code that members do not articulate through structured interviews. Depending on historical and cultural contexts, codes may be differently valued, and members may display ambivalent feelings towards one or more of these codes in their everyday speech practices. Our point is that language acquiring children acquire values associated with each code through participation in social activities involving code selection and this cultural knowledge impacts their acquisition of codes. With the increasing number of diaspora communities world-wide and the spread of international languages and literacies, the acquisition and maintenance of minority and indigenous languages is becoming increasingly problematic (Dorian 1989). Psycholinguistic studies of children's bilingual acquisition need to attend to the fact that grammatical development takes place in a world market of languages, where different languages, like other cultural commodities, carry different economic and political values.

In summary, while grammatical development does not depend upon a simplified speech environment, cultural values attached to particular codes do impact the acquisition (or nonacquisition) of those codes. Furthermore, cultural systems of belief, knowledge, and social order profoundly affect the acquisition of particular grammatical constructions. Earlier, we suggested that even very young children appear to be sensitive to the ways in which grammatical constructions within a code index social identity, in that they select forms that appropriately constitute their identity as "child" or as "male" or "female," or as one who is carrying out an appropriate role, such as "one who begs for food or things." A language socialization approach provides an analytic framework for assessing the social activities and identities that grammar indexes as well as the cultural norms, preferences, and expectations that define those activities and identities.

In this analysis, we have drawn primarily on ethnographic studies to make the point that culture affects grammatical development in surprising and subtle yet systematic ways. Culture is still missing from most accounts of grammatical development, and until more culturally sensitive accounts are available, we will only be guessing about the extent to which culture organizes the linguistic forms and practices of young children as speakers, addressees, and audiences over developmental time.[10] Until the cultural ecology of grammar is

---

[10] Slobin (1992: 6) comments in his crosslinguistic study of language acquisition: "This may be time to remember – as Ochs and Schieffelin (1984) have incisively argued – that language acquisition ALWAYS takes place in cultural and interpersonal contexts. The ethnographic content of chapters on 'exotic' languages shows how much ethnography is MISSING from our accounts of the acquisition of languages in more familiar settings."

better understood, grammatical development will continue to be viewed predominantly as an acultural process. Since language is a universal resource for constituting social life and cultural knowledge, and since members are deeply concerned with children's able participation in social life and command of cultural knowledge, then it makes good sense that analyses of children's production and comprehension of grammar seriously take these sociocultural universals into account and incorporate ethnographic methodology to capture the complexities of the social life of language (Sankoff 1980).

9

INTIMATE GRAMMARS:
ANTHROPOLOGICAL AND
PSYCHOANALYTIC ACCOUNTS OF
LANGUAGE, GENDER, AND DESIRE

ELIZABETH POVINELLI

Loco motion

The desert heat was oppressive. The flies were a constant presence on mouth, nostrils, and eyes. It is 1896. Baldwin Spencer and Frank Gillen are camped just west of Alice Springs, Australia. Gillen has arranged for Arrente men and women and their surrounding Aboriginal neighbors to gather nearby to perform a repertoire of their rituals in exchange for food, tobacco, tea and protection from pastoralists and police. Baldwin Spencer is a zoologist, Frank Gillen a telegraph operator. Both men aspire to be the intellectual leaders of an emergent Australian anthropology. So every day they direct photographers, scribble notes, sit with now nameless older Arrente men, who themselves sit and struggle to answer the river of questions Spencer and Gillen direct at them about the ceremonies they are performing. At times the heat must have overwhelmed everyone. But Spencer and Gillen were happy to sweat, to inhale flies, to stretch a cramped leg. They knew the unprecedented nature of what they were witnessing. Before their eyes was unfolding virtually the entire corpus of central desert male culture. The Arrente and their neighbors were performing and describing nearly every initiation, increase, and conception ceremony they owned. The ethnography Spencer and Gillen published based on these performances would become the touchstone of an ensuing generation of aspiring anthropologists.[1]

At times Spencer and Gillen's eyes must have wandered from their writing and passed over the distended bellies of Arrente children and over the buckshot scarred backs of Arrente men and women. When Spencer lay his wax matchsticks on the ground to help Arrente informants map out their genealogies he must have heard full or fragmentary stories of the epidemics, poisonings, and massacres which accounted for the dead ends of numerous Arrente family trees. But *Native Tribes of Central Australia* does not focus on these scandalously mistreated bodies. Instead it turns to what they and the emergent Australian settler nation considered to be the moral scandal of Aboriginal ritual practices.

---

[1] See Stocking (1995), pp. 94–8. See also Mulvaney *et al.* (1997).

The text turns and speaks to public anxieties about the secret truth of Aboriginal corroborees reported in a variety of mass-mediated texts: newspapers, popular settler memoirs, and amateur ethnologies. Aboriginal men's sacred corroborees included group sex. Yes, Spencer and Gillen write, it is true,

considerable license is allowed on certain occasions, when a large number of men and women are gathered together to perform certain corrobborees. When an important one of these is held, it occupies perhaps ten days or a fortnight; and during that time the men, and especially the elder ones, but by no means exclusively these, spend the day in camp preparing decorations to be used during the evening. Every day two or three women are told off to attend at the corrobboree ground, and, with the exception of men who stand in relation to them of actual father, brother, or sons, they are, for the time being, common property to all the men present on the corrobboree ground.[2]

Spencer, Gillen, and most of their successors took it to be self-evident that what they saw (or heard about) was "sex" between "men" and "women"; that when they and the Arrente pointed to a sex act they were pointing to the same field-of-action; that this sex act had a social syntax, men sexually exploiting women; and, finally, that an indigenous gender hierarchy could be read off this sexual activity. And though part of an emergent relativist paradigm in the social sciences, Spencer and Gillen also took as self-evident what constitutes a normal sexual relation.

The first is the normal one, when the woman is the private property of one man, and no one without his consent can have access to her, though he may lend her privately to certain individuals who stand in one given relationship to her. The second is the wider relation in regard to particular men at the time of marriage. The third is the still wider relation which obtains on certain occasions, such as the holding of important corrobborees.[3]

In *Across Australia* (1912), a book written for a general audience, Spencer and Gillen intensified their normative characterization of ritual sex, describing indigenous ceremonies as consisting of "naked, howling savages" engaged in bodily acts that were "crude in the extreme."[4] Why do Arrente men sexually use women during their sacred ceremonies?

The natives say that their presence during the preparations and the sexual indulgence, which was a practice of the Alcheringa, prevents anything from going wrong with the performance; it makes it impossible for the head decorations, for example, to become loose and disordered during the performance.[5]

Spencer and Gillen move on, but we might pause for a moment. What might the Arrente men have said and meant that Spencer and Gillen paraphrase as "it makes it impossible for the head decorations ... to become loose and disordered during the performance"? And why did they presume that it was sex that Arrente "men" were having with Arrente "women"?

---

[2] Spencer and Gillen (1899), p. 97.   [3] Ibid., p. 98.
[4] Spencer and Gillen (1912). See also Spencer and Gillen (1927).
[5] Spencer and Gillen (1899), p. 97.

It may seem odd to begin a review of contemporary studies of language, gender, and sexuality with a historical sex scandal. But it probably seems far less odd to most sociolinguists and linguistic anthropologists to begin this way than with Sigmund Freud's interpretation of Spencer and Gillen's texts or with Geza Roheim's Freudian interpretation of the phallocentric symbolism of Arrente rituals.[6] Who could blame them? Many contemporary scholars of language grind their teeth when they read or hear psychoanalytically informed accounts of language, especially Lacan's account of the signifier, of the phallus as the master signifier, of language as organized around lack, of desire as the difference between demand and need, of woman as (k)not (*la femme n'existe pas*). They revolt against Lacan's near exclusive reliance on and algebraic contortions of out-dated models of post-Saussurian linguistics, social theory, and continental philosophy; his extrapolation of universal psychic economies from particular European language structures; and his conflation of textual and locutionary aspects of denotation and predication.[7]

The unsettling sound of grinding teeth is heard even though, *maybe because* many scholars of gender and sexuality in linguistic anthropology share with Lacanian psychoanalysis a common intellectual genealogy and seem to share common intellectual interests; namely, to understand how gendered and sexual subjects (loosely, men and women) become gendered and sexual subjects *as such* through *language*;[8] how these gendered subjects come to have desires and to have these desires organized in normative and non-normative ways; and, finally, how, in certain cultural contexts, a sexed body and its sexual desires function as the defining index of social identity. Provide any further specificity to their accounts of language, the unconscious, gender, and sexuality, however, and psychoanalysis and contemporary linguistic anthropology quickly part company.

For their parts, Lacan and the *école freudienne* did not pretend an interest in language as a phenomenon in itself. Lacan was, instead, consumed with understanding the "passion of the signifier," a strangely catholic view of the psychic transubstantiations that human beings undergo as they become subjects *as such* through language.[9] Lacan's interest was in the psychic effects of the fact that human beings become sexed subjects through language. Thus while Lacan understood sexual difference to be the signifying difference of language (the Other), neither the linguistic details of how language signals sexual difference nor how it entails gendered subjects were what interested Lacan in the last instance. He chased what the subject's emergence into the linguistic order (having a language) foreclosed and set into motion: being and desire

[6] See Freud (1989); Roheim (1973, 1974).
[7] For critical attempts to read psychoanalysis against semiotics see Crapanzano (1993, 1998); Kristeva (1980); de Lauretis (1984); Cameron and Kulick (2003).
[8] Lacan (1977a), p. 78. See also Mitchell (1985); Grosz (1990); and Copjec (1994).
[9] Lacan (1977a), p. 79.

respectively. In contrast, it is exactly language that anthropologists working in the paradigms of sociolinguistics, linguistic anthropology, and pragmatics are interested in – the structure and function of language and their role in constituting the normative frameworks that contribute to the "laying down" of a person's gender and sexuality and to the ability of human subjects to make commonsense judgments such as: "Such-and-such gendered-person's desire and/or sexual practice is normal" and "Such-and-such gendered-person's desire and/or sexual practice is queer."

It is exactly these sharp divides between psychoanalytic and anthropological approaches to language and the subject that present a mutual challenge to each of these disciplines. The challenge Lacanian psychoanalysis poses to linguistic anthropology, sociolinguistics, and pragmatics is how to study language, desire and gender, without reducing them to each other. The challenge linguistic anthropology poses to psychoanalytic accounts is equally formidable: to reformulate an account of sex difference that is based exclusively neither on European language structures nor on post-Saussurean structural accounts of language; but, instead, situates an account of gender and sexuality in the semantic and pragmatic, metasemantic and metapragmatic conditions of being *and becoming* a human subject in the context of the coercive and consensual social institutions in which this being and becoming occurs. This chapter will barely tickle the still incubating surface of the monstrous beast I am proposing be born. I suggest two modest proposals as a way of beginning: first, that we attempt to theorize what I am provisionally describing as an *intimate pragmatics* by articulating recent work in metapragmatics and gender with a psychoanalytically inspired account of subjectivity and desire.

"Might be girl": the linguistic emergence of gender and sexuality

Over the last fifteen years or so anthropologically informed studies of language, gender, and sexuality have formulated a rigorous and robust methodological and theoretical apparatus for understanding the relationship between the semantic, pragmatic, and metapragmatic features of language and the social production, maintenance, and reproduction of normative gender and sexuality. They have examined in ever-finer detail grammatical and pragmatic systems of "gender," "sex acts," "sexuality," and "affect."[10] Scholars of language and gender have also begun to understand how grammatical and pragmatic aspects of language invest corporeal and psychic economies with particular gender, sexual, and affective systems; how they demarcate and entail social space (the private, the

---

[10] For a review of contemporary approaches to language and gender see Bergvall, Bing, and Freed (1996); Bucholtz, Mary and Kira Hall (1995); Cameron (1995); Hall and Bucholtz (1995); Hall, Bucholtz, and Moonwoman (1992); Harvey and Shalom (1997); Holmes (1995); McConnell-Ginet (1988); Mills (1995); Philips, Steele and Tanz (1987). For language and the emotions see Besnier (1993); Irvine (1990); Abu-Lughod and Lutz (1990); Lutz (1990); Rosenberg (1990).

public, the intimate and the ritual, the secular, the taboo); and how they con-
structively contribute to material and symbolic systems of value, domination,
and exploitation. We now have a fairly good idea of how languages signal the
gender of a noun phrase and its referent through various prefixes, suffixes, and
particles. Unfortunately, many anthropological studies of gender and sexuality do not situate the gender of Noun Phrases in other semantic senses and
levels, nor do they detail the dialectic between semantic and pragmatic structure and function. Instead, many studies of language and gender, linguistic or
otherwise, present fairly superficial gender and sex counts – three sexes and
four genders, two sexes and three genders, one sex, and two genders.[11] For all
the variation between linguistic structures suggested by these studies, Lacan's
basic argument that all human beings must enter through the doors of something
recognizable as grammatical gender seems unchallenged. All languages seem
to semantically encode gender and have the means to attach semantic gender
to human corporeal difference. What varies are the sociological and pragmatic
aspects of these semantic categorizations and indexical processes.

Whatever "gender" and "sexuality" are and whatever "critical linguistic"
projects develop in relation to them, these studies have demonstrated the useful-
ness of embedding an analysis of gender and sexuality in semantic, pragmatic,
and metapragmatic discourses and functions.[12] This framework allows us to
articulate the most delicate structures of grammar to the most dramatic social
contestations of power. Take for instance the intersection of metapragmatic discourse and function on social relations of gender. If pragmatic function refers
to those features of language that encode context and the context-presupposing
and entailing nature of language usage, metapragmatic discourse includes all
implicit and explicit references to such encodings, usages, and (im)proper
contexts of usage.[13] Likewise, metapragmatic function includes the means by
speakers, usually unconsciously, invest their interlocutionary acts with various
gender classes or gendered registers in order to cohere them into interpretable
(i.e., coherent) texts. Metapragmatic function is what provides speakers with
the means of building up from pragmatic acts higher order textual phenomena (genres, frames, conversations). Whereas in its pragmatic function "she"
entails and presupposes a context, in its metapragmatic function "she" points
to and in the process coheres (articulates) a here-and-now illocutionary action
to an external context and an internal unfolding text. Metapragmatic function
is, therefore, critical to how textual and interlocutionary phenomena (including individuals, their gender, their culture) are rendered coherent, durable, and
seemingly detachable from their local contexts.[14] Metapragmatic function also

[11] See, for instance, Trumbach (1994); Besnier (1993); Herdt (1994); Tan (1995).
[12] For "critical linguistics" see Cameron (1995); Harvey and Shalom (1997).
[13] See also Lucy (1993) and Lyons (1977) for "reflexive language." See Bakhtin (1986) for "speech
       genre."
[14] See Silverstein and Urban (1996); Lee (1997), esp. pp. 277–320; Derrida (1982).

creates a sense of a perduring temporal order out of the actual volatility and transience of sense-making. While every denotational sign can, indeed must, resignify an entire prior sequence of meaning ($s^1 \ldots s^2$ is in real-time $s^1 \ldots s^2$ modified by $^1 \ldots s^1$ modified by $^2 \ldots s^3 \ldots \sim$), metapragmatic function ensures that most communicative exchanges, indeed "culture" itself and identities within it, say gender, are experienced as a perduring coherent-enough totality.

In languages such as English, gender is part of the coherence-entailing metapragmatic apparatus of denotation and predication; that is, gender functions not only pragmatically and semantically, but it metapragmatically draws on these two linguistic dimensions – and usually unconsciously – to bind and cohere communicative action. For instance, in its standard average heteronormative English usage, "she" conveys a multiplex of semantic signals (number, person, gender) as it pragmatically indexes sign to context. But "she" is also drawn into metapragmatic work, regimenting ongoing pragmatic indexicality into a coherent interpretable text and interlocutionary event. To change the gender aspect while maintaining number and person – to switch to "he" or "it" or to switch randomly between "she," "he," and "it" – would seem to render meaningless the text's sense and value. Thus gender is a building block of the delicate intimate attachments of human society but not in the usual sense: gender delicately attaches conversational and grammatical texts to their internal and external contexts and cotexts – as it is, or seems to be, attaching one person to another. Conservative language critics of feminist language projects sense but misdiagnose this metapragmatic function of grammar when they accuse feminists or queer activists of incoherency or worse. They are not wrong in this limited sense: in standard average presumptively heteronormative English semantic and pragmatic coherence depends upon the formal indexical order of albeit ideologically loaded grammatical categories of gender.[15] But we see fairly immediately, however, that all "coherent" segments of language are in fact implicit metapragmatic discourses embedded in dominant or minority formal or informal social institutions. In English the refusal to abide by normative rules of pronominal usage only *seems* to render the semantics of an average English conversation, well, queer – ill-formed, dysfunctional insofar as it is contra-normative, if not anti-normative. In fact, it rends the implicit metapragmatic discourse of heteronormativity and its institutions while in the process building new speech genres and their subjects of enunciation.[16]

All these pragmatic and metapragmatic functions and forms along with their semantic senses and values are "neutral," if densely ideologically saturated, linguistic givens at any given moment of social spacetime. I use the term "neutral" to remind us that these functions and forms are non-intending semiotic

---

[15] See also Silverstein (1985).
[16] See Leap (1995); Livia and Hall (1997); Ogawa and Smith (1997).

architectures. They may be the explicit and implicit material on which we base our social presuppositions – the grounds upon which we make sense and meaning. Nevertheless, these linguistic facts simply are. And, insofar as they are, they can be regimented into new discursive forms. What social work they are pulled into is the emergent result of institutionally mediated interactional usage. Paraphrasing Ochs, the variable use of linguistic variants must be conventionalized before they can function as gender (or other social) deixes. A gender difference must be made out of a semiotic difference, linguistic and corporeal difference fashioned into gender ideology: the "ought to be" of corporeal and vocal normativity, the "how" of "this is how language and corporeal hexis ought to be articulated, where, for what purpose."

These denotational and indexical aspects of language use become, and are always already, a part of social relations when social agents who, often unknowingly, draw on the metapragmatic function of language and on one or another aspects of grammatical signaling to regiment indexical and semantic actualities into higher order gendered registers (or gendered speech genres). These genres are then part of the means by which subjects are disciplined in the how, who, when, where of *proper* gendered language usage and subsequently the proper meaning and usage of various social spaces (public, private, intimate, ritual, secular). Modals, qualifiers, quantifiers, negatives, and other aspects of language are a critical part of the apparatus of gender normativity and its contestations. These grammatical functions support and/or are themselves part of the signaling means by which new gendered registers are created. But whether nonsense indexicality is actually being used to lay out (entail) an actual semantic or social space or whether current structures of sense and meaning are being transformed into new senses and meanings, these always already existing pragmatic excesses and structures always already provide the means of potential new social spaces.

Studies on language socialization, linguistic ideology, and symbolic domination make clear that language is a key symbolic technology through which individuals are interpellated into hegemonic gendered social orders and, therefore, a key site of social struggle. Some of the best research in language and gender has focused on the social processes through which linguistic discourses and functions are drawn into social struggles over gender and sexual roles and values. Unfortunately, most of this research has focused exclusively on the metapragmatic discourses that link men and women to forms of talk, leaving uninvestigated how gender and sexuality emerged across global colonial and postcolonial spacetime. In order to suggest how gender and sexuality emerged in these contexts let us return to the conversations between Spencer, Gillen, and the Arrente as a case study of how persons are interpellated into gendered social orders. In particular, let us examine how these men mapped semantic structures across languages as they discussed ritual. How were gender and sexuality conveyed between English and Arrente? Does understanding the means of gender (and sexual) conveyance helps us understand the relationship between gender (and sexuality), subjectivity, and language? How did Spencer and Gillen contribute to the emergence of a "Western" entity-of-action (a sex act, gender, and sexuality as perduring essential qualities of humans rather than aspectival qualities of objects passing through states) from indigenous grammatical and pragmatic orders through the simple practice of pointing and through the simple desire to understand something about local ritual practices?

To begin with and to state the obvious, the Arrente were not simply speaking among themselves and with other regional indigenous groups. They, Spencer, and Gillen, were attempting to communicate across significantly different semiotic orders under real-time, often brutal, conditions of power, exploitation, and domination. Baldwin Spencer arrived in central Australia believing Frank Gillen to be a fluent speaker of Arrente only to find his "knowledge of Arunta (and several other Aboriginal languages) was in fact rather less fluent than Spencer had assumed."[17] Therefore, the Englishmen communicated with the Arrente men and their neighboring groups in an English-based pidgin. When speaking with Arrente men about their ritual practices, Spencer and Gillen describe themselves as using a pidgin form of English in order to point to and diagramming the action Spencer and Gillen understood to be "sex" or, perhaps, using a local Arrente term they understood to mean "copulation." And it is not unlikely that the Arrente men responded either with a series of codeswitches between the same pidgin and local languages or in some other form of English translation. If "sex" secured headdress to head, it did so only after "*that*" (or its English-based creole equivalents) secured two very different semantic fields to each other, that is, *before* any actual or significant meaningful realignment of either semantic system had occurred.

Let me bring the lens even closer and pause over what could be considered the most minor, if not meaningless, of colonial exchanges, the historical and grammatical substitution of "sex" for "that." At some point in time, whether before or after Spencer and Gillen arrived in Central Australia, indexical signs such as finger pointing or demonstratives opened a coherent-enough communicative channel between the Arrente and European settlers. These indexical signs secured two very different semantic realms of sense by first securing each semantic realm to an agreed upon point-of-reference. Again, in a strict sense, this agreed upon point-of-reference preceded any agreed upon sense-construal. Each group brought to the communicative event the conscious and unconscious "ought to be" of entities, actions and their modifications across contexts that marked the deep presuppositional normative structures of their "culture."[18] Thus, even the agreed upon point-of-reference would have taken time to secure as an entity-of-action was slowly detached from a local semantically and pragmatically embedded field-of-action.

---

[17] Stocking (1995), p. 92.
[18] For a fuller discussion of what these structures and practices might have entailed see Povinelli (2004).

As Spencer and Gillen pointed to the action they understood to be "sex" – using their fingers, diagrams, or demonstrative pronouns ("that") – the index "that" would be slowly replaced by the indexical and symbolic function of "sex." In other words, as the Arrente struggled to understand the referent of "that," "that" slowly worked its way into the sense-making structures of Arrente lives and it made a bridge across which "sex" could travel. Whether in their presence or out of the range of their hearing, the Arrente discussed what Spencer and Gillen could possibly mean by their questions, what their questions suggested about European views of humans and their environments, and what they themselves could and could not discuss as a matter of ceremonial law and interethnic "etiquette." Over time, the domain of excluded discourse would include the very actions Spencer and Gillen were so fascinated by – ritual sex, sex in public, sex out of the institutions of monogamous "marriage." And, over time, physical and corporeal spaces would be reoriented and differently inhabited. Sex would lay out space and social relations not in ritual terms but in terms associated with sex, privacy, intimacy, shame, and titillation.

The substitution of "sex" for "that" entailed a displacement not only of a demonstrative pronoun by a noun phrase but of one system of meaning by another. "Sex" slowly rearticulated the total order of indigenous semantic and pragmatic meaning, entextualizing new value-laden references and predications, the where, when, with whom (or what), for what, and meaning what aspects of British-derived understandings of normative and non-normative sex acts. As it did, space came to refold itself, the ritual less physical, the intimate a private property, the public as the hidden hand of power. In these real-time social interactions "that" appears anew as a grammatical grappling hook, a means of securing one semantic and pragmatic system to another, an instrument of seizure, a prelude to corporeal discipline proffered as the pragmatic means of escaping physical violence. In the light of these pragmatic practices, the question "why do you do *that*?" strays from its original referent and is resignified as a metalingual commentary on the act and orientation of translation in colonial contexts.

This resignification is masked, however, by the entextualization strategies of Spencer and Gillen. Sex expands its seemingly natural and universal sense-making reign because Spencer and Gillen utilize conventions of reported speech, quotation, and indirect quotation in such a way as to make the Arrente appear to be the authors of the very referential practices they are struggling to understand. Richard Parmentier reminds us "the quotation of authoritative discourse surrenders only momentarily to the hierarchical rank inherent in [the] reported discourse, for these official or traditional words are in fact put to uses unintended by their authors or not implied in their initial contexts".[19] Spencer and Gillen use direct and indirect quotation, in large part,

[19] Parmentier (1993), p. 263.

to signal the liberal scientific nature of their conversations with Arrente and their neighbors.

But the conversations in which the Arrente were engaged mock the liberal ideal of a rational communicative event excisable from fields of force. The Arrente were all too aware that one aspect of colonial power was being bracketed by another equal and opposing colonial force. As they danced and talked, the Arrente and their neighbors were in the midst of being systematically exterminated, having their ritual objects stolen, lost or destroyed, and having their lands taken and with them life-sustaining material and spiritual resources. In exchange for allowing them to record their rituals, Gillen and Spencer offered the Arrente and surrounding Aboriginal groups food and protection from police and settlers. Obviously, force was not removed from the scene. Quite the contrary. Force was the very condition of communicative action.[20] Vast inequalities of power provided an incentive for the Arrente to orient their utterances, if ever so subtly, to the context in which Spencer and Gillen were embedded and which they were creating. And it incited Arrente to detach, if in the beginning ever so slightly, a segment of their semiotic life-world and use this segment ("that"-"sex") as a means of building a somewhat coherent common language between themselves and these European men.

Focusing on these seemingly minor interlocutionary events and their semantic structures, at least in the first instance, allows for a more subtle model for thinking about the mechanics of sexual hegemony, especially for how normative systems are maintained or how they emerge through the articulation of dissimilar elements in a real-time social interactions.[21] These "utterances and their types" are "the drive belts" allowing us to develop a more rigorous methodology for maneuvering among vastly different scales of event and orders of social domination.[22] And they remind us that institutions of force are always part of the tacit presupposed background conditions of communication and corporeal hexis.

The subject of language

What then is the relationship between gender, metapragmatically understood, subjectivity and desire? To answer this question, it is important to view subjectivity as an order of phenomenon distinct from semantic and pragmatic orders of phenomena. This distinction suggests a limit within contemporary metasemiotic theories as they pertain to the (gendered, sexual) subject of language.[23] By the "subject of language" I do not mean the topic of language. I mean, instead, to refer to the human subject who is the product of language and to language

---

[20] See Calhoun (1995).   [21] See Laclau and Mouffe (1985), see esp. pp. 85–88.

[22] See Bakhtin (1986), p. 65.

[23] See Silverstein on the possible construal of the function(s) of semantic and metapragmatic orders of phenomena as distinct from each other in "every essential characteristic" (1993), p. 34.

as the dialectical product of being the communicative medium, instrument, or device of human subjects.

Let me review, briefly, the linguistic anthropological approach to the subject. As I noted above sociolinguists and linguistic anthropologists have side-stepped the formal relation between the pre- and post-linguistic, thus, gendered subject. But they have also bracketed the question of how natural human languages, in their pragmatic and semantic dimensions, bare the imprint of their status as a *human* language. Linguists do not ask: does the phenomenological condition of being the communicative medium of beings who become speaking subject leave its imprint on the structures and functions of language? Silverstein's understanding of the relationship between semantic and pragmatic orders of linguistic phenomena point us to the importance of this question and lays down the conceptual apparatus that demands it be answered. For, if we agree that a semantic order is not accessible except through some act of language usage (i.e. is inferred through pragmatic or metapragmatic acts), pragmatic and metapragmatic orders of natural human language usage likewise entail a *subject* using that language and a subject who once could not use that language. How might language, gender and desire reappear from the point-of-view of this subject? Let me suggest what is at stake in this shift in perspective from the sign's point-of-view to the subject's point-of-view by first discussing the dyshesion between language and context from the perspective of the subject.

Language cannot exhaustively master context in part because context is the always-shifting total result of a group's divergent denotational and predicational systems. From a semiotic perspective (a sign-eye's view) individual denotational and predicational presuppositions and entailments always diverge from others within the same linguistic group, even if ever so slightly. All subjects in a language group are certainly subjected to that language. But they are not subjected identically. As Ben Lee (1997) has noted though the "creative indexical properties of performatives bring about the conditions that make the utterances true" performatives also fail to bring about the conditions that would make them true without reserve, left-over, debris.[24] Performatives cannot saturate context because they, like all language acts, are linked to numerous, if delicate, differences in the presuppositional grounds of subjects, grounds on which subjects evaluate an event including its performative felicities. The bottle never hits the ship and the ritual percussionist never hits every beat according to the necessarily varied presuppositions and expectations of each and every member of the performing and on-looking crowd. They hit *"well enough," "better than last time," "in ways we can all agree on," "near perfectly, but did you see her shoes!," "well, true she should not have worn them, but that doesn't matter, does it?"*

---

[24] Lee (1997), p. 57. For Austin on performativity see Austin (1962, 1979). For gender and performativity see Butler (1985); Livia and Hall (1997).

The origin of these presuppositional differences can be accounted for, at least in part, in purely semiotic terms. As I noted above, the building blocks of new registers come from whatever pragmatic, semantic and metapragmatic forms and functions make up the linguistic material of a community of speakers. All the possible "types of interactions," "types of social identities," "types of agential states associated with type of social identity" and all the semantic and pragmatic means by which these types are regimented provide speakers with the material to inlay one speech genre into the domain of another and thus create new speech and text genres. These entextualizations may be the result of an intentional creative subject, the visions of a psychotic, or part of a social movement. In any case, one normative register is laid into another and in the process resignifies the entire discursive contour of the speaking community.

Entextualization is an ongoing feature of everyday language usage as speakers draw on metapragmatic functions to articulate what they are doing, where, and with whom. The quotidian nature of these semiotic mappings and re-mappings are a critical part of social struggle. For example, feminists have used the quotidian ideals and expectations of how "humans" or "liberal democratic peoples" ought to speak to one another to resignify normative ideals and expectations of how women and men ought to speak to one another. Habermas's discussion of the emergence of a particular form of bourgeois liberal subjectivity in eighteenth-century Europe is another relevant example of these genre extensions, entextualizations, and refigurations. The long-distance free traffic in economic news created by early capitalist trade led to aesthetic innovations in public and private textual forms and to subsequent social expectations about how speech should be regulated in the emergent space of the public sphere.[25]

But if language provides speakers the means of producing interactionally coherent texts, it also provides them the means of producing syntactically coherent sentences that challenge or flaunt social norms or usages. Take for instance the perfectly grammatical: "He might be a man" or "Some men are men" the implication being that "At least one man is not a man."[26] These social deictics may or may not have an obvious corporeal or behavioral context or reference. But they do have a social effect. If little else the listener wonders their meaning. "What do you mean some men are men? What are you saying? What or who could make a man otherwise than a man and what would this 'otherwise' consist of? No. A man is a man. Unless . . ." This imaginary fragment of introspection demonstrates, once again, that a divergent space between normative grammatical and social gender simply exists. It is. Its actuality makes it available for mean-making if social agents find it, deploy it, make something of it. Lacan certainly did with such infamous propositions as "*La femme n'existe pas*" and

[25] Habermas (1993); Fraser (1993); Hanson (1993); Gal (1998); Berlant (1997).
[26] See Levinson (1983), pp. 97–166; Lacan (1977b).

"*Il y a d'l'Un*." In the first moment, the pragmatic function of "some men are men" might be little more than a thin interpretive wedge driven into normative masculinity. But over time the silent, oft debilitating, interrogation of the interrogative, "Are you the one?" might reconstitute the normative expectations not only of masculinity but the social institutions regimenting and regimented by this genre.[27]

Grammar itself provides speakers with the means of signaling the conditionality of any and every given instance of language structure and usage, every proposition whether normatively or counter-normatively structured. Consider this stretch of modals: "Maybe I should talk like this to be a woman. Maybe I shouldn't"; "Maybe I am a woman, maybe I am not"; "Maybe I shouldn't have, but it's too late now"; "These might be the right contexts, conditions, people for me to express myself in this way. They might not be." These "might bes" and "maybes" mark a potential "otherwise" that speakers can always index *no matter there exists no actual content* for that otherwise *as of yet*. Whether used to buttress normative linguistic regimes or to show the ongoing failure of gender normativity, these grammatical features provide the material stuff of real-time social struggle. They point to a "condition of uncertainty" and thus possibility residing in the perduring presuppositional structures of language and society even if, in the first instance, this condition of possibility is nothing more than an empty grammatical space.

The source of this feeling of uncertainty (or, possibility) is in part the result of a speaker's metapragmatic sense: her sense of the implicit and explicit alternative forms that exist in her language and of the metapragmatic mapping that coheres and recoheres these forms. But this feeling, this modal pulsion, also derives from another order of phenomena: subjectivity. It is certainly true that before a subject is even partially aware of it doing so, language is laminating into her tacit rules of gender that become the strongly presuppositional structures she must assume to emerge as a proper subject-of-(an)-enunciation. A purely grammatical presupposition and entailment of gender becomes the condition of being-articulate and articulated into the recognizable. Gender designations entail. They are performative. In English, for instance, grammatical gender makes adjectival common sense in at least three ways: It makes sense to her. It makes sense for her. It makes sense of her.

However, as social agents (parents, teachers, day-care workers, ritual celebrants) are mediating the lamination of tacit rules of gender into individuals,

---

[27] Susan Gal has noted that these mappings across discursive registers are always already implicated in structures of power. She notes that although "the ability to make others accept and enact one's representation of the world" is a critical "aspect of symbolic domination . . . such cultural power rarely goes uncontested" especially when "devalued practices propose or embody alternate models of the social world." Gal (1991), p. 177. For the negotiation of meaning see Ehrlich and King (1996); Goodwin (1993); Herring, Johnson, and DiBenedetto (1995). See Povinelli (1993) for a socially situated discussion of the use of modals in Aboriginal society.

individuals are laminating language with the traumas and corporeal sensations they associate with the intimates who make up their lives. Remember, from the subject's point of view, linguistic grammar is initially only inferable through pragmatic and metapragmatic instances of language usage. For instance, the prelinguistic subject must infer from the use of the term "he" a system of number, person, and gender. That is, the grammatical sense and value only appears through the pragmatic and metapragmatic practices of other subjects and in the contexts of differential risks to the prelinguistic subject herself.

A strong version of the "subject of language" would argue that the various orders of linguistic phenomena themselves must carry in the signal form, function, or capacity the condition of being the communicative medium of a particular form of beings, a human being who becomes speaking subject. How we would demonstrate this imprint is not altogether clear to me. Nor is it clear what implications should be drawn from the difficulty of methodologically accounting for what makes phenomenological sense. But let us not worry, at this point, about these numerous dangers and instead re-examine modality from the perspective I am proposing. As we know, modality grammatically marks the degree of commitment a speaker has to a proposition. But modality might also be seen as a metalingual signal of language's dependence on a subject who must become a speaking subject. The childish form of "might not be" might signal not only a logical–semantic aspect of language, but first and foremost the experience of becoming entailed by a semiotic form as a necessary condition of being social and, at the same time, the experience of being before such an entailment. In short, the pulsion Lacan termed desire might be grammaticalized in linguistic forms like mood and desiderata.

I call these early and subsequent disturbances and grammaticalizations of social language norms a person's intimate pragmatics. Roman Jakobson referred to a related phenomenon as "individual langue" – a personalized linguistic code demarcated by a person's avoidance of "certain forms or certain words that are accepted by society but that seem unacceptable to him for whatever reason or to which he has an aversion."[28] If "social langue" maintains the unity of a society, "individual langue" reflects and maintains "the unity, that is, the continuity, of the individual identity."[29] A person's intimate pragmatics would include the specific delicate structures of a grammar, such as the learning of proper and improper gender classification, reference, and identity; and it would include the fine phonological features of a social register that lays out social space in the act of speaking.[30] But it would also include the fragmentary specters of countless microdiscursive and corporeal encounters, part subjects and trace memories, non-linguistic hopes, aspirations, disappointments, corporeal surfaces, and contours laminated into phonological features, lexical

---

[28] Jakobson (1990), p. 90.   [29] Jakobson (1990), p. 91.
[30] Such as do polite registers, for instance, see Errington (1988); Keating (1994); Siddell (1998).

choices, syntactic patterns. Inversely, the grammar itself would signal the pro-
visionality of every actual proposition – metapragmatically shaped segment of
meaning.

These intimate pragmatics are critical to understanding the dynamism of society, for they destabilize the very language of normative intimate community that
regimenting institutions of language are meant to stabilize. They do so because
a person projects, or more precisely, extends her intimate pragmatics into every
scene she enters. These intimate pragmatics migrate unperceived with individuals as they enter and transgress public and intimate spheres, orienting their
expectations, and demands, accounting in part for why no one ever quite "gets"
what they are trying to say. "Why don't you understand what I am asking of
you? Don't we both speak the same language?" Strictly speaking the answer
is "no." But again, the answer is no not simply because social langue is the
totality of the divergent individual langue composing it. The answer is strictly
no because language is not simply a semiotic phenomena. It is a phenomenon
whose material conditions, as well as social conditions, make it otherwise than
simply itself.

In other words, an individual's intimate pragmatics is not simply the code
itself, but rather the code and the desires it disturbs and is disturbed by. What disturbs social langue and transforms it into individual langue is not language *per
se* but, at least in part, the pre- and non-linguistic affective and corporeal attachments, needs, imaginaries, and material surfaces that language marks-marked
and impedes-impeded. These affects and imaginaries are certainly regimented
in the individual code, but strictly speaking, they are not identical with that
code. Here, psychoanalytic and dominant anthropological approaches to language, gender and sexuality diverge. Psychoanalytic desire does not refer. It
is not any specific encoding of emotion, feeling, emotional categories, emotional discourse, or discourses on emotions.[31] It cannot be reduced to "linguistic encodings" which "constitute distinct and describable phenomena," to
"discourse on emotions," or "emotional discourse" (phatic function), although
these provide a trace of its movement. Emotion may be a useful translation of
desire, but only if emotion is understood in its root sense as an incitement, a
movement defined by a motion not towards any specific thing, but out and away
from every positioning; i.e. every proposition such as "I am a woman," "This is
not sex," "Doing this makes headdress stick to head." Or not, depending upon
how effective the glue is.

In sum, rather than normative grammatical and social gender articulating
neatly with each other across diverse contexts, and both of these semiotic phenomena neatly articulating with the phenomena of subjectivity, each order must
be continually secured to the other and to the corporeal substances, psychic

---

[31] See Abu-Lughod and Lutz (1990) for a typical approach.

economies, social spaces and actions that make up their presupposed and entailed contexts and referents. Pragmatic and metapragmatic discourses and functions provide language with delicate and robust means of "securing" denotational text to bodies, contexts, institutions, and psyches. And bodies, contexts, and material spaces provide surfaces, densities, malleability, lumpiness, hollows, and solidities against which language must contend. But a variety of social agents and agencies are needed to regiment and discipline the use of these linguistic and non-linguistic forms to impede or prod the inherent play of linguistic innovation and its resultant social modifications. These agents and agencies include our most intimate allies, teachers, friends, lovers, who prod us to speak like a *proper* he or she, gay or straight, and our most distant consociates, academic or state officials legislating excitable or pornographic speech in the public sphere, on campus, in town commons, through the internet and parcel post.[32]

In these ordinary and extraordinary circumstances, in these intimate and intimidating spaces, children and adults learn not only the particular content of linguistic domination/incitation but also its specific form ("do not to speak like that" or "say it this way") and the variegated risks entailed in speaking otherwise. They then extend this form of linguistic domination and risk across various social institutions of work, intimacy, and gender and sexual identity. But insofar as language has the means for subjects to secure it to context, it also provides a location and the means for social agents to uncouple these indexical attachments of gender. Because a fundamental indexical nonsense form under-girds gender sense, every site where a speaking subject secures gender to a social context also provides a site where another speaking subject can contest the linkage. Countless studies in language and gender have now documented the diversity in semiotic form, content, and mediation of these struggles.

To become a gendered subject in language is, then, to entail a context for the subject of language and the conditions in which that subject will *suffer*. This subject will suffer for purely linguistic reasons. Semantic, pragmatic, and metapragmatic features and functions and the social agents who mediate them regiment the presuppositional conditions of the *proper* gendered subject. But these regimentations of normative gender and sexuality are also always subject to modification, question, interrogation, and accusation based on these same features, functions, institutions, and agents. Language may denote and predicate gender but it also provides the ever-present means of its insecurity and indetermination. But this subject of language will also suffer on account of language. Doomed to be *actual* only through language, the subject will be forced to enunciate herself as a full and truly human subject in a communicative medium

---

[32] See MacKinnon (1993); Butler (1997).

necessarily partial and particularizing. The subject will be forced to engage a social language with an intimate pragmatics that irritates and is irritated by that social language. Thus, to speak like a proper woman may be to become a proper woman. But if so, to be a woman is strictly impossible. But no more or less so than a man who, for all the indexically obviousness of his Thing, suffers the fact and security of its pragmatic attachment.

MAXIMIZING ETHNOPOETICS: FINE-TUNING ANTHROPOLOGICAL EXPERIENCE

PAUL FRIEDRICH

Ethnopoetics was coined if not defined by Jerome Rothenberg, Dennis Tedlock and their friends in 1967. Seeking to expand and advance the concept and its descendants, the word will be taken to mean, not just the intersection of poetry and anthropology, but the study and the creation of relations and interactions between three phenomena: first, *poetic language* in the largest sense, from self-conscious lyric to a political speech to the latent figures in any verbal communication – even a recipe for apple pie; second, a social group with its ethnicity and culture, ranging from a Tamil family to the Hatfield and McCoy clans to France to groups of ethnically defined nations – the Caucasus, China; the third phenomenon is the *individual* making the connection between the first two through his poetry or language in general: poet, orator, ethnopoetician, Everyman (always uniquely creative by definition).

Before launching into the map below with its road signs, let me state right off the gist of this chapter in simple terms. It runs from writing poems and doing translations that involve, in particular, distant and different worlds, to the analysis of poetic matter in terms of linguistics and anthropology, specifically ethnography. I then turn to several general questions, including theory in ethnopoetics and some possible relations between ethnopoetic and anthropological theory, and theory in other fields. Problems that pervade the chapter and animate it are the dilemma of poetic nuance versus universals, the role of tropes or figures, the harmonization of verbal art and scientific approaches, and the possible relations between ethnopoetry and politics. In the course of these discussions, I point out many connections to allied phenomena and the poetic substrata in phenomena not typically seen as poetic.

What follows now is a map with some road signs for the complexities suggested, and the problems and the dilemmas posed by any ethnopoetics when taken in this sweeping sense. Ethnopoetics will first of all be defined and discussed in terms of a rough division between the *synthetic* and the *analytic*, synthesis and analysis. The first, *synthetic* division includes highly subjective activities of two kinds. It may be creating a poem that is relatively anthropological

For their comments on this chapter I stand grateful to John Attinasi, Barney Bate, James Fernandez, Gwen Layne-Seeley, and Paul Liffman.

(of which more below). Or it may be translating or at least transposing something ethnopoetic from one language and culture world to another. *Analytic*, in
contrast, means taking apart and inspecting something ethnopoetic in terms of
the language or of the society and its culture: the *linguistic* and *ethnographic*
analyses. Either analysis or synthesis draws from some part of the world sample.
The following chapter specifically favors the Anglophone and Russian worlds
while including others, notably T'ang China (e.g. Wang Wei), Native America
(e.g. Eskimo, Quechua, Mayan, Zuni, Tarascan), Africa and East India (Tamil,
the Rig-Veda), and many, many more. In other words, depth and scope is of
necessity compromised when it comes down to individual players, fields of
knowledge and the sense of issue. Throughout a major concern will be with –
depending on your point of view – the dilemma or paradox or dialectic or
contradiction that obtains between (1) maximizing generality, universality of
meaning and audience, as against (2) maximizing embeddedness in the local and
concrete, the historically situated, the culturally unique gossamers of nuance.

   Both analysis and synthesis are entangled with the last two components of
ethnopoetics, the first of which is: how can ethnopoetic theory and practice be
reciprocally interconnected with general theory in anthropology and its sister
social sciences? Particularly, how can it fit with theories of verbal aesthetics
and the figuration and configurations of culture? How can ideas in ethnopoetics
articulate in an exciting way with methods and concepts even further afield,
for example, chaos theory or even the calculus? The second of these final
components delves into the etymological roots and resonances of the term itself:
how can the native theories of the poetic – of poetic language, the ethnicity and
culture, the poet or other agent – be inferred and stated as philosophies or world
views in their own right? Note the heuristic formula, to which we will recur
below: Marquesan navigation is to Marquesan ethnonavigation as Bantu poetry
is to Bantu ethnopoetics.

Synthesis

Ethnopoetic poetry

The writing of poetry inspired by distant reaches of the world sample should
be included at the outset of ethnopoetic theorizing. It is the alpha of maximally
intuitive and emotional synthesis versus the omega of objective criticism and
analysis. While some early poetries with a deep time line, notably Chinese, were
almost self-contained in their ethnocentricity, it is also true that the creative
response to the strange other's winged words is as old as the Akkadian Semitic
response to Sumerian (about 2100 BC), or the Hebrew to the Ugaritic or the
Hellenic to the Phoenician or the Indic to the Dravidian (all second millennium
BC). The response of Tamil and other Dravidian systems to Sanskrit began as
early and continues down through time to this day. Recent centuries, notably of
the Renaissance, and recent decades, notably since the 1950s, have witnessed

an acceleration of these processes of ethnopoetic response that often veer into
the exponential – from the hundreds of unpublished ethnopoetic poems of
Edward Sapir, to the Pulitzer Prize work of Gary Snyder and Dereck Walcott,
to the thousands of anthropologically oriented poems published annually in the
United States. Such ethnographic poetry can take off from the poems of a distant
tradition, but can also be inspired by other aspects of remote cultures, including
archaeological ruins as in the following by Gary Snyder on cliffdwellers in the
Southwest:[1]

> ANASAZI
> Anasazi,
> Anasazi,
>
> tucked up in clefts in the cliffs
> growing strict fields of corn and beans
> sinking deeper and deeper in earth
> up to your hips in Gods
> > your head all turned to eagle-down
> > & lightning for knees and elbows
> your eyes full of pollen
>
> > the smell of bats.
> > the flavor of sandstone
> > grit on the tongue.
>
> > women
> > birthing
> at the foot of ladders in the dark.
>
> trickling streams in hidden canyons
> under the cold rolling desert
> corn-basket   wide-eyed
>
> > red baby
> > rock lip home,
>
> Anasazi

Let us glance at a few concrete moments of the synthetic. Over a dozen far-
flung anthropologist poets and poet anthropologists were brought more fully in
touch with each other during the 1970s, mainly because of the organizational
initiative and energies of Stanley Diamond. It jumped off, a memorable two
days of poetry reading and discussion at the New School, followed in 1983
by a massive reading at the annual meeting of the American Anthropological
Association, and, for the next decade or so, by a spate of readings, reviews,

---

[1] Snyder majored in Anthropology at Reed under the illustrious guru David French and, with his
friend Dell Hymes, studied anthropology and linguistics for one year at Indiana University under
the Americanist Carl Voeglin, before he veered off and went to sea, worked as a forest ranger,
lead in the Beat movement, and did advanced work in Chinese and Japanese at Berkeley, then
residing for many years in Japan, where he became a Zen priest; anthropology and ethnopoetics
have been continuous co-presences throughout his long life.

journal essays, conferences and anthologies.[2] The full scope was integrated in an anthology, *Reflections. The Anthropological Muse*, with 48 contributers (Prattis 1985).

These little explosions had counterparts elsewhere. About the same time, several dozen linguists, led by Donna Jo Napoli and Bill Bright were giving readings and publishing what eventuated as four volumes (e.g. Rando and Napoli 1983). There was, naturally, some overlap between the two groups (Friedrich, Hymes, Tedlock). Also about the same time, again with some overlap scores, perhaps hundreds, of professional poets led by Jerome Rothenberg (1985), William Merwin (1979), David Wagoner (1998), and others, were writing and publishing hundreds of poems in response to Native American, African, Asian and other non-Western verbal art of all kinds. The 1980s, then, saw a great deal of synthesis.

Just as striking as the parallel and often confluent courses of the anthropological, linguistic, English language and creative writing streams, however, was the widespread lack of aesthetic and intellectual integration and sense of community at deeper levels: with a couple of exceptions, notably Nathaniel Tarn, no professional anthropologist or linguist competed in the professional "poetry mags" and "po biz" of the poets, and, again with a few exceptions, no professional poet worked through and internalized the language and culture from which (via translation) the new post-Postmodern lyrics were being extracted. A weird but well-attended reading at the New School in 1988 by Diamond, Friedrich, Hollander and Ashbery (the latter then the idol of the critical marketplace) was haunted or should we say plagued by a lack of empathy between the straight poetic and the poetic anthropological camps. In other words, various negative forces were interacting with natural tendencies toward synthesis, such as the Tedlock cum Rothenberg case.

Ethnographic poetry still lights up the pages of journals in diverse fields, on occasion, and, within anthropology, has been institutionalized with the annual awards for poetry by *Humanistic Anthropology* and, during Tedlock's editorship, by the publication of many poems in the *American Anthropologist*, but, speaking of it overall, the "small but bright" explosion of the 1980s, with readings attended by hundreds in auditoriums and ballrooms, subsided almost as quickly as it surfaced. The creative–synthetic response, which depends heavily on disregarding the walls between ethnography, linguistics, and the arts of poiesis, has suffered and is suffering more and more from the increasing professionalism of younger anthropologists in their (post)doctoral anxieties, and younger poets trapped within the paradigms and constraints of MFA programs and "po biz." Nonetheless, the creative–synthetic response, in poetic prose as

---

[2] The poets I recall at these anthropology readings are A. L. Becker, Stanley Diamond, Dell Hymes, Anthony Lewis, Dan Rose, Jerome Rothenberg, Gary Snyder, Nathaniel Tarn, Dennis Tedlock, and Ed Wilmsen. At the readings by linguist-poets, Dona Jo Napoli and Deborah Tannen stand out in my memory.

well as lyric poetry, continues to emerge as an insidious and far-branching ethnopoetics. Its questions and answers, its images and irreverencies find their way onto otherwise unpoetic pages, sound tracks, or film strips – just as in the 1950s Pablo Neruda's long and slender "Elemental odes" were squeezed in alongside the editorials of Santiago's leading leftist newspaper.

Ethnopoetic translation

The foregoing problems of form in poetry get us back to the second kind of synthetic, intuitive poetics, to wit, the practice and theory of translating from the world sample. Translation from distant tongues has, of course, been flourishing since ancient times, as in the Ugaritic to Hebrew example above, or in sub-Saharan Nilotic to Egyptian, long before "The Age of Discovery." The translation harvest or often hunting and gathering, or just poaching, accelerated greatly during the nineteenth century partly as a result of massive contact with Native American, African, Asian, and Near Eastern literatures, both written and oral, within the ideologies of Western Romanticism. "The Rubiat of Omar Khayam" from the Persian and similar translations of genius commingled with hundreds of volumes of mediocre work by scholars, poets, explorers, and polyglots who, like the missionaries, often worked hand in hand with or at least walked in the footprints of the forces of colonialism and imperialism. Today ethnopoetic translation comes in the extreme form, be it of excellent poems in the target language or scientific "literal" translations with no literary pretensions, but the great majority lie somewhere in between. The old adage that to translate is to traduce obscures the more basic fact that translation is linguistically and mathematically impossible and that any success even when it borders on the miraculous, remains a matter of degree.

Some of the more recent trends and traditions in anthropology and literary studies, if not the crypto-colonialism, were gathered together and catalyzed in the 1970s by the founding of the journal, *Alcheringa* (1976), by poet-anthropologist Dennis Tedlock and anthropological poet Jerome Rothenberg. Hundreds of poems were carried over from exotic and not so exotic languages. The journal became a symbol and synecdoche for more ambitious kindred enterprises, outstandingly the Penn Prize winning translation of the *Popol Vu* (Mayan epic of creation; Tedlock 1985) and Rothenberg's enormously creative and influential anthologies of poems from the world sample, from Inuit to Job, from Hottentot to Haiku, with extensive footnotes and annotations from anthropological and literary sources. While his anthologies have been criticized for yanking poems out of context, he usually does give some context and, context or no context, has had the effect of opening up potential publics to a huge range of ethnopoetic reality.

Roughly contemporaneous with these intense anthropological activities were those of professional poets in departments of English. Led by Karl Kroeber,

Bryan Swan, and others, a host of poet translators strove, like the anthropologists, to transport the gist or at least a snippet of alien aesthetic culture, the
poetic vision of "The Other," into our jaundiced, urban, Euro-American scheme
of things (institutionally speaking, the main stage has been sessions on Native
American, African, and other "non-Western" literature at the annual meetings
of the Modern Language Association). A prime example of the sophistication
that has resulted from these doings is *Nineteen Ways of Looking at Wang Wei*,
edited by a Harvard Sinologist and the Nobel Prize winning Mexican Octavio
Paz. *Nineteen Ways* takes a relatively timeless and universally valid classic by
the Chinese Buddhist Wang Wei (700–771 AD) and critically compares nineteen attempts at translation through two and a half centuries that culminate
with the masterpiece by Gary Snyder, to which I return below. Still, while fully
appreciating the quality of "the winner," we should also recognize the seriously
biased, historically and sociopolitically determined nature of their selections
and of Weinberger's often acidulous judgments.

Yet, again, one found a serious lack of confluence or even communication between anthropological and literary translators that reflects, as in the
case of poets, a profound antithesis between universalism and linguacultural
situatedness: the more generally accessible and acceptable the translation, the
farther it tends to be from the linguacultural reality of the original. In other
words, the truer the translation is to the linguistic and cultural reality of the
original, the more difficult and obscure it may seem to the speaker in the
target language. The near miracle of translations that are both highly accurate and great literature, has happened. As John Milton wrote back in 1673
of his incredible recreation of Horace's Ode I. 5: "Rendered almost word for
word without rhyme according to the Latin measure as nearly as the language
will permit" (Carne-Ross and Haynes 1996: 88). Blok's translations of some
Heine poems and lines in the *Iliad*'s of Pope and Chapman are similarly preter-
natural. But such miracles have rarely if ever been achieved by the translators from Native American or African poetry and few players in these fields
possess an appreciation for what might be called Miltonian standards. In an
anecdote cast in a poem, Gary Snyder, after wrestling with Milton, throws his
copy into a campfire in the high sierra. But the important overall result is that
the Sumerian Gilgamesh epic and love songs from Aboriginal Australia, the
Confucian Odes and the *Bhagavad Gita*, have been moved to the scholarly
front stage of comparative poetics and cultural and symbolic anthropology –
at least for those open-minded enough to take cognizance of such "data."

Ethnopoetic translation, often exclusivistically called "Americanist," actually
originated in the philology of earlier centuries and traditions (e.g. Böhtlink)
where native (e.g. Siberian) texts were carefully translated and commented
on in terms of phonetics, grammar, lexicology, ethnography, and even literary components. Typically the texts in question were tales, myths, or ritual
sequences where the form remains conveniently more or less fixed for the

scholar without electronic tape – as contrasted with conversation and other free-flowing discourse. By some global collusion these texts were usually taken to be prose until – by a flip reminiscent of the Molière character who didn't know he'd been talking prose all his life – Monro Edmondson pointed out to a mesmerized audience at an AAA meeting that the *Popul Vu*, our major New World text, could be read as consisting of lines, that it was a poem (Edmondson 1971). His discovery was rapidly exploited by dozens of scholars led by Hymes and Tedlock who examined hundreds of texts in dozens of languages. Much of the discussion centered on whether the line was set off by overt markers, or syntactic features, or prosodic ones (e.g. rising or falling intonation), the more reasonable arguing that all three variables were relevant (Bright 1979). These controversies ramify in many directions because the line, for all its apparent simplicity, is one of the firmest criteria for what makes poetry poetry.

Intertangled with questions of the demarcation of the line were those of how to represent its overall sound. Recognizing that the usual devices omit a great deal, some pioneers in the area, notably Dennis Tedlock (1972), devised notations that would capture – for performance – the basic musical variables of length, pitch and stress, as illustrated by the following excerpt from his first endeavor (length is indicated by dashes and the repetition of elements, pitch by height above the line, and stress by the size of the letter), a Zuni tale called "The Boy and the Deer":

```
SON'AHCHI
(audience) Ee_____so.
                LO_____NG A
SONTI                   GO
(audience) Ee_____so.
                VIL       HE'
THERE WERE    LAGERS AT   SHOKTA
and
up on the Prairie-Dog Hills
the deer
had their home.
The daughter of a priest
        sit         room        fourth       down
was    ting in a         on the        story        weaving
      bas
          ket plaques.
She was always sitting and working there, and the Sun
              came up
every day            Sun came up
          when the
      girl            working
the       would sit
at the place where he came in
It seems the Sun made her pregnant.
```

Such a notation, if followed faithfully, may bring us closer to the sound of the Zuni and was presumably instrumental in elevating a Zuni tale to a world audience. Yet such a system raises many questions – for example, that of the differential status of the three variables in the two languages, and of the comparability or even the gross similarity between the English transcription as pronounced by the ordinary reader and the Zuni original. Ethnopoetics has mainly turned to other fields today, partly because few linguists are interested in lyric effects, just as few poet-translators, especially the so-called "professionals," are interested in mastering the languages, particularly the tough ones, as most native American languages are, or the correspondingly tough technical linguistic features of the native texts they are translating. But the questions remain as alive and disturbing as before, as do those of relating such translations and notations to contemporary phonology (e.g. metrical phonology), lexicology (e.g. word grammars), or even postmodern ethnography, "critical anthropology" and literary criticism.

Analyses

Linguistic Ethnopoetics, or Linguapoetics

Some potential or implicit translation accompanies a third major part of ethnopoetics: the comparatively objective linguistic analysis of poetic texts or of the poetry necessarily inheres in any text – from an Eskimo cooking receipt for "Eskimo icecream" to a live performance in Malayalam of a Sanskrit epic. In the first or stricter sense linguistic ethnopoetics subdivides into three familiar parts, all of them illustrated by hundreds if not thousands of exemplary empirical studies. It may be sound patterns as in the analyses of Ob-Ugric song by Austerlitz (1958). It may be semantics as in the Jakobson-cum-Lévi-Strauss (1987) analysis of Baudelaire's sonnet "Les chats." It may be pragmatics as in Beeman's many analyses of emotion and performance in Persian (1986, 2000) or Irvin's on West African sociolinguistics. It may, finally, be those rarer studies that synthesize linguistic formalism, semantics, particularly of words in myth, and pragmatics, even a "breakthrough into performance" (Hymes 1981: 79–142, 200–263). All of these approaches, be it taking a sonnet apart or dissecting the tropology of a sermon or a political speech, raise in acute shape many age-old problems: what is the constructive relation between poetry and prose, between poetics and rhetoric, between song and conversation, between poiesis and logos – as well as challenging and problematizing the categories themselves of poetry, prose, poetics and rhetoric, song, discourse, conversation, poiesis, logos, and mythos – even ethnopoetics. In exploring these diverse fields and alleys it is fruitful to consider what is obvious and recognizably ethnopoetics and also the much greater information that is potentially or partially so.

Linguistic ethnopoetics thus extends into many fields and comes in many forms and is by no means limited to what is labeled or self-labeled as "ethnopoetic." It intersects with much of the work on iconicity, as illustrated, for example, by Quechua where ejective and aspirate sounds were borrowed and then spread through lexical networks where they were variously iconic with the processes involved in the expulsion of air (Mannheim 1991); in Quechua as in Chechen, ejectives would be ideal raw material for poetic effects. Similarly, much of Quechua patterning of ideophones is ipso facto poetic: the ideophone particle *tak* ranges in meaning from the sound of a gourd tapped for ripeness to the "sound of someone grabbing a machete" to a position within a definite point in a spatial field – like "the tail of a snake about to strike" (Nuckolls 1999: 242; 1996). Ideophones with direct reference to "the sound of a waterfall or the call of a toucan (Feld 1982) transcend "the arbitrariness of the symbol" to create a direct reference that is potentially as powerful as the "buzz" in Emily Dickinson's "I heard a Fly buzz when I died." Ethnopoetics, then, often involves processes – here of iconic reference – outside the boundaries of linguistic laws in the conventional sense.

Ethnopoetics similarly includes much of the work on indexicality because the innumerably different ways deixis can be handled in a given language, be it Mayan (Hanks 1990) or Homeric Greek and may, like iconic nuance, constitute a critical if aesthetically subtle component of meaning: looking down from the walls of Troy, old Priam uses a deictic pronoun that assumes only himself, the speaker, whereas Helen, dealing with a reality that "exists before her" uses a different pronoun that "actually points out the object of her reference, in the direct sense of deixis . . . Helen and Priam's joint seeing (of Agamemnon) is in fact the very point of the use of *houtos*" (Bakker 1999: 7).

Since conversation and similar use of natural language always has a poetic aspect, it follows that the research under the rubric of "pragmatics" and "discourse" also intersects with the ethnopoetic project, from Tannen's analytical versions of a Thanksgiving repast to Becker's chapter-length philology of a Malay sentence – both of which suggest the linguistic music, respectively, of a pleasant dinner-time dialogue and a beautiful sentence. Similar claims would be justified in the case of "formal linguistics," be it Chomsky's take-off from "Flying planes can be dangerous" to any article on phonology or syntax chosen at random from the latest issue of *Language* since all of them involve poetic (i.e. analogical) patterning. Ideally, the diverse linguistic approaches should be synthesized holistically and calibrated with ancillary cultural and political factors, as in Hill's tour de force on the text of a reported tragedy in a Nahuatl/Mexicano peasant village: the "art" of the eighteen levels of voice of a perhaps unusual speaker are analyzed in terms of many linguistic dimensions, including prosodic "shadow," and contextualized to community, culture and national politics, not to omit the art of the author herself and her treatment of how the second person pronoun breaks out at the climactic instant when old Don Gabriel sees his son lying under a blanket on the road, dead.

Within this multiplex and eclectic scene, special status accrues to Slavic and Native American studies for four reasons: partly because in the former linguistics and literary criticism continue to be practiced as two sides of the one coin, partly because of the inherent poetry of so many of the Native American texts; partly because of the long-standing ties that bind Americanist linguistics to anthropology (their annual meetings are part of the American Anthropological Association); finally, because of the seminal role of Jakobson and Sapir and their intellectual heirs such as Hanks and Hymes. These indicate that linguistic poetics has long been an integral part of all ethnopoetics. To adapt Jakobson's paraphrase of Horace: "I do ethnopoetics and am no stranger to anything in the poetry of language or the language of poetry."

The content of linguistic ethnopoetics varies extravagantly depending on what part of language is in the focus. Often enough this involves sound in the sense of metrics, rhyme and rhythm. Yet a focus on sound, while it may be enjoined by one's phonological model, also depends on the facts of the language: the poetics of Kabardian with its 69 consonants, is predictably more complex than that of Hawaiian with eleven, and a simpler phonotactics. The same rough correlation between linguistic and poetic structure also holds for morphology: languages like Russian or Sanskrit, or Inuit and Yupik, with their enormously productive systems of derivational (e.g. word-formative) morphology enjoin a poetics that would be inconceivable for simpler systems: many long words in the Sanskrit *Bhagavad Gita* cover an entire line, some run over two lines: the following from the *Bhagavad Gita* (11.14.b) is fairly typical

śítoṣṇasukhaduḥkhadáh
cold heat pleasure pain causing

A major Russian poem is built around derivations from the prefix *ras/raz*. In the realm of syntax – roughly, the order of free forms in a phrase or sentence – a language such as English or Chinese, with relatively fixed orders governed by mainly obligatory rules, will have a poetics that differs drastically from Latin or *Gita* Sanskrit with relatively free order governed by relatively probabilistic rules. Etymology, finally, is of consuming ethnopoetic interest given the ways poets and poetic speakers of all sorts play with etymological and related lexical relations as in *double entendre*.

At the level of style the differences between languages and their traditions entail categorically and correspondingly different poetics – as we move from the extraordinarily allusive language of the Late T'ang or Medieval Javanese to styles that minimize such allusiveness, be it the anti-poetic Nícanor Parra or the relative starkness of the Puritan Plain Style (Miller 1967) or of American objectivism or American country lyrics or the problematic "cool" of some of the recent American minimalism. Linguistic ethnopoetics thus calls for a judicious coordination between the structural facts of language, the skewings of a poet or a tradition – notably bilingual or multilingual ones – and the sociolinguistics and the linguistic demand of the audiences.

Saliently original work on the borderlands of linguistic poetics has been Woodbury's, who, after years of extensive and intensive analysis, argues that all Yupik conversation is not only poetic, but, in his strict sense, poetry (1985). His conclusions resemble those of Coleman researching the admittedly unusual Irish community of Roth Cairn. These and kindred studies provide a firm, analytical backstop to the theory behind Robert Frost's "The sound of sense" (1964), or, more explicitly, the fixed prosody of formulaic phrases. All of which harks back to one of the main contentions in European Romanticism, notably the preface to *Lyrical Ballads* by Coleridge and Wordsworth and, beyond that, of a long tradition of linguistic relativism that goes back to Plato's *Cratylus* and some early Indian thinkers about language. Between the extremes of those who contend that the poetic is ubiquitous and indeed obvious and those who fail to see it anywhere, there lies the much larger population of scholars who see poetry in language as important, but clearly a matter of degree. For this central majority the study of tropes promises much for linking the pro-poetic and anti-poetic theorists, the maximizers and the minimizers (Fernandez 1986, 1991).

Ethnographic or cultural ethnopoetics

Contemporaneous and entangled with linguistic ethnopoetics have been the many analyses by diverse anthropologists and some other social scientists of the cultural orchestration, content, contexts and functions of more or less poetic texts – and the poetics of texts that do not seem to be poetic. Outstanding instances of such analyses have been Bauman's work on American Protestant sermons and related religious language, and Tannen's (1989) treatment of the tropes in key political speeches by Martin Luther King, Jr. ("I had a dream") and Jesse Jackson Jr. ("My grandmother's quilt"). Both authors pinpoint the origins of these rhetorics in the sermon suggest how it draws audiences into passionate acceptance, resentful rejection. The verse of African-American preaching, incidentally, is very much in the breath-phrase structure of the blues and ballads of the same culture.

More generally, a wide front of scholarship with the most diverse approaches and models has involved two kinds of potentially reciprocal contextualization. First, speeches, songs and other literary expressions have been set in the context of their cultures. Second, turning the tables, cultural patterns and social events have been set in the poetic imagination and expressions of a given people. In these twinned operations of contextualization, ethnopoetics and "literary studies" in anthropology (e.g. Daniel and Peck 1996) have often intersected with "cultural studies" in comparative literature and many fields of language nad literature (reflected, for example, by many panels at the Modern Language

Association). A notable example of such crossings-over was the work of the
Shapiros on the acoustic patterns of Shakespeare's sonnets (1998) and the Ital-
ianate phonology in Pushkin – contextualized in the relevant cultural values.
The cross-fertilization between "literary studies" and "cultural studies" has
been enriching for all concerned, and highlights problems that are crucial for
ethnopoetics: what degree of specificity will be worthwhile? It may be one
uncannily unique individual (Hill 1995), or one stratum of a society such as
sessile Bedouin women, or one activity such as the political rhetoric and poetics
of Yemeni Arab men at war, or the ambivalences and strong feelings in a Tamil
family (Trawick 1992), or the semantics of "wine and conversation" in Austria
(Lehrer 1983).

As these examples suggest, ethnopoetics is willy-nilly going to involve the
functions and relations of the verbal aesthetics of any sphere of activity. True,
the extremes of "functionalism" have been excoriated, but the excoriations often
throw out the baby of priceless insight with the bathwater of dated theoretical
models and methods. In other words, the functionalist model, used judiciously
as a discovery procedure, can and has revealed significant analogies. From
discourse to phonetics, from the synchronic to the diachronic and historical,
ethnopoetics to some extent is and certainly could emerge as a crossroads for
anthropology and other social sciences, for linguistics in many of its guises,
and for the study of aesthetic functions, structures and associative relations in
comparative literature and kindred approaches to poetic art and its performance.
Ethnopoetics and poetry itself, like engineering, are everywhere implicit in the
phenomenal world.

Cultural ethnopoetics can be illustrated by two exemplary pieces of research
from the Islamic area. For Bedouins of North Africa, Abu-Lughod demonstrated
compellingly how a single poetic form, the two-line *ginnawa*, functions as an
idiom for reciprocal support and personal, intimate expression among women
and other less empowered categories of people; this is a way of resisting the
dominant, patriarchal culture while, at another level, helping to make it run.

> "I built, when despair was away,
> castles it knocked down when it came . . ."
>
> . . .
>
> "Blinded by the sandstorm of despair
> the wells of love were plugged . . ."
>
> . . .
>
> "I wonder, is despair
> a phantom or my companion for life . . ."
> (Abu-Lughod, 1986: 269)

A second example is Caton's demonstration for the Yemeni Arabs that poetry,
both in oratory and verbal dueling, can facilitate interaction within and between
groups in politics and war. Both studies are founded on the bedrock of the anthropologist's near native fluency in Arabic, and long-term, in-depth fieldwork,

Abu-Lughod conversing with women in their kitchens for thousands of hours, Caton memorizing much of the Koran and participant observing sheiks and their men during a war.

Congruous with these facts of method, culture covaries, works synergistically with language in aesthetically diverse ways that are captured in analyses. Sometimes, as in most sociolinguistics and linguistic ethnography, language and speech are taken as dominant whereas culture and society (and politics) are dealt with in a fragmentary and anecdotal way. In other studies the sociocultural aspects may be dealt with in great depth and extent while the linguistic "data" play an illustrative and contextualizing, even heuristic, role-like local color in romantic–realistic literature. In yet other cases, language/speech and culture/society are analyzed and represented as coordinate and interacting phenomena, each bringing out and realizing the meanings of the other. It is of course impossible to capture and integrate both of the infinitely extending sides of this one empirical interface, yet a comprehensive coordination has proven feasible in restricted domains, be it the semiotics of material culture or political rhetoric (Beeman 1986; Caton 1990; Coleman 1999; Bate 2000). In the main, such cultural ethnopoetics has been realized, not by linguists, but by linguistic or at least linguistically sensitized anthropologists who reject both the stifling positivist objectivism and positivism of earlier decades and the diluted, diffuse, and shallow subjectivism of much (post-) postmodernism and post-postmodernism.

Culture, like similar powerful ideas, has folk meanings and *a priori* or axiomatic meanings in many contexts, but also reflects ineluctable facts: the drastic differences in cuisine when landing in Berlin from Paris, or vice versa, are as convincing empirical evidence as barking one's shin was to Samuel Johnson (and Bertrand Russell). Beyond such crude realities lie deeper levels that are not made less deep by being put in plain language: that culture is a worldview or a way of life; that culture is what people do as against what they say they do as against what they say one should do; that every individual is in part like everyone else in the world, in part like someone in his or her culture (e.g. family, nation), and, of course, in part totally unique. Beyond such gnomic wisdom as rephrased by humanistic anthropologists like E. E. Evans-Pritchard and Clyde Kluckhohn, culture, including ethnopoetic culture, has the transcendental values that are suggested by its figures and other imaginative constructions. The "ethnic" in ethnopoetics is involved in all these meanings of culture.

Culture is a part of language just as language is a part of culture and the two partly overlapping realities can intersect in many ways – for which process the term "linguaculture" may serve. In any case, since culture in a full anthropological sense includes ethnopoetics, the reader deserves at this point an explicit working definition of the term since it is currently suffering the proverbial fate of the baby in the bathwater. Culture is the sets, associations and cybernetic networks of patterns, regularities, symbols and values (and ideas about them), behavioral, linguistic, and ideological, explicit and implicit, rational and emotional, conscious, unconscious and subconscious, that are differentially shared, transmitted in history, and created (or recreated) by the members, as individual agents or collectively, of a given society situated in concrete time and space (compare Kluckhohn and Kelly 1945).

Syntheses and Analyses

Ethnopoetic cum anthropological theory

We have now reviewed the field of ethnopoetics from ethnopoems to cultural analysis. Two meanings remain, at once the most general and, like most truths, the least obvious. I am talking of the at least potential reciprocity between ethnopoetic and anthropological theory.

First, here comes the ethnopoetics that has already gone far in achieving the integration in question: from Jakobson and Sapir to Tedlock and Fernandez. These flourishing traditions often interdigitate with generic literary aesthetics, from Longinus and Kant to, for example, contemporary critics of Asian and African literature. Can we achieve a tropology of tropes and of the individual imagination or character as originally launched in Plato's *Republic* (Book VIII)? How can our understandings of the dynamics of culture be deepened by seeing them in terms of processes in the minds of individual agents?

That the first set of connections promises much has been shown by recent research, be it the complex analogies between an Irish and a Russian novel (Coleman 1999), or the even more complex analogies between Dostoievsky's meanings of "soul" in Russia and the ethnography of the meanings of soul in the formerly closed city of Omsk, Siberia (where, over a century ago, he served four years time as a political prisoner). In these and myriad other instances, ethnopoetics in its interface with anthropological theory has been laced by detailed documentation and analyses of verbal and other evidence, in Pesmen's brilliant analyses of Russian ethnopoetics that integrates everything from the culture of Russian saunas and truck gardens to police practices and state political economy to a culling of insight from Russian poetry to a philology of *krutit'* and other key words, in order to elucidate the meanings of Russian *dusha*, roughly "soul" (Pesmen 2000) – in what is probably the most thorough and profound lexical pragmatics, "word in context," in world history.

Closely coupled with such studies of the poetry in culture have been the equally numerous postmodernist enterprises of taking anthropological texts, including ones that are about literature, and assuming that they are basically literary with, for example, the figures and other formal traits of a novel (Geertz 1986). Contrariwise, a work of literature, even Shakespeare's plays, is taken as importantly if not dominantly ethnographic (Bock 1984). It is in fact impossible to draw a clear line between the rigor of the first examples above and the more diffuse but equally insightful achievements of some "critical anthropology" as in Fabian's (1990) research on African proverbs and proverbial wisdom. Both types of literary anthropology are ethnopoetic to a high degree.

Within the conventional orbits of anthropology, to continue, most research past and present is significantly, often obviously ethnopoetic. Take the decisively influential analyses of color categories in Hanonóo by Conklin (1955) and in Ndembu by Turner (1966), where, among other things, a few powerful categories were shown to underlie a profusion of surface chromaticity with its many associations. Or take the work on chromatic continua by Berlin and Kay (1969) which, despite its rigid positivism, was early on recognized as relevant to ethnopoetics. All good ethnography and related descriptions contribute substantially to ethnopoetics; indeed, in most cases an ethnography has merited the adjectives "great" or "classic" precisely because of the persuasive power of its underlying ethnopoetics – the work of Malinowski, from *Coral Gardens and their Magic* to *Argonauts of the South Pacific*. This extended, diffuse or maximized ethnopoetics, this poetry in cognitive structures, or ethnography of poetic structures, is where the meanings of the ethnopoetic enterprise are most interesting intrinsically and acquire their largest purchase. Yet the professional ethnoscientist and the professional ethnopoetic critic usually and typically exclude each other in a parochial manner.

The extended scope of macro ethnopoetics, from another angle, is illustrated by a long tradition of analyses in anthropology and related fields, of categories and classification and, in some cases, of the dynamics and processes that relate and integrate them (Fernandez 1986). The great tradition runs from Frazer's *Golden Bough* (e.g. homeopathic versus sympathetic magic) and Durkheim and Mauss on so-called "primitive classification" to Douglas's work on purity and danger and the many volumes by Lévi-Strauss; and let us not forget the legions of lesser known toilers in the vineyards of taxonomy (e.g. Matisoff, 1978, Senft 1996). Man and woman are classifying animals, to be sure, but the classes and classifications, after the tables and paradigms, turn out to be interrelated and interanimated by tropes. To take this deeper, when powerful categories such as purity, caste, incest, totem and taboo, and honor and shame, are explored relentlessly and imaginatively, they and their subcategories turn out to be orchestrated in terms of basic tropes like synecdoche. The use of these tropes by individuals is itself ordered in the tropological deep structures of analogy and mood. Tropes go "all the way down."

Which brings me to the second part of "Synthesis and Analysis": the large body of theory in anthropology and related (and apparently unrelated) social and natural sciences where writers with an ear for the poetic have noticed and demonstrated, for example, that Darwin's perceptions and theorizing about variation among finches on Galapagos Island was supremely poetic (Weiner

1995), as have been the researches on the double helix and chaos theory. A huge and burgeoning theory and semi-theory in anthropology and other sciences, including the natural sciences and mathematics, bears witness to a poetic turn or revolution of which ethnopoetics is a part – a relatively small part at that. A proliferating literature on the poetics of law and politics, social reform, and social injustice, agriculture, and cooking, manners and family problems, religion and therapy, and physics and calculus, is concerned with opening up the poetics of these experiences and other fields – scan any issue of *Scientific American* or *American Scientist*. This poetics of knowledge often deals with the actual patterns of a given language or culture, as in the new field of ethnomathematics (D'Ambrósio 1992; Urton 1997): the ramifications of Zeno's paradox which underlies so much in modern mathematics (Belinsky 1995: 4 and *passim*; Hofstadter 1980) could equally well illuminate a poetics of interpersonal relations, including love, as suggested by Carson (1986).

The poetry of calculus or quantum physics joins ethnopoetics in a particularly exciting way when the facts of a natural language such as Hopi, Chinese or Latin are interpreted as significant variables (Chao 1976; Whorf 1997). This is not a matter of "physics for poets" or "the poetry of physics" but of poetic stuff within the innermost recesses of the thought in these fields.

Let us push further the connection between ethnopoetics and ethnoscience. To begin on the ground, the most comprehensive analyses of material culture with its intricacies of pottery design, fishtraps, and weaving, fairly teem with an aesthetics that is ethnopoetic. Similarly, the most comprehensive analyses of poetic culture, notably of metrics, metaphorical fields, rhyme patterns, and syntactic ambiguation, correspondingly teem with an implicit science of language and culture that is nothing if not ethnoscience. At one extreme, for example, Wallace Stevens' subtly mathematical "Thirteen ways of looking at a blackbird" has its counterpart in B. L. Whorf's often poetic statements about linguistic relativism and "linguistics as an exact science." At a yet higher level of abstraction, Gödel, Escher, and Bach drew on and to some extent shared a complex tropology that, as expounded by Hofstadter, makes contemporary anthropological theorizing on the subject seem formally crude; we have much to learn. Given the seriously cognitive aspects of ethnopoetics and the profoundly tropological aspects of all knowledge, including that of primitive peoples, it follows that ethnopoetics and ethnoscience pervasively and potentially intersect with each other, are two sides of one reality. This synergism, explicit or latent, artful or serendipitous, conscious or unconscious, has informed the best anthropology from early on and will continue to do so as the fields, becoming more mature, recognize the fact of indeterminacy and the interpretive power of polymathean holography and, for that matter, playfulness. And yet, as noted, the fields of ethnopoetics and ethnoscience have pursued paths that, while parallel, cross only on occasion, so deeply entrenched is the opposition between art and science.

Metapoetics and poetic revolution

The final meaning of "ethnopoetics" is also the first that many would think of when trying to define this protean term: "ethnopoetics" is that part of a society's ideas that deal with the construction and interpretation of its poetry and poetic language generally, or, more exactly, with the forms, functions and meanings of poetry in its narrower senses – lyric, or epic, tale or fable, parable or riddle. Ethnopoetics is roughly analogous, then, as noted above, to ethnonavigation, the native (e.g. Marquesan) theory of navigation. But how does making an outrigger or an early East Mediterranean sailing raft differ from making an epic poem or any kind of poem – and it does – when, as in a key page of the *Odyssey* (v. 228–261), the poem is about making a boat? It is here that the multiple contrasts and complementarities between ethnopoetics, linguistics, and ethnoscience become most edifying.[3]

A long line of linguistic and poetic relativists have intensely documented how languages and poetries are qualitatively comparable. The phonology of the Chechen mountaineer and the morphology of the Inuit hunter-bard are in fact, at a purely structural ("phonemic") level, more complex than the corresponding English systems of T. S. Eliot, or Milton. An individual lyric poem in a so-called "primitive" culture, moreover, may be not only comparable but qualitatively equal to a poem by Eliot or Milton. Western poets, as noted early on above, have been inspired by their analogies in other aesthetic worlds, be it Ezra Pound and Gary Snyder responding to High T'ang poetry or Mark Strand and Pablo Neruda doing a creative take on images in Quechua civilization.

In other ways, however, the occasionally incarnated ideals of linguistic and poetic relativism wither away or are at least problematized. To begin, the comparability of phonologies, as a sort of synecdoche for the comparability of structures, rides fallaciously on the assumption that such structures are isolable from their contexts; if we take into account the myriad nuances and associations of English sounds, then the phonology, or better, sociophonology, of Milton or Eliot is indeed vastly more complex than that of the Yupik bard. The opposite side of this anti-relativism runs as follows: many kinds of poetry reflect intentional erudition and richness of allusion, be it to a literary past and tradition or to the intricacies and often confused and anomic realities of urban life in a huge political economy: poems by Milton, Mandelshtam or Li Shang-Yin are difficult *prima facie* to compare with those of so-called "primitives" (or primitivists). Yet even this tentative anti-relativism is sown with theoretical landmines. Edward Sapir once wrote a review (1925) entitled "Emily Dickinson, a primitive," the tone of which reflected the then wide-spread downgrading of this giant of "The American Renaissance" (e.g. Matthieson 1941). Recent years have witnessed a

---

[3] As for the link to ethnoscience, using archaeological evidence has demonstrated conclusively that the boat-raft that Odysseus built matches pretty exactly Egyptian structures of the same time period.

torrent of scholarship that proves not only the aesthetic but the ideological, particularly religious, profundity, intricacy, and scope of most of her poems (often involving specific Christian symbols). In addition, the symbolic complexity of some Pacific Northwest myths and tales has been demonstrated by Dell Hymes and his students, colleagues and predecessors, a superb early example being Snyder's *He Who Hunted Birds in his Father's Village*. On a wider front, a palimpsest of brilliant scholars has more than demonstrated the subtle multi-vocalism and multilayeredness of the *Bhagavad Gita*, *Genesis*, the *Rig Veda* (Doniger 1991), the *Odyssey*, and other ancient texts. Poetic quality, in short, need not covary with the quality or technological complexity of the encapsulating culture society and political economy. By an ironic paradox, it is the great poetry that firmly buttresses both a radical, naïve relativism, since many poems from the world sample are not just comparable but equal to each other, and a radical, essentializing universalism whereby, as an empirical fact, many poems from the world sample speak deeply to us all. All of this gives a peculiar depth, and charm, to the often cited lines by Edward Sapir, a minor poet and a major phonologist, about the comparability of the linguistic structure of the headhunter of Assam and the Chinese Brahmin.

This brings us to the other side of the problem: poetics in the sense of comparative criticism. Great poetry, it is true, can arise in diverse cultures and cultural circumstances, but there are also hundreds if not thousands of poetic cultures with little or none of the annotation, explication, criticism and metacriticism that we take for granted and live with to the deplorable point where the readership for "po talk" exceeds that for "po." Between the extremes of criticism-saturated urban traditions and criticism-meager primitive and archaic poetic cultures, there lies and seethes the larger intermediate field where the practice and theory of poetry are more or less coordinate and are mutually fructifying: again, parts of classical Arabic and Hebrew, Chinese and Japanese, Tamil and Sanskrit poetic cultures. One goal for the future would be for ethnopoetics to move further toward a grasp of the conceptual categories and oral theoretical traditions of criticism-meager cultures, ethnopoetics in this critical sense drawing on the poetry itself, on statements by native poets and their audiences, on related bodies of knowledge in these cultures (for example, ethnopsychology), and on other methods in the comparative method.

Final problem: political ethnopoetics

Although not shackled to the word "ethnopoetics," one has to recognize that it not only connotes but denotes a politics. That is why it is so strange that most professionals in the field are mute on politics in their scholarship – no matter how activist as private citizens. To put the issue as generally as possible: all politics engenders poetic texts and all poetic texts are at least potentially political, when not charged with politics.

Let me change the pace by starting with a general definition of politics. Politics, like ethnopoetics, is concerned with "the creation of relations and interactions between" – analogously – politics in a generic sense, a social group with its culture, and the individual or "agent" – citizen, hobo, orator, farmer, president, everyman.

(1) Politics is struggle for power (Thomas Hobbes)

(2) Politics is who gets what when where and how (Harold Lasswell)

(3) Politics is the struggles and cooperation, processes and structures – be they conscious, subconscious or unconscious, ideological or behavioral, rational or emotional, overt or covert – for influence, control and power over material, human beings or minds, and other information – for example, to assign categories to self and other. Politics in this sense transpires in groups ranging from the family to the supra-national – and the pattern of and ideas about those struggles and cooperation – all of which are differentially shared, transmitted through history, and created, recreated, and used by the members of a given society and culture situated in concrete time and space.

Taking off from this, ethnopoetics would refer to the linguistic, sociolinguistic and linguacultural aspects of a given politics, or of politics in general.

There are many sides to political ethnopoetics. To begin, it may be internal or external. It is internal when it mainly distills and represents the envy, ambition or other passions of the power struggle, be it the initial standoff in the *Iliad* or the *Bhagavad Gita* (Biardeau 1982), or a praise poem in a Yoruba polity (Apter 1998) or a Communist orator in Tamilnadu today (Bate 2000). Such ethnopoetics is of states of mind, allegories of good and evil, peaks of glory and the depths of defeat and annihilation – with relatively little attention to the social and political context which may, as in the first two examples, be largely unknown and unknowable.

Political ethnopoetics is external when it mainly deals with or emanates, for example, from struggles between local factions or ethnic or other groups, or the encroachments of colonial powers or global capitalism. Its categories run parallel to those of political anthropology except that, while bypassing the institutional levels of government, hierarchy and bureaucracy, it intersects at such emotion-laden nodes as land reform and blood vengeance, family loyalty and betrayal, gender affinities and conflicts, and the defiance of tyranny and the praise of democracy or some kind of anarchism. How is the poetics of ethnicity, the metaphors, emblems and synecdoches of indigenous status exploited when negotiating with higher powers (Friedlander 1975)? What is the complex inter-play between Roma Gypsy verbal art, Russian racism, state autocracy and the poetry of Pushkin (Lemon 2000)?

External and internal can be variously synthesized. One level are the many anthologies by Rothenberg and others that assume that the poetries of the world are equal and comparable and can be collocated as one internally coherent corpus: the Chechen songs recorded by Tolstoy stand shoulder to shoulder with their Great Russian peasant counterparts, as does Inuit Eskimo Orpingalik to Sappho and Dickinson. This authentically anthropological view sharply differentiates political ethnopoetics both external and internal, from the great bulk of work and thinking in comparative literature; the latter is still usually unabashedly and even unselfconsciously ethnocentric. External and internal are compellingly synthesized in Derek Walcott's *Omeros*: Homer at his most universal, global problems of ideology, colonialism, and imperialism, a local scene with its Caribbean patois, a view from within of the mind sets of Caribbean fishermen, are woven together by this bard of the Nobel Prize of 1993 (who began as a lad of fifteen peddling his first chapbook of poems from door to door in his native island of Santa Lucía). Political ethnopoetics in its more analytical manifestations needs to emulate the synthesis achieved by Walcott in his very contemporary epic.

The field of ethnopoetics, because of its typically aesthetic, literary, and linguistic biases in the majority of cases tended to ignore politics or to deal with it in an anecdotal, fragmentary or marginal way. Yet all the texts, be it the *Rig Veda* or the T'ang anthology, the *Popol Vu* or Xhosa oral poetry, have always arisen and live on in a politically charged context. The Yucatec Mayan shamans who patiently interpreted the *Popol Vu* to the Tedlocks were motivated, as the Tedlocks indicate, by their image of the greatness of Mayan culture and with questions of cultural integrity as intense and profound as those of Chiapas Mayans fighting for land reform, cultural integrity and political liberty.

This leads to an emotion-laden dilemma that has agitated poets and critics in many traditions through the centuries and, indeed, millennia, even though, as so often, the counterposed principles turn out to be not necessarily, mutually contradictory. At one extreme is the total commitment to aesthetic form, to the beauty of language and the music of language. As one Russian Parnassian put it, "The idea of social and political meaning in a poem, is meaningless to me." As an American Parnassian, that is, total aesthete, exclaimed to me once, "Gary Snyder can't write poetry, he doesn't understand form, people just like him *because of what he stands for*" [emphasis mine].

Contrasting with this maximizing aestheticism is a total commitment to politics until the poetic process and the political process are seen as interdependent and integral to each other – until poetry and politics are bonded in a healthy way, or poetry is made totally subservient to politics, or is practically banished from it. The interdependence is obvious when the poem's themes and the intentions of the poet feed and promote political reform and revolution – or reaction, or, on the contrary, when the political extremes and middle ground of centrist politics feed into the culture of poets and poetry. Such reciprocating feedback happened with poems that depicted and condemned massacres, be it Milton on a massacre in the Piedmont or Bly on napalm bombing in Vietnam – or Tu Fu on press gang military conscription in Han – really T'ang – China:

the mother and little son clinging desperately to their husband-father as he is led away to almost certain death in war. Poems such as these are inspired by politics and war and they can also affect it.

Poems can affect politics directly. American poets hastened the end of the war in Vietnam and today contribute to ecological sanity: the Sierra Club and its poets such as Gary Snyder have influenced the fate of the Redwood Forests. But poets can affect us just as much when they act indirectly, as when, in the face of cruel punishments, they articulated the need for individual creativity, social decency, free will, sensitivity and conscience in Nazi Germany, and in China and Russia through the centuries to this day. One poetic giant in Stalinist Russia quipped a few years before dying in a Siberian concentration camp, "We must be dangerous or they wouldn't be so afraid of us." Later, regarding a religious dissident-poet, the first thing the then American president said to the then Russian premier was, "Has Ratushinskaya been freed yet?" Poetry can threaten vested interests and their threat or the potential for it should be included in ethnopoetic poetry.

Even apolitical or antipolitical poetry implicitly or potentially expounds what it denies: hiding one's head hermetically in the sands of aestheticism entails a passivity and noncommitment with serious political consequences. Yet the impact of poetry on political organization varies enormously by context as does the immediacy of its effects. On the one hand, the import may be shallow and scattered, practically and pragmatically nil: could any American poet affect the sometimes manic-depressive swings of the stock market and its consequences for our political economy?

Why ethnopoetics?

Beyond the Robert Southey poem that ends, "And what was the good of it after all? Quoth little Peterkin. Why that I do not know said he, / But t'was a famous victory," the maximization label exploited above may well have been a restricting or reducing metaphor for additional phenomena of deepening, fine tuning, sharpening, toughening, expanding, loosening up, relativizing, transcending – ethnopoetics. Be that as it may, "maximizing," with or without its cargo of paraglosses, may suggest four values that should now be listed. To begin, "the study and creativity" with which I began deepens and expands the consciousness, the interpretive subjectivity of the linguist or anthropologist. Secondly, ethnopoetics will increase and toughen the cords of the net for the details and the big picture of the linguacultural phenomena at issue: intense reading of *Omeros* or *Ulysses* or the *Odyssey*, for example, will sharpen one's senses for the nuance, the everyday and the ultimate axioms, respectively, of Afro-Caribbean, Modern Irish, or rural Greek society. In the third place, ethnopoetics, by its nature, has the effect of loosening or opening up the definitions and the perceptions of the dozens of subfields in question: rather than pre-scribed, prefigured and predelimited domains approached non-eclectically in terms of one (often simple-minded) model, the phenomenon itself and the experience of it will be seen more hesitantly and generously in terms that include potential and bridging meanings. Ethnopoetics tends to relativize knowledge, to recognize its subtlety. Fourth and last, ethnopoetics in the generic or maximized sense can connect linguistics, sociolinguistics, and cultural and interpretive anthropology with what was above called the poetic revolution (or turn), the ubiquitous trend over the last three decades to see the poetic aspect of everything from conservativism to cuisine to calculus, be it metonymy, vivid images, questions of mood and mode, formal operations or what may be the queen of them all: analogy. In these four senses, then, of enhanced consciousness, maximization of data out there, the opening or loosening up of one's field of investigation and an aware participation in the poetic revolution, the question, "Why ethnopoetics?" is provisionally answered.[4]

---

[4] The foregoing discussion, while including many recognized problems, does not, like translation theory in general (Schulte and Biguenet 1992), address many kinds of complexity that are found in many cultures: How to translate a Chinese tapestry with 400-odd characters that can be read forward and backward and obliquely? How to translate a "triple-decker" Sanskrit story that tells three entirely different stories at the same time, or another Sanskrit text that reads forward as an admonition to lead a perfect ascetic life and backward as a digression on eroticism? How to translate the criss-crossing nuances of a long poem by an exile in the language of his country about a native land that was only seen as a child, or has never been seen at all? How to make explicit the differences between Snyder writing his Anasazi poem in English as against in Anasazi if he could have learned it, or an Anasazi – if one were alive today – writing that poem in English originally or in Anasazian and then translated into English? These and other facts and hypothetical situations show how far ethnopoetics, including this chapter, is from dealing with or even acknowledging many of the complexities of "the real world" (thanks to Indologists Gwen and Clinton Seeley for this take on the problem).

INTERPRETING LANGUAGE
VARIATION AND CHANGE

KEVIN TUITE

Historical linguistics is a historical discipline, and the writing up of hypotheses about past states of languages in the form of etymologies and diachronic grammars is a type of historiography (Lass 1997: 17). The assertions contained in the preceding sentence seem tautological, yet surprisingly few practitioners of historical linguistics take an interest in current debates among historians, philosophers, and some anthropologists, over the nature of history as a social science, and the appropriate methods for reconstructing elements of the past and expressing them in writing. The focus of this chapter will be on etymology, as history and as historiography. Far from being a marginal antiquarian diversion for a handful of philological puzzle-solvers, etymological research operates along the fault-line separating the natural and human sciences, and for this reason alone an examination of etymological methodology and argumentation will be of interest to anthropologists working in this interstitial zone.

Throughout this chapter, I am intentionally employing the word "historiography" in its older sense, as defined in the *OED*: "the writing of history." The choice is motivated by my intention to distinguish "history" (or historical reconstruction) as a type of reasoning, from the process of writing it up for the purpose of publication. The critical study of historical linguistics as a historical discipline is concerned with fundamental issues akin to those Wylie (1985: 483) identified for the neighboring field of archaeology:

what is it that makes an account explanatory, what evidence constitutes grounds for accepting an hypothesis, what the limits are of empirical knowledge, and what the status is of theoretical claims about unobservable phenomena.

As concerns the historiographic component of historical linguistics, the pertinent questions center on issues of the ideological context of writing, intended

This chapter was supposed to have been the English translation of my *Anthropologie et sociétés* article, but after only a few lines, it began to take on a life of its own, or so it seemed, and it ended up as something very different. Much thanks to those who commented on earlier editions, answered questions on various matters or responded to my query on the HISTLING list about the etymology of "trouver": Konrad Koerner, Eric Hamp, Charles Taylor, Wolfgang Settekorn, Birte Lönneker, Marc Picard, Miguel Carrasquer, Mark Southern, Paul Lloyd, Maria Rosa Menocal, Robert Ratcliffe, Laurent Sagart, Britt Mize, Carol Justus, Roger Wright, Russon Wooldridge, John Leavitt, and Christine Jourdan.

readership, style of argumentation, choice of genre, gatekeeping and access to publication venues, and so forth. In practice, historical reconstruction and historiography are not so readily separable. The presuppositions underlying a given historical method largely dictate the contours of historiographic genres (non-narrative vs. narrative, etc.; White 1984). In return, the consolidation of historiographic traditions around model practitioners, canonical writings, preferred journals, and so on, reinforces certain historical approaches, while disfavoring or excluding others. It is my view that two distinct tendencies can be discerned in the practice of etymology, the tension – one might say, dialectic – between which informs the work of any given practitioner investigating a given problem. On the one hand, the "Neo-grammarian" approach favors a narrow encirclement of the object of study, limiting the explanatory apparatus as much as possible to law-like regularities of language change, the functioning of which can be described without reference to human subjects. Counterbalancing this is the approach I call "Schuchardtian," which favors a broadening of the hermeneutic circle to include not only linguistic, but also cultural, social, historical and other types of information. The investigators themselves, by dint of their specialized knowledge, and more fundamentally, by their nature as culturally, socially, historically situated beings, become an integral part of the process of interpretation. The goal of the Schuchardtian approach is to detect any convergence of implications and patterns recognized in the various data domains upon a single hypothesis concerning the history of the forms under investigation. The emergence of standards for the writing and publication of etymologies has been accompanied by a highly critical and agonistic style of debate. The effects have been salutary for the most part, although one detects occasional slippages toward the politically motivated deployment of etymology, or the lack of engagement with unorthodox points of view.

The chapter begins with a brief history of etymology, followed by a case study of an etymological crux which drew the attention of a number of leading specialists in Romance linguistics. Included in this chapter are some remarks on variationist sociolinguistics, a field of enquiry which is in many ways the offspring of nineteenth-century historical linguistics, and which is presently confronting similar issues in the modelling and interpretation of language change. I will limit my treatment in this chapter to etymology, and the study of sound change to which it gave birth, because of the exceptionally long history of inquiry into word origins, and because the methodological and historiographic issues pertinent to etymology are shared by historical syntax, morphology and other branches of diachronic linguistics.

Etymology and comparative grammar

The roots of the discipline of historical linguistics go back to ancient times. This is especially true of etymology, the study of word origins, which has been practiced, after a fashion, since at least Plato's time. As now practiced, etymology is the reconstruction of the history (and prehistory) of words and word elements. The modern English word *water*, for example, goes back to Old English *wœter*. From there, specialists take it back to a putative antecedent **watar* (the asterisk indicates a reconstructed form unattested in documents), the common ancestor of *water*, High German *Wasser* and other Germanic cognates. Germanic **watar* is itself but one of several descendants of the more remote ancestor **wed-/wod-/ud-*, whence Greek *hydōr*, Russian *voda*, and words for water in numerous other Indo-European languages. In its earliest recorded manifestations, of which the most celebrated is Plato's dialogue *Cratylus*, etymology had the more ambitious goal of revealing not only the ancestors of modern words, but also their true meanings, as they were known to the ancients believed to have created them (Lallot 1991; Sedley 1998; Barney 1998). Most of the dozens of word derivations tossed off by Socrates in the *Cratylus* are laughable by modern standards, but those proposed by Western scholars throughout the following two millennia were hardly much better. One especially long-lived, and notoriously inaccurate, technique was the reconstitution of collapsed originary definitions from the syllables of a word. In the *Cratylus*, the Greek word for moon, *selēnē*, also pronounced *selanaia*, was derived by Socrates from the word sequence *sela(s)* "brightness" + *enon* "old" + *neon* "new" + *aei* "always," i.e. the moon has "a light which is always old and always new." This chain of four words, after it has been "hammered into shape" phonetically, gives the name of the moon [*Cratylus* 409]. Over a thousand years later, medieval scholars were still explaining the form of the Latin word "cadaver" as the contraction of the phrase CAro DAta VERmibus "flesh given to worms" (Buridant 1998; Bloch 1983). The discipline as we now know it came about from the combined effect of two major developments: (1) the elaboration of criteria for evaluating the plausibility of etymologies; (2) the recognition that shared morphology and basic lexical inventory is evidence that certain languages are descended from a common ancestor.

The early Greek etymologies were for the most part derivations from synonymous expressions in the contemporary language or one of its dialects. Later Western investigators into linguistic matters operated with a richer diachronic perspective, which included Greek, Hebrew, and then Latin, as languages known to have been spoken in earlier times, and from which the contemporary tongues were believed to have somehow arisen. From the comparison of modern and ancient languages grew an awareness of formal change across time, although it was conceived in orthographic rather than phonetic terms. The guide to Latin orthography in Isidore's seventh-century *Etymologiarum libri* [i.xxvii], written for readers whose vernaculars had already diverged so far from Latin as to constitute distinct languages, reflected an awareness, at some level, of phonetic subclasses of consonants and vowels. Isidore, drawing on the work of early grammarians, pointed out alternations between voiced and voiceless stops with the same place of articulation (e.g. /c/ [k] and /g/ in *trecentos* "300," but *quadrigentos* "400"), and the substitution of /r/ for /s/ – now recognized as the result of rhotacization in prehistoric Latin – in such words as *honor* (older form *honos*), *arbor* (older form *arbos*). Unfortunately, systematic use of phonetic features was not made by medieval etymologists. The seventeenth-century philologist Gerhard Vossius invoked phonetically nonsensical, and inconsistently applied, "letter permutations" to account for the derivation of Latin words from their purported Greek ancestors, e.g. /m/ > /s/ in Greek *mimēlos* "imitative" > Latin *similis* "resembling"; /t/ > /v/ in Greek *tillō* "pull, pluck (hair)" > Latin *vello* (same meaning) (Curtius 1866: 8–9). The mid seventeenth-century French lexicographer Gilles Ménage has an unfairly poor reputation in the eyes of many modern readers, having been made an object of parody by Molière in his *Femmes savantes*. In fact, no less than seventy percent of his etymologies are still accepted today (Baldinger 1995). He introduced an additional degree of control on word histories by searching for antecedents of French words in later, post-classical varieties of Latin, and sought to verify his derivations by comparison with other Romance languages (Leroy-Turcan 1991: 20–22). A century later, Anne-Robert-Jacques Turgot, one of the more important and original thinkers on language of his time, endeavored to place the "art of etymology" on more solid methodological footing in his entry on the topic for Diderot's *Encyclopédie* of 1756 (Turgot 1966; Droixhe 1989). Turgot began from the premise that etymology has two chief components: that of formulating hypotheses about word origins, and that of criticizing them. Turgot's insistence that proposed etymologies be consistent with the derivations proposed for other words of the language, be phonetically reasonable, and that possible sources of borrowing also be considered, would be deemed sound advice by any historical linguist of the present. He advocated the investigation of all languages that might be historically linked to the one under study, and was aware of striking similarities between words in the European languages known to him, such as Greek, Latin, German and the Scandinavian languages (Turgot 1966: 101). He held in his hand, one could say, the same pieces of the puzzle that Rask and Bopp were to assemble into the Indo-European language family sixty years later. What held him back was the unwillingness to apply the concept of linguistic kinship in prehistory, at a chronological depth intermediate between that of comparatively shallow groupings such as Romance and Germanic, and the origin of language in the human species. Turgot apparently believed that languages could only be grouped into families if one knew their parents, that is, if they could be traced back to an attested ancestral language like Latin. The lexical correspondences among Greek, Latin and the Germanic "languages of the North" were interpreted by Turgot as the result of migration and contact in the remote past, rather than common descent from a long-lost ancestor.

The writing of word histories in the premodern period served a wide range of purposes, few of which are continued in a serious way in present-day practice.

Socrates's exuberant display of etymological prowess in the *Cratylus* has been interpreted by some classicists as a parody of pre-Socratic philosophies of language (Baxter 1992: 94–98), or even as an "agonistic display, in which Socrates is seen to beat etymology-mongers at their own game" (Barney 1998: 66). Some centuries later, Jerome and Augustine employed etymological analysis to ascertain the mystic significance of Hebrew proper names in the Bible, a practice consonant with the belief that "Hebrew, the original language, is [. . .] as close as any tongue can be to the thoughts of God at the time of creation" (Bloch 1983: 39). Perhaps the last serious exponent of philosophically-motivated etymology – at least until Heidegger – was the late eighteenth-century English philologist John Horne Tooke, who sought to demonstrate through linguistic analysis that "all the operations of thought reside in language alone" (Aarsleff 1983: 53). Well before his time, however, French etymologists such as Jacques Dubois (Dubois 1531/1998) and Gilles Ménage were endeavoring to employ a historical and comparative method relatively free from theologically- or philosophically based presuppositions in the reconstruction of word histories, an approach subsequently made explicit and methodologically more rigorous by Turgot. On the other hand, the rise of etymological dictionaries in sixteenth to eighteenth-century Europe cannot be explained in isolation from the new modes of imagining national identity that followed the dethronement of Latin in favor of vernacular-based written languages, and which were fostered by what Anderson (1991) calls "print-capitalism." The word lineages contained in the dictionaries of Dubois and Ménage furnished proof that the new medium of written and printed communication in France had a pedigree no less illustrious than that of its predecessor, Latin.

In the early years of the eighteenth century, the philosopher Leibniz was advising researchers and explorers to collect lexical material from as wide a range of languages as possible, with the goal of comparing and grouping them. He offered for this purpose the remote ancestor of Swadesh's core-vocabulary list, enumerating categories of words to collect: kinterms, numerals, names for body parts, animals, climate phenomena and common verbs (Gulya 1974). Throughout the century this plan was put into action, notably in the Russian Empire, where the tsars encouraged the collection of word lists from the indigenous peoples of Siberia, Central Asia, and the Caucasus. Comparison of lexical material, and, by the end of the eighteenth century, morphology as well, induced investigators to sort languages into genealogical groupings. Unlike the classifications of earlier centuries, such as Dante's grouping of Romance languages by their words for "yes," these new comparative studies revealed unanticipated kinships among noncontiguous languages spoken by speech communities with very different cultures and types of civilization. Samuel Gyarmathi's demonstration of the affinity among Hungarian, Finnish, Saamic, and Siberian languages such as Cheremis – along with his argument that Turkish-Hungarian lexical resemblances were due to borrowing – was a crowning achievement of the

new science of historical and comparative linguistics. Gyarmathi's insistence
that agreement in inflectional systems be considered a privileged criterion for
assessing linguistic relationship was a crucial methodological advance (Pedersen 1983: 34). The Danish linguist Rasmus Rask, who had read Gyarmathi,
applied the same method of lexical and inflectional comparison to the European
languages accessible to him in the early years of the nineteenth century, and
arrived at a "comparative grammar in embryo" (Pedersen 1983: 39) of a portion of what would come to be called the Indo-European family (Greek, Italic,
Germanic, Baltic, and Slavic) (Rask 1992). But it was only when the languages
of India and Iran became sufficiently known in the West that Indo-European
linguistics in particular, and historical linguistics in general, grew to maturity.
The postulation of such a kinship by William Jones in 1786 is commonly cited
by linguists as the birthdate of Indo-European Studies. Jones was not the first
European to study Sanskrit – some Catholic clergymen had compiled grammatical sketches much earlier – nor even the first to discern parallels with European
languages (Pedersen 1983: 40; Sergent 1995: 21). Jones's discourse followed
the English conquest of India, which made the study of the history and institutions of the subcontinent a matter of political and economic relevance. Joining
the "purely" scientific motives for the comparative linguistic analysis of Sanskrit and Greek, Latin, Germanic, and so forth were impulses of a different
sort, a European fascination with India that went back to Antiquity, and the
Romantic obsession with deep origins.

The new method of historical–comparative linguistics was inspired by the
recognition of systematic resemblances not only in vocabulary – which could
be due to extensive borrowing – but also in inflectional morphology (declension and conjugation) among noncontiguous languages. Furthermore, as Rask
(1818/1992) demonstrated in his pioneering study, these features were *not*
shared with all other languages, and thus not attributable to a putative proto-
language ancestral to all human tongues (as Hebrew had once been thought to
have been). Consider the following partial declensional paradigms of the word
for "tooth" in four languages, spoken by communities as far apart as India,
Italy and the Baltic coast (based on Szemerényi (1996: 166–167)). Not only are
the roots of strongly similar phonetic shape (contrast Georgian /k'bil-/, Basque
/hortz/, Saami /pääni/, all meaning "tooth"), but, what is more significant, the
suffixes indicating case and number have numerous shared features. Furthermore, the shift of accent between stem syllable and suffix, noted in Sanskrit,
is paralleled by a comparable shift in Lithuanian. (In the orthography of the
Lithuanian forms, the tilde and grave accent indicate two types of accented
syllable; the subscript cedilla on the final vowels of the accusative singular and
genitive plural marks a historically nasalized vowel.)

The demonstration of relatedness set in motion the exhaustive examination
of the lexical and morphological inventories of the Indo-European languages.
The comparative grammars of Rask and Bopp were followed less than twenty

Table 11.1. *Declension of word for "tooth" in four Indo-European languages*

case, number	Sanskrit	Latin	Gothic	Lith.	PIE
nominative singular	dán	dēns	tunþus	dantìs	*dōn
accusative singular	dántam	dentem	tunþu	dañtį	*dónt-m̥
genitive singular	datás	dentis	tunþáus	dantiẽs	*dn̥t-ós
nominative plural	dántas	dentēs	tunþius	dañtys	*dónt-es
accusative plural	datás	dentēs	tunþuns	dantìs	*d(o)nt-n̥s
genitive plural	datā́m	dent(i)um	tunþiwe	dantū̃	*dn̥t-óm

later by the *Etymological Investigations* of August Friedrich Pott, which began to appear in 1833. By yoking the ancient art of etymology to the project of historical-comparative linguistics, Pott and his colleagues sought to confirm the hypothesis of genetic relatedness by showing not only that formal similarities such as the above ran through the vocabularies of the Indo-Iranian, Greek, Romance, Germanic, Balto-Slavic, Celtic, and several other language groups, but also that related forms were associated by regular sound correspondences. This was a highly significant advance beyond the "letter permutations" proposed by pre-modern etymologists such as Vossius on a case-by-case, essentially ad-hoc basis, with little attention paid to more general patterns, or to phonetic plausibility.

The major breakthrough was the recognition of the large-scale shift of consonants in the Germanic languages, detected by Rask and confirmed by Jacob Grimm (Krahe 1960 I: 80–81; Petersen 1992: 28). The shift, now commonly known as "Grimm's First Sound Law," affected consonants at several places and modes of articulation, as shown in Table 11.2 (where English represents Common Germanic).

The new etymological method proved its efficacy by uncovering hitherto unsuspected cognates (one of the more startling being Armenian *erku* "two," which can be associated with Latin *duo*, etc. through perfectly regular sound correspondences [Meillet 1954: 31–32]). Equally important, if not more so, was the demonstration on the same grounds that certain formally similar sets of words with near-identical meanings are almost certainly false cognates. It had been thought since Antiquity, for example, that Greek $t^h eos$ and Latin *deus*, both meaning "god," were related words. (Rask appears to have been the last reputable linguist to have believed this (Rask 1992: 72)). The new comparative approach soon indicated that no regular sound law associated Greek /tʰ/ with /d/ in Latin, Sanskrit, Balto-Slavic, etc. Furthermore, Greek already had a good near-cognate for Latin *deus*, Sanskrit *devas* in the theonym *Zeus* (< **dyeu-*; cp. the genitive-case form *Dios*) (Pott 1833 I: 99; Curtius 1866: 213, 543). On the other hand, several robust sets of cognates link Greek /tʰ/ to Sanscrit /dʰ/ and Latin /f/ in initial position (e.g. Gk. *tʰur-a*, Lat. *for-es* "door"). Following

Table 11.2. *Germanic sound shift (Grimm's first sound law)*

Greek	Latin	English	Proto-Indo-European
I.VOICED STOP	VOICED STOP	VOICELESS STOP	
duo	duo	two	*dwō
gen-os	gen-us	kin	*gen-
II.VOICELESS ASPIRATE	VOICELESS FRICATIVE	VOICED STOP	
p^{h}rātēr "phratry member"	frāter	brother	*b^{h}rāter
t^{h}ur-a	for-es	door	*d^{h}wer- / d^{h}wor-
k^{h}ēn	(h)āns-er	goose	*g^{h}ans
III.VOICELESS STOP	VOICELESS STOP	VOICELESS FRICATIVE	
pod-	ped-	foot	*ped- / pod-
tria	tria	three	*trei
kōp-ē "handle"	cap-ere "seize"	haf-t	*kap-

the direction indicated by the sound laws and semantic features, linguists uncovered another Latin root, *fēs-* (in *fēstus* "festive," *fēriæ*, [Old Latin *fēsiæ*] "holidays"), which pointed to an ancestral root **d^{h}ēs-*, with some sort of religious signification. This supposition is supported by the Armenian plural *di-k'* "gods" (< IE **d^{h}ēs-es*), which goes back to the same Indo-European root. Since intervocalic /s/ was already known to have been lost in prehistoric Greek, the derivation *t^{h}eos* < pre-Greek **t^{h}es-os* < IE **d^{h}es-os* made the juxtaposition to Latin root *fēs-* < IE **d^{h}ēs-* yet more attractive (Hofmann 1966: 113), although the difference in vowel length between the Greek and Latin forms continues to make many experts uncomfortable (Frisk 1960: 662–663; Chantraine 1990: 429–430).

The victory of the new historical–comparative linguistics was assured by the founding of university chairs in pertinent subjects, most notably in Germany, accompanied by the emergence of the norms of admission and argumentation, and venues for the exchange of ideas among peers, that mark an academic discipline. Journals and monograph series began to be published, professional societies were organized, and practitioners policed the frontiers of the new field. A. F. Pott, who "laid the cornerstone for modern-day 'pure etymology'" (Malkiel 1993: 12), manifested an almost indefatigable zeal in the defense of the new approach to the historical study of language, as expressed in hundreds of pages of merciless criticism of those he deemed guilty of flawed, scientifically unsound methodology, the "champions of pseudo-etymologies, the comparative-linguistic quacks [. . .] who let themselves be seduced by the Sirens of phonetic similarity" [cited in Horn 1888: 321]. Such polemics reinforced standards for the evaluation of explanations and the use of evidence, and also set the tone for the debating styles of future generations.

The Neo-grammarians and the doctrine of the "exceptionless sound law"

The first generations of linguists to work on Indo-European were aware that even the most regular of sound correspondences had exceptions. Some such exceptions were attributed to the borrowing of words from other languages, especially those used in writing, administration or commerce. As shown in Table 11.2, the initial /t/ of English *two* is the regular counterpart of Latin initial /d/, as in *duo*; the /d/ of *double* is not (cp. Latin *duplus*). The word "double," as is well known, was borrowed from French well over a millennium after the Germanic consonant shift had ceased to be operative. Numerous other exceptions could not be so easily accounted for, but linguists felt that a modicum of irregularity was to be expected in a social phenomenon such as human language. A group of linguists centered at the University of Leipzig in the 1870s sought to bring greater rigor to the diachronic investigation of language by introducing a new model of change, comparable to those employed in the natural sciences. The "Neo-grammarians" (*Junggrammatiker*), as they came to be called, distinguished two fundamentally distinct classes of phenomena which modified the sound-shape of words. The Germanic sound shift and similar changes characterized by relatively regular sound correspondences were modelled as the output of "sound laws" (*Lautgesetze*), which spread mechanically throughout the effected speech community, being adopted by all members of the community, and affecting all words in which the target sound occurs in the appropriate context, without exception (Osthoff/Brugmann 1878: xiii). The other principal type of change was qualified as "analogical," the outcome of system-internal pressure to associate similar word-shapes to similar meanings (Kuryłowicz 1964, 1966).

The proponents of the *Lautgesetz* model acknowledged that sound laws were not "laws" in the same sense as the laws of chemistry or physics, and they provided explicitly for all sorts of exceptions, including borrowing and dialect splits as well as analogy. The proposal nonetheless was met with vigorous opposition from several quarters. Older linguists of a humanist, Humboldtian orientation, such as Pott and Georg Curtius, objected to the materialist determinism which they detected in the concept of exceptionless sound laws. Some younger specialists, notably Hugo Schuchardt and Otto Jespersen, believed that no clear, nor useful, demarcation could be made between mechanically regular, physiologically-conditioned *Lautgesetze*, and socially or psychologically conditioned varieties of sound change (see Wilbur 1977, and the papers reprinted in that volume). In practice, however, the major impact of the Neo-grammarian movement was to make "exceptionless sound laws" into the null hypothesis

Table 11.3. *Apparent exceptions to Grimm's first law*

Greek	Sanskrit	Latin	Old English	Proto-Indo-European
patēr	pitár	pater	fæDer	*pǝtér "father"
pʰrātēr	bhrátar	frāter	brōþor	*bʰráter "brother"

Greek	Sanskrit	Russian	Old High German	Proto-Indo-European
hekurā	śvaśrú	svekróvʲ	swiGar	*swekʲrúH- "husband's mother"
hekuro-s	śváśura	svékor	sweHur	*swékʲuro- "husband's father"

in etymological investigation, to the extent that exceptions to known sound correspondences were also to be examined from this point of view, before other scenarios could be entertained. The first successful demonstration of the new method was in connection with a sizeable class of exceptions to Grimm's First Law. The direction of the Germanic consonant shift, as reflected in initial consonants, was illustrated in Table 11.2. In internal position, however, the correspondences appeared less regular. Consider the kinship terms from Germanic (represented by Old English and Old High German), and other Indo-European languages, shown in Table 11.3.

The Germanic words for "brother" and "husband's father" contain the expected fricative reflexes of the voiceless stops *t and *kʲ. The words for "father" and "husband's mother," however, contain the voiced stops /d/ and /g/, respectively. This apparent irregularity was unravelled by the Danish linguist Karl Verner in 1875. Verner noticed that the realization of Indo-European voiceless stops and the fricative /s/ in medial position in Germanic was correlated with the stress placement in those languages which preserved the ancient Indo-European mobile accent (such as Sanskrit and Slavic). Where the cognate forms in these languages indicated that the syllable preceding the medial stop was unaccented, the latter appeared in Germanic as a voiced fricative, which in West Germanic languages such as English and German shifted further to the corresponding voiced stop. When preceded by a stressed syllable, the expected reflex (a voiceless fricative) appeared (Krahe 1960 I: 85–86; Meillet 1964: 141–142).

At the level of procedure, one of the principal differences between those historical linguists who identify themselves as (neo) Neo-grammarians, and those who situate themselves in the tradition of Pott, Curtius, and Schuchardt is their relative degree of discomfort with proposed etymologies that are not completely supported by recognized sound laws, and which invoke the effects of analogy, sound symbolism or frequency-related phonetic erosion (such as the evolution of "God be with you" to "good-bye" to a monosyllabic "bye" or reduplicated "bye-bye"). All of the latter phenomena are well-attested in languages from all parts of the globe, and linguists have identified the contexts which favor them, but they lack the sort of constraint that phonetics imposes upon regular sound laws. In the following section we will examine the debate surrounding one especially controversial etymological problem, which brought representatives of the two traditions into open conflict.

The etymology of *"trouver"*

The standard Latin words meaning "find" – *invenire* and *reperire* – went out of use in the first millennium of the Christian Era. Several different Latin verbs were recruited to fill the gap in the various Romance dialects: Spanish *hallar*, Portuguese *achar*, Rumanian *afla* < *afflare* "breathe upon" (then "detect by scent"); Romansch *kater* < *captare* "seek, try to get." There is no readily identifiable Latin antecedent, however, for French *trouver* and Occitan *trobar* (also Italian *trovare*, probably borrowed from French). Friedrich Diez saw in Latin *turbare* "stir up" the only plausible candidate, although a somewhat far-fetched sequence of meaning changes had to be assumed: "stir up" > "rummage through" > "seek" > "find" (Diez 1861 I: 427–429). In a paper first published in 1878, Gaston Paris challenged Diez's hypothesis on phonetic grounds. The transition from *turbare* to its alleged descendants would require (1) metathesis of the /r/: *turbare* > **trubare*; (2) lowering of the initial vowel to /o/: **trubare* > **trobare*; (3) retention of the intervocalic /b/ in Occitan: **trobare* > *trobar*. Metathesis of /r/ is sporadic but not rare in the history of the Romance languages, but the lenition of intervocalic /b/ to /v/ or zero appeared to be a highly regular sound change in Occitan (e.g. *probare* > *proar* "prove") (Paris 1909: 615–617). In keeping with Neo-grammarian doctrine, Paris believed it a methodologically sound principle to assume regularity of sound change unless there were compelling reasons to think otherwise. If one were to take *trouver* and *trobar* as the starting-point and work backwards in accordance with established sound laws, one arrives at the proto-form **tropare*. The vowels in the first syllable (especially the diphthong in the Old French present stem [il] *trueve*) point to a short /o/, and the intervocalic /b/ in Occitan normally comes only from the lenition of voiceless /p/. But could **tropare* have existed in Vulgar Latin, and if so, how could it have evolved to mean "find"? The clue to the answer, in Paris's opinion, was to be found in the name of the celebrated poets of medieval Provence, the troubadours (Occ. *trobaire*, Fr. *trouvère*). The classical Latin word *tropus*, borrowed from Greek, denoted a figure of rhetoric, but in later Latin it came to be used more commonly as a musical term, designating a melodic variation, and then music added to liturgical verses sung in plainchant. This specifically musical sense of the word "trope" was limited to the Latin of ancient Gaul. According to Paris, it was in the Gallo-Romance dialects that a presumed verb based on this root – **tropare*, meaning "compose a melody" – would have gradually acquired a more general sense: "compose" > "invent" > "discover, find" (Paris 1909: 616–617). Although no such verb was actually

attested in Latin, and despite the somewhat unusual semantic change required
by Paris's etymology (a technical term used by poets and musicians somehow
being adopted as the general Gallo-Romance verb for "find" in all its senses),
Paris believed that the historical phonology rendered all competing hypotheses
less probable or even impossible.

About twenty years after the publication of Paris's revised etymology,
Schuchardt reopened the investigation of *trouver/trobar*. In response to Paris's
objections on phonetic grounds, Schuchardt argued that Diez's initial proposal
might not have been so wrong-headed after all, if one admitted less regular
types of sound change, and if new evidence were introduced from the ethnography of European material culture. The sound-forms of the French and Occitan
verbs for "find" could be derived from *turbare* if allowance were made for
the deflection of sounds from their ordinary historical trajectories under the
influence of other elements. One such irregular change was the lowering of
short /u/ to /o/ – the second stage of Diez's derivation (see above) – for which
Schuchardt found parallels in other well-accepted etymologies, such as French
mot "word" < *muttum* "mumbled, inarticulate sound", where the lowering may
have been conditioned by a nearby labial consonant. The first and third stages,
which require the /r/ of the first syllable to shift position, and the /b/ to resist
weakening and eventual loss in the Occitan reflex, are explained by Schuchardt
as due to the influence of the closely-related verb *turbulare* > **trublare* "stir
up," whence French *troubler* and Occitan *treblar*. Such "contamination" of one
word-form by another that is phonetically and/or semantically similar to it is
not at all rare. In Schuchardt's reconstruction, the expected phonetic evolution
of *turbare* was deflected under the influence of the formally and semantically
related verb **trublare*. The most impressive aspect of Schuchardt's revision of
Diez's etymology, however, is not the phonetic argument so much as the rich
and varied documentation which he employed to justify the semantic shift of
turbare from its Latin meaning of "stir up" to that of its alleged Gallo-Romance
offspring. The initial clue was supplied by the words for "find" in the other
Romance languages. The Latin source words – *afflare* "detect by smell" and
captare "seek, try to get" – are associated with the semantic field of hunting.
Several Italian and Sardinian descendants of *turbare* have similar meanings,
e.g. the Sardinian verb *trubare*, which can denote "hunt game by beating the
bush to flush them out," and also "drive fish toward poisoned water (in order to
catch them)" (Gamillscheg 1969: 875). In Schuchardt's opinion, *turbare* underwent a meaning shift from "stir up" to the more specialized sense of "stir up
[water] in order to drive [fish toward a trap or net]," a meaning continued by
the Sardinian verb just mentioned. From there it followed an evolution comparable to those of *afflare* and *captare*: "seek [game]" > "seek (in general)" >
"find." Besides collecting linguistic evidence, Schuchardt undertook research
into traditional European fishing techniques. According to Malkiel (1993: 26),
he was said to have "temporarily transformed one of the rooms of his home into

a small-scale museum of fishing gear" while investigating the etymology of *trouver/trobar*.

Gaston Paris declared himself impressed by the wide-ranging erudition and brilliance of Schuchardt's contribution to the debate, but refused to change his opinion. The sequence of meaning changes from "stir up [water to catch fish]" to "find" did not strike him as more reasonable than those necessitated by a derivation from **tropare*. In any case, one consideration outweighed all others from his perspective. The phonetic evolution from **tropare* to *trouver/trobar* could be explained on the basis of highly-regular sound changes (or "sound laws," in Neo-grammarian parlance), solidly supported by the historical grammars of French and Occitan. The Diez–Schuchardt etymology required at least two "deviations" from those sound laws. While such exceptions were instantiated elsewhere in Gallo-Romance word histories, that was not good enough for Paris when a perfectly regular alternative was on the table: phonetic regularity must be accorded priority over semantic plausibility (Paris 1909: 618–626; cp. Thomas 1900).

The battlelines were drawn. Over the next several years, Paris and Antoine Thomas, publishing in the pages of *Romania*, defended the priority of regular sound change, while Schuchardt, writing in the *Zeitschrift für romanische Philologie*, used the example of *trouver/trobar* both as further ammunition in his long-standing battle against the Neo-grammarian doctrine of "exceptionless sound laws," and also as a first step toward putting the study of word meanings, and their likely trajectories of change, on sufficiently solid footing to make it a worthy partner of historical phonetics in etymological practice (see the blow-by-blow summary in Tappolet 1905/1977). To my knowledge, no etymology of *trouver/trobar* has as yet gained the universal acceptance of experts. The discovery of a Latin verb based on the root *trop-* – *contropare* "compare," attested in a work by the sixth-century Italian Cassiodorus and the Visigoth laws of the eighth century – gave added weight to Paris's conjecture (Spitzer 1940).

But *turbare* is not the only alternative to **tropare*. As early as 1928, the Spanish Arabist Julián Ribera y Tarragó hypothesized an Arabic source for Old Provençal *trobar* and its cognates, at least in their specialized use to denote the composing of verses, singing, etc. (whence, of course, the agent nouns *trobador*, *troubadour*). Ribera identified Arabic *tˤaraba* "song" (from the trilateral root Tˤ–R–B "provoke emotion, excitement, agitation; make music, entertain by singing") as the probable source (Menocal 1982). This lexeme would have borrowed into the Romance dialects spoken in Andalusia, thence into Catalan and Occitan, during the period of Arab occupation of Spain. In 1966, Lemay offered a similar proposal, but with a different Arabic etymon: Dˤ–R–B "strike, touch," by extension "play a musical instrument," alleged to have been borrowed into Old Spanish in or before the twelfth century to refer to singer-poets who accompany themselves on an instrument. More recently, the Hispanist María Rosa Menocal (1982, 1984) has revived Ribera's earlier proposal, although she entertains the possibility that the nearly homophonous D^Ω–R–B root may have contributed to the sense of the newly coined Romance verb *trobar* (1982: 147). If any one of these proposals is true, the implications for the history of medieval literature are considerable. Lemay and Menocal cite their etymologies in support of their theories that the origins of the art of the troubadours can be traced back to the Arabic culture of Al-Andalus (see also Menocal 1987). Neither Lemay nor Menocal, it should be noted, offer their Arabic etymon as the source for the Romance verb meaning "find." In their view, this lexeme was already present in the Romance dialects of Spain and the Provence, with something akin to its modern meaning, when the Arabic root was borrowed. Homophony led to overlapping usage and eventual fusion of the two verbs, one indigenous (*trobar₁*), one borrowed (*trobar₂*) (Lemay 1966: 1009). Aside from a handful of negative reviews (e.g. Le Gentil 1969), the Hispano-Arabic hypothesis has been ignored, rather than refuted, by the authors of the standard reference works in Romance historical linguistics. One can easily imagine why such an etymology, in either its Ribera-Menocal or Lemay version, would meet with the disfavor of "mainstream" specialists. The semantic fields associated with /T$^\Omega$–R–B/ and /D$^\Omega$–R–B/ most closely overlap that of **tropare*, in that all three roots could be employed to denote some sort of musical composition or performance, whereas they have no resemblance whatsoever with the meanings reconstructed by either Diez or Schuchardt for *turbare*. Hypothesizing an Arabic source, accompanied by the additional phonetic assumptions relating to the manner of its adoption into Hispano-Romance, would thus entail rejection of a Latin etymon with impeccable phonetic credentials, and a meaning no more problematic (Lemay 1966: 1004–1007; Menocal 1982: 146–147). The proposal has another, equally unfortunate, consequence. Having been pushed aside as the source of *trobar₂*, *trobador*, etc., **tropare* would be left to compete with *turbare* as the etymon of *trouver/trobar₁* "find" alone. On this reduced playing field **tropare* would be at a distinct disadvantage, indeed, partisans of the Hispano-Arabic hypothesis would be almost forced to acknowledge *turbare* as the sole likely source of the homophonous verb *trobar₁*. In other words, it requires overturning the stronger etymology in favor of the weaker one, and abandoning a single source for both senses of "trobar" for the less elegant solution of a split etymology. That being said, there is something disquieting about the silence of the etymologists, all the more so if one recalls the detailed presentation and criticism of Schuchardt's hypothesis by partisans of **tropare* in the etymological dictionaries and learned journals.

Etymologies, fossils, and narratives

I had a couple of purposes in mind when I selected the example of the *trouver/trobar* debate for this chapter. One of my goals was to illustrate some aspects of the practice of etymology. What the participants in the debate brought to bear on the problem under discussion was not only a thorough knowledge of the various stages of Latin, the medieval and modern Romance literary languages and numerous non-literary dialects, but also a familiarity with the diachronic trajectories of each phoneme in different contexts, as represented in the inventories of sound laws contained in the standard historical grammars. In addition, experienced practitioners will have a wide-ranging and rather eclectic acquaintance with the literature, art, history, archaeology, folklore and ethnography of the speech communities whose languages they study, and those of their principal neighbors. Even in the days when students routinely learned Greek in secondary school and defended their dissertations in Latin, specialists with the requisite knowledge base were not common. What distinguishes the masters of the etymological art is not so much the sheer quantity of the information they carry around in their heads, as their skill at bringing just the right bits of data to bear on a hitherto recalcitrant problem. While insisting on mastery of the necessary data-base, and on the rigorous testing of hypotheses for consistency with sound laws and semantic plausibility, Yakov Malkiel (1993) devoted particular attention to the "artistic" qualities of successful practitioners. Among those he mentioned are inventiveness, finesse, curiosity, and a special flair for digging out the pertinent facts from a mountain of raw data (Malkiel 1977: 353–354). Etymological studies of even a single word may run to hundreds of pages, but some of the most brilliant are only a few paragraphs long. Eric Hamp, for example, few of whose published etymologies exceed a half-dozen pages, has an uncommon gift for ferreting out the handful of well-hidden but crucially diagnostic cognate sets to support his reconstructions (Hamp 1998).

The summary of the *trouver* debate is also intended as an illustration of etymology as history. Historians and philosophers have carried on a lively discussion over the nature of historical explanation, the distinction between nomothetic, natural-scientific accounts and the hermeneutical or interpretive method characteristic of the human sciences, and of narrative, as the favored genre of the latter (Ricoeur 1978; Taylor 1979, 1991; White 1980, 1984). The philosophical pragmatist Richard Rorty (1982, 1983) has criticized the sharp ontological (or at least, methodological) differentiation maintained by most of his colleagues between those sciences which constitute their objects through natural laws, and those which situate their objects within a "web of meaning," and interpret them on that basis. Rorty discusses two types of historical inquiry: the study of fossils, as an example of an investigation undertaken according to the norms of the natural sciences, and the interpretation of a chronologically or culturally remote text, as an instance where the hermeneutic method is called for, that is, the application of interpretive techniques which attempt to bridge the gap between the reader's cultural-linguistic-historical "horizon," and that surrounding the production of the text (cp. Gadamer 1982). He argues that the study of fossils, like that of texts and other cultural artifacts, necessarily begins with their being situated in a web of meaning, in the sense that a fossil – as fossil (and not as a simple lump of rock) – is constituted as an object of inquiry through its placement in relation to other fossils. For Rorty, there is no fundamental distinction between the mode of inquiry appropriate to non-human objects such as fossils, and that appropriate to the reading of texts. At the level of practice, however, the construction by investigators of "interpretive" historical narratives is resorted to when no normalized, reductionist vocabulary has as yet been agreed upon which helps to reveal deeper connections among phenomena.

If we think of the fossil record as a text, then we can say that paleontology, in its early stages, followed "interpretive" methods. That is, it cast around for some way of making sense of what had happened by looking for a vocabulary in which a puzzling object could be related to other, more familiar, objects, so as to become intelligible. Before the discipline became "normalized," nobody had any clear idea of what sort of thing might be relevant to predicting where similar fossils might be found.

(Rorty 1982: 199)

It is regrettable that historical linguists, and especially the etymologists among them, have not been party to this discussion. The debate between Schuchardt and his French colleagues Paris and Thomas (and more generally, that between orthodox Neo-grammarians and those linguists who, like Schuchardt, consider all linguistic change, whether phonetic, morphosyntactic, or semantic, as a fundamentally social phenomenon) can be usefully examined from the standpoint of Rorty's philosophical parable. To what extent can etymology, as a type of historical inquiry, be likened to the study of fossils, or to the interpretation of texts? How fundamental is the difference between the two approaches? Should they be considered as complementary rather than opposed methods, at least at the level of etymological practice?

Let us begin with fossils. Rorty maintains that each fossil (or type of fossil) is constituted as an object of study through its positioning in a web of relations to other fossils. The system of relations thus formulated can be conceived as a "web of meaning" only if one adopts a very restricted, simplified Saussurean concept of meaning as determined contrastively within a stable, bounded semantic universe. After a sufficient number of fossils have been examined, parameters are recognized according to which each new specimen can be classified, and in terms of which investigators express regularities of morphological variation and change. In this way a new vocabulary, in Rorty's sense, is formulated. To the extent that this vocabulary accounts for the characteristics of newly discovered specimens, it will be adopted by other practitioners, bringing about the progressive normalization of the discipline. The developments in historical linguistic methodology sketched above contributed to a comparable process, with phonetics – synchronic and diachronic – supplying much of the new vocabulary. Also contributing to the normalization of etymological practice were the recognition of analogically driven change, and the factors favoring it; and also the study of such recurrent phenomena as sound symbolism and taboo effects.

In the relatively normalized context of orthodox Neo-grammarian-type historical linguistics, an etymology such as that proposed by Gaston Paris for *trouver/trobar* is expressed in the reductionist vocabulary of sound laws. The words under study are broken up into their component parts (phonemes), and the relations among them (phonological context). The web constructed around French *trouver* [tʀuve] is a bounded phonological system, defined in terms of contrastive features (voice, degree of occlusion, place of articulation, etc.), which is mapped via transformational rules onto the systems of anterior stages of the language. In this manner, French /v/ is mapped via /b/ onto Vulgar Latin /p/, /u/ via the Old French diphthong /ue/ onto Vulgar Latin short /o/, and so forth, with specification of the phonetic contexts in which the change occurs (the lenition of /p/ > /b/ > /v/ occurs between vowels; the fate of short /o/ is linked to the position of the accent). The above sequence of changes is presented in the form of a depersonalized history, with no plot-like narrative organization. Changes in form are recorded, or reconstructed, which are held to be consistent with observed regularities of the evolution of the species that left the fossils, or with the principles of diachronic phonetics or grammar. There is "no identifiable narrative voice" (White 1980: 11). This historiographic frame, in which evolution of word forms is treated like that of animal morphology, as read in the fossil record, is not seen as problematic by historical linguists, who share certain methodological assumptions. Consider the following example: One cannot prove that Parisian French [tyb] and Québec French [tsʏb], both meaning "tube," have a common ancestor, any more than (as Bertrand Russell once pointed out), one cannot prove that the universe has been in existence for more than five minutes. Linguists do, nonetheless, accept the common origin of [tyb] and [tsʏb], because doing so enables them to formulate sound laws (the lowering of high vowels in closed syllables, and the affricatization of the dental stops before high front vowels), which account in an elegant way for thousands of similar cases: [dis] and [dzɪs] "ten," [dyp] and [dzʏp] "dupe," etc. (on the phonetics of Québec French, see Picard 1987). Such hypotheses become more convincing to the extent that they account for other word histories, elegantly explain otherwise puzzling cases, and accommodate newly-discovered facts. It is the acceptance, by a community of practitioners, of ground rules concerning the role of economy and elegance as constraints on explanation, which makes historical reconstructions such as the above possible.

Schuchardt's arguments in support of his competing etymology show the workings of a very different strategy. Rather than limiting the explanatory apparatus to law-like regularities of sound change, as Paris had done, Schuchardt widened the explanatory circle within which the word history was to be reconstructed. His goal was to demonstrate that data from a number of distinct domains converged upon a single hypothesis. These included the verbs for "find" in other Romance languages, which originated in verbs associated with the semantic domain of hunting, and the evidence he collected on hunting and fishing techniques in medieval Europe. Schuchardt drew a wider circle around the phonetic trajectories as well, to include not only the sound laws of

Gallo-Romance, but also fields of lexemes with similar forms, and similar meanings, which can "deflect" the speech sounds from their expected paths of development. Within this wider circle, he believed, historical–phonetic, comparative–lexical and ethnographic facts independently converged on *turbare* as the most attractive antecedent for *trouver/trobar*. The plausibility of the historical account reconstructed by Schuchardt certainly owes a great deal to its author's erudition and investigative zeal. But in the final analysis, such an etymology is successful to the degree that it draws the readers themselves into the project of interpretation. This endeavor requires them to apply their imaginations, and instincts as social beings, to the task of bridging the gap from French *trouver* to a verb meaning "stir up."

Gaston Paris, to be sure, found himself obliged to make the same sorts of demands upon his readers, despite his insistence that sound laws trumped all other types of explanation in etymological reasoning. He examined the documentation of Latin *tropus*, and, drawing upon his knowledge of ancient rhetoric, poetics, music, and Catholic liturgy, traced the contexts of its use from the classical Latin of Rome to the medieval Latin of Gaul. The rest of the reconstructed semantic trajectory that led from "compose a melody" to "find" was a work of the imagination, but one that could only be convincing to the extent that other modern readers could trace out a similar path in their own minds, and deem it plausible. Paris and his readers were summoned to engage in the imaginative bridging of their contemporary cultural and linguistic "horizons" to the chronologically, culturally, and linguistically distant horizons within which are situated *tropare*, and the unattested intermediate forms preceding Old Provençal *trobar*. This, of course, is the sort of philologically informed sympathetic reading traditionally known as hermeneutics, although with the important difference that what is presented to the reader is not a textual artifact, but rather a historian's reconstruction of a word-form and its contexts of use. The success of the demonstration depends on the reader's powers of imagination, aided by knowledge of different languages, cultures, societies and historical periods.

Opening up the web of meaning in this manner, and the hermeneutic bridging of cultural–historic horizons that it entails, is a fundamental component of the etymological method. It is for this reason, as Meillet (1954: 104), Malkiel (1977), and Anttila (1988: 76–77) have acknowledged, that etymology is an art, or craft, as much as it is a science, and that recognition as a master practitioner depends as much on the intangible factors which Meillet lumped under the rubric "coefficient personnel," and Malkiel called "flair," as it does on the acquisition of a specific set of skills. As in ethnography, the etymologist him- or herself is the primary instrument of observation, of situating the object of study in the web of meaning that most elegantly accounts for its properties, and if possible, offers new insights into other puzzling questions. In the hands of acknowledged masters such as Schuchardt, Meillet, Benveniste, Malkiel, Szemerényi, Hamp, and Watkins, the hybrid technique illustrated here, conjoining the Neo-grammarian doctrine of sound laws to the reconstruction, aided by a multidisciplinary tool-kit, of the social contexts of language use, has proven highly successful, although numerous knotty problems remain, even in such extensively-worked language families as Indo-European.

The method has its weaknesses, nonetheless, which must not be overlooked. Presuppositions governing the range of explanations to be given explicit consideration, the sorts of information admitted as pertinent data, and the manner of its interpretation, typically go unchallenged if they are shared by the readership of historical reconstructions (or at least that segment of the readership whose opinions count). Menocal (1982, 1984) expressed dismay that the "third solution" to the *trobar* etymology – the Hispano-Arabic hypotheses of Ribera, Lemay and herself – had not received the kind of airing in Romance linguistic circles as had Schuchardt's *turbare* proposal. In her opinion, the problem was not the relative plausibility of either Arabic etymon compared to the Latin ones under consideration;

the real problem is the intellectual framework and set of scholarly assumptions and procedures which led to the complete ignoring of this possible Arabic etymon.

(Menocal 1984: 504)

One might question the extent to which the study of the Arabic influence on Hispano-Romance has been tainted by "the overtly anti-Semitic tendencies in Spanish history" (Menocal 1984: 504–505), or whether Romance etymologists have shown bad faith in refusing to discuss, in print at least, the merits of /Tˤ–R–B/ or /Dˤ–R–B/ as an antecedent of Old Provençal *trobar*. The silence of the etymologists might simply stem from their reluctance to reconfigure the imaginary scenarios they had postulated to accommodate the case of *trobar* in the absence of what they deem to be compelling justification for the shifting of the setting of the innovation from France to Spain, and the splitting of the etymology. It could, at least partially, be a consequence of the limitations on the hermeneutic reach of the tools they bring to bear on this type of problem. Menocal suspects that a disinclination on the part of Hispanists to learn Arabic (1984: 506–507), itself a reflection of bias, would leave them less able to detect any Arabic borrowings that might have been passed over by earlier scholars, which in turn, closing the vicious circle, would confirm their initial prejudices.

A more serious risk is inherent in the hermeneutic approach itself. The bridge linking the interpreter's horizon and that enclosing the culturally, geographically and/or historically remote object of study permits movement in both directions. Sympathetic interpreters in the present can open themselves to distant webs of meaning, but there is an ever-present risk that the scholar's prejudices or ideological agenda could be projected back into the remote horizon, thereby distorting the interpretation of the past (Sergent 1982; Anthony 1995; Lincoln 1999; Aerts 2000). The effect is magnified if the readers of these reconstructions, or the leadership of the institutions sponsoring the scholar's research, share the author's prejudices. Politically motivated amateur etymologies are depressingly common – especially on the Internet – but well-trained professional linguists have by no means been exempt from bias in the reconstruction of word histories, especially when political circumstances encouraged them to do so. Acting to reduce the risks of overlooking promising hypotheses, or of letting the ideological concerns of the present contaminate the reading of the past, is the argumentative, indeed agonistic, style favored by etymologists. The animated back-and-forth between Schuchardt and his French colleagues was nothing new in the field. It echoed the strident polemics of the *Lautgesetz* controversy of the 1870s and 1880s (Wilbur 1977), which were themselves informed by the uncompromising and sharp-tongued debating style effectively used by Pott and his colleagues in the first generation of historical–comparative linguists in the early nineteenth century.

The etymological approach, as historical method, can be summarized as a type of diachronic hermeneutics, the reconstruction of word histories through the projection of ancestral forms (usually unattested), situated in postulated webs of meaning which motivate their phonetic and semantic characteristics. Historical accounts are, of necessity, hypotheses. From this standpoint, the historical reasoning of linguists can be compared to that of archaeologists, who are likewise engaged in the reconstruction of past states of affairs from fragmentary evidence. The methodological issues singled out by Wylie (1985: 483), in the passage cited at the beginning of this chapter, provide a useful starting point for a summarizing of the degree of consensus among etymologists, and historical linguists in general, concerning the formation and constraining of hypotheses. I will add two further issues relating to historical methodology to Wylie's list:

(1) *What it is that makes an account explanatory, and what evidence constitutes grounds for accepting an hypothesis.* Historical phonetics has been remarkably successful in accounting for formal correspondences between cognate forms in related languages, and, on this basis, establishing likely trajectories of sound change. Although acoustics and articulatory physiology do not play a comparable constraining role in other domains of language structure, the diachronic study of morphological and syntactic typology has revealed favored directions of change, and the long-term stability of certain configurations of features (Nichols 1992; Harris/Campbell 1995). These regularities of language change impose limits of acceptability on historical reconstructions, although, as has been already shown, practitioners do not agree on the relative weighting of highly regular changes (sound laws) and the less regular, but well-documented, effects of analogy, sound symbolism, and the like. Constraints on semantic reconstruction are less well worked out. Schuchardt sought to refine the onomasiological approach, by

ascertaining regularities in the naming of particular classes of objects, animals, etc. As evidence in support of proposed etymologies in the Romance languages, he cited the practice of naming cereal varieties after the place where they were believed to have originated (hence French dial. *baillarc* "summer barley" < *balearicum* "Balearic"), and the frequent examples of species of fish named after birds they resemble in some manner (e.g. Occitan *siejo* "dace" < *acceia* "snipe") (Schuchardt 1902: 402–406; cp. Meyer-Lübke 1992: 6, 73). Etymologists have also made use of feature analysis, and the mutually defining relations among terms within semantic fields, as guides in the reconstruction of certain types of lexical sets, such as kinship terminology (Friedrich 1979; Benveniste 1969). In addition to the above factors, hypotheses are evaluated for the range of cases they cover, the number of unsupported, or thinly supported assumptions they entail, and their success in accommodating newly revealed facts.

(2) *The limits of empirical knowledge, and the status of theoretical claims about unobservable phenomena.* Since Turgot's time, the historical–comparative method has reached beyond attested ancestral languages, such as Latin, or alleged living fossils such as Vedic Sanskrit, to the reconstruction of linguistic elements which are not supported by documentary evidence, and extremely unlikely to ever be. Schleicher's formulation of more rigorous procedures of linguistic reconstruction, accompanied by his adoption of the asterisk to mark unattested ancestral forms, was an important advance in this direction (Schleicher 1967; Koerner 1982). Since then, hundreds of linguists, working in dozens of countries, have been occupied with reconstructing the phonology, morphology, syntax, and lexicon of a language which was presumably extinct for at least two millennia before the earliest trace of any of its daughter tongues. What these scholars label "Proto-Indo-European" is not so much a language in the usual sense as it is an operating model, continually subject to revision (or even abandonment), which represents regularities of sound correspondences, and elements of lexicon, affixation and morphological paradigms common – to greater or lesser degrees – to a large number of living and dead Eurasiatic languages. Specialists differ somewhat in the degree of realism they accord their reconstructions of the ancestral language. For some, the "phonemes" of Proto-IE are little more than markers of regular sound correspondences; on this view, an asterisked form such as *$k^w ek^w los$ "wheel" is essentially a conventional shorthand to specify the regular correspondences among Old English *hweol*, Greek *kuklos*, Sanskrit *cakrá-*, Tocharian *kukäl*, etc., and little interest is taken in how it might have been pronounced (Pulgram 1959). Others credit reconstructed forms with at least some measure of phonetic precision, and even go so far as to account for distributional features of the PIE sound system on phonetic grounds (Gamkrelidze and Ivanov 1984; Vennemann 1989).

The debate over limits to linguistic reconstruction is particularly heated with respect to the question of "long-range comparison," by which is meant the search for evidence of genetic links between languages at time depths significantly beyond that proposed for the ancestor of the Indo-European family (six to eight millennia before the present). Comparative work at these depths requires such substantial changes in methodology, that many linguists simply declare that the historical–comparative method cannot provide useful hypotheses that go back more than about 10,000 years before the present. To understand why long-range comparison arouses skepticism, it should be juxtaposed to comparison at shallow and middle-range time depths, which correspond to the genetic groupings Nichols (1992) calls "families" and "stocks," respectively. The first of these is exemplified by Romance historical linguistics, where the number of well-studied languages and dialects, rich documentary evidence, and recent origin of the genetic grouping (less than 2000 years), present optimal conditions for historical study. The basic sound correspondences are for the most part unproblematic, but the abundance of documentary, dialectological, and historical data affords ample material for etymologists to do detailed, even book-length, word histories. Middle-range comparison, at the level of the Indo-European, Uralic, Austronesian, and Northeast Caucasian language groups, relies more heavily on the evidence of shared morphology and the establishment of sound correspondences, many of them non-obvious, on the basis of smaller numbers of identifiable lexical cognates. Even very small sets of related forms can play a crucial role in reconstruction if they show sufficiently robust parallelism in form (according to the expected sound correspondences), meaning and grammatical categorization, to rule out coincidence as an acceptable explanation (Hamp 1998). At the range of what Matisoff (1990) calls "megalocomparison," large phyletic groupings ancestral to recognized stocks are postulated, at estimated time depths well beyond ten millennia. The more far-fetched of these include Greenberg's (1987) "Amerind", and even Bengtson and Ruhlen's (1994) "Proto-World." It seems at first glance paradoxical that the hypothesized sound correspondences linking the far-flung members of these mega-families are characteristically much simpler than those detected in Indo-European; one never encounters anything comparable to the complex, but regular, sound correspondences that link Armenian *erku* "two" to Latin *duo*. The reason behind this is the small number of possible cognates which can be identified in languages which separated from their common ancestor – if in fact they had one – in the Mesolithic or earlier. Megalocomparativists exhibit sets of phonetically similar words with similar meanings, but have difficulty convincing their colleagues that they have eliminated chance resemblances from their data base, or even that the proposed cognates have been correctly glossed and analyzed. In the absence of sufficiently robust cognate sets, strong parallels in morphological paradigms, and supporting data from written texts, archaeology, etc., the regular etymological approach cannot be used, or, to be more precise, does not yield the sort of results that would encourage traditionally trained linguists to continue their inquiry.

(3) *The enforcing of high standards of erudition and familiarity with neighboring disciplines considered relevant for etymological inquiry: history, archaeology, ethnology, sociology, etc.* Experienced practitioners can undertake broad-based examinations of the social, cultural and historical context of the phenomena being investigated in search of facts that converge upon a particular hypothesis (cp. Williams 2002: 256–257). This means of constraining hypotheses is familiar to those archaeologists, who, in response to criticism of archaeology's cooptation in the service of imperialism and nationalism, have sought to reconcile a realist view of history with the necessarily contingent and socio-historically conditioned nature of historical reconstruction (Kohl 1998: 233). Anthony (1995: 87), for example, has argued in favor of "convergent realism" as a methodological control on the distorting effects of bias and interpretive inaccuracy in reconstructing the past:

When the "facts" that are consistent with a particular explanation derive from many different sources [. . .] it becomes increasingly unlikely that all the evidence is tainted the same way.

(4) *The agonistic style of scholarly exchange favored by etymologists for almost two centuries.* In a disciplinary setting prone to criticism, and even hyper-criticism, it is natural that practitioners train themselves to resist "the Sirens of phonetic similarity," unless strong supporting arguments are adduced. Chartraine's refusal to endorse the etymological relation of Greek t^heos to the Latin root *fēs-*, for no other reason than the difference in vowel length, might strike outsiders as an exaggerated case of finickiness. No doubt some philologists felt the same way when Pott and his colleagues called into question the erstwhile undisputed kinship of t^heos and Latin *deus*. Such cases should serve as a reminder that not yielding too quickly to the Sirens' song can leave the investigator open to explore hypotheses that are less obvious at first glance, but more fruitful in the long run.

Research on variation and change since Saussure

The career of Ferdinand de Saussure serves to mark, both chronologically and intellectually, the transition from the nineteenth to the twentieth century in historical linguistics. The young Saussure trained at Leipzig under the leading linguists of the Neo-grammarian movement. Although Saussure was doing original linguistic research in his adolescence, it was at Leipzig that he learned of the *"fait étonnant"* of the sound law, as the core doctrine of the Neo-grammarian approach to the historical study of language (Saussure 1960). One of the more brilliant successes of this approach was Saussure's *Mémoire*, although its most daring proposals were not generally accepted until after the discovery of the long-lost Indo-European language Hittite a decade after Saussure's death. Later in his career, he undertook the exploration of a new approach to the study of language, one based upon a rigorous methodological distinction between language seen as the constantly changing speech habits of a community and language as a *system*, a virtual structure extracted from time and from the minds of its speakers. He imagined a corresponding split in the discipline of linguistics, between a *synchronic linguistics*, which "will concern itself with the logical and psychological relations among the coexisting terms which form a system, as perceived by the same collective conscience," and a *diachronic linguistics* which "will study the relations among successive terms not perceived by the same collective conscience, each of which substitutes [for the one before it] without forming a system among themselves" (Saussure 1974).

It has become a commonplace of academic jargon to apply the adjective "Saussurian" to idealized synchronic structural descriptions, such as Lévi-Strauss's analysis of myth, or Chomsky's generative grammar. In fact, Saussure's most celebrated disciples were historical linguists who faithfully practiced the Neo-grammarian craft. Despite the criticism it has received since its proclamation in the 1870s, the Neo-grammarian model of sound laws, conjoined to the hermeneutic approach to reconstructing word histories, dominates historical linguistic research on both sides of the Atlantic up to the present. At the same time, significant advances in the technology of speech recording and analysis, accompanied by the development of new research techniques, has opened a new chapter in the discipline of historical linguistics. Linguists have been able not only to demonstrate the fundamental correctness of Schuchardt's postulate concerning the ubiquity of synchronic variation, but have also undertaken extensive studies of the factors correlated with that variation.

"As far as can be ascertained by direct observation of ourselves or others," Schuchardt wrote, "the speech production of the individual is never free from variation" (Schuchardt 1928: 60). The new sociolinguistic methodology has confirmed that the speech repertory of each society, and even of each individual in each society, consists in a range of "lects" or "registers," distinguished by phonetic, lexical and other linguistic markers. William Labov and others working within his paradigm have for the most part conducted their research in Western urban settings such as New York (Labov 1972); Montréal (Thibault/Daveluy 1989); Belfast (Milroy[s]); and Norwich (Trudgill); this research has revealed in each case at least some linguistic markers which vary – often to a surprising degree – within what one would otherwise consider the same community of speakers (e.g. the pronunciation – even in the repertoire of a single speaker from New York City – of the vowel in "bad" ranging from a low [æ] right up to a high, diphthongized [Iə]). Of particular interest is the discovery by anthropological linguists that the phenomenon of variation is by no means limited to such settings. Consider, for example, the Imonda language of Papua-New-Guinea, spoken by 274 speakers who inhabited, until 1962, a single village. Seiler (1985: 20) noted how a phonetic feature – the centralization of high vowels – varied regularly with age. As speakers grow older, they modify certain markers in their speech to signal their position in the community (Seiler 1985: 11). Recent research has also revealed the correlation of linguistic variation with social categories even in speech communities of very recent origin. The case of Honiara, the capital of the Solomon Islands, is instructive. This town was founded after the Second World War, and its first indigenous inhabitants spoke a rich variety of rural forms of Solomon Islands Pijin, which they had acquired while working on plantations and in similar contexts. In the new urban environment, where Pijin was installed as the principal means of communication of a population comprising speakers from sixty or more ethnic groups, it underwent a number of modifications: phonetic changes linked to a more rapid speech tempo, increased vocabulary, and so forth. Interestingly, the structural homogenization of Solomons Pijin was accompanied by a new diversification of the urban varieties, leading to "the stabilization of levels of speech and markers of social class" in the varieties studied by Christine Jourdan in the late 1980s and 1990s (Jourdan and Keesing 1997: 415; cp. Jourdan 1994).

Labov insists that the minute observation of sound changes in progress has only confirmed the hypothesis of the Neo-grammarians concerning the distinction between regular, gradual phonetic change and other types of change, which are less regular and frequently conditioned in complex ways (Labov 1981, 1994). The shift of the vowel in "bad," mentioned above, is an example of the first type of change in the speech communities of those North American cities where the radical restructuration of the vowel system known as the "Northern Cities Shift" is underway (Labov 1991). The use of sophisticated techniques of sound recording and analysis has enabled Labov and his colleagues to pinpoint extremely subtle factors conditioning the pronunciation of certain vowels, but the correlation is said to be regular and predictable. On the other hand, a superficially similar sound shift in Philadelphia represents the second class of phonetic changes: the raising of [æ] is discrete, sensitive to the grammatical context, and limited to certain words. More exactly, the raising of [æ] in Philadelphia represents a *phonological*, rather than a phonetic, change: the mental representation of the word "bad," which undergoes the shift, contains a different vowel phoneme from that of "sad," which does not. After a change of the first (phonetic) type has run its course and ceased to be active, it is typically the case that all, or nearly all, words with the target sound in the appropriate context have been affected. A linguist, comparing the "before" and "after" stages of the language sometime in the future, would likely have the impression that an exceptionless and seemingly instantaneous "sound law" had swept through the speech community. The Neo-grammarian model of the

Lautgesetz is an illusory simplification, like the Ideal Gas Law in chemistry, but one that has descriptive adequacy under most circumstances.

Variationist research has provoked numerous commentaries, criticisms and field studies, most of which address themselves to one or the other of these questions: (i) How are Neo-grammarian-style phonetic changes to be explained in the context of the sociolinguistic framework? (ii) How are sociolinguistic correlations to be explained in terms of the social life of speakers? With regard to the first question, linguists have come to the somewhat paradoxical conclusion that the most "natural" sound changes – assimilation and weakening ("lenition") – are particularly susceptible to social evaluation despite their gradualness and relative imperceptibility, whereas more complex and abstract linguistic changes are less likely to be sociolinguistically marked, since they are more likely to be filtered out as speech errors (Hock 1991: 653–654). Regular sound changes tend to follow an "S"-shaped trajectory, from an initial phase of slow, incremental change through a middle period of rapid shift, to a final phase where the pace of change once again slows, and may not even go all the way to completion (Labov 1994: 65–67).

As for the link between sociolinguistic phenomena and the social lives of speakers, recent studies have sought to shed light on the narratives behind the statistical regularities detected by variationist studies. This is comparable to the historiographic genre shift noted above in connection with the practice of etymology: The social context of the sound change is described in greater detail, and the members of the speech community appear as social actors, even agents, rather than abstract clusters of demographic and socio-economic parameters. For example, the Milroys and others have pointed to the importance of social networks in accounting for the social and regional distribution of linguistic variables (L. Milroy 1987; Lippi-Green 1989; J. Milroy 1993). Other researchers have investigated the deployment of differently valorized forms of speech in the context of competition for prestige – "symbolic capital" – in what Bourdieu has termed the "linguistic marketplace" (Bourdieu 1983; Sankoff *et al* 1989). Highly interesting studies have been conducted on attitudes of identification, or resistance, on the part of more or less marginalized communities with respect to those groups holding higher prestige and/or power (Labov 1972 on the inhabitants of Martha's Vineyard; Eckert 1991 on the "jocks" and "burnouts" at an American high school). The phenomenon of linguistic distantiation, or boundary maintenance, is by no means uniquely urban. In some small-scale speech communities of Oceania, William Thurston (1987, 1989) observed instances of what he terms "esoterogeny," or the modification of language in order to make it more distinct, in terms of vocabulary or grammar, from the languages of neighboring communities (and by the same token less easily learned by outsiders; cf. Ross and Durie 1996: 21–22; Andersen 1988). Another type of linguistic differentiation has been attributed by Kroch (1978) and Chambers (1995: 250–253) to an ideology of resistance, although in this instance it is the privileged group which resists the adoption of sound changes originating in more popular varieties of speech. As a consequence, "the standard dialect typically differs from other dialects in the community by being more restricted or more tightly constrained in its grammar and phonology" (Chambers 1995: 246).

For all of its successes in bringing fascinating and extremely useful language data to light, sociolinguistics has been accused of having an unsure epistemological footing. Generative linguistics, including that branch which applies Chomskyan models of grammar to the investigation of language change (e.g. Lightfoot 1997), draws on a confident, almost naïve, empiricism, and a fundamental methodological consensus among its diverse schools. Sociolinguistics, on the other hand, seems to meander between structural and generative linguistics and sociology in search of tools of analysis – from the one side come "variable rules," from the other, network theory and notions of identification and resistance – or, more fundamentally, between a positivist epistemology and a hermeneutics appropriate to the human and historical sciences.

But is it necessarily a bad thing if sociolinguistics brings both natural-scientific and hermeneutic approaches to bear on the study of language variation and change? As summarized in the first two volumes of Labov's *Principles of linguistic change* (1994, 2001), the discipline is confronting the same issues as its predecessors of a century ago:

(1) Variation and change is a ubiquitous characteristic of language. Change inheres in its triple nature as system, activity and social institution (Lüdtke 1986, Keller 1994, Tuite 1999).

(2) Physiological and cognitive factors act as constraints upon certain types of change. Consonant lenitions are far more frequent than fortitions (Trask 1996: 55–60). Shifts in vowel features, such as height and anteriority, tend to follow predictable trajectories, as argued by Martinet (1964) and Labov (1994).

(3) Although the constraints in (2) assure a degree of regularity, even predictability, of linguistic change, the phenomenon is nonetheless fundamentally social in nature. Change is enacted and diffused in the intersubjective context of communication. Language use has an inherent indexical component, in that it continually signals, constructs, maintains and problematizes the multifaceted cluster of representations subsumed under the notion of "identity" (Silverstein 1996, 1998). Variation – different ways of saying "the same thing" – is the primary resource exploited in this process.

(4) For the above reason, among others, natural-science-like, desubjectivized models of variation and change must be complemented by hermeneutic approaches, which draw upon knowledge of various elements of the context of the phenomenon under study, as well as the investigators' own instincts and imaginative capabilities as socially, historically, and culturally situated actors.

Not surprisingly, therefore, divergent points of view comparable to those that enlivened etymological debates have surfaced in the sociolinguistic community. Some researchers have emphasized the role of universal or near-universal constraints on the direction of sound change. Gordon and Heath (1998) point to the evidence, from a large number of studies, that women generally lead men in changes marked by the raising and fronting of vowels, whereas men tend to lead in the lowering and backing of vowels, and also favor uvular and pharyngealized consonants. They argue that sexual differences in the adoption of phonetic changes can be explained to a considerable extent by differential preferences for acute and grave sounds, which are rooted in sexual dimorphism. As in the Schuchardt–Paris debate, Gordon and Heath's proposal has been met with discussion over the relative priority of regular phonetic trajectories compared to social and semantic factors in explaining language change (see the commentaries on Gordon and Heath 1998; and Labov 2001: 291–292, 307–308). A more interpretive approach informs the research of Penelope Eckert (2000) on the distribution of phonetic variables among high-school students near Detroit. Eckert's analysis makes extensive use of interviews, social-network maps, and two years of ethnographic observation. Rather than look for general constraints on sound change, she seeks to understand how individuals deploy linguistic features in the construction of their social personae, as markers of group affiliation and stance vis-à-vis the school as institution, and its associated values. Labov himself has contributed to both directions of inquiry. His comparative investigations of the directions of vowel-feature changes has introduced significant refinements to Martinet's theory of chain shifts (Labov 1994). The more "Schuchardtian" and interpretive aspect of Labov's research methodology is evident in his pioneering study of the social significance of particular phonetic features among the permanent residents of the island of Martha's Vineyard (1972: 1–42), and, more recently, in the collecting of life histories from the upper-working-class women who produce the most advanced forms of certain sociolinguistic variables in Philadelphia (Labov 2001: 385–411). Seen in historical perspective, against the backdrop of the debates over sound laws or the etymology of *trouver*, the hybrid methodology of sociolinguistics has proven itself to be a source of vitality, not weakness.

REFERENCES

Aarsleff, Hans. 1983. *The study of language in England, 1780–1860*. London: Athlone Press.

1988. "Introduction." In Wilhelm von Humboldt, *On language*, vii–lxv. Cambridge: Cambridge University Press.

Abramov, Israel. 1997. "Physiological mechanisms of color vision." In C. L. Hardin and Luisa Maffi (eds.), *Color categories in thought and language*. Cambridge: Cambridge University Press.

Abu-Lughod, Lila. 1986. *Veiled sentiments: honor and poetry in a Bedouin society*. Berkeley: University of California Press.

1995. *Writing women's worlds. Bedouin stories*. Berkeley: University of California Press.

Abu-Lughod, Lila and Catherine Lutz. 1990. "Introduction: emotion, discourse, and the politics of everyday life." In C. Lutz and L. Abu-Lughod (eds.), *Language and the politics of emotion*, 1–23. Cambridge: Cambridge University Press.

Adam, Lucien. 1883. *Les idiomes négro-aryen et maléo-aryen*. Paris.

Adone, Dany and Ingo Plag (eds.). 1994. *Creolization and language change*. Tübingen: Niemeyer.

Aerts, Romana. 2000. "L'Histoire des Perses de A. de Gobineau dans le cadre de la mythologie de l'impérialisme Indo-européen." In Sylvie Vanséveren (ed.), *Modèles linguistiques et Idéologie: "Indo-Européen"*, 97–108. Bruxelles: Éditions Ousia.

Alford, Danny K. H. Moonhawk. 1978. "The demise of the Whorf hypothesis (a major revision in the history of linguistics)." *Proceedings of the Annual Meeting of the Berkeley Linguistics Society* 4: 485–499.

1981. "Is Whorf's relativity Einstein's relativity?" *Proceedings of the Berkeley Linguistics Society* 7: 13–26.

2002. "The great Whorf hypothesis hoax: sin, suffering and redemption in academe." (Available at www.enformy.com/dma-Chap7.htm.)

Alleyne, Mervyn C. 1966. "La nature du changement phonétique à la lumière du créole français d'Haïti." *Revue de linguistique romane* 30: 279–303.

1971. "Acculturation and the cultural matrix of creolization." In Dell Hymes (ed.), *Pidginization and creolization of languages*, 169–187. Cambridge: Cambridge University Press.

1980. *Comparative Afro-American: an historical comparative study of some Afro-American dialects in the New World*. Ann Arbor: Karoma.

Althusser, Louis. 1968 (1970). "The object of *Capital*." In Louis Althusser and Etienne Balibar, *Reading Capital*, 71–198. Ben Brewster, trans. London: NLB.

Alvarez-Cáccamo, Celso. 1998. "From 'switching code' to 'code-switching': towards a reconceptualization of communicative codes." In Peter Auer (ed.), *Code-switching in conversation*, 29–50. London: Routledge.

Andersen, Henning. 1988. "Center and periphery: adoption, diffusion, and spread." In Jacek Fisiak (ed.), *Historical dialectology: regional and social.* New York: Mouton de Gruyter, 39–84.

Anderson, Benedict. 1991. *Imagined communities: reflections on the origin and spread of nationalism.* Revised edition. London and New York: Verso.

Anderson, Jeffrey. 2001. *The four hills of life: Northern Arapaho life, knowledge, and personhood.* Lincoln: University of Nebraska Press.

Anthony, David W. 1995. "Nazi and eco-feminist prehistories: ideology and empiricism in Indo-European archaeology." In Philip L. Kohl and Clare Fawcett (eds.), *Nationalism, politics, and the practice of archaeology,* 82–96. Cambridge: Cambridge University Press.

Anttila, Raimo. 1988. "The type and the comparative method." In Jorn Albrecht, Harald Thun, and Jens Lüdtke (eds.), *Eugenio Coseriu. Energeia und Ergon: sprachliche Variation, Sprachgeschichte, Sprachtypologie,* 43–56. Band II. Tübingen: G. Narr.

Apter, Andrew. 1998. "Discourse and its disclosures: Yoruba women and the sanctity of abuse." *Africa* 68(1): 68–97.

Aracil, Lluis. 1982. *Papers de sociolinguistica.* Barcelona: La Magrana.

Arends, Jacques. 1993. "Towards a gradualist model of creolization." In F. Byrne and J. Holm (eds.), *Atlantic meets Pacific: a global view of pidginization and creolization,* 371–380. Amsterdam: John Benjamins.

    (ed.). 1995. *The early stages of creolization.* Amsterdam: John Benjamins.

    2001. "Social stratification and network relations in the formation of Sranan." In N. Smith and T. Veenstra (eds.), *Creolization and Contact,* 291–307. Amsterdam: John Benjamins.

Atran, Scott. 1984. *Bilingual conversation.* Amsterdam: Benjamins.

    1990. *Cognitive foundations of natural history.* Cambridge: Cambridge University Press.

Auer, J. C. P. 1988. "A conversational approach to code-switching and transfer." In M. Heller (ed.), *Code-switching: anthropological and sociolinguistic perspectives,* 187–213. Berlin: Mouton.

    (ed.). 1998. *Code-switching in conversation.* London: Routledge.

Austerlitz, Robert. 1958. *Ob-Ugric metrics.* Helsinki: Suomalainen Tiedeakatemina Scientium Fennila.

Austin, J. L. 1962. *How to do things with words.* Oxford: Oxford University Press.

    1975. *How to do things with words.* Cambridge, Mass.: Harvard University Press.

    1979. "Performative utterances." *Philosophical Papers,* 233–252. Oxford: Oxford University Press.

Baker, Colin. 2001. *Foundations of bilingual education and bilingualism.* 3rd edn. Clevedon, U.K.: Multilingual Matters.

Baker, Philip. 1983. "Commentaire sur Chaudenson 1983." *Etudes Créoles* 6(2): 230–236.

    1990. "Off target." *Journal of Pidgin and Creole Languages* 5: 105–119.

    1993a. "Assessing the African contribution to French-based creoles." In Salikoko S. Mufwene (ed.), *Africanisms in Afro-American language varieties,* 123–155. Athens/London: The University of Georgia Press.

    1993b. "Australian influence on Melanesian pidgin English." *Te Reo* 36: 3–67.

    1995. "Directionality in pidginization and creolization." In Arthur Spears and Donald Winford (eds.), *The structure and status of pidgins and creoles,* 91–109. Amsterdam: John Benjamins publishing company.

    2000. "Theories of creolization and the degree and nature of restructuring." In Ingrid Neumann-Holzschuh and Edgar W. Schneider (eds.), *Degrees of restructuring in creole languages*, 41–63. Creole language library. Amsterdam/Philadelphia: John Benjamins.

Baker, Philip and Chris Corne. 1982. *Isle de France creole: affinities and origins*. Ann Arbor: Karoma.

Baker, Philip and Anand Syea (eds.). 1996. *Changing meanings, changing functions*. Westminster creolistics series, 2. London: University of Westminster Press.

Bakhtin, M. M. 1986. "The problem of speech genres." In Caryl Emerson and Michael Holquist (eds.), *Speech genres and other late essays*, 60–102. Austin: University of Texas Press.

Bakker, Egbert. 1999. "Homeric *outos* (ΟΥΤΟΣ) and the poetics of deixis." *Classical Philology* 94: 1–19.

Bakker, Peter and Maarten Mous (eds.). 1994. *Mixed languages. Studies in language and language use*, 13. Dordrecht: ICG Printing.

Baldinger, Kurt. 1995. "Gilles Ménage, grammairien et lexicographe: Ouverture du Colloque." In Isabelle Leroy-Turcan and Terence R. Wooldridge (eds.), *Gilles Ménage (1613–1692) grammairien et lexicographe: le rayonnement de son oeuvre linguistique*, 1–8. Lyon: Université Jean Moulin.

Balibar, Renée. 1984. *Galilée, Newton lus par Einstein. Espace et relativité*. Paris: PUF.

Barkow, Jerome H. 1994. "Evolutionary psychological anthropology." In P. K. Bock (ed.), *Psychological anthropology*, 121–37. Westport, CT: Praeger.

Barney, Rachel. 1998. "Socrates Agonistes: the case of the *Cratylus* etymologies." *Oxford Studies in Ancient Philosophy* 16: 63–98.

Barth, Fredrik (ed.). 1969. *Ethnic groups and boundaries*. Boston: Little, Brown.

Basilius, Harold. 1952. "Neo-Humboldtian ethnolinguistics." *Word* 8: 95–105.

Bate, John Bernard. 2000. "Meedaittamil: oratory and democratic practice in Tamil-nadu." Ph.D. thesis, University of Chicago.

Bates, E., L. Camaioni, and V. Volterra. 1979. "The acquisition of performatives prior to speech." In E. Ochs and B. B. Schieffelin (eds.), *Developmental pragmatics*, 111–129. New York: Academic Press.

Bauman, Richard. 1984. *Verbal arts as performance*. Prospect Heights, IL: Waveland Press.

Bauman, Richard and Charles Briggs. 1990. "Poetics and performance as critical perspectives on language and social life." *Annual Review of Anthropology* 19: 59–88.

2000. "Language philosophy as language ideology: John Locke and Johann Gottfried Herder." In Paul V. Kroskrity (ed.), *Regimes of language: ideologies, polities, and identities*, 139–204. Santa Fe: School of American Research Press.

Bavin, E. 1989. "Some lexical and morphological changes in Walpiri." In N. Dorian (ed.), *Investigating obsolescence: studies in language contraction and death*, 267–286. Cambridge: Cambridge University Press.

1992. "The acquisition of Walpiri." In D. Slobin (ed.), *The crosslinguistic study of language acquisition*, 309–372. Vol 3. Hillsdale, NJ: Lawrence Erlbaum Associates.

Baxter, Timothy M. S. 1992. *The Cratylus: Plato's critique of naming*. Leiden: E. J. Brill.

Becker, A. L. 1995. *Beyond translation: essays toward a modern philology*. Ann Arbor: University of Michigan Press.

Beeman, William O. 1986. *Language, status and power in Iran*. Bloomington: Indiana University Press.

2000. "Emotion and sincerity in Persian discourse: accomplishing the representation of inner states." *International Journal of the Sociology of Language* 148: 1–26.

Benedict, Ruth. 1934. *Patterns of culture*. Boston: Houghton Mifflin.

Bengtson, John D. and Merritt Ruhlen. 1994. "Global etymologies." In *On the origin of languages: studies in linguistic taxonomy*, 277–336. Stanford: Stanford University Press, Benjamins.

Bentolila, André. 1971. *Les systèmes verbaux créoles: comparaisons avec les langues africaines*. Thèse de 3ème cycle. Paris: Université René Descartes.

Benveniste, Emile. 1958 (1966). "Catégories de pensée et catégories de langue." In Emile Benveniste, *Problèmes de linguistique générale*, 63–74. Paris: Gallimard.

1969. *Le vocabulaire des institutions indo-européennes, Vol. 1. Économie, parenté, société*. Paris: Éditions de Minuit

Bergvall, Victoria, Janet Bing, and Alice Freed (eds.). 1996. *Rethinking Language and Gender Research, Theory and Practice*. New York; London: Longman.

Berlant, Lauren. 1997 "Introduction: the intimate public sphere." *The Queen of America Goes to Washington City, Essays on Sex and Citizenship*. 1–24. Durham: Duke University Press.

Berlin, Brent. 1992. *Ethnobiological classification*. Princeton NJ: Princeton University Press.

Berlin, Brent and Elois Ann Berlin. 1975. "Aguaruna color categories." *American Ethnologist* 2: 61–87.

Berlin, Brent and Paul Kay. 1969. *Basic color terms: their universality and evolution*. Berkeley: University of California Press.

Berlin, Brent, Dennis Breedlove and Peter H. Raven. 1973. "General principles of classification and nomenclature in folk biology." *American Anthropologist* 75: 214–242.

1974. *Principles of Tzeltal plant classification*. New York: Academic Press.

Berlinski, David. 1995. *A tour of the calculus*. NY: Random House (Vinton).

Berman, Ruth and Dan I. Slobin. 1994. *Relating events in narrative: a crosslinguistic developmental study*. Hillsdale, NJ: Erlbaum.

Berndt, Ronald M. 1976. *Love songs of Arnhem land*. Chicago: University of Chicago Press.

Bernstein, Charles. 1998. *Clare listening. Poetry and the performed word*. New York: Oxford University Press.

Bertrand, Frédéric. 2002. *L'anthropologie soviétique des années 20–30. Configuration d'une rupture*. Pessac: Presses universitaires de Bordeaux.

Besnier, Niko. 1993. "Reported Speech and Affect on Nukulaelae Atoll." In Jane Hill and Judith Irvine (eds.), *Responsibility and evidence in oral discourse*, 161–181. Cambridge: Cambridge University Press.

1994. "Polynesian gender liminality through time and space." In G. Herdt, *Third sex, third gender: beyond sexual dimorphism in culture and history*, 285–328. New York: Zone Books.

Bhabha, Homi K. 1994. *The location of culture*. London: Routledge.

Biardeau, Madeleine. 1982. *Hindouisme: anthropologie d'une civilization*. Editions Champs-Flammarion.

Bickerton, Derek. 1977. "Pidginization and creolization: language acquisition and language universals." In Albert Valdman (ed.), *Pidgin and creole linguistics*, 49–69. Bloomington/London: Indiana University Press.

1980. *Roots of language*. Ann Arbor: Karoma.

1984. "The language bioprogram hypothesis." *Brain and Behavioural Sciences* 7: 173–221.

1986. "Creoles and West African languages: a case of mistaken identity?" In Pieter C. Muysken and Norval Smith (eds.), *Substrata versus universals in Creole genesis*, 25–40. Creole language library, 1. Amsterdam/Philadelphia: John Benjamins.

1988. "Creole languages and the bioprogram." In Frederick J. Newmeyer (ed.), *Linguistic theory: extensions and implications*, 268–284. Linguistics: The Cambridge Survey, 2. Cambridge: Cambridge University Press.

1990a. *Language and species*. Chicago: University of Chicago Press.

1990b. "On Mufwene's response to Bickerton." *The Carrier Pidgin* 17(1,2): 6–7; 18(1): 3–4.

Billiez, Jacqueline. 1998. "L'alternance des langues en chantant." *LIDIL* 18: 125–140.

Black, Max. 1962. *Models and metaphors: studies in language and philosophy*. Ithaca: Cornell University Press.

Bloch, Maurice E. F. 1994. "Language, anthropology, and cognitive science." In *Assessing cultural anthropology*, ed. Robert Borofsky, 276–282. NY: McGraw-Hill.

1998. *How we think they think: anthropological approaches to cognition, memory, and literacy*. Boulder, Colorado: Westview Press.

Bloch, Ralph Howard. 1983. *Etymologies and genealogies: a literary anthropology of the French Middle Ages*. Chicago: University of Chicago Press.

Blom, Jan-Petter and John Gumperz. 1972. "Social meaning in linguistic structures: code-switching in Norway." In John Gumperz and Dell Hymes (eds.), *Directions in sociolinguistics: the ethnography of communication*, 407–434. New York: Holt, Rinehart and Winston.

Blommaert, Jan (ed.). 1999. *Language ideological debates*. Berlin: Mouton de Gruyter.

2001. "The Asmara declaration as a sociolinguistic problem: Reflections on scholarship and linguistic rights." *Journal of Sociolinguistics* 5(1): 131–142.

Bloom, A. H. 1981. *The linguistic shaping of thought: a study in the impact of language on thinking in China and the West*. Hillsdale, N.J.: Erlbaum.

Bloom, K. 1990. "Selectivity and early infant vocalization." In J. T. Enns (ed.), *The development of attention: research and theory*, 121–136. B. V. North-Holland: Elsevier Science Publishers.

Bloom, L. 1970. *Language development: form and function in emerging grammar*. Cambridge, Mass: MIT Press.

Bloom, Paul, Mary A. Peterson, Lynn Nadel, and Merrill F. Garrett (eds.). 1996. *Language and space*. Cambridge, MA: MIT Press.

Bloomfield, Leonard. 1933. *Language*. New York: Holt, Rinehart, and Winston.

Blount, Ben G. (ed.). (1995). *Language, culture, and society*. 2nd edn. Prospect Heights, IL: Waveland Press.

Blust, Robert. 1996. "The Neogrammarian hypothesis and pandemic irregularity." In Mark Durie and Malcolm Ross (eds.), *The comparative method reviewed: regularity and irregularity in language change*, 135–156. New York: Oxford University Press.

Boas, Franz. 1887 (1974). "Museums of ethnology and their classification." In George W. Stocking, Jr. (ed.), *The shaping of American anthropology, 1883–1917*, 63–67. New York: Basic Books.

1889 (1940). "The aims of ethnology." In Franz Boas, *Race, language, and culture*, 626–638. New York: Basic Books.

1889 (1974). "On alternating sounds." In George W. Stocking, Jr. (ed.), *The shaping of American anthropology, 1883–1911*, 72–77. New York: Basic Books.

1899. "Advances in methods of teaching." In *Race, language, culture*, 621–625. New York: Free Press.

1910. "Publicaciones nuevas sobre la lingüística americana." In *Reseña de la segunda sesión del XVII Congreso Internacional de Americanistas*, 225–232. Mexico: Museo Nacional de Arqueología, Historia y Etnología.

1911. "Introduction." In Franz Boas (ed.), *Handbook of American Indian languages*. Washington: Government Printing Office, 1–83. [Bureau of American Ethnology, Bulletin 40, Part 1.]

Bock, Philip R. 1984. *Shakespeare and Elizabethan culture*. New York: Schocken Books.

1994. *Psychological anthropology*. Westport, CT: Praeger.

Bohannon, Paul. 1963. *Social anthropology*. New York: Holt, Rinehart and Winston.

Böhtlink, Otto. 1964 (1815). *Über die Sprache der Yakuten*. The Hague: Mouton.

Boix, Emili and F. Xavier Vila. 1998. *Sociolingüística de la llengua catalana*. Barcelona: Ariel Lingüística.

Bornstein, M. H., W. Kessen, and S. Weiskopf. 1976. "Color vision and hue categorization in young human infants." *Journal of Experimental Psychology: Human Perception and Performance* 2: 115–129.

Boroditsky, L. 2001. "Does language shape thought? English and Mandarin speakers' conceptions of time." *Cognitive Psychology*, 43(1): 1–22.

Bourdieu, Pierre. 1975. "Le fétichisme de la langue." *Actes de la recherche en sciences sociales* 4: 2–3.

1977. *Outline of a theory of practice*. Cambridge: Cambridge University Press.

1983. "Vous avez dit 'populaire'?" *Actes de la recherche en sciences sociales* 46: 98–105.

Bowerman, Melissa. 1985. "What shapes children's grammars?" In D. I. Slobin (ed.), *The crosslinguistic study of language acquisition*, vol. 2, 1257–1320. Hillsdale, N.J.: Erlbaum.

1996a. "The origins of children's spatial semantic categories: Cognitive versus linguistic determinants." In J. Gumperz and S. C. Levinson (eds.), *Rethinking linguistic relativity*, 145–176. Cambridge: Cambridge University Press.

1996b. Learning how to structure space for language. In P. Bloom, M. A. Peterson, L. Nadel, and M. F. Garrett (eds.), *Language and space*, 385–436. Cambridge, MA: MIT Press.

2000. "Where do children's word meanings come from? Rethinking the role of cognition in semantic development." In L. Nucci, G. Saxe, and E. Turiel (eds.), *Culture, thought, and development*, 199–230. Mahwah, NJ: Erlbaum.

Bowerman, Melissa and Soonja Choi. 2001. "Shaping meanings for language: universal and language specific in the acquisition of spatial semantic categories." In M. Bowerman and S. C. Levinson (eds.), *Language acquisition and conceptual development*, 475–511. Cambridge: Cambridge University Press.

2003. "Space under construction: language-specific spatial categorization in first language acquisition." In D. Gentner and S. Goldin-Meadow (eds.), *Language in mind: advances in the study of language and thought*, 387–427. Cambridge MA: MIT Press.

Bowerman, Melissa and Stephen C. Levinson (eds.). 2001. *Language acquisition and conceptual development*. Cambridge: Cambridge University Press.

Boyer, Henri. 1991. *Langues en conflit*. Paris: L'Harmattan.

Boyer, Pascal (ed.). 1993. *Cognitive aspects of religious symbolism*. Cambridge: Cambridge University Press.

Brenneis, Donald and Ronald H. S. Macaulay (eds.). 1996. *The matrix of language: contemporary linguistic anthropology*. Boulder, Colorado: Westview Press.

Briggs, Charles. 1988. *Competence and performance: the creativity of tradition in Mexican verbal art*. Philadelphia: University of Pennsylvania Press.

Bright, William O. 1979. "A Karok myth in measured verse: the translation of a performance." *Journal of California and Great Basin Anthropology* 1: 117–123.

Brown, Penelope. 1998. "Conversational structure and language acquisition: the role of repetition in Tzeltal." *Journal of Linguistic Anthropology* 8(2): 197–221.

2001. "Learning to talk about motion UP and DOWN in Tzeltal: is there a language-specific bias for verb learning?" In M. Bowerman and S. C. Levinson (eds.), *Language acquisition and conceptual development*, 512–543. Cambridge: Cambridge University Press.

2002a. "Everyone has to lie in Tzeltal." In S. Blum-Kulka and C. E. Snow (eds.), *Talking to adults: the contribution of multiparty discourse to language acquisition*, 241–275. Mahwah, NJ: Lawrence Erlbaum Associates.

2002b. "Language as a model for culture: lessons from the cognitive sciences." In B. King and R. Fox (eds.), *Anthropology beyond culture*, 169–192. Oxford: Berg.

Brown, Penelope and S. C. Levinson. 1987. *Politeness: some universals in language usage*. Cambridge: Cambridge University Press.

1993a. "Linguistic and nonlinguistic coding of spatial arrays: explorations in Mayan cognition." Cognitive Anthropology Research Group, Max Planck Institute for Psycholinguistics, Working Paper 24, Oct. 1993.

1993b. " 'Uphill' and 'downhill' in Tzeltal." *Journal of Linguistic Anthropology* 3(1): 46–74.

2000. "Frames of spatial reference and their acquisition in Tenejapan Tzeltal." In L. Nucci, G. Saxe, and E. Turiel (eds.), *Culture, thought, and development*, 167–197. Mahweh, NJ: Erlbaum.

Brown, R. 1977. "Introduction." In C. Ferguson and C. Snow (eds.), *Talking to children: language input and acquisition*, 1–30. Cambridge: Cambridge University Press.

Brown, R., C. Cazden, and U. Bellugi. 1968. "The child's grammar from I to III." In J. P. Hill (ed.), *The second annual Minnesota symposium on child psychology*. Minneapolis: University of Minnesota Press, 28–73.

Brown, Roger Langham. 1967. *Wilhelm von Humboldt's conception of linguistic relativity*. The Hague: Mouton. [Janua Linguarum, Series minor, 65.]

Brown, Roger W. and Eric H. Lenneberg. 1954. "A study of language and cognition." *Journal of Abnormal and Social Psychology* 49: 454–462.

Bucholtz, Mary and Kira Hall. 1995. "Introduction: twenty years after *Language and woman's place*." In Hall, *Gender articulated*, 1–22.

Bunzl, Matti. 1996. "Franz Boas and the Humboldtian tradition: from *Volksgeist* and *Nationalcharakter* to an anthropological concept of culture." In George W. Stocking, Jr. (ed.), *Volksgeist as Method and Ethic: Essays on Boasian Anthropology and the German Anthropological Tradition*, 17–78. Madison: University of Wisconsin Press.

Buridant, Claude. 1998. "Les paramètres de l'étymologie médiévale." *L'étymologie, de l'antiquité à la Renaissance*, 11–56. Numéro coordonné et présenté par C. Buridant *et al.* Villeneuve d'Ascq: Presses Universitaires du Septentrion.

Butler, Judith. 1990. *Gender trouble, feminism and the subversion of identity*. New York: Routledge.

1997. *Excitable speech, a politics of the performative*. New York and London: Routledge.

Bynon, Theodora. 1966. "Leo Weisgerber's four stages in linguistic analysis." *Man* n.s. 1: 468–483.

Byrne Francis and Thom Huebner (eds.). 1991. *Development and structures of creole languages. Creole language library*, 10. Amsterdam/Philadelphia: John Benjamins.

Byrne, R. and A. Whiten (eds.). 1988. *Machiavellian intelligence*. Oxford: Clarendon Press.

Calame-Griaule, Geneviève. 1987. *Ethnologie et langage. La parole chez les Dogon.* Paris: Gallimard.

Calhoun, Craig. 1995. *Critical social theory, culture, history and the challenge of difference.* Oxford: Blackwell.

Cameron, Deborah. 1995. *Verbal hygiene.* London and New York: Routledge.

Cameron, Deborah and Don Kulick. 2003. *Language and sexuality.* Cambridge: Cambridge University Press.

Capro, Fritjof. 1977. *The Tao of physics.* New York: Bantam Books.

Carne-Ross, D. S. and Kenneth Haynes. 1996. *Horace in English.* New York: Penguin.

Carruthers, Peter, and Jill Boucher (eds.). 1998. *Language and thought: interdisciplinary themes.* Cambridge: Cambridge University Press.

Carson, Anne. 1986. *Eros the bittersweet: an essay.* Princeton: Princeton University Press.

Casasola, Marianella, 2005. "Can language do the driving? The effect of linguistic input on infants' categorization of support spatial relations." *Developmental Psychology* 41(1): 183–192.

Cassirer, Ernst. 1923 (1955). *The philosophy of symbolic forms.* I. *Language.* Ralph Mannheim, trans. New Haven: Yale University Press.

Casson, R. W. (ed.). 1981. *Language, culture and cognition.* New York: Macmillan.
1983. "Schemata in cognitive anthropology." *Annual Review of Anthropology* 12: 429–462.

Castonguay, Charles. 1996. "L'intérêt particulier de la démographie pour le fait français au Canada." In Jürgen Erfurt (ed.), *De la polyphonie à la symphonie. Méthodes, théories et faits de la recherche pluridisciplinaire sur le français au Canada*, 3–18. Leipzig: Leipziger Universitätsverlag.

Caton, Steven. 1990. *"Peaks of Yemen I Summon."* Berkeley: University of California Press.

Cazden, C. 1965. "Environmental assistance to the child's acquisition of grammar." Unpublished Ph.D. thesis. Harvard University.

Chafe, Wallace and Johanna Nichols (eds.). 1986. *Evidentiality: the linguistic coding of epistemology.* Norwood, NJ: Ablex.

Chambers, J. K. 1995. *Sociolinguistic theory: linguistic variation and its social significance.* Oxford: Blackwell.

Chantraine, Pierre. 1990. *Dictionnaire étymologique de la langue grecque: histoire des mots.* (Nouv. tirage). Paris: Klincksieck.

Chao, Yuen-Ren. 1976. "Philosophical perspectives." *Aspects of Chinese sociolinguistics.* Selected and Introduced by Anwar S. Dil. Stanford: Stanford University Press.

Chatterjee, Ranjit. 1985. "Reading Whorf through Wittgenstein: a solution to the linguistic relativity problem." *Lingua* 67: 37–63.

Chaudenson, Robert. 1974. *Le lexique du parler créole de la Réunion.* Paris: Champion. 2 vols.
1977. "Toward the reconstruction of the social matrix of Creole language." In Albert Valdman (ed.), *Pidgin and creole linguistics*, 259–277. Bloomington/London: Indiana University Press.
1979. *Les créoles français.* Paris: Nathan.
1983. "Où l'on reparle de la genèse et des structures des créoles de l'Océan Indien." *Études créoles* 6(2): 157–224.
1988. "Le dictionnaire du créole Mauricien: où l'on reparle (à nouveau mais pour la dernière fois) de la genèse des créoles réunionnais." *Etudes Créoles* 11(2): 35–54.
1992. *Des îles, des hommes, des langues. Langues créoles/cultures créoles.* Paris: L'Harmattan.

Choi, Soonja and Melissa Bowerman. 1991. "Learning to express motion events in English and Korean: the influence of language-specific lexicalization patterns." *Cognition* 41: 83–121.

Choi, Soonja, Laraine McDonough, Melissa Bowerman, and Jean Mandler. 1999. "Early sensitivity to language-specific spatial categories in English and Korean." *Cognitive Development* 14(2): 241–268.

Chomsky, Noam. 1980. *Rules and representations*. New York: Columbia University Press.

1981. *Lectures on government and binding*. Dorbrecht, The Netherlands: Foris.

Clancy, Patricia. 1985. "The acquisition of Japanese." In D. Slobin (ed.), *The cross-linguistic study of language acquisition*, 373–524. Hillsdale, NJ: Lawrence Erlbaum Associates.

1986. "The acquisition of communicative style in Japanese." In B. B. Schieffelin and E. Ochs (eds.), *Language socialization across cultures*, 213–250. Cambridge: Cambridge University Press.

1999. "The socialization of affect in Japanese mother–child conversation." *Journal of Pragmatics* 31(11): 1397–1421.

Clancy, P. M., N. Akatsuka, and S. Strauss. 1997. "Deontic modality and conditionality in discourse: A cross-linguistic study of adult speech to young children." In Akio Kamio (ed.), *Directions in functional linguistics*, 19–57. Philadelphia: John Benjamins Publishing.

Clark, Eve V. and O. Garnica. 1974. "Is he coming or going? On the acquisition of deictic verbs." *Journal of Verbal Learning and Verbal Behavior* 13: 559–572.

Clark, Herbert H. 1973. "Space, time, semantics and the child." In Timothy E. Moore (ed.), *Cognitive development and the acquisition of language*, 28–64. New York: Academic Press.

Clifford, James and George Marcus (eds.). 1986. *Writing culture: the poetics and politics of ethnography*. Berkeley: University of California Press.

Cloeren, Hermann J. 1988. *Language and thought: German approaches to analytic philosophy in the 18th and 19th centuries*. Berlin: Walter de Gruyter.

Cole, Michael and Sylvia Scribner. 1974. *Culture and thought*. New York: Wiley.

1977. "Cross-cultural studies of memory and cognition." In R. V. Kail and J. W. Hagen (eds.), *Perspectives on the development of memory and cognition*, 239–72. Hillsdale, NJ: Lawrence Erlbaum.

Coleman, Steve. 1999. *Return from the West. A poetics of voice in Irish*. Ph.D. thesis. Department of Anthropology, University of Chicago.

Conklin, Harold C. 1955. "Hanunóo color categories." *Southwestern Journal of Anthropology* 11: 339–344.

Cook, H. M. 1988. "Sentential particles in Japanese conversation: a study of indexicality." Unpublished Dissertation. University of Southern California.

1996. "Japanese language socialization: indexing the modes of self." *Discourse Processes* 22(2): 171–197.

Copjec, Joan. 1994. "Sex and the euthanasia of reason." In *Read my desire, Lacan against the historians*. 201–236. Cambridge, MA: MIT.

Corne, Chris. 1983. "Commentaire sur Chaudenson 1983." *Etudes Créoles* 6(2): 22–59.

Corris, Peter. 1973. *Passage, port and plantation: a history of Solomon Islands migration, 1870–1904*. Melbourne: Melbourne University Press.

Crago, Martha. 1988. "Cultural context in communicative interaction of Inuit children." Unpublished Dissertation. McGill University, Montreal.

Crapanzano, Vincent. 1993. "Text, transference, and indexicality." In J. Lucy (ed.), *Reflexive language*, 293–314. New York: Cambridge University Press.

1998. "'Lacking now is only the leading idea, that is – we, the rays, have no thoughts': interlocutory collapse in Daniel Paul Schreber's *Memoirs of my nervous illness.*" *Critical Inquiry* 24(3): 737–767.

Cross, T. 1977. "Mothers' speech adjustments: the contribution of selected child listener variables." In C. Ferguson and C. Snow (eds.), *Talking to children: language input and acquisition*, 151–188. Cambridge: Cambridge University Press.

Crowley, Terry. 1990. *Beach-la-mar to Bislama*. Oxford: Oxford University Press.

Cuervo Marquez, Carlos. 1924. "La percepcion de los colores in algunas tribus indígenas de Colombia." *Proceedings of the International Congress of Americanists* 20: 49–51.

Curtius, Georg. 1866. *Grundzüge der griechischen Etymologie* (2. erweiterte aufl.) Leipzig: B. G. Teubner.

D'Ambrósio, Ubiratan. 1992. "Ethnomathematics: a research program on the history and philosophy of mathematics with pedagogical implications." *Notices of the American Mathematical Society* 39.10: 1183–1185.

D'Andrade, Roy. 1984. "Cultural meaning systems." In R. A. Shweder and R. A. Levine (eds.), *Culture theory: essays on mind, self, and emotion*, 88–119. Cambridge: Cambridge University Press.

1989. "Culturally based reasoning." In A. Gellatly, D. Rogers, and J. A. Sloboda (eds.), *Cognition and social worlds*, 132–143. Oxford: Clarendon Press.

1995. *The development of cognitive anthropology*. Cambridge: Cambridge University Press.

D'Andrade, Roy and Claudia Strauss (eds.). 1992. *Human motives and cultural models*. Cambridge: Cambridge University Press.

Daniel, E. Valentine and Jeffrey M. Peck. 1996. *Culture/contexture. Explorations in anthropology and literary study*. Berkeley: University of California Press.

Danziger, Eve. 2001. "Cross-cultural studies in language and thought: is there a metalanguage?" In C. Moore and H. Matthews (eds.), *The psychology of cultural experience*, 199–222. Cambridge: Cambridge University Press.

Darnell, Regna. 1974. "Rationalist aspects of the Whorf hypothesis." *Papers in Linguistics* 7: 41–50.

1989. "Stanley Newman and the Sapir School of Linguistics." In Mary Ritchie Key and Henry Hoenigswald (eds.), *General and Amerindian linguistics: in remembrance of Stanley Newman*, 71–88. Berlin: Mouton de Gruyter.

1990. *Edward Sapir: linguist, anthropologist, humanist*. Berkeley and Los Angeles: University of California Press.

1998a. "Camelot at Yale: the establishment and dismantling of the Sapirian synthesis (1931–1939)." *American Anthropologist* 100: 361–372.

1998b. "Mary Haas and the 'first school of Yale linguistics.'" *Anthropological Linguistics* 39: 566–575.

1998c. *And along came Boas: continuity and revolution in Americanist anthropology*. Amsterdam and Philadelphia: John Benjamins.

2001. *Invisible genealogies: a history of Americanist Anthropology*. Lincoln: University of Nebraska Press.

Davidoff, Jules. 2001. "Language and perceptual categorisation." *Trends in Cognitive Sciences*, 5: 382–387.

Davidoff, Jules, Ian Davies, and Debi Roberson. 1999. "Colour categories in a stone age tribe." *Nature*, 398: 203–204.

Davidson, Donald. 1974 (1984). "On the very idea of a conceptual scheme." In Donald Davidson, *Inquiries into truth and interpretation*. Oxford: Oxford University Press, 183–198.

DeGraff, Michel (ed.). 1999. *Language creation and language change: creolization, diachrony and development*. Boaston: MIT Press.

— 2001. In *Kenttale: a life in language*, ed. Michael Keastowicz. Cambridge, MA: MIT University Press, pp. 53–121.

— 2003. "Against creole exceptionalism." *Language*, 79:(2): 391–410.

De Houwer, A. 1990. *The acquisition of two languages from birth: a case study*. New York: Cambridge University Press.

De Lauretis, Theresa. 1984. *Alice doesn't, feminism, semiotics, cinema*. Bloomington: Indiana University Press.

de León, Lourdes. 1994. "Exploration in the acquisition of geo-centric location by Tzotzil children." In *Space in Mayan languages*, Special issue ed. John Haviland and Stephen C. Levinson, *Linguistics* 32 (4/5): 857–885.

— 1998. "The emergent participant: interactive patterns in the socialization of Tzotzil (Mayan) infants." *Journal of Linguistic Anthropology* 8(2): 131–161.

— 2001. "Finding the richest path: language and cognition in the acquisition of verticality in Tzotzil (Mayan)." In M. Bowerman and S. C. Levinson (eds.), *Language acquisition and conceptual development*, 544–565. Cambridge: Cambridge University Press.

de León, Lourdes and Stephen C. Levinson (eds.). 1992. Spatial description in Mesoamerican languages. Special issue of *Zeitschrift für Phonetik, Sprachwissenschaft und Kommunikationsforschung* 45(6): 590–611.

De Mejía, Anne-Marie. 2002. *Power, prestige and bilingualism: international perspectives on elite bilingual education*. Clevedon, UK: Multilingual Matters.

De Valois, Russell L., Israel Abramov, and G. H. Jacobs. 1966. "Analysis of responses patterns of LGN cells." *Journal of the Optical Society of America* 59: 966–977.

De Valois, Russell L., H. C. Morgan, M. C. Polson, W. R. Mead, and E. M. Hull. 1974. "Psychophysical studies of monkey vision–I. Macaque luminosity and color vision tests." *Vision Research* 14: 53–67.

Demuth, C. 1986. "Prompting routines in the language socialization of Basotho children." In B. B. Schieffelin and E. Ochs (eds.), *Language socialization across cultures,* 51–79. Cambridge: Cambridge University Press.

Deprez, Christine. 1994. *Les enfants bilingues: langues et familles*. Paris: Didier.

Derrida, Jacques. 1967. "La structure, le signe et le jeu dans le discours des sciences humaines." In Jacques Derrida, *L'écriture et la différence*. Paris: Seuil, 409–428.

— 1982. "Signature Event Context." In *The Margins of Philosophy*. Alan Bass, trans. 307–330. Chicago: University of Chicago.

Derrington, A. M., J. Krauskopf, and P. Lennie. 1984. "Chromatic mechanisms in lateral geniculate nucleus of macaque." *Journal of Physiology* 357: 241–265.

Diamond, Stanley. 1986. "Special issue on poetry and anthropology." *Dialectical Anthropology* 11: (2–4).

Diez, Friedrich. 1861. *Etymologisches Worterbuch der romanischen Sprachen* (2 verbesserte Ausgabe). Bonn: Weber.

Dirven, René, Roslyn Frank, and Martin Pütz (eds.). 2003. *Cognitive models in language and thought*. Mouton de Gruyter.

Doniger, Wendy. 1991. *The Rig Veda. An anthropology*. New York: Penguin.

Dorian, N. (ed.). 1989. *Investigating obsolescence: studies in language contraction and death*. Cambridge: Cambridge University Press.

Dougherty, Janet W. D. 1975. "A universalist analysis of variation and change in color semantics." Ph. Dissertation, University of California, Berkeley.

1977. "Color categorization in West Futunese: variability and change." In B. G. Blount and M. Sanches (eds.), *Sociocultural Dimensions of Language Change*, 133–148. New York, London: Plenum.

(ed.). 1985. *Directions in cognitive anthropology*. Urbana: University of Illinois Press.

Dougherty, Janet W. D. and Charles M. Keller. 1985. "Taskonomy: a practical approach to knowledge structures." In J. W. D. Dougherty (ed.), *Directions in cognitive anthropology*, 161–174. Urbana: University of Illinois Press.

Douglas, Mary. 1984. *Purity and danger: an analysis of the concepts of pollution and taboo*. New York: Routledge.

Droixhe, Daniel. 1989. "Le primitivisme linguistique de Turgot." In textes réunis par Chantal Grell et Christian Michel, *Primitivisme et mythes des origines dans la France des lumières 1680–1820*, 59–87. Paris: Presse de l'Université de Paris-Sorbonne.

Dubois, Jacques (Sylvius). 1531/1998. *Introduction à la langue française suivie d'une grammaire*. Ed. and trans. Colette de Demaiziere. (Textes de la Renaissance, 22; Traités sur la langue française, 1.) Paris: Honore Champion.

Duranti, Alessandro. 1997. *Linguistic anthropology*. Cambridge: Cambridge University Press.

(ed.). 2001a. *Linguistic anthropology: a reader*. Oxford: Oxford University Press.

(ed.). 2001b. *Key terms in language and culture*. Malden, MA: Blackwell Publishers.

2003. "Language as culture in US anthropology: three paradigms." *Current Anthropology* 44(3): 323–335.

Duranti, Alessandro and Charles Goodwin (eds.). 1992. *Rethinking context: language as an interactive phenomenon*. Cambridge: Cambridge University Press. [Studies in the Social and Cultural Foundations of Language, 11.]

Durham, William. 1991. *Coevolution*. Stanford University Press.

Durkheim, Emile and Marcel Mauss. 1987. *Primitive classification*. Trans. Rodney Needham. Chicago: University of Chicago Press.

Dutton, Tom. 1983. "Birds of a feather: a pair of rare pidgins from the Gulf of Papua." In E. Woolford and W. Washabaugh (eds.), *The social context of creolization*, 77–105. Ann Arbor: Karoma.

Eberwein, T. D. 1998. *An Emily Dickinson encyclopedia*. Greenwood Press.

Eckert, Penelope. 1991. "Social polarization and the choice of linguistic variants." In Penelope Eckert (ed.), *New ways of analyzing sound change*, 213–231. San Diego: Academic Press.

2000. *Linguistic variation as social practice: the linguistic construction of identity in Belten High*. Oxford: Blackwell Publishers.

Edmondson, Monro. 1971. *The book of counsel: the Popol Vu of the Quiche Maya of Guatemala*. Tulan University Middle American Research Institute. Publication no. 35.

Ehrlich, Susan and Ruth King. 1996. "Consensual sex or sexual harassment: negotiating meaning." In Bergvall, Bing, and Freed (eds.), *Rethinking Language*, 153–172. London: Longman.

Eisenberg, A. 1986. "Teasing: verbal play in two Mexican homes." In B. B. Schieffelin and E. Ochs (eds.), *Language socialization across cultures*, 182–198. Cambridge: Cambridge University Press.

Emeneau, Murray. 1969. "Onomatopoetics in the Indian linguistic area." *Language* 45: 224–99.

England, Nora C. 1978. "Space as a Mam grammatical theme." In Nora England (ed.), *Papers in Mayan linguistics*, 225–38. Columbia: University of Missouri Press.

Erickson, Jon, Marion Gymnich, and Ansgar Nünning. 1997. "Wilhelm von Humboldt, Edward Sapir, and the Constructivist Framework." *Historiographia Linguistica* 24: 285–306.

Errington, Joseph J. 1988. *Structure and style in Javanese: a semiotic view of linguistic etiquette.* Philadelphia: University of Pennsylvania Press.

Escure, Geneviève. 1997. *Creole and dialect continua.* Amsterdam; Philadelphia: John Benjamins.

Essock, S. M. 1977. "Color perception and color classification." In D. M. Rumbaugh (ed.), *Language learning by a chimpanzee.* New York, San Francisco, London: Academic Press.

Everett, Daniel L. 2005. "Cultural constraints on grammar and cognition in Pirahã: another look at the design features of human language." With discussion and reply. *Current Anthropology* 46: 621–646.

Fabian, Johannes. 1983. *Time and the other: how anthropology makes its object.* New York: Columbia University Press.

　1986. *Language and colonial power.* Berkeley: University of California Press.

　1990. *Power in performance: ethnographic explorations through proverbial wisdom and theater in Shaba, Zaire.* Madison: University of Wisconsin Press.

　1993. "Crossing and patrolling: thoughts on anthropology and boundaries." *Culture* XIII (1): 49–54.

Fader, A. 2001. "Literacy, bilingualism and gender in a Hasidic community." *Linguistics and Education* 12 (3): 261–283.

Fatnowna, Noël. 1989. *Fragments of a lost heritage.* North Ryde, Aus.: Angus and Robertson Ltd.

Feld, Steven. 1982. *Sound and sentiment, birds, weeping: poetics and song in Kaluli expression.* Philadelphia: University of Pennsylvania Press.

Ferguson, Charles A. 1964. "Baby talk in six languages." *American Anthropologist* 66(6): 103–114.

　1964. "Diglossia." In Dell Hymes (ed.), *Language in culture and society*, 429–439. New York: Harper and Row.

　1977. "Baby talk as a simplified register." In C. Ferguson and C. Snow (eds.), *Talking to children: language input and acquisition*, 209–235. Cambridge: Cambridge University Press.

　1982. "Simplified registers and linguistic theory." In L. K. Obler and Lise Menn (eds.), *Exceptional language and linguistics*, 49–66. New York: Academic Press.

Fernandez, James. 1986. *Persuasion and performance: the play of tropes in cultures.* Bloomington: Indiana University Press.

　(ed.) 1991. *Beyond metaphor: the theory of tropes in anthropology.* Stanford: Stanford University Press.

Ferraz, Luiz. 1983. "The origin and development of four creoles in the Gulf of Guinea in the social context of creolization." In Ellen Woolford and William Washabaugh (eds.), *The social context of creolization*, 120–125. Ann Arbor: Karoma.

Feuer, Lewis S. 1953. "Sociological aspects of the relation between language and philosophy." *Philosophy of Science* 20: 85–93.

Field, M. 1999. "Maintenance of indigenous ways of speaking despite language shift: language socialization in a Navajo preschool." Unpublished Ph.D. Dissertation, University of California, Santa Barbara.

Finck, Franz Nikolaus. 1899. *Der deutsche Sprachbau als Ausdruck deutscher Weltanschauung: Acht Vorträge.* Marburg: N. G. Elwert.

　1910. *Die Haupttypen des Sprachbaus.* Leipzig: B. G. Teubner.

Finnegan, Ruth. 1977. *Oral poetry: its nature, significance and social context*. Cambridge: Cambridge University Press.

Fishman, Joshua (ed.). 1968. *Readings in the sociology of language*. The Hague: Mouton.

Fodor, Jerry A. 1983. *Modularity of mind: an essay on faculty psychology*. Cambridge, MA: MIT Press.

Foley, William A. 1988. "Language birth: the processes of pidginization and creolization." In Frederick J. Newmeyer (ed.), *Language: the socio-cultural context*, 162–183. Linguistics: The Cambridge survey, 4. Cambridge: Cambridge University Press.

1997. *Anthropological linguistics: an introduction*. Oxford: Blackwell.

Fornel, Michel de. 2002. "Le destin d'un argument. Le relativisme linguistique de Sapir-Whorf." In Michel de Fornel and Jean-Claude Passeron (eds.). *L'argumentation. Preuve et persuasion*, 121–147. Paris: Editions de l'Ecole des Hautes Etudes en Sciences Sociales.

Foucault, Michel. 1975. *Surveiller et punir: naissance de la prison*. Paris: Gallimard.

1977. *Language, counter-memory, practice: selected essays and interviews* by Michel Foucault. Edited by Donald Bouchard. Ithaca, NY: Cornell University Press.

1979. *The history of sexuality*: Vol. 1: An introduction. London: Allen Lane.

Fournier, Robert. 1987. "Le bioprogramme et les français créoles." Ph.D. thesis. Sherbrooke: Département de linguistique, Université de Sherbrooke.

Fox, Richard G. and Barbara J. King (eds.). 2002. *Anthropology beyond culture*. Oxford: Berg.

Frake, Charles O. 1971 [1985]. "Cognitive maps of time and tide among medieval seafarers." *Man* 20: 254–270.

Franciscan Fathers. 1910. *An ethnological dictionary of the Navaho language*. Arizona: St. Michaels.

Franklin, A. and I. R. L. Davies (2004). "New evidence for infant colour categories." *British Journal of Developmental Psychology* 22(3): 349–377.

Franklin, A., A. Clifford, E. Williamson, and I. R. L. Davies (2005). "Colour term knowledge does not affect Categorical Perception of colour in toddlers." *Journal of Experimental Child Psychology* 90: 114–141.

Fraser, Nancy. 1993. "Rethinking the public sphere: a contribution to the critique of actually existing democracy." In Craig Calhoun (ed.), *Habermas and the public sphere*, 109–142. Cambridge, MA: MIT Press.

Freud, Sigmund. 1989. *Totem and taboo*. New York: Norton.

Friedlander, Judith. 1975. *Being an Indian in Hueyapan*. New York: St. Martin's Press.

Friedrich, Paul. 1969. "On the meaning of the Tarascan suffixes of space." *International Journal of American Linguistics* 35(4): 5–28. Memoir 23.

1970. "Shape in grammar." *Language* 46: 379–407.

1971. *The Tarascan suffixes of locative space: meaning and morphotactics*. Bloomington: Indiana University Press.

1972. "Shape categories in grammar." *Linguistics* 77: 5–22.

1979. "Poetic language and the imagination: a reformulation of the Sapir Hypothesis." In Anwar S. Dil (ed.), *Language, context and the imagination: essays by Paul Friedrich*, 441–517. Stanford: Stanford University Press.

1979 [1966]. "Proto-Indo-European kinship." *Language, context and the imagination*, 201–252. Stanford: Stanford University Press.

1986. *The language parallax: linguistic relativism and poetic indeterminacy*. Austin: University of Texas Press.

1989. "The Tao of language." *Journal of Pragmatics* 13: 833–858.

1998. *Music in Russian poetry*. New York: Peter Lang.

Frisk, Hjalmar. 1960. *Griechisches etymologisches Wörterbuch*. Heidelberg: Carl Winter.

Frost, Robert. 1964. "Letter to John Bartlett." *Selected letters of Robert Frost*, ed. Lawrence Thompson. New York: Holt.

Gadamer, Hans Georg. 1982. "Hermeneutics as a theoretical and practical task." *Reason in the age of science*, 113–138. Trans. Frederick G. Lawrence. Cambridge: MIT Press.

Gadet, Françoise. 1990. *Saussure. Une science de la langue*. Second edition. Paris: PUF.

Gal, S. 1979. *Language shift: social determinants of linguistic change in bilingual Austria*. New York: Academic Press.

1991. "Problematics of research on language and gender." In di Leonardo (ed.), *Gender at the Crossroads of Knowledge*, 175–203. Berkeley: University of California Press.

1993. "Diversity and contestation in linguistic ideologies: German speakers in Hungary." *Language in Society* 22(3): 337–360.

1995. "Lost in a Slavic sea: linguistic theories and expert knowledge in 19th century Hungary." *Pragmatics* 5(2): 155–166.

1998. "Multiplicity and contestation among linguistic ideologies." In Bambi Schieffelin, Kathryn A. Woolard, and Paul Kroskrity (eds.), *Language ideologies: practice and theory*, 113–138. New York: Oxford University Press.

Galenson, David W. 1986. *Traders, planters and slaves: market behaviour in early English America*. Cambridge: Cambridge University Press.

Gamillscheg, Ernst. 1969. *Etymologisches Wörterbuch der französischen Sprache* (2, vollständig neu bearb. Auflage). Heidelberg: C. Winter.

Gamkrelidze, Tamaz and Vjacheslav V. Ivanov. 1984. *Indoevropejskij jazyk i indoevropejcy*. Tbilisi State University Press. (English translation: *Indo-European and the Indo-Europeans: A reconstruction and historical analysis of a proto-language and a proto-culture*, trans. Johanna Nichols. Berlin: Mouton de Gruyter.)

Gardner, Howard. 1989. *The mind's new science*. New York: Basic Books.

Garrett, Paul. B. 1999. "Language socialization, convergence and shift in St. Lucia, West Indies." Unpublished Ph.D. dissertation, New York University.

2000. "High Kwéyol: the emergence of a formal creole register in Santa-Lucia, West Indies." In John McWhorter (ed.), *Language change and language contact in pidgins and creoles*, 63–101. Amsterdam and Philadelphia: John Benjamins.

In press. "What a language is good for: language socialization, language shift, and the persistence of code-specific genres in St. Lucia." *Language in society*.

Garrett, P. B. and P. Baquedano-Lopez. 2002. "Language socialization: reproduction and continuity, transformation and change." *Annual Review of Anthropology*, 31: 339–361. Palo Alto: Annual Reviews Inc.

Geertz, Clifford. 1973. *The interpretation of cultures*. New York: Basic Books.

1986. *Works and lives: the anthropologist as author*. Stanford: Stanford University Press.

Genesee, F. 1989. "Early bilingual development: one language or two." *Child Language* 16: 161–179.

Genishi, C. 1981. "Code-switching in Chicano six year olds." In R. Duran (ed.), *Latino language and communicative behavior*, 133–152. Norwood: Ablex.

Gentner, Dedre, and Susan Goldin-Meadow (eds.). 2003. *Language in mind*. Cambridge, MA: MIT Press.

Giddens, Anthony. 1984. *The constitution of society*. Berkeley, Los Angeles: University of California Press.

Gipper, Helmut. 1972. *Gibt es ein sprachliches Relativitätsprinzip? Untersuchungen zur Sapir-Whorf-Hypothese*. Frankfurt: Fischer.

Gladstone, William E. 1858. *Studies on Homer and the Homeric age*. London: Oxford University Press.

Gleason, H. A. 1961. *An introduction to descriptive linguistics*. New York: Holt, Rinehart and Winston.

Glieck, James. 1987. *Chaos: making a new science*. New York: Viking.

Goldstein, Tara. 1997. *Two languages at work: bilingual life on the production floor*. Berlin: Mouton de Gruyter.

Goodenough, Ward. 1964 (1957). "Cultural anthropology and linguistics." In D. Hymes (ed.), *Language in culture and society*, 36–39. New York: Harper and Row.

1971. *Culture, language and society*. Reading, MA: Addison-Wesley.

1981. *Culture, language, and society*. Menlo Park, CA: Benjamin/Cummings.

Goodman, Morris F. 1964. *A comparative study of Creole French dialects*. The Hague: Mouton.

1984. "Are creole structures innate?" *Behavioural and Brain Sciences* 7(2): 19–35.

1987. "Pidgin origins reconsidered." *Journal of Pidgin and Creole Languages* 2(2): 149–162.

1988. "A response to Naro." *Journal of Pidgin and Creole Languages* 3(1): 10–38.

Goodwin, Marjorie. 1993. "Tactical uses of stories: participation frameworks within boys' and girls' disputes." In D. Tannen (ed.), *Gender*, 110–143. New York: Oxford University Press.

Goody, Esther. 1995. *Social intelligence and interaction*. Cambridge: Cambridge University Press.

Goody, Jack. 1977. *The domestication of the savage mind*. Cambridge: Cambridge University Press.

1989. *The logic of writing and the organization of society*. Cambridge: Cambridge University Press.

Goodz, N. 1989. "Parental language mixing in bilingual families." *Infant Mental Health Journal* 10(1): 25–44.

Gordon, Matthew and Jeffrey Heath. 1998. "Sex, sound symbolism and sociolinguistics." *Current Anthropology* 39 (4): 421–450.

Gossen, Gary. 1974. "'To speak with a heated heart': Chamula canons of style and good performance." In Richard Bauman and Joel Sherzer (eds.), *Explorations in the ethnography of speaking*, 389–413. Cambridge: Cambridge University Press.

Gottlieb, Alma and Philip Graham. 1994. *Parallel worlds: an anthropologist and a writer encounter Africa*. Chicago: University of Chicago Press.

Greenberg, Joseph. 1987. *Language in the Americas*. Stanford University Press.

Grether, W. F. 1939. "Color vision and color blindness in monkeys." *Comparative Psychology Monographs* 15: 1–38.

Grice, Paul. 1975. "Logic and conversation." In P. Cole and J. Morgan (eds.), *Syntax and semantics*, vol. 3, 41–58. New York: Academic Press.

Grillo, Ralph. 1989. *Dominant languages*. Cambridge: Cambridge University Press.

Grin, François. 1999. *Compétences et récompenses: la valeur des langues en Suisse*. Fribourg: Éditions universitaires Fribourg.

Grosz, Elizabeth. 1990. *Jacques Lacan: a feminist introduction*. New York and London: Routledge.

Gruppe, Otto Friedrich. 1831 (1914). *O. F. Gruppe Philosophische Werke. I. Antäus*. Fritz Mauthner (ed.). Munich: Georg Müller.

Gudschinsky, Sarah. 1967. *How to learn an unwritten language*. New York: Holt, Rinehart and Winston.

Gulya, Janos. 1974. "Some eighteenth century antecedents of nineteenth century linguistics: the discovery of Finno-Ugrian." In Dell Hymes (ed.), *Studies in the history of linguistics: traditions and paradigms*, 258–276. Bloomington: Indiana University Press.

Gumperz, John. 1964. "Speech variation and the study of Indian civilization." In Dell Hymes (ed.), *Language in culture and society*, 416–428. New York: Harper and Row.

1971. *Language in social groups*. Stanford: Stanford University Press.

1982a. *Discourse strategies*. Cambridge: Cambridge University Press.

(ed.). 1982b. *Language and social identity*. Cambridge: Cambridge University Press.

1992. "Contextualization and understanding." In A. Duranti and C. Goodwin (eds.), *Rethinking context: language as an interactive phenomenon*, 229–252. New York: Cambridge University Press.

Gumperz, John J. and Stephen C. Levinson. 1991. "Rethinking linguistic relativity." *Current Anthropology* 32(5): 613–622. [Studies in the Social and Cultural Foundation of Language, 17.]

(eds.). 1996. *Rethinking linguistic relativity*. Cambridge: Cambridge University Press.

Haas, Mary. 1998. Interview with Stephen O. Murray. *Anthropological Linguistics* 39 (4): 695–713.

Habermas, Jürgen. 1983. "Interpretive social science vs. hermeneuticism." In Norma Haan *et al.* (eds.), *Social science as moral inquiry*, 251–269. New York: Columbia University Press.

1993. *The structural transformation of the public sphere, an inquiry into a category of bourgeois society*. Cambridge: MIT Press.

Hage, Per and Kristen Hawkes. 1975. "Binumarin color categories." *Ethnology* 24: 287–300.

Hall, Kira and Mary Bucholtz (eds.). 1995. *Gender Articulated, Language the Socially Constructed Self*. New York and London: Routledge.

Hall, Kira, Mary Bucholtz, and Birch Moonwoman (eds.). 1992. *Locating power: proceedings of the second Berkeley women and language conference*. Berkeley Women and Language Group: Berkeley, CA.

Hamill, James F. 1990. *Ethno-logic: the anthropology of human reasoning*. Urbana/Chicago: University of Illinois Press.

Hamp, Eric P. 1998. "Whose were the Tocharians? Linguistic subgrouping and diagnostic idiosyncrasy." In Victor H. Mair (ed.), *The Bronze Age and Early Iron Age peoples of eastern Central Asia*, 307–346. (Journal of Indo-European Studies Monograph no. 26). Washington, DC: Institute for the Study of Man.

Hancock, Ian F. 1986. "The domestic hypothesis, diffusion and componentiality: an account of Atlantic Anglophone creole origins." In P. Muysken and N. Smith (eds.), *Substrata versus universals in creole genesis*, 71–102. Amsterdam: John Benjamins.

Hanks, William. 1990. *Referential practice: language and lived space among the Maya*. Chicago: University of Chicago Press.

1995. *Language and communicative practice*. Boulder, CO: Westview Press.

1996. "Language form and communicative practices." In John J. Gumperz and Stephen C. Levinson (eds.), *Rethinking linguistic relativity*, 232–270. Cambridge: Cambridge University Press. [Studies in the Social and Cultural Foundations of Language, 17.]

Hanson, Miriam. 1993. "Foreward." In Oskar Negt and Alexander Kluge, *Public sphere and experience, toward an analysis of the bourgeois and proletarian public sphere*, ix-xli. Minneapolis: University of Minnesota Press.

Harkness, Sara. 1973. "Universal aspects of learning color codes: a study in two cultures." *Ethos* 2: 175–200.

1992. "Human development in psychological anthropology." In T. Schwartz, G. White, and C. Lutz (eds.), *New directions in psychological anthropology*, 102–122. Cambridge: Cambridge University Press.

Harkness, Sara and Charles M. Super. 1996. Introduction. In S. Harkness and C. M. Super (eds.), *Parents' cultural belief systems: their origins, expressions, and consequences*, 1–23. New York: Guilford.

Harris, Alice C. and Lyle Campbell. 1995. *Historical syntax in cross-linguistic perspective*. Cambridge: Cambridge University Press.

Harris, Marvin. 1968. *The rise of anthropological theory*. New York: Crowell.

Hart, R. A. and G. T. Moore. 1973. "The development of spatial cognition: a review." In R. M. Downs and D. Stea (eds.), *Image and environment: cognitive mapping and spatial behavior*, 246–288. Chicago: Aldine.

Harvey, Keith and Celia Shalom (eds.). 1997. *Language and desire, encoding sex, romance and intimacy*. London and New York: Routledge.

Haviland, John, and Stephen C. Levinson (eds.). 1994. *Spatial conceptualization in Mayan languages*. Special issue of *Linguistics*, 42(4/5).

Hawkes, David. 1967. *A little primer of Tu Fu*. Oxford: Renditions Paperback.

Heath, S. B. 1982. "What no bedtime story means: narrative skill at home and school." *Language in Society* 11: 49–76.

1983. *Ways with words: language, life and work in communities and classrooms*. Cambridge: Cambridge University Press.

Heider, Eleanor Rosch. 1972a. "Universals in color naming and memory." *Journal of Experimental Psychology* 93: 1–20.

1972b. "Probabilities, sampling and the ethnographic method: the case of Dani colour names." *Man* 7: 448–466.

Heider, Eleanor Rosch and Donald C. Olivier. 1972. "The structure of the color space for naming and memory in two languages." *Cognitive Psychology* 3: 337–354.

Heinrich, Albert C. 1972. "A non-European system of color classification." *Anthropological Linguistics* 14: 220–227.

Heller, Monica (ed.). 1988. *Codeswitching: anthropological and sociolinguistic perspectives*. Berlin: Mouton de Gruyter.

1989. "Aspects sociolinguistiques de la francisation d'une entreprise montréalaise." *Sociologie et sociétés* 21(2): 115–128.

2002a. "L'écologie et la sociologie du langage." In Annette Boudreau, Lise Dubois, Jacques Maurais and Grant McConnell (eds.), *L'Écologie des langues. Ecology of languages*, 175–192. Paris: L'Harmattan.

2002b. *Éléments d'une sociolinguistique critique*. Paris: Didier.

Heller, Monica and Laurette Lévy. 1994. "Mariages linguistiquement mixtes: les stratégies des femmes franco-ontariennes." *Langage et société* 67: 53–88.

Heller, Monica and Marilyn Martin-Jones (eds.). 2001. *Voices of authority: education and linguistic difference*. Greenwood CT: Ablex.

Heller, Monica and Carol Pfaff. 1996. "Code-switching and code-mixing." In Peter Nelde, Hans Goebl, Wolfgang Wölck and Z. Stary (eds.), *Internationales Handbuch der Kontaktlinguistik*, 594–610. Berlin: Walter de Gruyter.

Hendel, Charles W. 1955. "Introduction." In Ernst Cassirer, *The Philosophy of Symbolic Forms*. I. *Language*. New Haven: Yale University Press, 1–65.

Hendrikson, John. 2001. "Pushkin and the Koran: Dialogic imagination." *Pushkin Review*.

Herdt, Gilbert (ed.). 1994. *Third sex, third gender, beyond sexual dimorphism in culture and history*. New York: Zone Books.

Herring, Susan, Deborah A. Johnson, and Tamra DiBenedetto. 1995. "This discussion is going too far!: Male resistance to female participation on the internet" In Hall and Bucholtz (eds.). *Gender Articulated*, 67–96. New York: Routledge.

Herskovits, Melville J. 1975. *Life in a Haitian valley*. New York: Octagon Books.

Herzfeld, Michael. 1985. *The poetics of manhood: context and identity in a Cretan mountain village*. Princeton: Princeton University Press.

Heynick, Frank. 1983. "From Einstein to Whorf: space, time, matter, and reference frames in physical and linguistic relativity." *Semiotica* 45(1–2): 35–64.

Hickerson, Nancy. 1975. "Two studies of color: implications for cross-cultural comparability of semantic categories." In D. Kinkade, K. Hale and O. Werner (eds.). *Linguistics and anthropology: in honor of C. F. Voegelin*, 317–330. Lisse: de Ridder.

Higonnet, Patrice. 1980. "The politics of linguistic terrorism and grammatical hegemony during the French Revolution." *Social Theory* 5: 41–69.

Hill, Jane. 1988. "Language, culture and world view." In F. Newmeyer (ed.), *Linguistics: The Cambridge Survey*, vol. IV: *Language: The cultural context*, 14–36. Cambridge: Cambridge University Press.

1995. "The eighteen voices of Don Gabriel: Responsibility and self in a modern Mexican narrative." In Tedlock and Mannheim (eds.), 97–147.

Hill, Jane and Kenneth Hill. 1986. *Speaking mexicano: dynamics of syncretic language in central Mexico*. Tucson: University of Arizona Press.

Hill, Jane and Bruce Mannheim. 1992. "Language and world view." *Annual Review of Anthropology* 21: 381–406.

Hobsbawm, Eric. 1990. *Nations and nationalism since 1760*. Cambridge: Cambridge University Press.

Hock, Hans Henrich. 1991. *Principles of historical linguistics*, 2nd ed. New York: Mouton de Gruyter.

Hofmann, Johann Baptist. 1966. *Etymologisches Wörterbuch des Griechischen*. München: Oldenbourg.

Hofstadter, Douglas. 1980. *Gödel, Escher, Bach: an eternal golden braid*. New York: Random House.

Hoijer, Harry *et al.* (ed.) 1946. *Linguistic structures of native America*. New York: The Vileing Fund.

(ed.). 1954. *Language in culture*. Chicago: University of Chicago Press.

Holden, Constance. 2004. "Life without numbers in the Amazon." *Science* 305: 1093.

Holland, Dorothy and Naomi Quinn (eds.). 1987. *Cultural models in language and thought*. Cambridge: Cambridge University Press.

Holland, Dorothy, William Lachicotte, Jr., Debra Skuiner, and Carole Cain 1998. *Identity and agency in cultural worlds*. Cambridge MA: Harvard University Press.

Holmes, Janet. 1995. *Women, men and politeness*. London: Longman.

Hopper, Paul J. (ed.). 1982. *Tense-aspect: between semantics and pragmatics*. Amsterdam: John Benjamins. [Typological Studies in Language, 1.]

Horn, Paul. 1888 [1974]. August Friedrich Pott (necrology). *Einleitung in die allgemeine Sprachwissenschaft*, by A. G. Pott; newly edited together with a bio-bibliographical sketch of Pott by Paul Horn, by E. F. K. Koerner. Amsterdam: Benjamins.

Hudson, Richard, Andrew Rosta, Jasper Holmes, and Nikolas Gisborne. 1996. "Synonyms and syntax." *Journal of Linguistics* 32: 439–446.

Hugh-Jones, Christine. 1988. *From the Milk River: spatial and temporal processes in Northwest Amazonia*. Cambridge: Cambridge University Press.

Humboldt, Wilhelm von. 1795 (1903). "Theorie der Bildung des Menschen." In Albert Leitzmann (ed.), *Wilhelm von Humboldts Gesammelte Schriften*, I.282–287. Berlin: B. Behr.

1820 (1905). "Ueber das vergleichende Sprachstudium in Beziehung auf die verschiedenen Epochen der Sprachentwicklung." In Albert Leitzmann (ed.), *Wilhelm von Humboldts Gesammelte Schriften*, IV.1–34. Berlin: B. Behr.

1825 (1906). "Notice sur une grammaire japonaise imprimée à Mexico." In Albert Leitzmann (ed.), *Wilhelm von Humboldts Gesammelte Schriften*, V.237–248. Berlin: B. Behr.

1829 (1907). "Von dem grammatischen Baue der Sprachen." In Albert Leitzmann (ed.), *Wilhelm von Humboldts Gesammelte Schriften*, VI.337–486. Berlin: B. Behr.

1836 (1988). *On language: the diversity of human language-structure and its influence on the development of mankind*. Peter Heath, trans. Cambridge: Cambridge University Press.

Hunn, E. 1985. "The utilitarian factor in folk biological classification." In J. W. D. Dougherty (ed.), *Directions in cognitive anthropology*, 117–40. Urbana, Ill.: University of Illinois Press.

1995. "Ethnoecology: the relevance of cognitive anthropology for human ecology." In B. Blount (ed.), *Language, culture, and society*. 2nd edition, 439–455. Prospect Heights, IL: Waveland Press.

Hutchins, Edwin. 1980. *Culture and inference*. Cambridge, MA: Harvard University Press.

1983. "Understanding Micronesian navigation." In D. Gentner and A. L. Stevens (eds.), *Mental models*, 191–225. Hillsdale, NJ: Erlbaum.

1995. *Cognition in the wild*. Cambridge, MA: MIT Press.

Hutton, Christopher M. 1999. *Linguistics and the Third Reich: mother-tongue fascism, race and the science of language*. London: Routledge.

Huxley, Aldous. 1937. "Words and behaviour." *The olive tree*, 84–103. New York and London: Harper and Brothers.

Hymes, Dell. 1961. "On typology of cognitive styles in language." *Anthropological Linguistics* 3 (1): 22–54.

(ed.). 1964. *Language in culture and society: a reader in linguistics and anthropology*. New York: Harper and Row.

1966. "Two types of linguistic relativity." In William Bright (ed.), *Sociolinguistics*, 114–167. The Hague: Mouton.

1981. *"In vain I tried to tell you." Essays in native American ethnopoetics*. Philadelphia: University of Pennsylvania Press.

Hymes, Dell and John Fought. 1975. "American structuralism." In Thomas Sebeok (ed.), *Current trends in linguistics: historiography of linguistics*, 903–1176, 13. The Hague: Mouton.

Hymes, Virginia. 1987. "Warm Springs Sahaptin narrative analysis." In Joel Sherzer and Anthony Woodbury (eds.), *Native American discourse: poetics and rhetoric*, 62–102. New York: Cambridge University Press.

Irvine, Judith. 1990. "Registering affect: heteroglossia in the linguistic expression of emotion." In Lutz (ed.), *Language and the politics of emotion*, 126–161.

Isidore of Seville. 1957. *Etymologiarum sive originum libri XX*. W. M. Lindsay (ed.). Oxford: Clarendon.

Jaffe, Alexandra. 1999. *Ideologies in action: language politics on Corsica*. Berlin: Mouton de Gruyter.

Jakobson, Roman. 1959 (1971). "Boas' view of grammatical meaning." In Roman Jakobson, *Selected writings*. II, 490–496. The Hague: Mouton.

1960 (1971). "The Kazan' school of Polish linguistics." In Roman Jakobson, *Selected writings.* ii, 394–428. The Hague: Mouton.

1960. "Linguistics and poetics." In Thomas E. Sebeok (ed.), *Style in language*, 350–377. Cambridge: MIT Press.

1982 (1985). "Einstein and the science of language." In Roman Jakobson, *Selected writings.* vii, 254–264. Berlin: Mouton.

1987. *Language in literature.* Krystyna Pomorska and Stephen Rudy (eds.). Cambridge: Harvard University Press.

1990. "Langue and parole: code and message." In Linda Waugh and Monique Monville-Burston (eds.), *On language, Roman Jakobson*, 80–109. Cambridge, MA: Harvard University Press.

Johnston, Judith R. and Dan L. Slobin. 1979. "The development of locative expressions in English, Italian, Serbo-Croatian and Turkish." *Journal of Child Language* 6: 529–545.

Joseph, John. 1996. "The immediate sources of the Sapir–Whorf Hypothesis." *Historiographia Linguistica* 23: 365–404.

Jourdan, Christine. 1983. "Mort du Kanaka Pidgin English à Mackay (Australie)." *Anthropologie et sociétés* 7 (3): 77–96.

1985. "Sapos Yumi Mitim Yumi: urbanization and creolization of Solomon Islands pidgin." Ph.D. thesis, Australian National University, Canberra.

1988. "Langue de personne, langue de tout le monde: le Pijin à Honiara (Iles Salomon)." *Etudes Créoles* 11(2): 128–147.

1991. "Pidgins and creoles: the blurring of categories." *Annual Review of Anthropology* 20: 187–209.

1994. "Créolisation, urbanisation et identité aux îles Salomons." *Journal de la Société des Océanistes* 99: 177–186.

2000. "'My nephew is my aunt': features and transformations of kinship terminology in Solomon Islands pijin." In Jeff Siegel (ed.), *Processes of language contact.* Montreal: Fides, 99–121.

2001. "Contact." In S. Duranti (ed.), *Key terms in language and culture*, 40–44. Oxford: Oxford University Press.

In press. "The cultural in pidgin genesis." In J. Singler and S. Kouwenberg (eds.), *The handbook of pidgins and creoles.* London: Blackwell Publishers.

Jourdan, Christine and Roger Keesing. 1997. "From Fisin to Pijin: creolization in progress in the Solomon Islands." *Language in Society* 26: 401–420.

Junod, Henri A. 1927. *The life of a South African tribe.* New York: Macmillan and Co.

Kant, Immanuel. 1991 (1768) "Von dem Ersten Grunde des Unterschiedes der Gegenden im Raume" (Translation "On the first ground of the distinction of regions in space.") In *The philosophy of right and left*, 27–33. J. van Cleve and R. E. Frederick (eds.). Dordrecht: Kluwer.

Kay, Paul. 1975. "Synchronic variability and diachronic change in basic color terms." *Language in Society* 4: 257–270.

1996. "Intra-speaker relativity." In John J. Gumperz and Stephen C. Levinson (eds.), *Rethinking linguistic relativity*, 97–114. Cambridge: Cambridge University Press.

1999. "The emergence of basic color lexicons hypothesis." In Alexander Borg (ed.), *The language of colour in the Mediterranean*, 76–90. Stockholm: Almquist and Wiksell International.

(in press) "Color categories are not arbitrary." *Color cognition and culture* a special issue of the *Journal of Cross-Cultural Research*, ed. Kimberly Jameson and Nancy Alvarado.

Kay, Paul and Brent Berlin. 1997. "Science? Imperialism: there are non-trivial constraints on color categorization." *Behavioral and Brain Sciences* 20: 196–201.

Kay, Paul and Luisa Maffi. 1999. "Color appearance and the emergence and evolution of basic color lexicons." *American Anthropologist* 101: 743, 760.

Kay, Paul and Chad K. McDaniel. 1978. "The linguistic significance of the meanings of basic color terms." *Language* 54: 610–646.

Kay, Paul and Willett Kempton. 1984. "What is the Sapir–Whorf hypothesis?" *American Anthropologist* 86: 65–79.

Kay, Paul, Brent Berlin, and William Merrifield. 1991. "Biocultural implications of systems of color naming." *Journal of Linguistic Anthropology* 1: 12–25.

Kay, Paul and Terry Regier. 2003. *Resolving the question of color naming universals* (pdf). *Proc. Nat. Acad. Sci.* 100, 9085–9089.

Kay, Paul, Brent Berlin, Luisa Maffi, and William Merrifield. 1997. "Color naming across languages." In C. L. Hardin and Luisa Maffi (eds.), *Color categories in thought and language*, 21–57. Cambridge: Cambridge University Press.

2005. *The world color survey.* CSLI Publications.

Keating, Elizabeth. 1994. "Language, gender, rank, and social space: honorifics in Pohnpei, Micronesia." In Mary Bucholtz (ed.), *Cultural performances: proceedings of the third Berkeley women and language conference*, 367–377. Berkeley: Berkeley Woman and Language Press.

1998. *Power sharing: language, rank, gender and social space in Pohnpei, Micronesia.* Oxford: Oxford University Press.

Keesing, Roger. 1972. "Paradigms lost: the new anthropology and the new linguistics." *Southwestern Journal of Anthropology* 28(4): 299–332.

1981. *Cultural anthropology: a contemporary perspective.* New York: Holt, Rinehart, Winston.

1987. "Models, 'folk' and 'cultural': paradigms regained?" In D. Holland and N. Quinn (eds.), *Cultural models in language and thought*, 369–93. Cambridge: Cambridge University Press.

1988. *Melanesian pidgin and the oceanic substrate.* Stanford: Stanford University Press.

1992. "Anthropology and linguistics." In M. Pütz (ed.), *Thirty years of linguistic evolution*, 593–602. Amsterdam: John Benjamins.

1993. "The lens of enchantment." *Culture* 13(1): 57–59.

Keil, Frank. 1984. "Of pidgins and pigeons." *Behavioural and Brain Sciences* 7(2): 197–198.

Keller, Charles M. and Janet Dixon Keller. 1996. *Cognition and tool use: the blacksmith at work.* Cambridge: Cambridge University Press.

Keller, Rudi. 1994. *On language change: the invisible hand in language.* Trans. Brigitte Nerlich. London: Routledge.

Kluckhohn, Clyde. 1961. *Anthropology and the classics.* Providence: Brown University Press.

Kluckhohn, Clyde and William H. Kelly. 1945. "The concept of culture." In *The science of man in the world crisis*, 78–107. New York: Columbia University Press.

Knobloch, Clemens. 2000. "Begriffspolitik und Wissenschaftsrhetorik bei Leo Weisgerber." In Klaus D. Dutz (ed.), *Interpretation und re-interpretation. Aus Anlass des 100. Geburtstages von Johann Leo Weisgerber (1899–1985)*, 145–174. Münster: Nodus.

Koerner, E. F. Konrad. 1977. "The Humboldtian trend in linguistics." In Paul J. Hopper (ed.), *Studies in descriptive and historical linguistics: Festschrift for Winfred P. Lehmann*, 145–158. Amsterdam: John Benjamins. [Amsterdam Studies in the Theory and History of Linguistic Science, Series IV, 4.]

1982. "The Neogrammarian doctrine: breakthrough or extension of the Schleicherian paradigm." In J. Peter Maher, Allan R. Bombard and E. F. K. Koerner (eds.), *Papers from the 3rd International Conference on Historical Linguistics*, 129–152. Amsterdam: John Benjamins.

(ed.). 1992. "The Sapir–Whorf hypothesis: a preliminary history and a bibliographic essay." *Journal of Linguistic Anthropology* 2: 173–98.

Kohl, Philip L. 1998. "Nationalism and archaeology: on the constructions of nations and the reconstructions of the remote past." *Annual Review of Anthropology* 27: 223–246.

Kouwenberg, Sylvia. 2004. *L1 transfer and the cut-off point for L2 acquisition: processes in creole formation*. Paper presented in the Montréal Dialogues conference, August.

Krahe, Hans. 1960. *Germanische Sprachwissenschaft, I. Einleitung und Lautlehre*. Berlin: Sammlung Göschen.

Krauss, Robert M. 1968. "Language as a symbolic process." *American Scientist* 56: 265–278.

Kristeva, Julia. 1980. *Language in desire, a semiotic approach to literature and art*. New York: Columbia University Press.

Kroch, Anthony. 1978. "Toward a theory of social dialect variation." *Language in Society* 7: 17–36.

Kroeber, Karl. 1997. *Traditional literatures of the American Indian: texts and interpretations*. Lincoln: University of Nebraska Press.

Kroskrity, P. (ed.). 2000. *Regimes of language: ideologies, polities, and identities*. Santa Fe: School of American Research Press.

Kulick, D. 1992. *Language shift and cultural reproduction: socialization, self, and syncretism in a Papua New Guinean Village*. Cambridge: Cambridge University Press.

Kulick, Don and Bambi B. Schieffelin. 2004. "Language socialization." In A. Duranti (ed.) *A companion to linguistic anthropology*, 349–368. Malden, MA: Blackwell.

Kurytowicz, Jerzy. 1964. *The inflectional categories of Indo-European*. Heidelberg: Carl Winter.

1966. "La nature des procès dits 'analogiques'." In Eric P. Hamp, Fred W. Householder and Robert Austerlitz (eds.), *Readings in linguistics II*, 158–174. Chicago: University of Chicago Press.

Kuschel, Rolf and Torben Monberg. 1974. "'We don't talk much about colour here': a study of colour semantics on Bellona Island." *Man* 9: 213–242.

Labov, William. 1972. *Sociolinguistic patterns*. Philadelphia: University of Pennsylvania Press.

1981. "Resolving the neogrammarian controversy." *Language* 57(2): 267–308.

1984. "Intensity." In D. Shiffrin (ed.), *Meaning, form, and use in context: linguistic applications*, 43–70. Georgetown University Round Table on Languages and Literature. Washington: Georgetown University Press.

1991. "The three dialects of English." In Penelope Eckert (ed.), *New ways of analyzing sound change*, 1–44. San Diego: Academic Press.

1994. *Principles of linguistic change*, Volume 1. *Internal factors*. Oxford: Blackwell.

2001. *Principles of linguistic change*, Volume 2. *Social factors*. Oxford: Blackwell.

Lacan, Jacques. 1977a. "The signification of the phallus." *Ecrits, a selection*, 281–291. New York: Norton.
1977b. "The agency of the letter in the unconscious or reason since Freud." *Ecrits, a selection*, 146–178. New York: Norton.
Laclau, Ernesto and Chantal Mouffe. 1985. *Hegemony and socialist strategy*. London and New York: Verso.
Lafont, Robert. 1997. *Quarante ans de sociolinguistique à la périphérie*. Paris: L'Harmattan.
Lakoff, George. 1987. *Women, fire and other dangerous things: what categories reveal about the mind*. Chicago: University of Chicago Press.
Lakoff, George and Mark Johnson. 1980. *Metaphors we live by*. Chicago: University of Chicago Press.
Lallot, Jean. 1991. "ΕΤΥΜΟΛΟΓΙΑ: L'étymologie en Grèce ancienne d'Homère aux grammairiens alexandrins." In Jean-Pierre Chambon and Georges Lüdi (eds.), *Discours étymologiques: actes du colloque international organisé à l'occasion du centenaire de la naissance de Walther von Wartburg*, 135–147. Tübingen: M. Niemeyer.
Landry, Rodrigue and Réal Allard. 1996. "Vitalité ethnolinguistique: une perspective dans l'étude de la francophonie canadienne." In Jürgen Erfurt (ed.), *De la polyphonie à la symphonie. Méthodes, théories et faits de la recherche pluridisciplinaire sur le français au Canada*, 61–88. Leipzig: Leipziger Universitätsverlag.
Lass, Roger. 1997. *Historical linguistics and language change*. Cambridge: Cambridge University Press.
Laurendeau, Monique and Adrien Pinard. 1970. *The development of the concept of space in the child*. New York: International Universities Press.
Lave, Jean. 1988. *Cognition in practice*. Cambridge: Cambridge University Press.
Lave, Jean and E. Wenger. 1991. *Situated learning: legitimate peripheral participation*. Cambridge: Cambridge University Press.
Le Gentil, Pierre. 1969. "Compte rendu de Richard Lemay. A propos de l'origine arabe de l'art des troubadours." *Romania* 90: 425–426.
Leap, William (ed.). 1995. *Beyond the lavender lexicon: authenticity, imagination, and appropriation in lesbian and gay languages*. Buffalo, N. Y.: Gordon and Breach.
Leavitt, John. 1991. "The shapes of modernity." *Culture* 11(1–2): 29–42.
(ed.). 1997. *Poetry and prophecy: the anthropology of inspiration*. Ann Arbor: University of Michigan Press.
Lee, Benjamin. 1997. *Talking heads, language, metalanguage and the semiotics of subjectivity*. Durham and London: Duke University Press.
Lee, Dorothy Demetracopoulou. 1938. "Conceptual implications of an Indian language." *Philosophy of Science* 5: 89–102.
1944. "Linguistic reflection of Wintu thought." *International Journal of American Linguistics* 10: 181–187.
Lee, Penny. 1991. "Whorf's Hopi tensors: subtle articulators in the language/thought nexus?" *Cognitive Linguistics* 2: 123–147.
1996. *The Whorf theory complex: a critical reconstruction*. Amsterdam: John Benjamins. [Amsterdam Studies in Theory and History of Linguistic Science, Series III, 81.]
Lefebvre, Claire. 1984. "Grammaires en contact: définition et perspectives de recherche." *Revue québécoise de linguistique* 14(1): 11–49.
1986. "Relexification in creole genesis revisited: the case of Haitian Creole." In Pieter C. Muysken and Norval Smith (eds.), *Substrata versus universals in creole genesis*, 279–301. Amsterdam; Philadelphia: John Benjamins.

1998. *Creole genesis and the acquisition of grammar: the case of Haitian creole.* Cambridge: Cambridge University Press.

2004. *Issues in the study of pidgins and creoles.* Studies in language comparison series. Amsterdam: John Benjamins Publishing Company.

Lefebvre, Claire and John S. Lumsden. 1989. "Les langues créoles et la théorie linguistique." In "La créolisation. Theme issue." *Revue canadienne de linguistique* 34(3): 249–272.

Lehrer, Adrienne. 1983. *Wine and conversation.* Bloomington: Indiana University Press.

Lemay, Richard. 1966. "A propos de l'origine arabe de l'art des troubadours." *Annales Economies, Sociétés, Civilisations* 21: 990–1011.

Lemon, Alaina. 2000. *Between two fires: gypsy performance and Romani memory from Pushkin to postsocialism.* Durham: Duke University Press.

Lenneberg, Eric H. 1953. "Cognition in ethnolinguistics." *Language* 29: 463–471.

Lenneberg, Erik H. and John M. Roberts. 1956. *The language of experience: a study in methodology.* Memoir 13 of *International Journal of American Linguistics.*

Leroy-Turcan, Isabelle. 1991. *Introduction à l'étude du "Dictionnaire étymologique ou Origines de la langue française" de Gilles Ménage (1694). Les étymologies de Ménage: science et fantaisie.* Lyon: Centre d'études linguistiques Jacques Goudet.

Levinson, Stephen C. 1983. *Pragmatics.* Cambridge: Cambridge University Press.

1995. "Cognitive anthropology." In J. Verschueren, J.-O. Ostman, and J. Blommaert (eds.), *Handbook of Pragmatics*, 100–105. Amsterdam: John Benjamins.

1996a. "Relativity in spatial conception and description." In J. Gumperz and S. C. Levinson (eds.), *Rethinking linguistic relativity*, 177–202. Cambridge: Cambridge University Press.

1996b. "Frames of reference and Molyneux's question: crosslinguistic evidence." In Paul Bloom, Mary A. Peterson, Lynn Nadell, and Merrill F. Garrett (eds.), *Language and space*, 109–169. Cambridge, MA: MIT Press.

1996c. "Language and space." *Annual Review of Anthropology* 25: 353–382.

1997a. "Language and cognition: The cognitive consequences of spatial description in Guugu Yimithirr." *Journal of Linguistic Anthropology* 7(1): 98–131.

1997b. "From outer to inner space: linguistic categories and non-linguistic thinking." In J. Nuyts and E. Pederson (eds.), *Language and conceptual representation*, 13–45. Cambridge: Cambridge University Press.

1998. "Studying spatial conceptualization across cultures: anthropology and cognitive science." In E. Danziger (ed.), *Language, space and culture*, special issue. *Ethos* 26(1): 7–24.

1999. "The theory of basic color terms and Yélî Dnye." *Journal of Linguistic Anthropology* 10: 3–55.

2003a. *Space in language and cognition: explorations in cognitive diversity.* Cambridge: Cambridge University Press.

2003b. "Language and mind: let's get the issues straight!" In D. Gentner and S. Goldin-Meadow (eds.), *Language in mind*, 25–46. Cambridge MA: MIT Press.

Levinson, Stephen C. and Penelope Brown. 1994. "Immanuel Kant among the Tenejapans: anthropology as empirical philosophy." *Ethos* 22(1): 3–41.

Levinson, Stephen C. and David Wilkins (eds.) (in press). *Grammars of space.* Cambridge: Cambridge University Press.

Levinson, Stephen C., Sotaro Kita, Daniel Haun, and B. Rasch. 2002. "Returning the tables: language affects spatial reasoning." *Cognition* 84: 155–188.

Lévi-Strauss, Claude. 1960. "Four Winnebago myths: a structural sketch." In Stanley Diamond (ed.), *Culture in history: essays in honor of Paul Radin*, 351–362. New York: Published for Brandeis University by Columbia University Press.

1967. *The Savage Mind*. London: Weidenfeld and Nicholson.

Levy, Robert I. 1984. "Emotion, knowing, and culture. " In R. A. Shweder and R. A. Levine (eds.), *Culture theory: Essays on mind, self, and emotion*, 214–237. Cambridge: Cambridge University Press.

Lieberman, Philip. 1984. *The biology and evolution of language*. Cambridge, MA: Harvard University Press.

Lightfoot, David. 1979. *Principles of diachronic syntax*. Cambridge studies in linguistics, 23. Cambridge: Cambridge University Press.

1997. "Catastrophic change and learning theory." *Lingua* 100: 171–192.

Lincoln, Bruce. 1999. *Theorizing myth: narrative, ideology and scholarship*. Chicago: University of Chicago Press.

Lippi-Green, Rosina. 1989. "Social network integration and language change in progress in a rural alpine village." *Language in society* 18: 213–234.

Liss, Julia E. 1996. "German culture and German science in the *Bildung* of Franz Boas." In George W. Stocking, Jr. (ed.), *Volksgeist as Method and ethic: essays on Boasian ethnography and the German anthropological tradition*, 155–184. Madison: University of Wisconsin Press.

Livia, Anna and Kira Hall (eds.). 1997. *Queerly phrased, language, gender and sexuality*. Oxford: Oxford University Press.

Lock, A. 1981. *The guided reinvention of language*. London: Academic Press.

Lovejoy, Paul E. and David. V. Trotman. (2002). "Enslaved Africans and their expectations of slave life in the Americas." In V. Shepherd and G. Richards (eds.), *Questioning creole: creolisation discourses in Caribbean culture*, 67–88. Kingston: Ian Randle Publishers.

Lowenstein, Tom and Knut Rasmussen. 1973. *Eskimo poems from Canada and Greenland*. Pittsburgh: University of Pittsburgh Press.

Lucy, John A. 1985. "Whorf's view of the linguistic mediation of thought." In B. Blount (ed.), *Language, culture, and society*. 2nd edn, 415–438. Prospect Heights, IL: Waveland Press.

1992a. *Language diversity and thought*. Cambridge: Cambridge University Press.

1992b. *Grammatical categories and cognition: a case study of the linguistic relativity hypothesis*. Cambridge: Cambridge University Press.

(ed.). 1993. *Reflexive language: reported speech and metapragmatics*. Cambridge: Cambridge University Press.

1996. "The scope of linguistic relativity: an analysis and review of empirical research." In J. Gumperz and S. C. Levinson (eds.), *Rethinking linguistic relativity*, 37–69. Cambridge: Cambridge University

1997a. "The linguistics of 'color'." In C. L. Hardin and Luisa Maffi (eds.), *Color categories in thought and language*, 320–346. Cambridge: Cambridge University Press.

1997b. "Linguistic relativity." *Annual Review of Anthropology* 26: 291–312.

Lucy, John A. and Suzanne Gaskins, 2001. "It's later than you think: the role of language-specific categories in the development of classification behavior." In M. Bowerman and S. C. Levinson (eds.), *Language acquisition and conceptual development*, 257–283. Cambridge: Cambridge University Press.

2003. "Interaction of language type and referent type in the development of nonverbal classification preferences." In D. Gentner and S. Goldin-Meadow (eds.), *Language in mind*, 465–492. Cambridge MA: MIT Press.

Lucy, John and R. A. Shweder. 1979. "Whorf and his critics: linguistic and nonlinguistic influences on color memory." *American Anthropologist* 81: 581–615.

Lucy, John A. and James V. Wertsch. 1987. "Vygotsky and Whorf: A comparative analysis." In Maya Hickmann (ed.), *Social and functional approaches to language and thought*, 67–86. New York: Academic.

1988. "The effect of incidental conversation on memory for focal colors." *American Anthropologist* 90: 923–931.

Lüdtke, Helmut. 1986. "Esquisse d'une théorie du changement langagier." *La linguistique* 22 fasc. 1: 3–46.

Lutz, Catherine. 1990. "Engendering emotion: gender, power and rhetoric of emotional control in American discourse." In C. Lutz (ed.), *Language and the politics of emotion*, 69–91. Cambridge: Cambridge University Press.

Lyons, John. 1977. *Semantics*. Cambridge: Cambridge University Press.

1999. "The vocabulary of colour with particular reference to ancient Greek and classical Latin." In Alexander Borg (ed.), *The language of colour in the Mediterranean*, Wiesbaden: Otto Harrassowitz.

MacDonald, Marion. 1990. *"We are not French!."* London: Routledge.

Mackey, William. 1968. *The description of bilingualism*. In Joshua Fishman (ed.), *Readings in the sociology of language*. The Hague: Mouton, 554–584.

MacKinnon, Catherine. 1993. *Only words*. Cambridge: Harvard University Press.

MacLaury, Robert E. 1986. "Color in Meso-America: vol I. A theory of composite categorization." Unpublished Ph.D. thesis. University of California, Berkeley.

1987. "Color-category evolution and Shuswap yellow-with-green." *American Anthropologist* 89: 107–124.

1997. *Color and cognition in Mesoamerica*. Austin: University of Texas.

Maffi, Luisa. 1990a. "Cognitive anthropology and human categorization research: the case of color." Department of Anthropology, University of California, Berkeley.

1990b. "Somali color term evolution: grammatical and semantic evidence." *Anthropological Linguistics* 32: 316–334.

Maffi, Luisa and C. L. Hardin. 1997. "Closing thoughts." In C. L. Hardin and Luisa Maffi (eds.), *Color categories in thought and language*, 347–372. Cambridge: Cambridge University Press.

Majid, Asifa. 2002. "Frames of reference and language concepts." *Trends in Cognitive Science*, 6(12): 503–504.

Majid, A., M. Bowerman, S. Kita, D. Haun, and S. Levinson. 2004. "Can language restructure cognition? The case for space." *Trends in Cognitive Sciences*, 8(3), 108–114.

Malkiel, Yakov. 1974. "Editorial comment: a Herder–Humboldt–Sapir–Whorf hypothesis?" *Romance Philology* 28: 199.

1977. "Etymology and general linguistics." In Rüdiger Schmitt (ed.), *Etymologie*, 347–376. Darmstadt: Wissenschaft.

1993. *Etymology*. Cambridge: Cambridge University Press.

Malkoc, Gohkan. 2003. "Color categories and the structure of color space." Ph.D. thesis. University of Nevada at Reno.

Malkoc, G., P. Kay, and M. A. Webster. 2002. "Individual differences in unique and binary hues." OSA *Fall Vision Meeting, Palace of Fine Arts, San Francisco, CA.*

Malkoc, G., M. A. Webster, and P. Kay. 2002. "Individual differences in color categories." *2nd Annual Meeting of Vision Sciences Society*, Sarasota, FL.

Malotki, Ekkehart. 1983. *Hopi Time: a linguistic analysis of the temporal concepts in the Hopi language*. Berlin: Mouton. [Trends in Linguistics, Studies and Monographs, 20.]

Mannheim, Bruce. 1991. *The language of the Incas since the European invasion*. Austin: University of Texas Press.

Marantz, Alec. 1984. "Special evidence for innateness." *Behavioural and Brain Sciences* 7(2): 199–200.

Martin, Laura. 1986. "Eskimo words for snow: a case study in the genesis and decay of an anthropological example." *American Anthropologist* 88: 418–423.

Martinet, André. 1964. *Économie des changements phonétiques; traité de phonologie diachronique*. Berne: A. Francke.

Matisoff, James. 1978. *Variational semantics in Tibeto-Burman*. Philadelphia: Institute for the study of Human Issues.

1990. "On megalocomparison." *Language* 66(1): 106–120.

Matsuzawa, T. 1985. "Colour naming and classification in a chimpanzee (*Pan troglodytes*)." *Journal of Human Evolution* 14: 283–291.

Matthiesen, F. O. 1941. *American renaissance*. Oxford: Oxford University Press.

McClure, Erica. 1977. "Aspects of code-switching in the discourse of bilingual Mexican-American children." In M. Saville-Troike (ed.), *Linguistics and anthropology: Georgetown University round table on languages and linguistics*, 93–115. Washington: Georgetown University Press.

1981. "Formal and functional aspects of the code-switched discourse of bilingual children." In Richard Duran (ed.), *Latino language and communicative behavior*, 69–94. Norwood NJ: Ablex.

McConnell-Ginet, Sally. 1988. "Language and gender." In Frederick J. Newmeyer (ed.), *Linguistics: the Cambridge survey, IV. Language: the socio-cultural context*, 75–99. Cambridge: Cambridge University Press.

McDonald, Terrence J. 1996. "Introduction." In *The historic turn in the human sciences*, 1–14. Ann Arbor: University of Michigan Press.

McDonough, Laraine, Soonja Choi, and Jean M. Mandler. 2003. "Understanding spatial relations: flexible infants lexical adults." *Cognitive Psychology* 46: 229–259.

McLaughlin, B. 1984. "Early bilingualism: methodological and theoretical issues." In M. Paradis and Y. Lebrun (eds.), *Early bilingualism and child development*, 19–45. Lisse: Swets and Zeitlinger.

McNeill, D. 1970. *The acquisition of language: the study of developmental psycholinguistics*. New York: Harper and Row.

McWhorter, John. 1992. "Substratal influences on Saramaccan." *Journal of Pidgin and Creole Languages* 7(1): 1–54.

1998. "Identifying the creole prototype: vindicating a typological class." *Language*.

2001. "The world's simplest grammars are creole grammars." *Linguistic Typology* 5(3/4): 125–156.

Meek, B. 2001. "Kaska language socialization, acquisition and shift." Unpublished Ph.D. thesis, University of Arizona.

Meeuwis, Michael and Jan Blommaert. 1994. "The 'Markedness Model' and the absence of society: remarks on codeswitching." *Multilingua* 14(4): 387–423.

Meillet, Antoine. 1954 [1925]. *La méthode comparative en linguistique historique*. (Instituttet for sammenlingnende kulturforskning, Oslo. Ser. A: Forelesninger 2) Paris: H. Champion.

1964. *Introduction à l'étude comparative des langues indo-européennes*. University, Ala.: University of Alabama Press.

Menocal, María Rosa. 1982. "The etymology of Old Provençal *trobar, trobador*: a return to the 'third solution'." *Romance Philology* 36 (2): 137–148.

1984. "The mysteries of the Orient: special problems in Romance etymology." In Philip Baldi (ed.), *Papers from the XIIth Linguistic Symposium on Romance Languages*, 501–515. Amsterdam: Benjamins.

1987. *The Arabic role in medieval literary history: a forgotten heritage*. Philadelphia: University of Pennsylvania Press.

Merwin, William S. 1979. *Selected translations*. New York: Athaneum.

1998. *East window. The Asian translations*. Port Townsend: Copper Canyon Press.

Meyerhoff, Miriam. 2000. *Constraints on null subjects in Bislama (Vanuatu)*. Canberra: Pacific Linguistics.

Meyer-Lübke, Wilhelm. 1992 [1935]. *Romanisches etymologisches Wörterbuch*. (6th edition). Heidelberg: Carl Winter Universtitäsverlag.

Miller, George A. and Philip N. Johnson-Laird. 1976. *Language and perception*. Cambridge, MA: Harvard University Press.

Miller, Peggy, J. 1982. *Amy, Wendy, and Beth: learning language in South Baltimore*. Austin: University of Texas Press.

Miller, Perry. 1967. "An American language." In *Nature's nation*, 208–40. Cambridge: Harvard University Press.

Miller, Robert L. 1968. *The linguistic relativity principle and Humboldtian ethnolinguistics: a history and appraisal*. The Hague: Mouton. [Janua Linguarum, Series minor, 67.]

Mills, Sara. 1995. *Language and gender: interdisciplinary perspectives*. London and New York: Longman.

Milosz, Czeslaw (ed.). 1996. *A book of luminous things. An international anthology of poetry*. New York: Harcourt Brace and Co.

Milroy, James. 1993. "On the social origins of language change." Charles Jones (ed.), *Historical linguistics: problems and perspectives*, 215–236. London: Longman.

Milroy, Lesley. 1987. *Language and social networks*. 2nd edn. Oxford: New York: B. Blackwell.

Mintz, Sidney W. 1971. "The socio-historical background to pidginization and creolization." In Dell Hymes (ed.), *Pidginization and creolization of languages*, 481–498. Cambridge: Cambridge University Press.

1974. *Caribbean transformations*. Chicago: University of Chicago Press.

1982. "Caribbean marketplaces and Caribbean history." *Radical History Review* 27: 110–120.

Mintz, Sydney and Richard Price. 1992. *The birth of African-American culture: anthropological perspective*. Boston: Beacon Press.

Mishra, Ramesh C., Pierre Dasen, and Shanta Niraula. 2003. "Ecology, language, and performance on spatial cognitive tasks." *International Journal of Psychology* 38(6): 366–383.

Mitchell, Juliet. 1974. *Psychoanalysis and feminism, Freud, Reich, Laing and women*. New York: Vintage.

1985. "Introduction – 1." In Juliet Mitchell and Jacqueline Rose (eds.). *Feminine sexuality, Jaques Lacan and the école freudienne*, 1–26. New York and London: Norton.

Moitt, Bernard. 2001. *Women and slavery in the French Antilles, 1635–1848*. Bloomington: Indiana University Press.

Monberg, Torben. 1971. "Tikopia color classification." *Ethnology* 10: 349–358.

Moore, Clive. 1985. *Kanaka Maratta: a history of Melansian Mackay*. Port Moresby: Institute of Papua New Guinea studies and the University of Papua New Guinea Press.

Morgan, Lewis Henry. 1877. *Ancient society*. New York: Henry Holt.

Morissey, Marietta. 1989. *Slave women in the New World: gender stratification in the Caribbean.* Lawrence, Kansas: University Press of Kansas.

Mougeon, Raymond and Edouard Beniak. 1991. *Linguistic consequences of language contact and restriction: the case of French in Ontario, Canada.* Oxford: Oxford University Press.

Mufwene, Salikoko. 1984. "The language bioprogram hypothesis, Creole studies, and linguistic theory." *Behavioural and Brain Sciences* 7(2): 20–23.

1986. "The universalist and substrate hypotheses complement one another." In Pieter C. Muysken and Norval Smith (eds.), *Substrata versus universals in Creole genesis*, 129–162. Amsterdam/Philadelphia: John Benjamins.

1989. "Response to Bickerton." *The Carrier Pidgin* 17(2,3): 6–7.

(ed.). 1993. *Africanisms in Afro-American language varieties.* Athens/London: The University of Georgia Press.

1999. "On the language bioprogram hypothesis: hints from Tazie." In M. DeGraff (ed.), *Language variation and language change: creolization, diachrony, and development*, 95–127. Cambridge, Mass.: The MIT Press.

Mühlhäusler, Peter. 1978. "Samoan plantation pidgin English and the origin of Papua New Guinea pidgin." *Papers in pidgin and creole linguistics.* Canberra: Pacific Linguistics 28(4): 67–120.

Mulvaney, John, Howard Morphy, and Alison Petch (eds.). 1997. *"My Dear Spencer": The letters of F. J. Gillen to Baldwin Spencer.* Melbourne: Hyland.

Murray, Stephen O. 1994. *Theory groups and the study of language in North America.* Amsterdam and Philadelphia: John Benjamins.

Muysken, Pieter. 1984. "Do creoles give insight into the human language faculty?" *Behavioural and Brain Sciences* 7(2): 20–34.

1995. "Code-switching and grammatical theory." In Lesley Milroy and Pieter Muysken (eds.), *One speaker, two languages: cross-disciplinary perspectives on code-switching*, 177–198. Cambridge: Cambridge University Press.

Muysken, Pieter and Norval Smith (eds.). 1986. *Substrata versus universals in creole genesis.* Amsterdam: John Benjamins.

1990. "Question words in Pidgin and Creole languages." *Linguistics* 28(4): 883–903.

Myers-Scotton, Carol. 1993a. *Social motivations for code-switching: evidence from Africa.* Oxford: Oxford University Press.

1993b. *Duelling languages: grammatical structure in code-switching.* Oxford: Oxford University Press.

Napoli, Donna Jo and Eminly Nawood Rando. 1983. *Meliglossa.* Edmonton, Alberta, Canada: Linguistic Research, Inc.

Naro, Anthony J. 1978. "Study of the origins of pidginization." *Language* 54: 314–347.

1988. "A reply to Pidgin origins reconsidered" by Morris Goodman. *Journal of Pidgins and Creole Languages* 3(1): 95–102.

Needham, Rodney. 1973. *Right and left: essays on dual symbolic classification.* Chicago: University of Chicago Press.

Nelson, K. (ed.). 1986. *Event knowledge: structure and function in development.* Hillsdale: Lawrence Erlbaum.

Neumann-Holzschuh, Ingrid and Edgar W. Schneider (eds.). 2000. *Degrees of restructuring in creole languages.* Creole language library, 22. Amsterdam; Philadelphia: John Benjamins.

Newman, Stanley. 1954. "Semantic problems in grammatical systems and lexemes: a search for method." In H. Hoijer (ed.) *Language in culture*, 82–91. Chicago: University of Chicago Press.

Newport, E. L., H. Gleitman and L. R. Gleitman. 1977. "Mother, I'd rather do it myself: some effects and non-effects of maternal speech style." In C. Ferguson and C. Snow (eds.), *Talking to children: language input and acquisition*, 109–150. Cambridge: Cambridge University Press.

Nichols, Johanna. 1992. *Linguistic diversity in space and time*. Chicago: University of Chicago Press.

Nida, Eugene A. 1959. "Principles of translation as exemplified by Bible translating." In Reuben A. Brower (ed.), *On Translation*. Cambridge, MA: Harvard University Press.

Niemeier, Susanne and René Dirven (eds.). 2000. *Evidence for linguistic relativity*. Amsterdam: Benjamins.

Nuckolls, Janis. 1996. *Sounds like life: sound–symbolic grammar, performance, and cognition in Pastaza Quechua*. New York: Oxford.

1999. "The case for sound symbolism." *Annual Review of Anthropology*, 28: 225–252.

O'Brien, Flann. 1977. *The hair of the dogma*. London: Hart-Davis.

Ochs E. 1982. "Talking to children in Western Samoa." *Language in Society* 11: 77–104.

1985. "Variation and error: a sociolinguistic study of language acquisition in Samoa." In D. Slobin (ed.), *The crosslinguistic study of language acquisition*, 783–838. Hillsdale: Lawrence Erlbaum Associates.

1988. *Culture and language development: language acquisition and language socialization in Samoan village*. Cambridge: Cambridge University Press.

1990. "Cultural universals in the acquisition of language." *Papers and Reports on Child Language Development* 29: 1–19

1993. "Constructing social identity: a language socialization perspective." *Research on Language and Social Interaction* 26(3): 287–306.

Ochs, E. and B. B. Schieffelin. 1984. "Language acquisition and socialization: three developmental stories and their implications." In R. Shweder and R. Levine (eds.), *Culture theory: essays on mind, self and emotion*, 276–320. New York: Cambridge University Press.

1989. "Language has a heart." *Text* 9(1): 7–25.

(eds.). 1990. *Language socialization across cultures*. Cambridge: Cambridge University Press.

1995. "The impact of language socialization on grammatical development." In P. Fletcher and Brian MacWhinney (eds.), *Handbook of child language*, 73–94. Oxford: Blackwell.

Ogawa, Naoko and Janet S. Smith. 1997. "The gendering of the gay male sex classing Japan: a case study based on *Rasen No Sobyo*." In Livia and Hall, *Queerly phrased, language, gender and sexuality*, 402–415.

Öhman, Suzanne. 1953. "Theories of the 'linguistic field'." *Word* 9: 123–134.

Ohnuki-Tierney, Emiko. 1990. "Introduction: the historicization of anthropology." In Emiko Ohnuki-Tierney (ed.), *Culture through time: anthropological approaches*, 1–25. Stanford: Stanford University Press.

Opland, Jeff. 1983. *Xhosa oral poetry*. Cambridge: Cambridge University Press.

Orlove, Benjamin S. 1980. "Ecological anthropology." *Annual Review of Anthropology* 9: 235–273.

Ortner, Sherry. 1984. "Theory in anthropology since the sixties." *Comparative Studies in Society and History* 26: 126–166.

Osthoff, H. and K. Brugmann. 1878 [1974]. *Morphologische Untersuchungen auf dem Gebiete der indogermanischen Sprachen. Erster Theil*. Hildesheim: Georg Olms.

Paris, Gaston. 1909. *Mélanges linguistiques. Latin vulgaire et langues romanes; langue française; notes étymologiques.* Paris: Champion.

Parmentier, Richard. 1993. "The political function of reported speech: a Belauan example." In J. Lucy (ed.), *Reflexive language*, 261–286.

Patrick, Peter. 1999. *Urban Jamaican creole: variation in the mesolect.* Amsterdam: John Benjamins.

Paugh, Amy. 2001. "'Creole day is every day': language socialization, shift, and ideologies in Dominica, West Indies." Unpublished Ph.D. thesis, New York University.

Paul, Hermann. 1920 [1960]. *Prinzipien der Sprachgeschichte.* 6th edn. Tübingen: M. Niemeyer.

Pedersen, Holger. 1983. *A glance at the history of linguistics, with particular regard to the historical study of phonology.* Trans. Caroline C. Henriksen; ed. with an introduction by Konrad Koerner. Amsterdam: J. Benjamins.

Pederson, Eric, Eve Danziger, Stephen Levinson, Sotaro Kita, Gunter Senft, and David Wilkins. 1998. "Semantic typology and spatial conceptualization." *Language* 74: 557–589.

Peirce, C. S. 1938–58. *Collected papers*, vols. 1–8, C. Hartshorne and P. Weiss (eds.). Cambridge, MA: Harvard University Press.

Penn, Julia M. 1972. *Linguistic relativity versus innate ideas: the origins of the Sapir–Whorf hypothesis in German thought.* The Hague: Mouton. [Janua Linguarum, series minor, 120.]

Pesmen, Dale. 2000. *Russia and soul. An exploration.* Ithaca: Cornell University Press.

Petersen, Uwe. 1992. "Rasks Stellung in der Sprachwissenschaft." In von Rasmus Rask; herausgegeben und übersetzt von Uwe Petersen (eds.), *Von der Etymologie überhaupt: Eine Einleitung in die Sprachvergleichung*, 9–29. Tübingen: Gunter Narr.

Philips, S. U. 1983. *The invisible culture: communication in classroom and community on the Warm Springs Indian reservation.* New York: Longman.

    2001. "Power." In Alessandro Duranti (ed.). *Key terms in language and culture*, 190–192. Oxford: Blackwell.

Philips, Susan, Susan Steele, and Christine Tanz (eds.). 1987. *Language, gender and sex in comparative perspective.* Cambridge: Cambridge University Press.

Piaget, Jean and Barbel Inhelder. 1967 (1948). *The child's conception of space.* New York: Norton.

Picard, Marc. 1987. *An introduction to the comparative phonetics of English and French in North America.* Amsterdam: J. Benjamins Pub. Co.

Pick, H., and L. Acredolo (eds.). 1983. *Spatial orientation: theory, research and application.* New York: Plenum Press.

Pierrehumbert, Janet and Paul Gross. 2003. "Community phonology." (Presented at the 39th meeting of the Chicago Linguistic Society, April 12, 2003.)

Pinker, Steven. 1994. *The language instinct: how the mind creates language.* New York: William Morrow.

Pinxten, R., I. van Dooren, and F. Harvey. 1983. *The anthropology of space.* Philadelphia: University of Pennsylvania Press.

Platt, M. 1986. "Social norms and lexical acquisition: a study of deictic verbs in Samoan Child Language." In B. B. Schieffelin and E. Ochs (eds.), *Language socialization across cultures*, 127–151. Cambridge: Cambridge University Press.

Pokorny, Julius. 1959. *Indogermanisches etymologisches Worterbuch.* Bern: Francke.

Poplack, Shana. 1988. "Contrasting patterns of code-switching in two communities." In Monica Heller (ed.), *Codeswitching: anthropological and sociolinguistic perspectives*, 215–244. Berlin: Mouton de Gruyter.

Pott, August Friedrich. 1833–1836. *Etymologische forschungen auf dem gebiete der indogermanischen sprachen, mit besonderem bezug auf die lautumwandlung im sanskrit, griechischen, lateinischen, littauischen und gothischen.* Lemgo: Meyersche hof-buchhandlung. (2nd, completely revised version published in 1859–67).

1856. *Die Ungleichheit menschlicher Rassen haupt-sächlich vom Sprachwissenschaftlichen Standpunkte, unter besonderer Berücksichtigung von des Grafen von Gobineau gleichnamigem Werke.* Lemgo: Detmold, Meyer.

Povinelli, Elizabeth A. 1993. "'Might be something': the language of indeterminacy in Australian Aboriginal land use." *Man* December 28(4): 679–704.

2004. *The cunning of recognition: indigenous alterity and the making of Australian multiculturalism.* Durham, NC: Duke University Press.

Prattis, J. Iain (ed.). 1985. *Reflections. The anthropological muse.* Washington, D. C.: American Anthropological Association.

Price, Charles and Elizabeth Baker. 1976. "Origins of Pacific islands labourers in Queensland, 1863–1904." *Journal of Pacific History* 9(1): 106–111.

Price, Richard. 1983. *First-time: the historical vision of an Afro-American people.* Baltimore: The Johns Hopkins Press ltd.

Prost, André. 1956. "La Langue Sonay." *Mémoires de l'Institut d'Afrique Noire*#47. Dakar.

Pulgram, Ernst. 1959. "Proto-Indo-European reality and reconstruction." *Language* 35(3): 421–426.

Pullum, Geoffrey. 1989. "The great Eskimo vocabulary hoax." *Natural Language and Linguistic Theory* 7: 275–281.

Pütz, Martin and Marjolijn Verspoor (eds.). 2000. *Explorations in linguistic relativity.* Amsterdam: Benjamins.

Pye, C. 1992. "The acquisition of K'iche' Maya." In D. Slobin (ed.), *The crosslinguistic study of language acquisition,* 221–308. Hillsdale NJ: Lawrence Erlbaum Associates.

Quine, W. V. 1969. *Ontological relativity and other essays.* New York: Columbia University Press.

Quinn, Naomi. 1991. "The cultural basis of metaphor." In James W. Fernandez (ed.), *Beyond metaphor: the theory of tropes in anthropology,* 56–93. Stanford, CA: Stanford University Press.

1996. "Culture and contradiction: the case of Americans reasoning about marriage." *Ethos* 24: 391–425.

1997. "The mainstreaming of cultural models." Paper delivered at the plenary session: Psychological Anthropology: State of the Art, at the 1997 biennial meeting of the Society for Psychological Anthropology, Oct. 9–12, San Diego.

Ramanujan, A. K. 1967. *The interior landscape. Love poems from the Classical Tamil anthology.* Bloomington: Indiana University Press.

1969. *The collected essays of A. K. Ramanujan.* Oxford: Oxford University Press.

Rampton, Ben. 2002. "Ritual and foreign language practices at school." *Language in Society* 31(4): 491–526.

Rask, Rasmus Kristian. 1992. *Von der Etymologie überhaupt: Eine Einleitung in die Sprachvergleichung.* Uwe Petersen, trans. Tübingen: Gunter Narr. (German tr. of Chapter 1 of *Undersögelse om det gamle Nordiske eller Islandske Sprogs Oprindelse,* publ. 1818).

Raudo, Emily Narwood and Donna Jo Napoli (eds.). 1983. *Meliglossa.* Edmonton, Alberta, Canada: Linguistic Research, Inc.

Ray, Verne. 1952. "Techniques and problems in the study of human color perception." *Southwestern Journal of Anthropology* 8: 251–959.

1953. "Human color perception and behavioral response." *Transactions of the New York Academy of Sciences* (series 2) 16: 98–104.

Regier, Jerry, Paul Kay, and Richard S. Cook. 2005. "Focal colors are universal after all." *Proceedings of the National Academy of Sciences* 102, 8386–8391.

Rickford, John R. 1987. *Dimensions of a creole continuum: history, texts and linguistic analysis of Guyanese creole.* Stanford: Stanford University Press.

Ricoeur, Paul. 1978. "Explanation and understanding: on some remarkable connections among the theory of the text, theory of action, and theory of history." In Charles Reagan and David Stewart (eds.), *The philosophy of Paul Ricoeur: an anthology of his work*, 149–166. Boston: Beacon Press.

Ridington, Robin. 1991. "On the language of Benjamin Lee Whorf." In Ivan Brady (ed.), *Anthropological poetics*, 241–261. Savage: Rowan and Littlefield.

Riley, K. C. 2001. "The emergence of dialogic identities: transforming heteroglossia in the Marquesas, F.P." Unpublished Ph.D. thesis, City University of New York.

Rindler-Schjerve, Rosita (ed.). In press. *Explorations in historical sociolinguistics: language and power in the Habsburg Empire.* Berlin: Mouton de Gruyter.

Roberson, Debi, Ian Davies, and Jules Davidoff. 2000. "Colour categories are not universal: replications and new evidence from a stone age culture." *Journal of Experimental Psychology: General*, 129: 369–398.

Rogoff, B. 1990. *Apprenticeship in thinking.* New York: Oxford University Press.

Rogoff, Barbara, and Jean Lave (eds.). 1984. *Everyday cognition.* Cambridge, MA: Harvard University Press.

Rogoff, Barbara and Gilda A. Morelli. 1994. "Cross-cultural perspectives on children's development." In P. K. Bock (ed.), *Psychological anthropology*, 231–242. Westport, CT: Praeger.

Roheim, Geza. 1973. *Psychoanalysis and anthropology.* New York: International Universities Press.

1974. *Children of the desert.* New York: Harper and Row.

Romaine, Suzanne. 1989. *Bilingualism.* Oxford: Basil Blackwell.

Romney, A. K. and Roy G. D'Andrade (eds.). 1964. "Transcultural studies in cognition." *American Anthropologist* 66(3), pt. 2.

Ronjat, J. 1913. *Le développement du langage observé chez un enfant bilingue.* Paris: Champion.

Rorty, Richard. 1982. "Method, social science and social hope." *Consequences of pragmatism (Essays: 1972–1980)*, 191–210. Minneapolis: University of Minnesota Press.

1983. "Method and morality." In Norma Haan *et al.* (eds.), *Social science as moral inquiry*, 155–176. New York: Columbia University Press.

Rosch, Eleanor. 1977. "Linguistic relativity." In P. N. Johnson-Laird and P. C. Wason (eds.), *Thinking: readings in cognitive science*, 501–22. Cambridge: Cambridge University Press.

1978. "Principles of categorization." In *Cognition and categorization*, ed. E. Rosch and B. Lloyd, 28–48. Hillsdale, NJ: Erlbaum.

Rosenberg, Daniel. 1990. "Language in the discourse of the emotions." In C. Lutz and L. Abu-Lughod, *Language and the politics of emotions*, 162–185.

Ross, Malcolm and Mark Durie. 1996. "Introduction." In Mark Durie and Malcolm Ross (eds.), *The comparative method reviewed: regularity and irregularity in language change*, 3–38. New York: Oxford University Press.

Rossi-Landi, Ferruccio. 1973. *Ideologies of linguistic relativity.* The Hague: Mouton. [Approaches to Semiotics, 4.]

Roth Pierpont, Claudia. 2004. "The measure of America: how a rebel anthropologist waged war on racism." *The New Yorker*, March 8, 2004, 48–63.

Rothenberg, Jerome. 1967. *Essays.* Stony Brook, NY.

1985. *Technicians of the sacred.* Berkeley: University of California Press.

1986 (1972). *Shaking the pumpkin. Traditional poetry of Indian North Americans.* Revised edn. New York: Alfred van der March Editions.

Rothenberg, Jerome and Diane Rothenberg. 1983. *Symposium of the whole. A range of discourse toward an ethnopoetics.* Berkeley: University of California Press.

Sacks, Harvey, Emanuel A. Schegloff, and Gail Jefferson. 1974. "A simplest systematics for the organization of turn-taking for conversation." *Language* 50: 696–735.

Sahlins, Marshall. 1976. "Colors and cultures." *Semiotica* 16: 1–22.

1981. *Historical metaphors and mythical realities. Structure in the early history of the Sandwich Islands Kingdoms.* Ann Arbor: University of Michigan Press.

2000. *Culture in practice.* New York: Zone Books.

Samarin, William. 1982a. "Colonization and pidginization on the Ubangui river." *Journal of African languages and linguistics* 4: 1–42.

1982b. "Goals, roles, and language skills in colonizing Central Equatorial Africa." *Anthropological linguistics* 24: 410–422.

1989. *The black man's burden: African colonial labor on the Congo and Ubangi Rivers 1880–1900.* Boulder, CO: Westview Press.

Sandell, J. H., C. G. Gross, and M. H. Bornstein. 1979. "Color categories in macaques." *Journal of Comparative and Physiological Psychology* 93: 626–635.

Sankoff, D., H. Cedergren, W. Kemp, P. Thibault, and D. Vincent. 1989. "Montréal French: language, class and ideology." In Ralph W. Fasold and Deborah Schiffrin (eds.), *Language change and variation*, 107–118. Amsterdam: J. Benjamins.

Sankoff, Gillian. 1979. "The genesis of a language." In K. C. Hill (ed.), *The genesis of language*, 23–47. Ann Arbor: Karoma.

1980. *The social life of language.* Philadelphia: University of Pennsylvania Press.

1990. "The grammaticalization of tense and aspect in Tok Pisin and Sranan." *Language variation and change* 2(3): 295–312.

Sankoff, Gillian and Suzanne Laberge. 1973. "On the acquisition of native speakers by a language." *Kivung* 6 (1): 32–47 reprinted in Gillian Sankoff (ed.), *The social life of language*, 195–209. Philadelphia: University of Pennsylvania Press.

Sapir, Edward. 1907. "Herder's Ursprung der Sprache." *Modern Philology* 5: 109–142.

1916. *Time perspective in aboriginal American culture: a study in method.* Ottawa: Canadian Geological Survey Memoir 90.

1921. *Language: an introduction to the study of speech.* New York: Harcourt, Brace and World.

1924 (1949). "The grammarian and his language." In David G. Mandelbaum (ed.), *Selected writings of Edward Sapir in language, culture and personality*, 150–159. Berkeley: University of California Press.

1925. "Emily Dickinson: a primitive." Review of *The complete poetry of Emily Dickinson. Poetry* 26: 97–105.

1929a (1949). "The status of linguistics as a science." In David G. Mandelbaum (ed.), *Selected writings of Edward Sapir in language, culture and personality*, 160–166. Berkeley: University of California Press.

1929b (1949). "A study in phonetic symbolism." In David G. Mandelbaum (ed.), *Selected writings of Edward Sapir in language, culture and personality*, 61–72. Berkeley: University of California Press.

1933 (1949). "The psychological reality of phonemes." In David G. Mandelbaum (ed.), *Selected writings of Edward Sapir in language, culture and personality*, 46–60. Berkeley: University of California Press.

1949. *Selected writings of Edward Sapir.* David Mandelbaum (ed.). Berkeley: University of California Press.

1994. *The psychology of culture: a course of lectures by Edward Sapir*. Reconstructed and ed. Judith T. Irvine. Berlin: M. de Gruyter.

Saunders, B. A. C. and J. van Brakel. 1997. "Are there non-trivial constraints on colour categorization?" *Behavioral and Brain Sciences* 20: 167–228.

Saunders, Kay. 1974. "Uncertain bondage." Ph.D. thesis. Brisbane: University of Queensland.

Saussure, Ferdinand de. 1916 (1972). *Cours de linguistique générale*. Charles Bally and Albert Sechehaye (eds.). Paris: Payot.

1960. "Souvenirs de F. de Saussure concernant sa jeunesse et ses études." *Cahiers Ferdinand de Saussure* 17: 12–25.

1968. *Cours de linguistique générale*. R. Engler (ed.). Wiesbaden: Otto

1974. *Cours de linguistique générale. Appendice: Notes sur la linguistique générale*. R. Engler. (ed.). Wiesbaden: Otto Harrassowitz.

Schank, Roger C., and Robert P. Abelson 1977. *Scripts, plans, goals, and understanding: an enquiry into human knowledge structures*. Hillsdale, NJ: Erlbaum.

Schegloff, Emanuel A., Gail Jefferson, and Harvey Sacks. 1977. "The preference for self-correction in the organization of repair in conversation." *Language* 53: 361–382.

Schieffelin, Bambi, B. 1985. "The acquisition of Kaluli." In D. Slobin (ed.), *The crosslinguistic study of language acquisition*, 525–594. Hillsdale: Lawrence Erlbaum Associates.

1990. *The give and take of everyday life: language socialization of Kaluli children*. Cambridge: Cambridge University Press.

1994. "Code-switching and language socialization: some probable relationships." In J. Duchan, L. E. Hewitt, and R. M. Sonnenmeier (eds.), *Pragmatics: From theory to practice*, 20–42. New York: Prentice Hall.

Schieffelin, Bambi B. and E. Ochs. 1986a. "Language socialization." *Annual Review of Anthropology* 15: 163–191.

(eds.). 1986b. *Language socialization across cultures*. New York: Cambridge University Press.

Schieffelin, Bambi, Kathryn Woolard, and Paul Kroskrity (eds.). 1998. *Language ideologies: practice and theory*. Oxford: Oxford University Press.

Schlegel, August Wilhelm von. 1818. *Observations sur la langue et la littérature provençales*. Paris: Librairie grecque-latine-allemande.

Schlegel, Friedrich von. 1808. *Über die Sprache und Weisheit der Indier*. Heidelberg: Mohr und Zimmer.

Schleicher, August. 1967 [1871]. "Introduction to 'A compendium of the comparative grammar of the Indo-European, Sanskrit, Greek and Latin languages'." (From his *Compendium der vergleichenden Grammatik der indogermanischen Sprachen*; Weismar: Hermann Böhlau, 1871, 1–9.) *A reader in nineteenth-century historical Indo-European linguistics*, 87–96. ed. and trans. by Winfred P. Lehmann. Bloomington: Indiana University Press.

Schmidt, A. 1985. *Young people's Djirbal: an example of language death from Australia*. Cambridge: Cambridge University Press.

Schuchardt, Hugo. 1885. "Über die Lautgesetze. Gegen die Junggrammatiker." In T. H. Wilbur (ed.), *The Lautgesetz-controversy: a documentation*, 51–87. Amsterdam: J. Benjamins.

1902. "Etymologische Probleme und Prinzipien." *Zeischrift für romanische Philologie* 26: 385–427.

1903. Zur Wortgeschichte. "Trouver." *Zeischrift für romanische Philologie* 27: 97–105.

1928. *Hugo Schuchardt-Brevier; ein Vademacum der allgemeinen Sprachwissenschaft.* 2te. erweiterte Aufl. Leo Spitzer (ed.). Halle: Neimeyer.

1979. *The ethnography of variation: selected writings on pidgins and creoles.* Ann Arbor: Karoma.

1980. *Pidgin and creole languages.* Ed. and trans. Glenn Gilbert. Cambridge: Cambridge University Press.

Schulte, Rainer and John Biguenet. 1992. *Theories of translation. An anthology of essays from Dryden to Derrida.* Chicago: University of Chicago Press.

Schultz, Emily A. 1990. *Dialogue at the Margins: Whorf, Bakhtin, and linguistic relativity.* Madison: University of Wisconsin Press.

Scollon, S. 1982. "Reality set, socialization and linguistic convergence." Unpublished Ph.D. thesis. Honolulu: University of Hawaii.

Scribner, Sylvia. 1977. "Modes of thinking and ways of speaking: Culture and logic reconsidered." In P. N. Johnson-Laird and P. C. Wason (eds.), *Thinking: readings in cognitive science,* 483–500. Cambridge: Cambridge University Press.

1992. "Mind in action: a functional approach to thinking, and the cognitive consequences of literacy." *Quarterly Newsletter of the Laboratory of Comparative Human Cognition,* 14(4): 83–157.

Scribner, Sylvia and Michael Cole. 1981. *The psychology of literacy.* Cambridge, MA: Harvard University Press.

Sedley, David. 1998. "The etymologies in Plato's *Cratylus.*" *Journal of Hellenic Studies* 118: 140–154.

Seiler, Walter M. 1985. *The Imonda language, West Sepik Province, PNG.* Pacific Linguistics B-93. Canberra: Pacific Linguistics.

Sell, M. A. 1992. "The development of children's knowledge structures: events, slots, and taxonomies." *Journal of Child Language* 19(3): 659–676.

Senft, Gunther. 1987. "Kilivila color terms." *Studies in Language* 11: 313–346.

1996. *Classificatory particles in Kilivila.* New York: Oxford University Press.

Sergent, Bernard. 1982. "Penser – et mal penser – les Indo-européens." *Annales: économies, sociétés, civilisations* 37: 669–681.

1995. *Les Indo-Européens: histoire, langues, mythes.* Paris: Payot.

Seuren, Peter. 1984. "The bioprogram hypothesis: facts and fancy." *Behavioural and Brain Sciences* 7(2): 20–29.

Shapiro, Michael. 1998. "Sound and meaning in Shakespeare's sonnets." *Language* 74: 81–103.

Shatz, M. 1983. *Communication. Handbook of child psychology* Volume III: *Cognitive development.* New York: John Wiley and Sons, 841–890.

Sherzer, Joel. 1982. "Poetic structuring of Kuna discourse: the line." *Language in Society* 11: 371–90.

1983. *Kuna ways of speaking.* Austin: University of Texas Press.

Sherzer, Joel and Anthony Woodbury (ed). 1987. *Native American discourse: poetics and rhetoric.* Cambridge: Cambridge University Press.

Shore, Bradd. 1996. *Culture in mind: cognition, culture, and the problem of meaning.* Oxford: Oxford University Press.

Shweder, Richard A. 1990. "Cultural psychology – what is it?" In J. W. Stigler, R. A. Shweder, and G. Herdt (eds.), *Cultural psychology: essays on comparative human development,* 1–43. Cambridge: Cambridge University Press.

Shweder, Richard A. and Robert A. LeVine (eds.). 1984. *Culture theory: essays on mind, self, and emotion.* Cambridge: Cambridge University Press.

Siddell, Jack. 1998. "Organizing social and spatial location. Elicitations in Indo-Guyanese village talk." *Journal of Linguistic Anthropology* 7(2): 143–165.

1999. "Gender and pronominal variation in an Indo-Guyanese community." *Language in Society* 28(3), 367–399.

2001. "Conversational turn taking in a Caribbean English creole." *Journal of Pragmatics* 33(8), 1263–1290.

Siegel, Jeff. 1985. "Koines and koineization." *Language in Society* 14(3): 357–378.

1987. *Language contact in a plantation environment: a sociolinguistic history of Fiji.* Cambridge: Cambridge University Press.

1997. "Mixing, levelling and Pidgin/Creole development." In Arthur K. Spears and Donald Winford (eds.), *The structure and status of pidgins and creoles,* 111–149. Creole language library, 19. Amsterdam/Philadelphia: John Benjamins.

Silverstein, Michael.1972. "Chinook jargon: language contact and the problem of multilevel generative systems." *Language* 48: 378–406, 596–625.

1976. "Shifters, linguistic categories, and cultural description." In Keith H. Bass and Henry A. Selby (eds.), *Meaning in anthropology,* 11–55. Albuquerque: University of New Mexico Press.

1977. "Cultural prerequisites to grammatical analysis." In Muriel Saville-Troike (ed.), *Anthropology and linguistics,* 139–151. Washington: Georgetown University Press. [Georgetown University Round Table on Language and Linguistics, 1977.]

1979. "Language structure and linguistic ideology." In Paul Clyne, William Hanks and Carol Horbauer (eds.), *The elements: a parasession on linguistic units and levels,* 193–247. Chicago: Chicago Linguistic Society.

1981 (2001). "The limits of awareness." In Alessandro Duranti (ed.), *Linguistic anthropology: a reader,* 382–401. Oxford: Blackwell.

1985. "Language and the culture of gender: at the intersection of structure, usage and ideology." In Elizabeth Mertz and Richard Parmentier (eds.), *Semiotic mediation: sociocultural and psychological perspectives,* 219–259. New York: Academic Press.

1993. "Metapragmatic discourse and metapragmatic function." In J. Lucy, *Reflexive language: reported speech and metapragmatics,* 33–58. Cambridge: Cambridge University Press.

1996. "The indexical order and the dialectics of sociolinguistic life." *SALSA* (Symposium about language and society – Austin) 3: 266–295. Austin: University of Texas, Department of Linguistics.

1998. "The uses and utility of ideology: a commentary." In Bambi B. Schieffelin, Kathryn A. Woolard, and Paul Kroskrity (eds.), *Language ideologies: practice and theory,* 123–148. Oxford: Oxford University Press.

Silverstein, Michael and Greg Urban. 1996. "The natural history of discourse." In Michael Silverstein and Greg Urban (eds.), *Natural Histories of Discourse,* 1–17. Chicago: University of Chicago Press.

Singler, John V. 1988. "The homogeneity of the substrate as a factor in Pidgin/Creole genesis."*Language,* 64: 27–51.

1993a. "African influence upon Afro-American language varieties: a consideration of sociohistorical factors." In Salikoko S. Mufwene (ed.), *Africanism in Afro-American language varieties,* 235–253. Athens/London: The University of Georgia Press.

1993b. "The cultural matrix of creolization: evidence from Goupy des Marets." In *The African presence in Caribbean French colonies in the seventeenth century: documentary evidence,* 187–224. Travaux de recherche sur le créole haïtien. Montreal: UQAM, Groupe de recherche sur le créole haïtien.

1993c. "The African presence in Caribbean French colonies in the seventeenth century: documentary evidence." *Travaux de recherche sur le créole haïtien,* 16–17: 1–236.

1993d. "The setting for creole genesis in France's Caribbean colonies: evidence from seventeen century Marie-Galante." In *The African presence in Caribbean French colonies in the seventeenth century: documentary evidence.* Travaux de recherche sur le créole haïtien. Montreal: UQAM, Groupe de recherche sur le créole haïtien, 225–36.

1995. "The demographics of Creole genesis in the Caribbean: a comparison of Martinique and Haiti." In J. Arends (ed.), *The early stages of creolization*, 203–232. Amsterdam: John Benjamins.

Skutnabb-Kangas, Tove. 2000. *Linguistic genocide in education or worldwide diversity and human rights?* London: Lawrence Erlbaum.

Slobin, Dan I. 1985. *The crosslinguistic study of language acquisition*, vols. 1–2. Hillsdale, NJ: Erlbaum.

1992. *The crosslinguistic study of language acquisition*, vol. 3. Hillsdale, NJ: Erlbaum.

1996. "From 'thought and language' to 'thinking for speaking'." In J. Gumperz and S. C. Levinson (eds.), *Rethinking linguistic relativity*, 70–96. Cambridge: Cambridge University Press.

1997. *The crosslinguistic study of language acquisition*, vols. 4 and 5. Mahweh, NJ: Erlbaum.

2003. "Language and thought online: cognitive consequences of linguistic relativity." In D. Gentner and S. Goldin-Meadow (eds.), *Language in mind: advances in the investigation of language and thought*, 157–191. Cambridge, MA: MIT Press.

Smith, Geoff. 2002. *Growing up with Tok Pisin: contact, creolization and change in Papua New Guinea's national language.* London: Battlebridge.

Smith, Richard T. 1959. "Family structure and plantation systems in the new world." In *Plantation systems of the new world: papers and discussion summaries of the seminar held in San Juan, Puerto Rico*, 148–159. Social Science monograph, no. 7. Washington: Pan American Union.

Smith-Hefner, B. 1988. "The linguistic socialization of Javanese children." *Anthropological Linguistics* 30(2): 166–198.

Snow, D. L. 1971. "Samoan color terminology: a note on the universality and evolutionary ordering of color terms." *Anthropological Linguistics* 13: 385–390.

Snyder, Gary. 1974. *Turtle island.* San Francisco: New Directions.

1979. *He who hunted birds in his father's village. The dimensions of a Haida myth.* Bolinas, CA: Grey Fox Press.

1995. *The Gary Snyder reader.* Washington, DC: Counterpoint.

Spencer, Baldwin and Frank Gillen. 1899. *The native tribes of Central Australia.* New York: MacMillan and Co. Ltd.

1912. *Across Australia.* London: MacMillan and Co. Ltd.

Sperber, Dan. 1985. "Anthropology and psychology: towards an epidemiology of representations." *Man* 20: 73–87.

1987. *On anthropological knowledge.* Cambridge: Cambridge University Press.

1996. *Explaining culture: a naturalistic approach.* Oxford: Blackwell.

Sperry, L. and D. Sperry. 2000. "Verbal and nonverbal contributions to early representation." In N. Budwig, U. Uzgiris and J. Wertsch (eds.), *Communication: an arena of development*, 143–165. Stamford: Ablex.

Spitzer, Leo. 1940. "Trouver." *Romania* 66: 1–11.

Spradley, J. ed. 1972. *Culture and cognition: rules, maps, and plans.* San Francisco: Chandler.

Starr, Frederick. 1901. *Some first steps in human progress.* Cleveland: Chatauqua.

Stegmann von Pritzwald, Kurt. 1936. "Kräfte und Köpfe in der Geschichte der indogermanischen Sprachwissenschaft." In Helmut Arntz (ed.), *Germanen und*

Indogermanen: Volkstum, Sprache, Heimat, Kultur. Festschrift für Herman Hirt, 1–24. Heidelberg: Carl Winter. [Indogermanische Bibliothek, 50, Teil 2.]

Steiner, George. 1975. *After Babel: aspects of language and translation*. London: Oxford University Press.

Steinthal, Heymann. 1848. *Die Sprachwissenschaft Wilhelm von Humboldt's und die Hegel'sche Philosophie*. Berlin: Dümmler.

1860. *Charakteristik der hauptsächlichsten Typen des Sprachbaues*. Berlin: Dümmler.

Stern, D. 1977. *The first relationship: infant and mother*. London: Fontana Open Books.

Stewart, William A. 1967. "Sociolinguistic factors in the history of American negro dialects." *Florida FL Reporter* 5.

Stigler, James W., Richard A. Shweder, and Gilbert Herdt (eds.). 1990. *Cultural psychology: essays on comparative human development*. Cambridge: Cambridge University Press.

Stocking, George W., Jr. 1965 (1968). "From physics to ethnology." In George W. Stocking, Jr., *Race, culture, and evolution*, 133–160. New York: Basic Books.

1974. "Introduction: the basic concepts of Boasian anthropology." In George W. Stocking, Jr. (ed.), *The shaping of American anthropology, 1883–1911: A Franz Boas reader*, 1–20. New York: Basic Books.

1995. *After Tylor, British social anthropology 1888–1951*. Madison: The University of Wisconsin Press.

Stoller, Paul. 1985. "Toward a phenomenological perspective in Pidgin and Creole studies." In I. Hancock (ed.), *Diversity and development in English related creoles*, 1–12. Ann Arbor: Karoma.

Strauss, Claudia and Naomi Quinn. 1997. *A cognitive theory of cultural meaning*. Cambridge: Cambridge University Press.

Strömquist, Sven and Ludo Verhoeven (eds.). 2004. *Relating events in narrative, Vol. 2: typological and contextual perspectives*. Mahwah NJ: Erlbaum.

Suchman, Lucy. 1987. *Plans and situated actions: the problem of human machine interaction*. Cambridge: Cambridge University Press.

Swan, Brian. 1994. *Coming to light. Contemporary translations of the native literature of North America*. New York: Random House.

Swiggers, Pierre. 1985. "Catégories grammaticales et catégories culturelles dans la philosophie du langage de Humboldt: les implications de la 'forme grammaticale'." *Zeitschrift für Phonetik, Sprachwissenschaft und Kommunikationsforschung* 38: 729–736.

Sylvain, Suzanne. 1936. *Le créole haïtien: morphologie et syntaxe*. Wetteren, Belgium: Imprimerie De Meester/Port-au-Prince: By the author.

Szemerényi, Oswald J. L. 1996. *Introduction to Indo-European linguistics*. [tr. of *Einführung in die vergleichende Sprachwissenschaft*, enlarged, 5th ed.]. Oxford: Clarendon Press.

Talmy, Leonard. 1983. "How language structures space." In H. Pick and L. Acredolo (eds.), *Spatial orientation: theory, research and application*, 225–282. New York: Plenum Press.

Tan, Michael L. 1995. "From *Bakla* to gay, shifting gender identities and sexual behaviors in the Philippines." In Richard G. Parker and John H. Gagnon (eds.), *Conceiving sexuality, approaches to sex research in a postmodern world*, 85–96. New York: Routledge.

Tannen, Deborah. 1984. *Conversational style: analyzing talk among friends*. Norwood, NJ: Ablex Publishing Corporation.

1989. *Talking voices: repetition, dialogue, and imagery in conversational discourse.* Cambridge: Cambridge University Press.

Tappolet, Ernst. 1977 [1905]. "Phonetik und Semantik in der etymologischen Forschung." Rüdiger Schmitt (ed.), *Etymologie*, 74–102. Darmstadt: Wissenschaft.

Taylor, Charles. 1979 [1971]. "Interpretation and the sciences of man." In Paul Rabinow and William M. Sullivan (eds.), *Interpretive social science: a reader*, 25–72. Berkeley: University of California Press.

1991. "Ricoeur on narrative." In David Wood (ed.), *On Paul Ricoeur: narrative and interpretation*, 174–179. London: Routledge.

1997. "L'interprétation et les sciences de l'homme." In *La liberté des modernes*, 137–194. Paris: Presses universitaires de France.

Tedlock, Dennis. 1972. *Finding the center: narrative poetry of the Zuni Indians.* Philadelphia: University of Pennsylvania Press.

1983. *The spoken word and the work of interpretation.* Philadelphia: University of Pennsylvania Press.

1985. *Popol Vu. The definitive edition of the dawn of life and the glories of gods and kings.* New York: Simon and Schuster.

Tedlock, Dennis and Jerome Rothenberg. 1975. *Alcheringa. Ethnopoetics.* Boston: Boston University Press.

Thibault, Pierrette and Michelle Daveluy. 1989. "Quelques traces du passage du temps dans le parler des Montréalais. 1971–1984." *Language Variation and Change* 1: 19–45.

Thomas, Antoine. 1900. Compte rendu de H. Schuchardt *Romanische Etymologien, II. Romania* 29: 438–440.

Thomason, Sarah and Terence Kaufman. 1988. *Language contact, creolization and genetic linguistics.* Berkeley: University of California Press.

Thompson, Edgar T. 1975. *Plantation societes, race relations, and the South: the regimentation of population.* Durham: Duke University Press.

Thurston, William R. 1987. *Processes of change in the languages of north-western New Britain. Pacific linguistics.* Series B no. 99. Canberra: Research School of Pacific Studies, Australian National University.

1989. "How exoteric languages build a lexicon: esterogeny in West New Britain." In Ray Harlow and Robin Hooper (eds.), *VICAL 1, Oceanic languages: papers from the fifth International Conference on Austronesian Linguistics*, 555–579. Auckland: Linguistic Society of New Zealand.

Tilley, Christopher. 1999. *Metaphor and material culture.* Malden, MA: Blackwell.

Tornay, Serge (ed.). 1978. *Voir et nommer les couleurs.* Nanterre: Publications du Laboratoire d'Ethnologie et de Sociologie Comparative, Université de Paris X.

Trabant, Jürgen. 1986. *Apeliotes oder Der Sinn der Sprache. Wilhelm von Humboldts Sprach-Bild.* Munich: Wilhelm Fink.

1989. "Le courant humboldtien." In Sylvain Auroux (ed.), *Histoire des idées linguistiques*, 311–322 III. Brussels: Mardaga.

1990. *Traditionen Humboldts.* Frankfurt: Suhrkamp.

2000. "How relativistic are Humboldt's 'Weltansichten'?" In Martin Pütz and Marjolijn H. Verspoor (eds.), *Explorations in linguistic relativity*, 25–44. Amsterdam: John Benjamins.

Trask, Robert Lawrence. 1996. *Historical linguistics.* New York: Oxford University Press.

Trawick, Margaret. 1992. *Notes on love in a Tamil family.* Berkeley: University of California Press.

Trevarthen, C. 1979. "Communication and co-operation in early infancy: a description of primary intersubjectivity." In M. Bullowa (ed.), *Before speech*, 321–349. Cambridge: Cambridge University Press.

Troy, Jakelin. 1985. "Australian Aboriginal contact with the English language in New South Wales: 1788 to 1845." B.A. Honours thesis in Anthropology. Sydney: University of Sydney.

Trumbach, Randolph. 1994. "London's sapphists: from three sexes to four genders in the making of modern culture." In Herdt, *Third Sex, Third Gender*, 111–136. New York: Zone Books.

Tryon, Darrel T. and Jean-Michel Charpentier. 2004. *Pacific pidgins and creoles*. Berlin: Mouton de Gruyter.

Tuite, Kevin. 1999. "Au delà du *Stammbaum*: théories modernes du changement linguistique." *Anthropologie et sociétés* 23(3): 15–52.

n.d. "The meaning of Dæl. Symbolic and spatial associations of the South Caucasian Goddess of game animals." m.s.

Turgot, Anne-Robert-Jacques. 1966 [1756]. "Étymologie." In Denis Diderot and Jean D'Alembert (eds.), *Encyclopédie ou Dictionnaire raisonné des sciences, des arts et des métiers* vol. vi: 98–111. Stuttgart: F. Frommann Verlag.

Turner, David. 1978. "La catégorization de la couleur en Music." In Tournay, ed. 1978.

1980. "There's no such beast: cattle and colour naming among the Music." *Man* 15: 320–338.

Turner, Victor. 1966. "Color classification in Ndembu ritual." In Michael Banton (ed.), *Anthropological approaches to the study of religion*. London: Tavistock.

1967. *The forest of symbols*. Ithaca: Cornell University Press.

Tyler, Stephen A. (ed.). 1969. *Cognitive anthropology: readings*. New York: Holt, Rinehart and Winston.

Tylor, Edward Burnett. 1871. *Primitive culture*. London: John Murray.

Urton, Gary with Primitivo Nina Llanos. 1997. *The social life of numbers: a Quechua ontology of numbers and philosophy of arithmetic*. Austin: University of Texas Press.

Vaillancourt, François. 1996. "Le français dans un contexte économique." In Jürgen Erfurt (ed.), *De la polyphonie à la symphonie. Méthodes, théories et faits de la recherche pluridisciplinaire sur le français au Canada*, 119–136. Leipzig: Leipziger Universitätsverlag.

Valdman, Albert (ed.). 1977. *Pidgin and creole linguistics*. Bloomington/London: Indiana University Press.

Varro, Gabrielle. 1984. *La femme transplantée. Une étude du mariage franco-américain en France et le bilinguisme des enfants*. Lille: Le Septentrion.

Vennemann, Theo (ed.). 1989. *The new sound of Indo-European: essays in phonological reconstruction*. Berlin; New York: Mouton de Gruyter.

Voegelin, Carl F. and Florence M. Voegelin. 1957. *Hopi domains*. Indiana University Publication in Anthroplogy and Linguistics. Memoir no. 14 of the *International Journal of American Linguistics*.

Volterra, V. and T. Taeschner. 1978. "The acquisition and development of language in bilingual children." *Journal of Child Language* 5: 311–326.

Vygotsky, L. S. 1987 (1934). *Thought and language* (rev. edn. A. Kozulin). Cambridge, MA: MIT Press.

Wagoner, David. 1998. *The principles of concealment*. Poetry Magazine, May.

Walcott, Derek. 1990. *Omeros*. New York: Farrar, Strauss and Giroux.

Ward, M. 1971. *Them children: a study in language*. New York: Holt, Rinehart, and Winston.

Wassman, Jürg and Pierre R. Dasen. 1998. "Balinese spatial orientation: some empirical evidence for moderate linguistic relativity." *Journal of the Royal Anthropological Institute, Incorporating Man* (NS), 4: 689–711.

Watson-Gegeo, K. and D. Gegeo. 1986. "Calling out and repeating routines in the language socialization of Basotho children." In B. B. Schieffelin and E. Ochs (eds.), *Language socialization across cultures*, 17–50. Cambridge: Cambridge University Press.

Wax, Murray. 1956. "The limitations of Boas' anthropology." *American Anthropologist* 58: 63–74.

Weber, Eugene. 1976. *Peasants into Frenchmen*. Stanford: Stanford University Press.

Weinberger, Eliot and Octavio Paz. 1987. *Nineteen ways of looking at Wang Wei*. Wakefield, RI: Moyer Bell.

Weiner, Jonathan. 1995. *The beak of the finch*. New York: Viking.

Weinreich, Uriel. 1953a. *Languages in contact*. New York: Linguistics Circle of New York.

Weisgerber, Leo. 1926 (1965). "Das Problem der inneren Sprachform und seine Bedeutung für die deutsche Sprache." In Leo Weisgerber, *Zur Grundlegung der ganzheitlichen Sprachauffassung. Aufsätze 1925–1933*, 36–50. Helmut Gipper (ed.). Düsseldorf: Schwann.

1954. *Vom Weltbild der deutschen Sprache, 2 Halbband. Die sprachliche Erschliessung der Welt*. Düsseldorf: Schwann. [Von den Kräften der deutschen Sprache, 2nd edn., 2.]

Wertsch, J. 1985. *Culture, communication and cognition*. Cambridge: Cambridge University Press.

White, Geoffrey. 1980. "Conceptual universals in interpersonal language." *American Anthropologist*. 82: 759–81.

White, Hayden. 1980. "The value of narrativity in the representation of reality." *Critical Inquiry* 7: 5–27.

1984. "The question of narrative in contemporary historical theory." *History and Theory* 23(1): 1–33.

Whorf, Benjamin Lee. 1940. "Science and linguistics," *Technology Review* 42(6): 229–31, 247–8.

1941a (1956). "The relation of habitual thought and behavior to language." In John B. Carroll (ed.). *Language, thought and reality*. Cambridge, MA: MIT. Orig. pub. in *Language culture and personality, essays in memory of Edward Sapir*. Leslie Spier, ed. Menasha, WI: Sapir Memorial Publications Fund.

1941b (1956). "Languages and logic." In *Language, thought, and reality*, 233–245.

1956 (1936). "An American Indian model of the universe." In John B. Carroll (ed.), *Language, thought, and reality: selected writings of Benjamin Lee Whorf*, 57–64. Cambridge: MIT Press.

Wierzbicka, Anna. 1990. "The meaning of color terms: semantics, culture, and cognition." *Cognitive Linguistics* 1: 99–150.

1992. *Semantics, culture, and cognition: universals of human concepts in culture-specific configurations*. Oxford: Oxford University Press.

Wilbert, Johannes. 1993. *Mystic endowment: religious ethnography of the Warao Indians*. Cambridge: Harvard University Press.

Wilbur, Terence H. 1977. "Introduction." *The Lautgesetz-controversy: a documentation*. Amsterdam: J.

Williams, Bernard. 2002. *Truth and truthfulness: an essay in genealogy*. Princeton, N. J.: Princeton University Press.

Williams, Glyn. 1992. *Sociolinguistics: a sociological critique*. London: Routledge.

Williamson, S. G. 1979. "Tamil baby talk: a cross-cultural study." Unpublished Ph.D. Dissertation. University of Pennsylvania.

Winford, Donald. 2000. "'Intermediate' creole and degrees of change in creole formation: the case of Bajan." In Ingrid Neumann-Holzschuh and Edgar W. Schneider (eds.), *Degrees of restructuring in Creole languages*, 215–246. Creole Language Library, 22. Amsterdam/Philadelphia: John Benjamins.

Winteler, Jost. 1876. *Die Kerenzer Mundart des Kantons Glarus, in ihren Grundzügen dargestellt*. Leipzig: Carl Winter.

Witthoft, N., J. Winawer, L. Wu, M. Frank, A. Wade, and L. Boroditsky. 2003. "Effects of language on color discriminability." *Proceedings of the 25th Annual Meeting of the Cognitive Science Society*.

Woehrling, José. 1996. "Le droit et la législation comme moyens d'intervention sur le français: les politiques linguistiques du Québec, des autorités fédérales et des provinces anglophones." In Jürgen Erfurt (ed.), *De la polyphonie à la symphonie. Méthodes, théories et faits de la recherche pluridisciplinaire sur le français au Canada*, 209–232. Leipzig: Leipziger Universitätsverlag.

Woodbury, Anthony C. 1985. "Functions of rhetorical structure: a study of central Alaskan Yupik Eskimo discourse." *Language in Society* 14: 150–193.

Woolard, Kathryn and Bambi Schieffelin. 1994. "Language ideology." *Annual Review of Anthropology* 23: 55–82.

Woolford, Ellen and William Washabaugh. 1983. *The social context of creolization*. Ann Arbor: Karoma.

Wylie, Alison. 1985. "Between philosophy and archaeology." *American Antiquity* 50 (2): 478–490.

Zentella, A. C. 1990. "Integrating qualitative and quantitative methods in the study of bilingual code-switching." In E. Bendix (ed.), *The uses of linguistics: annals of the New York Academy of Sciences*, vol. 583, 75–92. New York: New York Academy of Sciences.

Zentella, Ana Celia. 1981. "Tá bien, you could answer me in cualquier idioma: Puerto Rican code-switching in bilingual classrooms." In Richard Duran (ed.), *Latino language and communicative behavior*, 109–131. Norwood NJ: Ablex.

   1997. *Growing up bilingual: Puerto Rican children in New York*. Malden: Blackwell.

INDEX

STUDIES IN THE SOCIAL AND CULTURAL
FOUNDATIONS OF LANGUAGE

Editors
JUDITH T. IRVINE
BAMBI SCHIEFFELIN

Printed in the United States
119112LV00003B/1-6/P

9 780521 849418